Anonymus

Return of judicial statistics of Ireland, 1883

Anonymus

Return of judicial statistics of Ireland, 1883

ISBN/EAN: 9783742810373

Manufactured in Europe, USA, Canada, Australia, Japa

Cover: Foto ©Suzi / pixelio.de

Manufactured and distributed by brebook publishing software
(www.brebook.com)

Anonymus

Return of judicial statistics of Ireland, 1883

CRIMINAL AND JUDICIAL STATISTICS.

1883.

IRELAND.

PART I.

POLICE—CRIMINAL PROCEEDINGS—PRISONS.

PART II.

CIVIL PROCEEDINGS IN CENTRAL AND LARGER AND SMALLER DISTRICT COURTS.

Presented to both Houses of Parliament by Command of Her Majesty.

DUBLIN:
PRINTED BY ALEX. THOM & CO. (LIMITED), 87, 88, & 89, ABBEY-STREET.
THE QUEEN'S PRINTING OFFICE.

To be purchased either directly or through any Bookseller, from any of the following agents, viz.:
Messrs. HANSARD, 13, Great Queen-street, W.C., and 32, Abingdon-street, Westminster;
Messrs. EYRE and SPOTTISWOODE, East Harding-street, Fleet-street, and Sale Office, House of Lords;
Messrs. ADAM and CHARLES BLACK, of Edinburgh;
Messrs. ALEXANDER THOM and Co. (Limited), or Messrs. HODGES, FIGGIS, and Co., of Dublin.

1884.

[C.—4161.] *Price 1s. 8d.*

GENERAL REGISTER OFFICE,

CHARLEMONT HOUSE, DUBLIN,

21st October, 1884.

SIR,

In compliance with your letter of the 21st of January, 1884, conveying the desire of His Excellency the Lord Lieutenant, that I should compile the report upon the Criminal and Judicial Statistics of Ireland for the year 1883, I have the honour to submit the following Report, with Tables appended thereto, for His Excellency's consideration.

I remain, Sir,

Your obedient servant,

THOMAS W. GRIMSHAW,

Registrar-General.

Sir R. G. C. HAMILTON, K.C.B.

Under Secretary,

&c., &c., &c.

CONTENTS OF REPORT.

PART I.—CRIMINAL STATISTICS.

CHAPTER I.—STATISTICS OF CRIME.

CHAPTER II.—MODES OF PROCEDURE FOR PUNISHING CRIME.

CHAPTER III.—CRIMINALS AND OTHERS IN CONFINEMENT, AND KNOWN CRIMINALS AT LARGE.

CHAPTER IV.—COST OF THE REPRESSION OF CRIME.

PART II.—JUDICIAL STATISTICS.

CONTENTS OF APPENDIX OF TABLES.

PART I.—CRIMINAL STATISTICS.

I. POLICE TABLES.

II. STATE PRISONS.

III. CRIMINAL PROCEEDINGS AT ASSIZES, THE DUBLIN COMMISSION COURT, AND QUARTER SESSIONS, WITH COSTS.

PART II.—JUDICIAL STATISTICS.—CIVIL PROCEEDINGS.

I. CENTRAL ADMINISTRATION OF JUSTICE.

High Court of Justice.

II. LOCAL ADMINISTRATION OF JUSTICE.

Larger Districts.

III. LOCAL ADMINISTRATION OF JUSTICE.

Smaller Districts.

INDEX TO SUBJECTS

IN

REPORT AND TABLES.

CRIMINAL AND JUDICIAL STATISTICS (IRELAND), 1883.

REPORT.

GENERAL REMARKS.

General Remarks.

The information dealt with in the following Report has been collected in the usual manner, and has been arranged so that it may be in accord with that contained in the previous reports upon the same subject. Care has been taken when arranging the various tables and statements that they may, as far as possible, be easily comparable with similar papers published for the other divisions of the United Kingdom.

The Report is, as on former occasions, divided into two principal divisions—that relating to the Criminal, and that dealing with the Judicial Statistics. Each of these portions has been again sub-divided so as to deal with the more important items in a somewhat detailed manner.

A general review of the tables contained in the Appendix points to the following conclusions.

1. That there has been an increase in the total number of Criminal offences in Ireland in 1883 as compared with 1882.
2. That this increase is among the less serious offences (those determined summarily).
3. That there has been a material diminution in the more serious offences (those not determined summarily) in 1883 as compared with 1882, there having been a decrease in each class of these offences, especially in offences "against the person," in "malicious offences against property," and in "miscellaneous offences."
4. That the judicial returns present no change of importance.

PART I.—CRIMINAL STATISTICS.

CHAPTER I.—STATISTICS OF CRIME.

Increase and Decrease of Criminal Offences.—The Criminal offences and charges of all kinds in Ireland are given in the following statement for the year 1883, as compared with each year during the past decade.

As regards charges determined summarily the figures indicate the number of persons proceeded against, including those cases in which the charges were dismissed. In the case of Indictable Offences the figures represent the number of crimes committed.

Year.	Estimated Population in middle of year.*	Criminal Offences: Indictable, not disposed of summarily — Number	Rate per 10,000 Population	Increase or decrease compared with preceding year — In number — Increase	Decrease	In Rate per 10,000 Population	Disposed of Summarily — Number	Rate per 10,000 Population	Increase or decrease compared with preceding year — In number — Increase	Decrease	In Rate per 10,000 Population	Total — Number	Rate per 10,000 Population	Increase or decrease compared with preceding year — In number — Increase	Decrease	In Rate per 10,000 Population
1874,	[illegible]	[illegible]	[illegible]	–	[illegible]	[illegible]	[illegible]	[illegible]	[illegible]	–	[illegible]	[illegible]	[illegible]	[illegible]	–	[illegible]
1875,	[illegible]	[illegible]	[illegible]	–	[illegible]	[illegible]	[illegible]	[illegible]	[illegible]	–	[illegible]	[illegible]	[illegible]	[illegible]	–	[illegible]
1876,	[illegible]	[illegible]	[illegible]	–	[illegible]	[illegible]	[illegible]	[illegible]	[illegible]	–	[illegible]	[illegible]	[illegible]	[illegible]	–	[illegible]
1877,	[illegible]	[illegible]	[illegible]	[illegible]	–	[illegible]	[illegible]	[illegible]	[illegible]	–	[illegible]	[illegible]	[illegible]	[illegible]	–	[illegible]
1878,	[illegible]	[illegible]	[illegible]	[illegible]	–	[illegible]	[illegible]	[illegible]	[illegible]		[illegible]	[illegible]	[illegible]	[illegible]	–	[illegible]
1879,	[illegible]	[illegible]	[illegible]	[illegible]	–	[illegible]	[illegible]	[illegible]	–	[illegible]	[illegible]	[illegible]	[illegible]	–	[illegible]	[illegible]
1880,	[illegible]	[illegible]	[illegible]	[illegible]	–	[illegible]	[illegible]	[illegible]	–	[illegible]	[illegible]	[illegible]	[illegible]	–	[illegible]	[illegible]
1881,	[illegible]	[illegible]	[illegible]	[illegible]	–	[illegible]	[illegible]	[illegible]	–	[illegible]	[illegible]	[illegible]	[illegible]	–	[illegible]	[illegible]
1882,	[illegible]	[illegible]	[illegible]	–	[illegible]	[illegible]	[illegible]	[illegible]	[illegible]	–	[illegible]	[illegible]	[illegible]	[illegible]	–	[illegible]
1883,	[illegible]	[illegible]	[illegible]	–	[illegible]	[illegible]	[illegible]	[illegible]	[illegible]	–	[illegible]	[illegible]	[illegible]	[illegible]	–	[illegible]

* Estimated population for the middle of each year from the Registrar-General's Returns.

From this statement it appears that the total number of criminal offences during the year 1883, was 232,739 or 464·0 per 10,000 of the estimated population, as compared with 228,157 or 447·5 per 10,000 of the population in 1882, showing an increase of 4,575 in number, and an increase of 16·5 in the rate per 10,000 persons. Thus, last year, as in 1882, criminal offences which had shown a decided and progressive tendency to decrease in the years 1879, 1880, and 1881, again showed the same tendency towards increase which was observable in the years previous to 1879, but the ratio to the population was not so great as the lowest ratio in any of the years between 1874 and 1881. Looking at the foregoing comparative statement it will be observed that the increase is altogether due to criminal offences disposed of summarily, which show an increase of 7,967 in 1883, as compared with 1882. Offences not disposed of summarily, constituting the more serious group of crimes, show the material decrease of 3,392 as compared with the year 1882, and the absolute number (7,214) and the ratio to the population (14·4 per 10,000) are lower than in any year since 1878.

General Distribution of Criminal Offences.—The following statement shows the distribution of criminal offences in Ireland by Provinces, Counties, and large Town Districts, such as the Dublin Metropolitan Police District, the Borough of Belfast, &c.

[illegible]	[illegible]	[illegible]			[illegible]	[illegible]	[illegible]			[illegible]	[illegible]	[illegible]		
		In-	De-	Rate [illegible]			In-	De-	Rate [illegible]			In-	De-	Rate [illegible]
[illegible]	[illegible]	.	[illegible]	[illegible]	[illegible]	[illegible]	[illegible]	. .	[illegible]	[illegible]	[illegible]	[illegible]	-	[illegible]
[illegible]	[illegible]	.	[illegible]	[illegible]	[illegible]	[illegible]	[illegible]	.	[illegible]	[illegible]	[illegible]	.	[illegible]	[illegible]
[illegible]	[illegible]	.	[illegible]	[illegible]	[illegible]	[illegible]	[illegible]	.	[illegible]	[illegible]	[illegible]	[illegible]	.	[illegible]
[illegible]	[illegible]	.	[illegible]	[illegible]	[illegible]	[illegible]	[illegible]	-	[illegible]	[illegible]	[illegible]	[illegible]	.	[illegible]
[illegible]	[illegible]	.	[illegible]	[illegible]	[illegible]	[illegible]	[illegible]	.	[illegible]	[illegible]	[illegible]	[illegible]	.	[illegible]
[illegible]	[illegible]	.	[illegible]	[illegible]	[illegible]	[illegible]	[illegible]	.	[illegible]	[illegible]	[illegible]	[illegible]	.	[illegible]
[illegible]	[illegible]	.	[illegible]	[illegible]	[illegible]	[illegible]	.	[illegible]	[illegible]	[illegible]	[illegible]		[illegible]	[illegible]
[illegible]	[illegible]	.	[illegible]	[illegible]	[illegible]	[illegible]	-	[illegible]	[illegible]	[illegible]	[illegible]	.	[illegible]	[illegible]
[illegible]	[illegible]	.	[illegible]	[illegible]	[illegible]	[illegible]	[illegible]	.	[illegible]	[illegible]	[illegible]	[illegible]	.	[illegible]
[illegible]	[illegible]	.	[illegible]	[illegible]	[illegible]	[illegible]	[illegible]	.	[illegible]	[illegible]	[illegible]	[illegible]	.	[illegible]
[illegible]	[illegible]	.	[illegible]	[illegible]	[illegible]	[illegible]	.	[illegible]	[illegible]	[illegible]	[illegible]	.	[illegible]	[illegible]
[illegible]	[illegible]	.	[illegible]	[illegible]	[illegible]	[illegible]	[illegible]	.	[illegible]	[illegible]	[illegible]	[illegible]	.	[illegible]
[illegible]	[illegible]	.	[illegible]	[illegible]	[illegible]	[illegible]	.	[illegible]	[illegible]	[illegible]	[illegible]	.	[illegible]	[illegible]
[illegible]	[illegible]	-	[illegible]	[illegible]	[illegible]	[illegible]	[illegible]	.	[illegible]	[illegible]	[illegible]	[illegible]	-	[illegible]
[illegible]	[illegible]	.	[illegible]	[illegible]	[illegible]	[illegible]	.	[illegible]	[illegible]	[illegible]	[illegible]	.	[illegible]	[illegible]
[illegible]	[illegible]	.	[illegible]	[illegible]	[illegible]	[illegible]	[illegible]	.	[illegible]	[illegible]	[illegible]	[illegible]	.	[illegible]
[illegible]	[illegible]	.	[illegible]	[illegible]	[illegible]	[illegible]	[illegible]	.	[illegible]	[illegible]	[illegible]	[illegible]	.	[illegible]
[illegible]	[illegible]	.	[illegible]	[illegible]	[illegible]	[illegible]	[illegible]	.	[illegible]	[illegible]	[illegible]	[illegible]	.	[illegible]
[illegible]	[illegible]	.	[illegible]	[illegible]	[illegible]	[illegible]	.	[illegible]	[illegible]	[illegible]	[illegible]	[illegible]	[illegible]	[illegible]
[illegible]	[illegible]	[illegible]	.	[illegible]	[illegible]	[illegible]	[illegible]	.	[illegible]	[illegible]	[illegible]	[illegible]	.	[illegible]
[illegible]	[illegible]	.	[illegible]	[illegible]	[illegible]	[illegible]	[illegible]	.	[illegible]	[illegible]	[illegible]	[illegible]	.	[illegible]
[illegible]	[illegible]	.	[illegible]	[illegible]	[illegible]	[illegible]	[illegible]	.	[illegible]	[illegible]	[illegible]	[illegible]	-	[illegible]
[illegible]	[illegible]	.	[illegible]	[illegible]	[illegible]	[illegible]	[illegible]	.	[illegible]	[illegible]	[illegible]	[illegible]	-	[illegible]
[illegible]	[illegible]	.	[illegible]	[illegible]	[illegible]	[illegible]	[illegible]	.	[illegible]	[illegible]	[illegible]	[illegible]	.	[illegible]
[illegible]	[illegible]	.	[illegible]	[illegible]	[illegible]	[illegible]	.	[illegible]	[illegible]	[illegible]	[illegible]	.	[illegible]	[illegible]
[illegible]	[illegible]	-	[illegible]	[illegible]	[illegible]	[illegible]	[illegible]	.	[illegible]	[illegible]	[illegible]	[illegible]	.	[illegible]
[illegible]	[illegible]	[illegible]		[illegible]	[illegible]	[illegible]	[illegible]	.	[illegible]	[illegible]	[illegible]	[illegible]	.	[illegible]
[illegible]	[illegible]	.	[illegible]	[illegible]	[illegible]	[illegible]	[illegible]	.	[illegible]	[illegible]	[illegible]	[illegible]	-	[illegible]
[illegible]	[illegible]	.	[illegible]	[illegible]	[illegible]	[illegible]	.	[illegible]	[illegible]	[illegible]	[illegible]	.	[illegible]	[illegible]
[illegible]	[illegible]	[illegible]	.	[illegible]	[illegible]	[illegible]	.	[illegible]	[illegible]	[illegible]	[illegible]	.	[illegible]	[illegible]
[illegible]	[illegible]	[illegible]	.	[illegible]	[illegible]	[illegible]	[illegible]	-	[illegible]	[illegible]	[illegible]	[illegible]	.	[illegible]
[illegible]	[illegible]	.	.	[illegible]	[illegible]	[illegible]	.	[illegible]	[illegible]	[illegible]	[illegible]	-	[illegible]	[illegible]
[illegible]	[illegible]	.	[illegible]	[illegible]	[illegible]	[illegible]	.	[illegible]	[illegible]	[illegible]	[illegible]	-	[illegible]	[illegible]
[illegible]	[illegible]	.	[illegible]	[illegible]	[illegible]	[illegible]	[illegible]	.	[illegible]	[illegible]	[illegible]	[illegible]	.	[illegible]
[illegible]	[illegible]	.	.	[illegible]	[illegible]	[illegible]	.	[illegible]	[illegible]	[illegible]	[illegible]	.	[illegible]	[illegible]
[illegible]	[illegible]	.	[illegible]	[illegible]	[illegible]	[illegible]	.	[illegible]	[illegible]	[illegible]	[illegible]	.	[illegible]	[illegible]
[illegible]	[illegible]	.	[illegible]	[illegible]	[illegible]	[illegible]	.	[illegible]	[illegible]	[illegible]	[illegible]	.	[illegible]	[illegible]
[illegible]	[illegible]	.	[illegible]	[illegible]	[illegible]	[illegible]	.	[illegible]	[illegible]	[illegible]	[illegible]	.	[illegible]	[illegible]
[illegible]	[illegible]	.	[illegible]	[illegible]	[illegible]	[illegible]	.	[illegible]	[illegible]	[illegible]	[illegible]	.	[illegible]	[illegible]
[illegible]	[illegible]	.	[illegible]	[illegible]	[illegible]	[illegible]	.	[illegible]	[illegible]	[illegible]	[illegible]	.	[illegible]	[illegible]
[illegible]	[illegible]	.	[illegible]	[illegible]	[illegible]	[illegible]	.	[illegible]	[illegible]	[illegible]	[illegible]	.	[illegible]	[illegible]
[illegible]	[illegible]	.	[illegible]	[illegible]	[illegible]	[illegible]	[illegible]	.	[illegible]	[illegible]	[illegible]	.	[illegible]	[illegible]
[illegible]	[illegible]	.	[illegible]	[illegible]	[illegible]	[illegible]	[illegible]	.	[illegible]	[illegible]	[illegible]	.	[illegible]	[illegible]
[illegible]	[illegible]	-	[illegible]	[illegible]	[illegible]	[illegible]	.	[illegible]	[illegible]	[illegible]	[illegible]	-	[illegible]	[illegible]
[illegible]	[illegible]	.	[illegible]	[illegible]	[illegible]	[illegible]	.	[illegible]	[illegible]	[illegible]	[illegible]	-	[illegible]	[illegible]
[illegible]	[illegible]	.	[illegible]	[illegible]	[illegible]	[illegible]	.	[illegible]	[illegible]	[illegible]	[illegible]	[illegible]	[illegible]	[illegible]
[illegible]	[illegible]	.	[illegible]	[illegible]	[illegible]	[illegible]	[illegible]	.	[illegible]	[illegible]	[illegible]	[illegible]	.	[illegible]
[illegible]	[illegible]	.	[illegible]	[illegible]	[illegible]	[illegible]	[illegible]	.	[illegible]	[illegible]	[illegible]	.	[illegible]	[illegible]

Part I. Criminal Statistics. — Chapter I. Statistics of Crime. — Distribution of crime.

Leinster, 84,593, or at the rate of 661·4 per 10,000 of the population in 1881; Munster, 63,971, or at the rate of 480·6 per 10,000; Ulster, 55,771, or 320·0 per 10,000; and Connaught, 28,297, or 345·5 per 10,000. Compared with the year 1882, there has been an increase of criminal cases in Leinster to the extent of 4,108, or 32·1 per 10,000 persons, and an increase of 4,250 or 31·9 per 10,000 in Munster, but there has been a decrease of 3,333, or 19·0 per 10,000 in Ulster, and a decrease of 445, or 5·4 per 10,000 in Connaught. The more serious cases (those not determined summarily) have decreased in all the Provinces. The less serious offences (those determined summarily) have increased in Leinster, Munster, and Connaught, but decreased in Ulster.

Criminal offences show a decrease in the total number in 22 counties and districts, and an increase in 21.

In the following list the counties and districts are arranged in order from that in which there was least crime (in 1883) to that in which there was most:—

1. Antrim.	12. Leitrim.	23. Dublin (County).	34. Galway, E.R.
2. Donegal.	13. Carlow.	24. Kilkenny.	35. Kildare.
3. Down.	14. Roscommon.	25. King's County.	36. Kerry.
4. Mayo.	15. Londonderry.	26. Louth.	37. Limerick City.
5. Wexford.	16. Monaghan.	27. Cork, E.R.	38. Belfast Town.
6. Fermanagh.	17. Meath.	28. Tipperary, N.R.	39. Waterford City.
7. Cavan.	18. Cork, W.R.	29. Queen's County	40. Drogheda Town.
8. Carrickfergus Town.	19. Waterford (County).	30. Longford.	41. Galway Town.
9. Armagh.	20. Wicklow.	31. Sligo.	42. Cork City.
10. Galway, W.R.	21. Clare.	32. Tipperary, S.R.	43. Dublin Metropolitan Police District.
11. Tyrone.	22. Limerick (County).	33. Westmeath.	

It will be observed that in the above list the seven principal Town Districts, occupy the most unfavourable position. This is owing to the greater criminality of town populations, which is more fully demonstrated in the following statement, where the rate of crime to the population in the principal Town Districts is compared with the rate in the adjacent Country Districts.

Excess of crime in urban districts.

Statement showing for the year 1883, the Proportion of Criminal Offences in each 10,000 of Population in the under-mentioned Districts, and the excess of crime in Urban Districts.

Districts.	Offences per 10,000 of Population.			Number of Offences in Urban District for every 100 Offences in an equal number of inhabitants of adjoining Counties.
	In Urban District.	Adjoining County.	Excess in Urban District.	
Dublin Metropolis,	1537·0	408·8	928·2	377
Cork City,	1005·0	396·2	609·8	254
Galway Town,	974·2	363·1	611·1	268
Drogheda,	937·6	421·8	515·8	222
Waterford City,	533·9	367·9	166·0	145
Belfast,	677·3	190·5	486·8	355
Limerick City,	603·0	401·6	201·4	150

It will be observed that the criminal offences in Belfast exceeded those among an equal number of the inhabitants of the adjacent County in the proportion of 355 to 100, and that even in Limerick, where the excess of crime in the Urban over the adjacent Rural District was least, the proportion was as 150 to 100.

Character of persons proceeded against. Table 10.

The character of the persons proceeded against is set forth in the following statement, from which it appears that the character of 13·3 per cent. of the persons proceeded against was unknown to the Police, and that the character of 89·4 per cent. of the remainder was ascertained to be previously good.

Statement showing the character of persons proceeded against.

STATEMENT showing the CHARACTER of PERSONS PROCEEDED AGAINST for CRIMINAL OFFENCES in IRELAND in 1883

CHARACTER OF PERSONS PROCEEDED AGAINST IN 1883	IRELAND IN 1883.	
	Total	Proportion of each Class to the Total Number
		Per cent.
Total number proceeded against,	218,979	100
Deduct persons whose character is unknown,	21,712	13·6
Total number whose character is known,	197,267	100
Previous Good Character,	176,445	89·4
Suspicious Characters,	7,306	3·7
Prostitutes,	4,694	2·4
Vagrants, Tramps, and others without any visible means of subsistence,	4,593	2·3
Habitual Drunkards (not under other heads),	2,831	1·4
Known Thieves,	1,498	0·8

NATURE OF CRIMES.

Nature of Crimes.

In Police Tables 6 and 7 of the Appendix, the nature of the Crimes committed is set forth in detail. The following abstract (see page 20) has been constructed from Table 6, which includes the more serious offences, namely those not dealt with summarily, and gives their distribution throughout Ireland in detail.

Distribution of the more serious offences throughout Ireland. Table 6.

The total number of these cases amounted to 7,211, or at the rate of 13·9 per 10,000 of the population, according to the Census of 1881. Of these, 1,197, or 2·3 per 10,000 of the population, were offences against the person; 416, or 0·8 per 10,000, against property with violence; 3,977, or 7·7 per 10,000, against property without violence; 753, or 1·4 per 10,000, were malicious offences against property. Cases of forgery and against the currency were only 44, or 0·1 per 10,000, and all other cases amounted to 837. It will be observed that the rate per 10,000 of all offences not disposed of summarily was in Leinster 26·9; Munster, 8·7; Ulster, 5·0; and Connaught, 5·6.

Offences against the person.

In the case of *Offences against the Person* the rates per 10,000 of the population were:—for Leinster 4·2 (including 10·8 in the Dublin Metropolitan District), Munster, 2·1; Ulster, 1·4; Connaught, 1·6. The largest number of these offences, both absolutely and relatively, were committed in the Dublin Metropolitan District, amounting to 378, or 10·8 per 10,000; the next largest, in proportion to population, in Limerick City, amounting to 5·1 per 10,000; while the rate in Cork City was 3·5, in Galway Town 3·3, and in Kilkenny County 3·0. In all the other counties and districts it was below 3 per 10,000, being below 1·0 in twelve.

Malicious offences.

In the case of *Malicious Offences against Property* it appears that the rates per 10,000 of the population were for Leinster 1·7, Munster 1·8, Ulster only 0·9, Connaught 1·6. The highest rate (3·5) was in Kilkenny and Longford, the next (3·1) in Kerry and the North Riding of Tipperary. The lowest was 0·1 in Cork City, and the next lowest 0·2 in the Town of Belfast. In the Cities of Limerick and Waterford, this class of crime was absent.

Part I.
Criminal Statistics.

Chapter I.
Statistics of Crime.

Distribution of the more serious offences throughout Ireland.
Table 8.

STATEMENT showing the DISTRIBUTION of the MORE SERIOUS OFFENCES throughout IRELAND.

Counties, Counties of Cities, with Ridings and Districts of Police	Population	Against the Person: Total	Against the Person: Rate	Against Property with Violence: Total	Against Property with Violence: Rate	Against Property without Violence: Total	Against Property without Violence: Rate	Malicious offences against Property: Total	Malicious offences against Property: Rate	Forgery and offences against the Currency: Total	Forgery and offences against the Currency: Rate	Not included in foregoing Classes: Total	Not included in foregoing Classes: Rate	Total of Offences: Total	Total of Offences: Rate
TOTAL OF IRELAND,	[illegible]	[illegible]	[illegible]	[illegible]	[illegible]	[illegible]	[illegible]	[illegible]	[illegible]	[illegible]	[illegible]	[illegible]	[illegible]	[illegible]	[illegible]
LEINSTER.															
Carlow,	[illegible]	[illegible]	[illegible]	[illegible]	[illegible]	[illegible]	[illegible]	[illegible]	[illegible]	[illegible]	[illegible]	[illegible]	[illegible]	[illegible]	[illegible]
Drogheda Town,	[illegible]	[illegible]	[illegible]	[illegible]	[illegible]	[illegible]	[illegible]	[illegible]	[illegible]	[illegible]	[illegible]	[illegible]	[illegible]	[illegible]	[illegible]
Dublin,	[illegible]	[illegible]	[illegible]	[illegible]	[illegible]	[illegible]	[illegible]	[illegible]	[illegible]	[illegible]	[illegible]	[illegible]	[illegible]	[illegible]	[illegible]
Dublin Metropolitan Police District,	[illegible]	[illegible]	[illegible]	[illegible]	[illegible]	[illegible]	[illegible]	[illegible]	[illegible]	[illegible]	[illegible]	[illegible]	[illegible]	[illegible]	[illegible]
Kildare,	[illegible]	[illegible]	[illegible]	[illegible]	[illegible]	[illegible]	[illegible]	[illegible]	[illegible]	[illegible]	[illegible]	[illegible]	[illegible]	[illegible]	[illegible]
Kilkenny,	[illegible]	[illegible]	[illegible]	[illegible]	[illegible]	[illegible]	[illegible]	[illegible]	[illegible]	[illegible]	[illegible]	[illegible]	[illegible]	[illegible]	[illegible]
King's County,	[illegible]	[illegible]	[illegible]	[illegible]	[illegible]	[illegible]	[illegible]	[illegible]	[illegible]	[illegible]	[illegible]	[illegible]	[illegible]	[illegible]	[illegible]
Longford,	[illegible]	[illegible]	[illegible]	[illegible]	[illegible]	[illegible]	[illegible]	[illegible]	[illegible]	[illegible]	[illegible]	[illegible]	[illegible]	[illegible]	[illegible]
Louth,	[illegible]	[illegible]	[illegible]	[illegible]	[illegible]	[illegible]	[illegible]	[illegible]	[illegible]	[illegible]	[illegible]	[illegible]	[illegible]	[illegible]	[illegible]
Meath,	[illegible]	[illegible]	[illegible]	[illegible]	[illegible]	[illegible]	[illegible]	[illegible]	[illegible]	[illegible]	[illegible]	[illegible]	[illegible]	[illegible]	[illegible]
Queen's County,	[illegible]	[illegible]	[illegible]	[illegible]	[illegible]	[illegible]	[illegible]	[illegible]	[illegible]	[illegible]	[illegible]	[illegible]	[illegible]	[illegible]	[illegible]
Westmeath,	[illegible]	[illegible]	[illegible]	[illegible]	[illegible]	[illegible]	[illegible]	[illegible]	[illegible]	[illegible]	[illegible]	[illegible]	[illegible]	[illegible]	[illegible]
Wexford,	[illegible]	[illegible]	[illegible]	[illegible]	[illegible]	[illegible]	[illegible]	[illegible]	[illegible]	[illegible]	[illegible]	[illegible]	[illegible]	[illegible]	[illegible]
Wicklow,	[illegible]	[illegible]	[illegible]	[illegible]	[illegible]	[illegible]	[illegible]	[illegible]	[illegible]	[illegible]	[illegible]	[illegible]	[illegible]	[illegible]	[illegible]
TOTAL OF LEINSTER,	[illegible]	[illegible]	[illegible]	[illegible]	[illegible]	[illegible]	[illegible]	[illegible]	[illegible]	[illegible]	[illegible]	[illegible]	[illegible]	[illegible]	[illegible]
MUNSTER.															
Clare,	[illegible]	[illegible]	[illegible]	[illegible]	[illegible]	[illegible]	[illegible]	[illegible]	[illegible]	[illegible]	[illegible]	[illegible]	[illegible]	[illegible]	[illegible]
Cork, East Riding,	[illegible]	[illegible]	[illegible]	[illegible]	[illegible]	[illegible]	[illegible]	[illegible]	[illegible]	[illegible]	[illegible]	[illegible]	[illegible]	[illegible]	[illegible]
Cork, West Riding,	[illegible]	[illegible]	[illegible]	[illegible]	[illegible]	[illegible]	[illegible]	[illegible]	[illegible]	[illegible]	[illegible]	[illegible]	[illegible]	[illegible]	[illegible]
Cork City,	[illegible]	[illegible]	[illegible]	[illegible]	[illegible]	[illegible]	[illegible]	[illegible]	[illegible]	[illegible]	[illegible]	[illegible]	[illegible]	[illegible]	[illegible]
Kerry,	[illegible]	[illegible]	[illegible]	[illegible]	[illegible]	[illegible]	[illegible]	[illegible]	[illegible]	[illegible]	[illegible]	[illegible]	[illegible]	[illegible]	[illegible]
Limerick,	[illegible]	[illegible]	[illegible]	[illegible]	[illegible]	[illegible]	[illegible]	[illegible]	[illegible]	[illegible]	[illegible]	[illegible]	[illegible]	[illegible]	[illegible]
Limerick City,	[illegible]	[illegible]	[illegible]	[illegible]	[illegible]	[illegible]	[illegible]	[illegible]	[illegible]	[illegible]	[illegible]	[illegible]	[illegible]	[illegible]	[illegible]
Tipperary, North Riding,	[illegible]	[illegible]	[illegible]	[illegible]	[illegible]	[illegible]	[illegible]	[illegible]	[illegible]	[illegible]	[illegible]	[illegible]	[illegible]	[illegible]	[illegible]
Tipperary, South Riding,	[illegible]	[illegible]	[illegible]	[illegible]	[illegible]	[illegible]	[illegible]	[illegible]	[illegible]	[illegible]	[illegible]	[illegible]	[illegible]	[illegible]	[illegible]
Waterford,	[illegible]	[illegible]	[illegible]	[illegible]	[illegible]	[illegible]	[illegible]	[illegible]	[illegible]	[illegible]	[illegible]	[illegible]	[illegible]	[illegible]	[illegible]
Waterford City,	[illegible]	[illegible]	[illegible]	[illegible]	[illegible]	[illegible]	[illegible]	[illegible]	[illegible]	[illegible]	[illegible]	[illegible]	[illegible]	[illegible]	[illegible]
TOTAL OF MUNSTER,	[illegible]	[illegible]	[illegible]	[illegible]	[illegible]	[illegible]	[illegible]	[illegible]	[illegible]	[illegible]	[illegible]	[illegible]	[illegible]	[illegible]	[illegible]
ULSTER.															
Antrim,	[illegible]	[illegible]	[illegible]	[illegible]	[illegible]	[illegible]	[illegible]	[illegible]	[illegible]	[illegible]	[illegible]	[illegible]	[illegible]	[illegible]	[illegible]
Armagh,	[illegible]	[illegible]	[illegible]	[illegible]	[illegible]	[illegible]	[illegible]	[illegible]	[illegible]	[illegible]	[illegible]	[illegible]	[illegible]	[illegible]	[illegible]
Belfast Town,	[illegible]	[illegible]	[illegible]	[illegible]	[illegible]	[illegible]	[illegible]	[illegible]	[illegible]	[illegible]	[illegible]	[illegible]	[illegible]	[illegible]	[illegible]
Carrickfergus Town,	[illegible]	[illegible]	[illegible]	[illegible]	[illegible]	[illegible]	[illegible]	[illegible]	[illegible]	[illegible]	[illegible]	[illegible]	[illegible]	[illegible]	[illegible]
Cavan,	[illegible]	[illegible]	[illegible]	[illegible]	[illegible]	[illegible]	[illegible]	[illegible]	[illegible]	[illegible]	[illegible]	[illegible]	[illegible]	[illegible]	[illegible]
Donegal,	[illegible]	[illegible]	[illegible]	[illegible]	[illegible]	[illegible]	[illegible]	[illegible]	[illegible]	[illegible]	[illegible]	[illegible]	[illegible]	[illegible]	[illegible]
Down,	[illegible]	[illegible]	[illegible]	[illegible]	[illegible]	[illegible]	[illegible]	[illegible]	[illegible]	[illegible]	[illegible]	[illegible]	[illegible]	[illegible]	[illegible]
Fermanagh,	[illegible]	[illegible]	[illegible]	[illegible]	[illegible]	[illegible]	[illegible]	[illegible]	[illegible]	[illegible]	[illegible]	[illegible]	[illegible]	[illegible]	[illegible]
Londonderry,	[illegible]	[illegible]	[illegible]	[illegible]	[illegible]	[illegible]	[illegible]	[illegible]	[illegible]	[illegible]	[illegible]	[illegible]	[illegible]	[illegible]	[illegible]
Monaghan,	[illegible]	[illegible]	[illegible]	[illegible]	[illegible]	[illegible]	[illegible]	[illegible]	[illegible]	[illegible]	[illegible]	[illegible]	[illegible]	[illegible]	[illegible]
Tyrone,	[illegible]	[illegible]	[illegible]	[illegible]	[illegible]	[illegible]	[illegible]	[illegible]	[illegible]	[illegible]	[illegible]	[illegible]	[illegible]	[illegible]	[illegible]
TOTAL OF ULSTER,	[illegible]	[illegible]	[illegible]	[illegible]	[illegible]	[illegible]	[illegible]	[illegible]	[illegible]	[illegible]	[illegible]	[illegible]	[illegible]	[illegible]	[illegible]
CONNAUGHT.															
Galway, East Riding,	[illegible]	[illegible]	[illegible]	[illegible]	[illegible]	[illegible]	[illegible]	[illegible]	[illegible]	[illegible]	[illegible]	[illegible]	[illegible]	[illegible]	[illegible]
Galway, West Riding,	[illegible]	[illegible]	[illegible]	[illegible]	[illegible]	[illegible]	[illegible]	[illegible]	[illegible]	[illegible]	[illegible]	[illegible]	[illegible]	[illegible]	[illegible]
Galway Town,	[illegible]	[illegible]	[illegible]	[illegible]	[illegible]	[illegible]	[illegible]	[illegible]	[illegible]	[illegible]	[illegible]	[illegible]	[illegible]	[illegible]	[illegible]
Leitrim,	[illegible]	[illegible]	[illegible]	[illegible]	[illegible]	[illegible]	[illegible]	[illegible]	[illegible]	[illegible]	[illegible]	[illegible]	[illegible]	[illegible]	[illegible]
Mayo,	[illegible]	[illegible]	[illegible]	[illegible]	[illegible]	[illegible]	[illegible]	[illegible]	[illegible]	[illegible]	[illegible]	[illegible]	[illegible]	[illegible]	[illegible]
Roscommon,	[illegible]	[illegible]	[illegible]	[illegible]	[illegible]	[illegible]	[illegible]	[illegible]	[illegible]	[illegible]	[illegible]	[illegible]	[illegible]	[illegible]	[illegible]
Sligo,	[illegible]	[illegible]	[illegible]	[illegible]	[illegible]	[illegible]	[illegible]	[illegible]	[illegible]	[illegible]	[illegible]	[illegible]	[illegible]	[illegible]	[illegible]
TOTAL OF CONNAUGHT,	[illegible]	[illegible]	[illegible]	[illegible]	[illegible]	[illegible]	[illegible]	[illegible]	[illegible]	[illegible]	[illegible]	[illegible]	[illegible]	[illegible]	[illegible]

The cases of *Forgery* and *Offences against the Currency* amounted to the small number of 44, or 0·1 per 10,000 of the population: of these, 16 were in Dublin Metropolitan Police District and 6 in Belfast; in other places this class of offence was of insignificant proportions.

Of offences of the *Miscellaneous class* there were 827, or at the rate of 1·6 per 10,000 of the population. The principal portion of this figure is made up of the offence of *Intimidation by Threatening Letters, Notices, or otherwise*, but the number of cases of this nature shows a great decline, amounting to but 535 as compared with 2,651 in 1882, and 8,093 in 1881. Of those miscellaneous offences, 290, or 2·3 per 10,000 of the population, were in Leinster, including 150 cases of intimidation by threatening letters, &c. (of which 30 were in the Dublin Metropolitan Police District, 28 in Longford, and 21 in Westmeath); 319, or 2·4 per 10,000 inhabitants, were in Munster, including 246 cases of intimidation (of which 125 were in Kerry, 24 in Clare, and 28 in the West Riding of Cork. In Ulster there were 122 miscellaneous offences, or only 0·7 per 10,000 of the population; of these 39 were cases of intimidation. In Connaught the number of miscellaneous offences was 96, or 1·2 per 10,000 of the population, including 80 cases of intimidation, of which 25 were in East Galway and 22 in Mayo.

For the indictable offences not disposed of summarily, there were 3,461 persons apprehended, being equal to 48 per cent. of the number of offences as compared with 46 per cent. in the previous year.

The following summary—also constructed from Table 6—showing the number of offences not determined summarily, classified according to their nature and compared with previous years—will give a fair idea of the variations which have taken place during the past five years in the number of more serious offences in Ireland:—

Offences	1883.	1882.	1881.	1880.	1879.
1. Against the Person, ...	1,187	1,642	1,475	1,369	1,457
2. Against Property with Violence, . . .	416	660	754	864	592
3. Against Property without Violence, . .	3,977	4,104	4,048	3,068	1,111
4. Malicious against Property, ...	753	1,860	1,676	1,133	704
5. Forgery and against Currency, . . .	44	55	60	91	104
6. Not included in foregoing, ...	827	8,104	3,964	3,267	1,121
Total, ...	7,214	10,605	11,915	8,677	5,089

A glance at this statement will show a gratifying decrease in all classes of serious crime, as compared with 1882, and the averages for the preceding three years.

A more minute consideration of Table 6 in the Appendix will show that there were 28 cases of *murders of infants*, which were very evenly distributed throughout Ireland: 7 occurred in Leinster, 9 in Munster, 10 in Ulster, and 2 in Connaught. In the case of *other murders* there were 17 in Ireland, in 1883, as compared with 40 in 1882, 40 in 1881, 22 in 1880, and 22 in 1879. Of these 17 murders, 8 were in Leinster, 4 in Munster, 4 in Ulster, and 1 in Connaught. There was 1 murder each in Dublin Metropolitan Police District, Kildare County, Westmeath, Wicklow, Cork, East Riding, Kerry, Limerick, Tipperary, South Riding, Belfast Town, Cavan County, Down, Fermanagh, and West Galway; and 2 each in Dublin County and Queen's County. There were not any such murders in Carlow County, Drogheda Town, Kilkenny County, King's County, Longford, Louth, Meath, or Wexford, in the Province of Leinster; nor in Clare County, West Cork, Cork City, Limerick City, Tipperary North Riding, or the County or City of Waterford, in the Province of Munster;

Part I. Criminal Statistics. — Chapter I. *Statistics of Crime.*

Offences against the currency and forgery.

Miscellaneous offences.

Offences not determined summarily in 1883 compared with previous years. Table 6.

Murders.

Part I. Criminal Statistics. — Chapter I. Statistics of Crime. — Attempts to murder, shooting at, wounding, &c.

nor in Antrim, Armagh, Carrickfergus Town, Donegal, Londonderry, Monaghan, or Tyrone, in the Province of Ulster; nor in Galway East Riding, Galway Town, Leitrim, Mayo, Roscommon, or Sligo, in the Province of Connaught. There were in all 11 *attempts to murder* in 1883, as compared with 35 in 1882; 19 in 1881; 16 in 1880, and 6 in 1879. There were 139 cases of *shooting at, wounding, stabbing, &c., with intent to do bodily harm* in 1883, compared with 232 in 1882; 246 in 1881; 226 in 1880, and 160 in 1879. The cases of *assault and inflicting bodily harm*, were 468 in 1883, compared with 574 in 1882; 426 in 1881; 418 in 1880, and 530 in 1879. In all cases of *offences against property with violence* there is a diminution, as compared with 1882, except as regards sacrilege, the cases of which (18) show an increase of 5, and "attempts to rob and demanding money by menaces," the number of which was the same in both years.

Offences against property without violence.

In cases of *offences against property without violence*, there is, on the whole, no remarkable variation as compared with the previous year. As usual, *simple larceny* contributes more than half the crime in this class. It is also to be noted that a very large proportion of this class of crime is committed in the Dublin Metropolitan Police District. Of the 3,977 offences against property without violence in Ireland, no less than 3,225, or more than three-fourths, were in that District, and of the 2,550 simple larceny cases 2,240 occurred there.

The classes of *malicious offences against property, offences against the currency* and *miscellaneous offences*, included in Table 6, have already been sufficiently dealt with in the general comments on crime not determined summarily.

Offences disposed of summarily. Table 7.

In Table 7 of the Appendix details are given of the cases determined summarily, which include those usually dealt with in police courts.

These, as previously shown, amount to a total of 225,516, and constitute 96·9 per cent. of the total crime of the country. It is also in this class that the preponderance of town over rural crime is specially noticeable. Among the offences disposed of summarily the more important are set out in the following statement, and a comparison instituted with the previous year.

	1883	1882
Common Assaults, . .	26,958	30,017
Drunkenness, . . .	70,343	67,497

Thus there has been a decrease of 3,059 in common assaults, but an increase of 2,846 cases of drunkenness and disorderly conduct in connexion therewith. As these cases constitute more than one half of all the cases dealt with in the police and Petty Sessions courts, are clearly connected with one another, and are the starting points of many other criminal actions, their import is very great when measuring the general condition of the criminal classes.

Habitual drunkards' convictions. Table 11.

In connexion with the statistics of drunkenness, a special return of habitual drunkards (Table 11, page 84) has been introduced, in continuation of a similar Return for the year 1882; it gives the number of persons convicted three times or upwards for being "Drunk" or "Drunk and Disorderly" in 1883.

The most important result of the habitual drunkenness return is the light it throws upon the causes of town crime, which has been noticed as excessive. Taking the seven town jurisdictions outside Dublin, of Belfast, Cork, Limerick, Waterford, Galway, Drogheda, and Carrickfergus, with an aggregate population of 391,000, the habitual drunkards were 675, or 17·3 per 10,000 of the population. In the rest of Ireland, outside the Metropolitan district, with a population of 4,434,000, the number was only 1,898, or 4·3 in the 10,000. In the Dublin Metropolitan Police District, with a population of 350,000, the number was 169, or 5·4 per 10,000 population. Compared with 1882 there was a decrease in the number in each of the town jurisdictions except the Cities of Limerick and Waterford, in the former of which there were 31 cases against 18 in 1882 (the number for 1881 amounted to 43) and in the latter 81 against 46. In the rest of Ireland there was a decrease, from 1,975 to 1,894. In all Ireland there was a decrease of 178—viz., from 2,940 to 2,762. Of this total, 2,236 were convictions three times and less than five times, 471 five times and less than ten times, and 55 ten times and upwards. It will be observed from Table 7 that the number of cases of "illegally selling intoxicating drinks" rose from 2,220 in 1882 to 3,349 in 1883.

PART I. GENERAL STATISTICS. — CHAPTER I. *Statistics of Crime.* — Offences against the Licensing Laws. Table 7.

Cases of *cruelty to animals* decreased from 1,695 in 1882 to 1,530 in 1883. *Offences against Local Acts and Borough By-laws* show an increase, from 13,214 in 1882 to 15,511 in 1883. Offences *against the Public Health and Nuisances Removal Acts*, numbered 4,328 in 1883, as compared with 3,979 in 1882: it is remarkable that of the 4,328 charges under these Acts 3,469 were in the Dublin Metropolitan district. In a large number of districts no offences against these Acts are recorded. *Unlawful possession of stolen goods* decreased from 1,060 cases in 1882 to 1,008 in 1883. The *offences against the Highway Act*, including Nuisances on Public Roads, increased from 17,196 in 1882 to 19,167 in 1883. The other statistics contained in Table 7 do not call for any special remark, but, nevertheless, contain many items of considerable interest.

Cruelty to animals. Local Acts and Borough Bye-laws. Public Health and Nuisances Removal Acts. Unlawful possession of stolen goods. Highway Act.

CHAPTER II.—MODES OF PROCEDURE FOR PUNISHING CRIME.

CHAPTER II. *Procedure.*

The Police act as public prosecutors in the great majority of cases in Ireland. In many cases they undertake the sole duty of prosecuting, and in most of the more serious offences the preliminary proceedings are instituted by them. In all the counties of Ireland, except the County and City of Dublin, there are two Crown Solicitors, one of whom deals with cases at Quarter Sessions, the other with the more serious cases which come before the Judges at Assizes.

Coroners' Courts still deal with cases where criminal offences are involved, and Coroners' Juries frequently find verdicts implicating or exonerating certain persons in cases of homicide, &c. It is not, however, the custom now to bring prisoners charged with homicide, &c., before Coroners' Courts, and in a large number of cases the finding of the Jury relates merely to the cause of death.

A special feature in the administration of Criminal Law in Ireland is the proclamation of certain Districts under special Acts of Parliament. The following is a general statement relating to these Special Acts and the extent of their application in Ireland during the last year.

Under the Act 6 Wm. IV., chap. 13, the following counties were proclaimed as requiring additional Police at end of 1883:—Clare, Cork, Galway, Kerry, King's County, Leitrim, Limerick, Mayo, Roscommon, Tipperary, and Westmeath, Limerick City, and portions of the counties of Donegal, Longford, Sligo, and Waterford.

Districts proclaimed under Act 6 Wm. IV., cap. 13. Table 13.

Under the Peace Preservation (Ireland) Act, 1881, prohibiting the having or carrying arms without a licence, three provinces, viz., Leinster (except Kilkenny City), Munster and Connaught, and parts of the counties of Armagh, Donegal, and Monaghan were proclaimed at end of 1883. In Ulster the prohibition against carrying arms included the Town of Belfast and Londonderry City, the counties of Cavan, Fermanagh, and Monaghan, one Barony in Down, and five Baronies in Tyrone.

Districts proclaimed under Peace Preservation (Ireland) Act, 1881. Tables 10 and 11.

PART I. GENERAL STATEMENT. — CHAPTER II. Procedure. — Prevention of Crime (Ireland) Act, 1882. Provisions of sections 6, 11, 12, and 14.

The Prevention of Crime (Ireland) Act 1882, provides for special proceedings in certain cases.

Section 6, refers to riots and other offences in a Proclaimed District.

Section 11, refers to arrest of persons found at night under suspicious circumstances in a Proclaimed District.

Section 12, refers to arrest of strangers found under suspicious circumstances in a Proclaimed District.

Section 14, refers to searches for arms and illegal documents in a Proclaimed District.

Localities proclaimed under the Prevention of Crime (Ireland) Act, 1882. Table 10.

In accordance with this Act, the following localities were proclaimed in the province of Leinster:—Under Sections 6, 11, 12 and 14, Kilkenny, King's County, Longford, Meath, Queen's County, Westmeath and the City of Dublin; under Sections 6, 12 and 14, the County of Dublin, the Town of Drogheda and City of Kilkenny; and under Sections 12 and 14, three Baronies in County Kildare. In Munster, under Sections 6, 11, 12 and 14, the Counties of Clare, Cork, Kerry, Limerick, Tipperary, and Waterford; under Sections 6, 12 and 14, the Cities of Cork, Limerick and Waterford. In Connaught, under Sections 6, 11, 12, 14, the Counties of Galway, Leitrim, Mayo, Roscommon and Sligo; and under Sections 6, 12, and 14, the Town of Galway. In Ulster under Sections 6, 11, 12 and 14, the County of Cavan, under Sections 11, 12 and 14, portions of the counties of Armagh and Monaghan, and under Sections 12 and 14 the City of Londonderry.

Offences against the Prevention of Crime (Ireland) Act, 1882.

The number of cases dealt with under this Act is given in Tables 12 to 14, in the Appendix. From these Tables it appears that in the year 1883, 841 persons were proceeded against, of whom 458 were discharged and 383 convicted, including 233 for intimidation under Section VII.; 12 for riot or unlawful assembly; 44 for holding forcible possession; 14 for aggravated acts of violence against the person; and 21 for assaults on constables, bailiffs, &c., under Section VIII.; 46 for being found out at night under suspicious circumstances, under Section XI.; and 10 for being strangers found under suspicious circumstances. The details of the punishments inflicted, and the number of appeals in these cases will be found in Tables 13 and 14, pages 85 and 86.

In the year 1882 there were 1,114 persons proceeded against under this Act, of whom 648 were discharged and 466 convicted; the total number for last year (841) therefore shows a decrease of 273 as compared with the number for the portion of the year 1882 (from the 12th July), during which the Act was in force.

Distribution of charges under the Prevention of Crime (Ireland) Act, 1882. Table 12.

The distribution of the charges under the Crimes Act throughout the country (in 1883) is shown in Table 12. It will be observed that of the 841 cases, 196 were in Leinster, including 5 in Dublin County, 6 in Dublin Police District, 10 in Kildare, 30 in Kilkenny, 26 in King's County, 22 in Longford, 4 in Louth, 19 in Meath, 21 in Queen's County, 33 in Westmeath, 14 in Wexford, and 6 in Wicklow; 387 were in the province of Munster, including 38 in Clare, 29 in East Cork, 21 in West Cork, 162 in Kerry, 54 in Limerick County, 4 in Limerick City, 12 in North, and 41 in South Tipperary, and 6 in Waterford County. In the province of Ulster there were 68 cases, including 29 in Cavan, 10 in Donegal, 7 in Down, 3 in Fermanagh, 16 in Monaghan, and 3 in Tyrone. In the province of Connaught there were 189 cases, including 81 in East Galway, 16 in West Galway, and 1 in Galway Town; 17 in Leitrim, 45 in Mayo, 29 in Roscommon, and 54 in Sligo.

Of the 1,114 cases under this Act in 1882, 178 were in Leinster, 601 in Munster, 29 in Ulster, and 306 in Connaught.

Of 3,461 persons apprehended in 1883 for offences punishable after Indictment and trial by jury, 1,131, or 33 per cent., were discharged, 237, or 7 per cent. were bailed or committed in default of finding bail pending further examination, 2,093, or 60 per cent., were committed for trial or admitted to bail pending trial.

The result of proceedings in 741 cases brought before Grand Juries was that in 236 cases no bill was found, in 283 cases no prosecution took place, and in 222 cases bail was accepted, and the cases not tried. In addition to those bailed and not tried, or where there was no prosecution, there were 63 cases in which trials were postponed after disagreement of the juries.

Of 2,221 persons tried by jury in 1883, 461, or 20·8 per cent. were acquitted: besides 20, or 0·9 per cent. who were found insane or acquitted on the ground of insanity, 1,740, or 78·3 per cent. were convicted.

The following statement shows for the past decade the number of persons tried by jury at Assizes, at the Dublin Commission Court and at Quarter Sessions, and how their cases were disposed of:—

Part I. Criminal Statistics. Chapter II. Procedure.

Results of preliminary enquiry as to offences. Table 1.

Disposal of bills of indictment by grand jury. Table 24.

Disposal of persons tried by jury. Table 14.

Year	Tried.	Convicted or Detained as Insane.	Acquitted.	Proportion per cent. of those Tried who were	
				Convicted or Detained as Insane.	Acquitted.
1874, . . .	3,389	2,353	1,036	69·3	30·7
1875, . . .	3,521	2,500	1,021	70·9	29·1
1876, . . .	3,475	2,357	1,118	67·8	32·2
1877, . . .	3,191	2,311	880	72·4	27·6
1878, . . .	3,128	2,259	869	72·1	27·9
1879, . . .	3,364	2,317	1,047	68·9	31·1
1880, . . .	3,453	2,397	1,056	69·5	30·5
1881, . . .	3,850	2,714	1,136	70·5	29·5
1882, . . .	3,162	2,279	883	72·1	27·9
1883, . . .	2,221	1,760	461	79·2	20·8

In the following statement the sentences inflicted on persons convicted, after trial by jury, in 1883, are set out in comparison with similar cases in 1882.

Part I.
Criminal Statistics.

Chapter II.
Procedure.

Disposal of men and boys for trial by jury compared with disposal of women and girls.
Table 24.

Disposal of Persons Committed for Trial by Jury.

How Disposed of.	1883: Total.	1883: Men and Boys.	1883: Women and Girls.	1883: Proportion disposed of: Men and Boys	1883: Proportion disposed of: Women and Girls	1882: Total.	1882: Men and Boys.	1882: Women and Girls.	1882: Proportion disposed of: Men and Boys	1882: Proportion disposed of: Women and Girls
				Per cent.	Per cent.				Per cent.	Per cent.
Total number of persons sent for trial	[illegible]	[illegible]	[illegible]	[illegible]	[illegible]	[illegible]	[illegible]	[illegible]	[illegible]	[illegible]
Total not tried,	[illegible]	[illegible]	[illegible]	[illegible]	[illegible]	[illegible]	[illegible]	[illegible]	[illegible]	[illegible]
Viz.—Bailed and not tried,	[illegible]	[illegible]	[illegible]	[illegible]	[illegible]	[illegible]	[illegible]	[illegible]	[illegible]	[illegible]
No bills found against,	[illegible]	[illegible]	[illegible]	[illegible]	[illegible]	[illegible]	[illegible]	[illegible]	[illegible]	[illegible]
Not prosecuted,	[illegible]	[illegible]	[illegible]	[illegible]	[illegible]	[illegible]	[illegible]	[illegible]	[illegible]	[illegible]
Trial postponed after discharge of jury,	[illegible]	[illegible]	[illegible]	[illegible]	[illegible]	[illegible]	[illegible]	[illegible]	[illegible]	[illegible]
Total tried and disposed of, I and II.,	[illegible]	[illegible]	[illegible]	[illegible] / [illegible]	[illegible] / [illegible]	[illegible]	[illegible]	[illegible]	[illegible] / [illegible]	[illegible] / [illegible]
I. Convicted or detained as insane,	[illegible]	[illegible]	[illegible]	[illegible]	[illegible]	[illegible]	[illegible]	[illegible]	[illegible]	[illegible]
Viz.—Sentenced to death,	[illegible]	[illegible]	[illegible]	[illegible]	[illegible]	[illegible]	[illegible]	[illegible]	[illegible]	[illegible]
Penal servitude—										
For life,	[illegible]	[illegible]	—	[illegible]	.	[illegible]	[illegible]	.	[illegible]	.
Above 10 years,	[illegible]	[illegible]	—	[illegible]	—	[illegible]	[illegible]	.	[illegible]	.
For 10 and above 5 years,	[illegible]	[illegible]	[illegible]	[illegible]	[illegible]	[illegible]	[illegible]	[illegible]	[illegible]	[illegible]
For 5 years,	[illegible]	[illegible]	[illegible]	[illegible]	[illegible]	[illegible]	[illegible]	[illegible]	[illegible]	[illegible]
Found insane, or acquitted on ground of insanity,	[illegible]	[illegible]	[illegible]	[illegible]	[illegible]	[illegible]	[illegible]	[illegible]	[illegible]	[illegible]
Imprisonment—										
Above 2 years,	[illegible]	[illegible]	[illegible]	[illegible]	[illegible]	[illegible]	[illegible]	[illegible]	[illegible]	[illegible]
For 1 year and above 6 months,	[illegible]	[illegible]	[illegible]	[illegible]	[illegible]	[illegible]	[illegible]	[illegible]	[illegible]	[illegible]
For 6 months and under,	[illegible]	[illegible]	[illegible]	[illegible]	[illegible]	[illegible]	[illegible]	[illegible]	[illegible]	[illegible]
Whipping, fined, discharged on sureties, &c. [illegible],	[illegible]	[illegible]	[illegible]	[illegible]	[illegible]	[illegible]	[illegible]	[illegible]	[illegible]	[illegible]
II. Acquitted on trial,	[illegible]	[illegible]	[illegible]	[illegible]	[illegible]	[illegible]	[illegible]	[illegible]	[illegible]	[illegible]
Sent to Reformatory Schools,	[illegible]	[illegible]	[illegible]	—	.	[illegible]	[illegible]	[illegible]	—	.

From this it appears that, exclusive of those detained as insane, 1,740 were punished for serious offences in 1883, as compared with 2,255 in 1882, showing a decrease of 515. Of these, 1,398 were males, and 342 females, being about the same proportion as in 1882. Of the persons convicted, 11 were sentenced to death; 123 (112 males and 11 females) to penal servitude—5 of these were for life, 4 for over 10 years, 33 for above 5 and up to 10 years, and 81 for 5 years; 1,181 (925 males and 256 females) were sentenced to various terms of imprisonment. Seventeen cases (12 males and 5 females) were sent to Reformatory Schools.

The following statement shows the results of proceedings for the punishment of crime dealt with summarily in 1883, as compared with 1882, distinguishing the sexes:—

DISPOSAL OF PERSONS PROCEEDED AGAINST SUMMARILY.

Proceedings for offences determined summarily: cases of men and boys compared with those of women and girls.
Table 2.

How Disposed of.	1883. Total.	1883. Men and Boys.	1883. Women and Girls.	1883. Proportion per Cent. to Total: Men and Boys.	1883. Proportion per Cent. to Total: Women and Girls.	1882. Total.	1882. Men and Boys.	1882. Women and Girls.	1882. Proportion per Cent. to Total: Men and Boys.	1882. Proportion per Cent. to Total: Women and Girls.
Total Number proceeded against.	[illegible]	[illegible]	[illegible]	[illegible]	[illegible]	[illegible]	[illegible]	[illegible]	[illegible]	[illegible]
Discharged.	[illegible]	[illegible]	[illegible]	[illegible]	[illegible]	[illegible]	[illegible]	[illegible]	[illegible]	[illegible]
Sent Convicted.	[illegible]	[illegible]	[illegible]	[illegible]	[illegible]	[illegible]	[illegible]	[illegible]	[illegible]	[illegible]
Unclassed Punishments.	[illegible]	[illegible]	[illegible]	-	-	[illegible]	[illegible]	[illegible]	-	-
Classed Punishments.	[illegible]	[illegible]	[illegible]	[illegible]	[illegible]	[illegible]	[illegible]	[illegible]	[illegible]	[illegible]
Number not Committed, viz.—Total.	[illegible]	[illegible]	[illegible]	[illegible]	[illegible]	[illegible]	[illegible]	[illegible]	[illegible]	[illegible]
Fined.	[illegible]	[illegible]	[illegible]	[illegible]	[illegible]	[illegible]	[illegible]	[illegible]	[illegible]	[illegible]
To find Sureties or Recognizances.	[illegible]	[illegible]	[illegible]	[illegible]	[illegible]	[illegible]	[illegible]	[illegible]	[illegible]	[illegible]
Delivered to Army or Navy.	[illegible]	[illegible]	-	[illegible]	-	[illegible]	[illegible]	-	[illegible]	-
Whipped.	[illegible]	[illegible]	-	-	-	[illegible]	[illegible]	-	-	-
Number Committed, viz.—Total.	[illegible]	[illegible]	[illegible]	[illegible]	[illegible]	[illegible]	[illegible]	[illegible]	[illegible]	[illegible]
To Prison, 14 days or under.	[illegible]	[illegible]	[illegible]	[illegible]	[illegible]	[illegible]	[illegible]	[illegible]	[illegible]	[illegible]
" 1 month and above 14 days.	[illegible]	[illegible]	[illegible]	[illegible]	[illegible]	[illegible]	[illegible]	[illegible]	[illegible]	[illegible]
" 2 months and above 1 month.	[illegible]	[illegible]	[illegible]	[illegible]	[illegible]	[illegible]	[illegible]	[illegible]	[illegible]	[illegible]
" 3 months and above 2 months.	[illegible]	[illegible]	[illegible]	[illegible]	[illegible]	[illegible]	[illegible]	[illegible]	[illegible]	[illegible]
" 6 months and above 3 months.	[illegible]	[illegible]	[illegible]	[illegible]	[illegible]	[illegible]	[illegible]	[illegible]	[illegible]	[illegible]
" Above 6 months.	[illegible]	[illegible]	[illegible]	-	-	[illegible]	[illegible]	[illegible]	-	-
To Reformatory Schools.	[illegible]	[illegible]	[illegible]	[illegible]	[illegible]	[illegible]	[illegible]	[illegible]	[illegible]	[illegible]
To Industrial Schools.	[illegible]	[illegible]	[illegible]	[illegible]	[illegible]	[illegible]	[illegible]	[illegible]	[illegible]	[illegible]

Of the 225,518 persons proceeded against summarily in 1883, there were 35,310 discharged, and 190,208 convicted, as compared with 37,888 and 179,663 respectively in 1882. Of those convicted in 1883, 161,607 were males and 28,601 females. Of unclassed punishments there were 18,695 (13,988 males and 4,707 females). Of classed punishments there were 171,513 (147,619 males and 23,894 females). Of 159,100 persons not committed, 155,938 (136,641 males and 19,297 females) were fined, 2,830 (2,050 males and 780 females) were required to find sureties or recognizances; 321 were given up to the military or naval authorities, and 11 were whipped. Of the persons committed 4,654 (3,317 males and 1,337 females) were committed to prison for 14 days or under; 4,162 (2,788 males and 1,374 females) for one month and above 14 days; 1,293 (1,021 males and 272 females) for 2 months and over 1 month; 770 (544 males and 226 females) for 3 months and above 2 months; 430 (353 males and 77 females) for 6 months and above 3 months; and 72 (61 males and 11 females) for above 6 months. There were 203 young persons, including 154 males and 49 females, sent to Reformatory Schools, and 829, including 358 males and 471 females, sent to Industrial Schools.

Court for consideration of Crown cases reserved.
Table 74.

In the Court for the consideration of Crown cases reserved, constituted under 11 & 12 Vic., cap. 78, there was but one case before the Court in 1883. The conviction was reversed. There were three cases before the Court in 1882.

CHAPTER III. Criminals, &c., in Confinement and at large.

CHAPTER III.—CRIMINALS AND OTHERS IN CONFINEMENT, AND KNOWN CRIMINALS AT LABOR.

The statistics of persons in confinement, with a view to punishment for or prevention of crime, include actual criminals, persons accused of criminal offences, debtors, children detained in industrial and reformatory schools, and criminal and dangerous lunatics.

Admissions to different places of detention compared.

In the following statement the number of prisoners admitted to various places of confinement is set out:—

Admissions to Places of Detention.	Men and Boys.	Women and Girls.	Total.	Per cent.
Total in all Ireland,	27,475	14,476	41,951	100·
†Into 34 General and Larger District Prisons,	21,341	11,833	33,174	79·1
†Into 31 Smaller District Prisons (Bridewells),	2,653	508	3,161	7·5
Into 14 Short Sentence Prisons,	1,951	560	2,511	6·0
Into Lunatic Asylums (as criminals or dangerous),	1,037	713	1,750	4·2
Into Industrial Schools,	439	688	1,127*	2·7
Into Reformatory Schools,	196	19	215	0·5

* Of this number 5 were re-committals.

† The number of admissions into larger and smaller district prisons includes ordinary prisoners only.

It would thus appear that there were 41,951 persons admitted to places of confinement during the year, but this number is somewhat in excess of the fact, as children sent to Reformatories and some lunatics were confined in District Prisons prior to their final disposal in schools and lunatic asylums. It must also be noticed that some of the prisoners confined in prison during the year were committed more than once during that period.

Persons in detention at one time compared.

The distribution of prisoners under detention, at the end of the year 1883, among the different kinds of places of confinement is shown in the following statement:—

Criminals, &c., under Detention at end of year.	Men and Boys.	Women and Girls.	Total.	Per cent.
Total in all Ireland,	9,086	6,788	15,874	100·
Ordinary Criminals in Central and larger District Prisons,	1,598	625	2,223	14·0
In Smaller District Prisons (Bridewells),	36	7	43	0·3
In Short Sentence Prisons,	27	12	39	0·2
Debtors and on Civil Process,	8	–	8	0·0
Convicts,	763	108	871	5·5
Military or Naval Prisoners,	97	–	97	0·6
In Lunatic Asylums (as criminals or dangerous),	3,234	2,105	5,339	33·6
In Reformatories,	906	193	1,099*	6·9
In Industrial Schools,	2,409	3,750	6,159†	38·8

* Not including 3 retained in School, sentence expired.

† Not including 63 retained in School, sentence expired.

It appears from this statement that at the close of the year 1883 there were 15,874 detained in places of confinement, either for the punishment or the prevention of crime. Of the 15,874 there were 6,168 children in Industrial schools and 5,329 lunatics, making a total of 11,497, or more than two-thirds of the entire number who were not actual criminals, but were detained as a preventive measure. PART I. CRIMINAL STATISTICS. CHAPTER II. Criminals, &c., in Confinement and at large.

PRISONS.

The Prisons of Ireland which have since the year 1877 been completely under the control of the General Prisons Board, consist of four classes, namely :—1st. Three Central Prisons used for the reception of convicts and other special cases. 2nd. Larger District Prisons, 31 in number. 3rd. Short Sentence Prisons, 14 in number. 4th. Bridewells or smaller District Prisons which number 34. Classification of Prisons.

The State Prisons Tables, Tables 19 to 23, pp. 89–91, give various particulars as to the inmates of those institutions.

The number of commitments of ordinary criminals to larger district prisons in the year 1883, compared with 1882, was as follows:—

	1882.	1883.	Increase in 1883.	Decrease in 1883.
Men and Boys, . . .	22,884	21,341	–	1,543
Women and Girls, . .	11,221	11,833	612	–
Total, . . .	34,105	33,174	–	931

The state of education of those committed in 1883 is given in the following summary by sexes:— Degree of education of prisoners. Table 19(d).

Degree of Instruction.	Total of both Sexes.	Men and Boys.	Women and Girls.	Proportion per cent.	
				Males.	Females.
Total, ...	33,174	21,341	11,833	100·	100·
Read and write well, ...	12,367	8,703	3,664	43·5	31·0
Neither read nor write, ...	13,113	7,410	4,723	34·7	49·6
Read, or read and write imperfectly, . .	6,326	4,835	2,431	19·1	20·6
Superior instruction, ...	233	227	6	1·3	0·0
Instruction not ascertained, ...	83	81	2	0·2	0·0

The ignorance of the criminal class is illustrated by these figures: the proportion of ignorance is much greater among the females than among the males.

From the following statement it appears that of 33,174 commitments to larger district prisons of ordinary criminals, 17,981, or 54·2 per cent., were recommitments. It is remarkable that the proportion of recommitments in the case of females is 78 per cent. of the total of that sex, while in the case of males it is only 44 per cent., showing a greater proportion of habitual criminals among females than among males:— Re-commitments of Ordinary Criminals. Table 19(e).

COMMITMENTS OF ORDINARY CRIMINALS.

—	Total.	Number.		Percentage 1883.	
		Men.	Women.	Men.	Women.
Total number, . .	33,174	21,341	11,833	100·	100·
First Commitments, .	15,193	11,943	3,250	56	27
Recommitments, . .	17,981	9,350	8,583	44	73

Part I. Criminal Statistics. — Chapter III. Criminals, &c., in Confinement and at large. — Re-commitments of ordinary criminals. Table 19 (a).

A more detailed statement is here given as to the number of recommitments of these criminals committed more than once.

Number of Times which Prisoners were previously Committed.	Total of both Sexes.	Men.	Women.	Proportion per cent. 1863. Total of both Sexes.	Men.	Women.
Total number of recommitments, .	17,981	9,[illegible]	8,663	100·	100·	100·
Once previously, . . .	4,255	2,944	1,311	23·7	31·3	15·8
Twice do., . . .	3,243	1,552	691	18·5	16·5	[illegible]
Thrice do., . . .	1,525	1,014	511	8·5	10·8	[illegible]
Four times previously, . .	1,080	883	197	5·7	6·4	[illegible]
Five times do., . . .	761	408	353	4·2	4·3	[illegible]
Six or seven times previously, .	1,134	617	517	6·3	6·6	6·0
Eight, nine, or ten times do., . .	1,269	658	611	7·1	7·0	7·1
Above ten times, . . .	5,764	1,603	4,161	32·0	17·1	48·5

From this it appears that of the 17,981 prisoners who were committed more than once, 4,255, or 23·7 per cent., were previously committed once; 3,243, or 18·5 per cent., twice; 1,525, or 8·5 per cent., three times; 1,080, or 5·7 per cent., *four times*; 761, or 4·2 per cent., *five times*; 1,134, or 6·3 per cent., *six or seven times*; 1,269, or 7·1 per cent., eight, nine, or ten times; and 5,764, or 32·0 per cent., above ten times. The greater proportion of re-commitments among females than males is more fully shown in this than in the previous statement; the percentage of males committed above ten times being 17·1 as compared with 48·5 among females.

Age and sex of ordinary prisoners. Table 19 (b).

The following summary shows the age and sex of the ordinary prisoners (other than debtors and persons charged with military and naval offences) committed to the larger District Prisons in Ireland in 1863, together with the proportions per cent. of each sex at the several age-periods:—

Ages.	Total of both Sexes.	Men and Boys.	Women and Girls.	Proportion per cent. 1863. Men and Boys.	Women and Girls.
Total, . . .	33,174	21,341	11,833	100·	100·
Under twelve years, . . .	99	80	19	0·4	0·1
Twelve years and under sixteen, . .	704	594	110	2·8	0·9
Sixteen years and under twenty-one, .	6,319	5,093	1,226	23·9	10·4
Twenty-one years and under thirty, .	10,971	7,063	3,919	33·1	33·1
Thirty years and under forty, . .	7,534	4,023	3,515	18·9	29·7
Forty years and under fifty, . .	4,461	2,411	2,050	11·3	17·3
Fifty years and under sixty, . .	1,857	1,184	673	5·5	5·7
Above sixty years, . . .	1,169	838	332	3·9	2·8
Age not ascertained, . . .	53	52	1	0·2	0·0

Occupations of ordinary prisoners. Table 19 (c).

The statistics of the occupations of prisoners are given in Table 19 (c), page 69. They show the usual large proportion of prostitutes and unoccupied [illegible] of bad character, the numbers under these heads being 5,843 and 2,491 respectively, out of a total of 11,833 female prisoners.

Part I. Criminal Statistics. — Chapter II. Criminals, &c., in Confinement and at large. — Criminal and Dangerous Lunatics in confinement. Table 31.

Criminal and Dangerous Lunatics.

The following summary shows the number of persons detained in lunatic asylums, the authority under which they were committed and the mode of their disposal during the year:—

Criminal Lunatics and Dangerous Lunatics charged with intent to commit Crime.	Ireland, 1883		
	Men.	Women.	Total.
Total number of such Lunatics under detention during year,	1,080	2,678	8,758
Under detention at commencement of year,	4,042	1,965	6,097
Committed by Justices, under 30 & 31 Vic., c. 118,	969	681	1,652
Received from Prisons under warrant of Lord Lieutenant,	67	29	96
Received from other Asylums,	2	-	2
Total number disposed of during year,	846	573	1,419
Discharged on recovery, on certificate of Resident Medical Superintendent.	111	253	543
Died,	271	213	484
Given to their friends,	120	70	190
Became ordinary patients on expiration of sentence,	16	11	27
Removed to workhouses, as sane,	15	23	38
Discharged as sane by warrant of Lord Lieutenant,	7	1	8
Removed to Prison for trial or punishment,	7	2	9
Escaped.	1	-	1
Transferred to other Asylums,	8	1	9
Remaining under detention at close of year,	3,224	2,105	5,329

The above statement shows an increase of 182 in the number under detention at the end of 1883, as compared with the number at commencement of the year.

Grounds of committal. Table 32.

The following summary shows the number of dangerous lunatics committed to asylums in 1883, and the offences which criminal lunatics committed to asylums during the year, were charged with having committed:—

Offences of Lunatics on Grounds of Committal.	Males.	Females.	Total of both Sexes.	Proportion per cent.
Total committed during the year,	1,067	713	1,780	100
Dangerous persons, having intent to commit crime,	969	684	1,653	91·5
Assaults and riot,	23	8	31	1·8
Offences against property,	11	9	20	1·1
Offences against human life,	9	6	15	0·9
Other offences than those here specified,	21	6	27	1·5
Vagrants and insane persons without control,	3	1	4	0·2

It appears from this table that the lunatics committed as dangerous persons at large having an intent to commit crime, formed 94·5 per cent. of the total number of criminal and dangerous lunatics committed during the year.

PART I. GENERAL STATISTICS. — CHAPTER II. *Criminals, &c., in Confinement and at large.* — Criminal and Dangerous Lunatics. Judgment or order of committal under which detained.

The following summary shows the judgments or orders under which criminal and dangerous lunatics were committed to asylums in Ireland in 1883:—

Judgment or Order of Committal.	Males.	Females.	Total of both Sexes.	Proportion per cent.
Total committed during year,	1,037	713	1,750	100·
Committed to asylums by Justices as dangerous, under sec. 10, 30 & 31 Vic., c. 118, s. 10,	969	634	1,652	94·5
Transmitted from prisons by Lord Lieutenant's warrant:—				
Became insane while undergoing sentence of imprisonment,	35	20	55	3·3
Found or declared insane,	14	1	15	0·9
Became insane after committal and before trial,	6	5	11	0·6
Acquitted as insane,	8*	5	13*	0·7

It appears that 94·5 per cent. of the lunatics were committed direct to asylums by Justices as dangerous with intent to commit crime, and that only 5·5 per cent. were sent by Lord Lieutenant's warrant.

REFORMATORY SCHOOLS.

Reformatory Schools. Number in confinement. Table 27.

With respect to institutions for the prevention of crime, namely, Reformatory and Industrial Schools, the following statement deals with juvenile criminals under Reformatory control in the year 1883, compared with 1882.

Number of Children in Reformatory or under Reformatory control in Ireland.	End of 1883. Boys.	End of 1883. Girls.	End of 1883. Total Boys and Girls.	End of 1882. Total.	Increase in 1883.	Decrease in 1883.
In School,	907	192	1,099	1,140	–	41
On licence,	88	1	89	92	–	3
Remained in School, sentence expired,	3	–	3	9	–	6
Absconded, sentence unexpired,	7	–	7	7	–	–
In Prison,	3	–	3	4	–	1
Total,	1,006	193	1,199	1,250	–	51

From this table it appears that there was a decrease of 51 in the number of children under Reformatory control in Ireland at the end of 1883, as compared with the close of the preceding year. There were 41 less in the schools under sentence; 3 less on licence; 1 less in prison; and 6 less were retained in school after sentence had expired (with their own consent), until provided with employment. Seven had absconded, with sentence unexpired, being equal to the number under this heading in 1882.

The total number of children under Reformatory control at the close of the year 1883 was 1,190 (1,006 boys and only 193 girls): the number committed during the year was 245—196 boys and 49 girls.

Degree of parental control. Table 28.

The position of the children committed in 1883 to *Reformatories* in Ireland, as regards parental control, is shown in the following table:—

	Boys.	Girls.	Proportion per cent. Boys.	Proportion per cent. Girls.
Total committed,	196	49	100·	100·
Illegitimate, deserted, or one or both parents destitute or criminal,	60	17	30	35
Under control of parents, other than above	84	22	43	45
One parent dead,	33	8	17	16
Total orphans,	19	2	10	4

Of the boys 43 per cent., and of the girls 45 per cent., were under parental control.

* Including one man transferred from a District Asylum.

The illegitimate, the deserted, and those having one or both parents destitute or criminal amounted to 30 per cent. of the boys and 35 per cent. of the girls. The orphans (or having one parent dead) were only 27 per cent. of boys and 20 per cent. of girls.

The degree of education of children committed to Reformatory Schools is shown in the following summary:—

	Boys.	Girls.	Proportion per cent. Boys.	Proportion per cent. Girls.
Total committed,	176	49	100·	100·
Neither read nor write,	83	26	47	53
Read or read and write imperfectly,	[illegible]	13	41	27
Read and write well,	[illegible]	10	12	20
Superior instruction,	-	-	-	-

The want of education is pointedly shown in this summary. Of the boys committed to Reformatories, 47 per cent. were wholly uneducated; only 12 per cent. could read and write well, while the remainder, 41 per cent., had received a small amount of education. Amongst the girls 53 per cent. were wholly uneducated, and 27 per cent. could only read, or read and write imperfectly, and only 20 per cent. could read and write well.

INDUSTRIAL SCHOOLS.

The institutions in which the largest number of persons were in custody at the end of the year were Industrial Schools.

The number of Industrial Schools in 1883, as compared with the number in 1882, shows an increase of 2, making 63,* of which 26 were in Munster, 19* in Leinster, 10 in Connaught, and 8 in Ulster.

The following summary shows the number of children under warrant of detention in Industrial Schools in Ireland at the end of 1883, as compared with similar statistics for the end of 1882:—

Children under Control of Industrial Schools in Ireland.	End of 1883. Boys.	End of 1883. Girls.	End of 1883. Total.	End of 1882.	Increase, 1883.	Decrease, 1883.
In School,	2,409	3,759	6,168	6,078	90	-
On Licence,	165	255	420	377	43	-
Absconded,	1	[illegible]	5	6	-	1
Retained in school, sentence expired,	7	56	63	69	-	6
Total,	2,588	4,068	6,656	6,530	126	-

It appears from this table that the number of children under control of Industrial Schools in Ireland at the end of 1883 (6,656) is higher by 126 than the number (6,530) at the end of 1882. Of the total number, 6,168 were in the schools undergoing their sentence of detention, 63 were retained in school by their own consent although their sentences had expired, 420 were on licence, and 5 had absconded.

The following figures show the ages of the children placed in these schools in 1883:—

Ages of Children.	Boys and Girls.	Boys.	Girls.	Percentage of Total. Boys.	Percentage of Total. Girls.
Total,	1,119	428	691	Per cent. 100·	Per cent. 100·
Under 6 years,	44	7	37	1·6	5·4
6 and under 8 years,	292	68	224	15·9	32·4
8 and under 10 years,	424	113	311	[illegible]	[illegible]
10 and under 12 years,	316	163	153	38·1	22·1
12 years and upwards,	153	87	66	20·3	9·6

* See Note (2), page 103.

Part I. Criminal Statistics.

It appears from these figures that 68 per cent. of the girls and 42 per cent. of the boys are brought under careful training in these schools at the early age of under ten years.

In 1882, 511 boys were sent to Industrial Schools, as compared with 744 girls; and in 1883, 420 boys were sent, as compared with 691 girls.

Thieves, &c., at large. Table 3.

Table 3 exhibits statistics of the number of known thieves, depredators, receivers of stolen goods, and suspected persons at large and of the houses they frequent.

Chapter IV. Cost of Repressing Crime.

CHAPTER IV.—COST OF THE REPRESSION OF CRIME.

Tables 1, 2, 22, 25, 27, 29, 31.

The cost of repression of crime is shown in the following statement:—

Cost of Repression of Crime.	1882.	1883.	Increase.	Decrease.
	£	£	£	£
Total cost, .	1,970,707	2,201,604	230,897	–
Police, ...	1,452,879	1,719,861	247,982	–
Prosecutions, ...	61,115	63,716	2,300	–
Prisons, ...	145,689	149,960	4,271	–
Lunatics, ...	111,664	123,723	8,049	–
Industrial Schools, . . .	113,845	114,297	452	–
Reformatory Schools, . . .	32,393	30,945	–	1,448

Police Establishments.

The following summary shows the Police Force in Ireland in 1883, compared with the number in 1882, at the periods of the year stated in the tables:—

Constabulary and Police.	1882.	1883.	Increase, 1883.	Decrease, 1883.
Royal Irish Constabulary. (Table 1.)				
Effective strength—Officers, ...	263	271	8	–
" Head-Constables, Constables, &c., .	14,343	13,735	–	608
Total, .	14,606	14,006	–	600
Dublin Metropolitan Police. (Table 2.)				
Superior Officers, ...	38	41	3	–
Sergeants and Constables, . . .	1,139	1,181	42	–
Total, .	1,177	1,222	45	–
Grand Total, .	15,783	15,228	–	555

Decrease in Royal Irish Constabulary and increase in Dublin Metropolitan Police.

The number of the Royal Irish Constabulary has been decreased by 608 men, and the number of the Dublin Metropolitan Police increased by 42 men, making a net decrease of 566 men in the total Police force* for Ireland, following an increase of 2,021 in 1882, 1,161 in 1881, 182 in 1880, and 101 in 1879, and a decrease of 125 in 1878.

Tables 1 and 2.

A column in the first table in the Appendix shows the proportion which the number of effective force of Constabulary bears to the population in the various counties, and is

* Exclusive of Officers.

towns with a separate Police force, in Ireland. In the following counties the proportion of Police to population is the smallest, as will be seen from the table :—

Antrim, ...	11 in every 10,000 of the population.
Armagh, ...	11 „ „
Down, ...	11 „ „
Londonderry, ...	11 „ „

In the following counties in Ireland the proportion of Police is the largest :—

Galway, ...	48 in every 10,000 of the population.
Westmeath	45 „ „
Limerick, ...	44 „ „
Tipperary, N.R., ...	[illegible] „ „
Tipperary, S.R., ...	[illegible] „ „
King's County, ...	[illegible] „ „

The proportion of Police in the principal Cities and Towns is as follows :—

Galway, ...	[illegible] in every 10,000 of the population.
Drogheda, ...	32 „ „
Dublin Metropolitan Police District, . .	31 „ „
Kilkenny, ...	29 „ „
Waterford, ...	29 „ „
Belfast Town Force, ...	29 „ „
Cork, ...	25 „ „
Limerick, ...	[illegible] „ „
Londonderry, ...	[illegible] „ „

The proportion of Police—excluding County Inspectors and District Inspectors (formerly Sub-Inspectors)—but including Depot and Reserve Force—to the estimated population of Ireland in 1883 was 30 in every 10,000 of the people.

In the Royal Irish Constabulary the members of the different branches of the Force are selected when necessary, to act as detectives; in the Police of the Dublin Metropolitan Police District there is an entire division of 39 effective men (23 Constables, 16 Sergeants,) with 4 Inspectors and 1 Superintendent, who are detectives.

The following table shows the total cost of the Police Establishments in Ireland in 1883, as compared with that for 1882 :—

[illegible]	[illegible]	[illegible]	[illegible]	[illegible]
	£	£	£	£
Total of all Ireland, .	[illegible]	[illegible]	[illegible]	-
Royal Irish Constabulary, .	[illegible]	[illegible]	[illegible]	-
Dublin Metropolitan Police, .	[illegible]	[illegible]	—	10,[illegible]

This table indicates an increase in the total cost of the Police Force of £267,232 in 1883, following increases of £144,545 in 1882, £76,720 in 1881, £13,958 in 1880, £21,131 in 1879, £8,744 in 1878, £20,307 in 1877, and decreases of £9,394 in 1876 and £34,644 in 1875.

There was some increase in the demand for extra Constabulary during the year ended 30th September, 1883: the greatest number chargeable in any month reached 3,300 in November, 1882, as against 3,248 in September, 1882, 1,677 in September, 1881, and 1,033 in September, 1880; the least number chargeable, 3,051 in August, 1883, was considerably above the minimum for the preceding year, which was 1,810 in October, 1881.

* Royal Irish Constabulary for year ended 31st March, 1883. Dublin Metropolitan Police for year ended 31st March, 1884.

Part I. General Statistics. — Chapter IV. Cost of Repressing Crime.

Cost of Criminal Lunatics in Asylums. Table 31.

The cost of criminal lunatics and dangerous lunatics charged with an intention to commit a crime, is £123,733.

Cost of Industrial Schools. Table 30.

In the case of Industrial Schools, the total expenditure returned is £144,337—Imperial Taxes,* £77,960; Local Rates,* £27,960; other sources £39,819.

Cost of Criminals in Confinement. Tables 23 and 27.

The following table shows the cost of criminal classes, other than lunatics, in confinement in 1883, as compared with 1882:—

Cost of Criminal Classes in Confinement.	1882.	1883.	Increase, 1883.	Decrease, 1883.
	£	£	£	£
Total of places of confinement,	178,083	180,925	2,813	–
Prisons,	145,489	149,980	4,591	–
Reformatories,	32,393	30,945	–	1,448

State Prisons. Table 23.

The cost of State Prisons in Ireland, including what were formerly Convict Prisons, County and Town Gaols, and the Bridewells that are still retained, is taken at £149,980, the sum in the Parliamentary Estimates for 1884–5; the particulars are given therein in detail.

Reformatories. Table 27.

As to Reformatories, the total costs in Ireland are returned as £30,945—£17,356 charged to Imperial Taxes, £7,920 to Local Rates, and £5,469 to other sources.

Costs of Criminal Prosecutions. Table 33.

The form of return as to costs of criminal prosecutions, settled in 1872, has been continued. It brings the information up to 31st March, 1883.

Criminal Courts.	Costs of Criminal Prosecutions.		Increase, 1882–83.	Decrease, 1882–83.
	1881–82.	1882–83.		
	£	£	£	£
Total of all Ireland,	61,416	63,716	2,300	—
Assizes and Commission Courts,	42,668	42,684	16	—
Quarter Sessions,	14,554	14,530	–	24
Petty Sessions, Inquests, and Police Courts,	4,296	6,504	2,208	—

This table shows an increase in the cost of criminal prosecutions in Ireland in 1882–83 above 1881–82 of £2,300, following an increase of £12,300 in 1881–82.

* The sum (£105,920) entered under "Imperial Taxes" and "Local Rates" includes £105 unexpended at close of year.

PART II.—JUDICIAL STATISTICS.

Part II. Judicial Statistics.

Arrangement of Tables.

The Tables in this part include Statistics relating to the Civil Jurisdiction of all Courts in Ireland.

The Courts and Offices are divided into those which relate to the Central Administration of Justice, and those which relate to the Local Administration of Justice. The latter are classified into larger and smaller District Administration of Justice, according to the size of the districts into which Ireland is divided for the Special Jurisdiction.

1.—CENTRAL ADMINISTRATION OF JUSTICE.

Central Administration of Justice.

Arrangement of Tables.

The Central Administration of Justice includes the High Court of Justice, with its five divisions—Chancery, Queen's Bench, Common Pleas, Exchequer, and the Probate and Matrimonial Division.

There are three outlying Courts:—The Court of the Land Commission, the High Court of Admiralty, and the Court of Bankruptcy.

The Central Appellate Jurisdictions, viz., Her Majesty's Court of Appeal, Ireland; Court for Crown Cases Reserved; Court for Cases Reserved for Judges of the Queen's Bench, Common Pleas, and Exchequer Divisions; the Privy Council in Ireland; Her Majesty in Council, and the House of Lords, have been grouped along with the other Central Jurisdictions, as they are closely connected with them.

In the arrangement of the Tables of the different Divisions of the High Court of Justice, the order followed in the English report has been, as far as possible, adopted.

The chief business of the Queen's Bench, Common Pleas, and Exchequer Divisions (the proceedings at the Plea side) is given in consecutive tables.

The proceedings at Jury Trials in Dublin of these three divisions, and the Dublin County Court Appeals, are grouped together, as the business is really transacted on a consolidated plan. With these, the proceedings at chambers before a single Judge, and the cases of minor importance remitted to County Courts are grouped together.

The Statistics regarding the exclusive jurisdiction of each of the three divisions:—on the Crown side of the Queen's Bench, as to election petitions and acknowledgements of married women in the Common Pleas, and at the Revenue side of the Exchequer, are given last, as the business is so small, compared with that transacted on the Plea side of these divisions.

The offices of Registration of Judgments and Record of Title are grouped together, and along with them is given the Registry of Deeds, as the functions performed by the three are somewhat similar.

The statistics as to the Chancery, Common Law, and Land Judges' Taxing Offices

JUDICIAL STATISTICS. — *General Administration of Justice.* — Business in Court before Lord Chancellor, Master of the Rolls, and Vice-Chancellor. Tables 33-4.

The following summary shows the Court business in the Chancery Division during the years 1882 and 1883, with the increase or decrease under each head in the latter year.

Court Business in Chancery Division.	1882.	1883.	Increase, 1883.	Decrease, 1883.
Before Lord Chancellor.				
Orders on motions special or from Chambers,	37	43	5	–
Orders on motions of course,	11	9	–	2
Orders on petitions of course,	–	1	1	–
Orders on petitions heard,	–	5	5	–
Causes, actions, &c., heard,	–	–	–	–
Motions for decree or judgment heard,	–	–	–	–
Causes, actions, &c., for further consideration heard,	1	1	–	–
	49	58	9	–
Before Master of the Rolls.				
Orders on motions special or from Chambers,	255	242	–	13
Orders on motions of course,	199	205	6	–
Orders on petitions heard,	74	80	6	–
Causes, actions, &c., heard,	71	43	–	28
Motions for decree or judgment heard,	34	28	–	6
Causes, actions, &c., for further consideration heard,	78	50	–	28
	711	648	–	63
Before Vice-Chancellor.				
Orders on motions special or from Chambers,	273	298	24	–
Orders on motions of course,	183	167	–	16
Orders on petitions heard,	78	73	–	
Causes, actions, &c., heard,	49	64	15	–
Motions for decree or judgment heard,	50	46	–	4
Causes, actions, &c., for further consideration heard,	55	55	–	–
County Court equity appeals heard,*	6	5	–	1
	694	708	13	–
Total,	1,456	1,414	–	42

This table shows a decrease of Court business of 42 proceedings, following a decrease of 49 in 1883. The arrears increased from 29 at the end of 1882, to 60 at the end of 1883.

Registrars' Office. Table 33.

In the office of the Registrars of the Chancery Division, the total number of Side Bar Orders was 530 as compared with 496 in 1882.

Appeals from Equity Actions in County Courts. Table 34.

From the County Court equitable jurisdiction, up to £500 property and £30 a year in land, there were 15 Appeals filed, 9 of which were heard before the Vice-Chancellor or one of the Land Judges, with the result that 5 were dismissed with costs and 4 reversed or varied. One case was struck out, and there were 5 pending at the end of the year.

* There were also 1 of such Appeals before Judge Flanagan in 1883, and 6 in 1882.

Part II. Judicial Statistics. — *Central Administration of Justice.* — *Chancery Division.* — Chief Clerks' Returns of proceedings in Chambers Table 26.

The following is a summary of the proceedings in the chambers of the Lord Chancellor, the Master of the Rolls, and the Vice-Chancellor :—

Proceedings in Chambers of Chancery Judges.	1882.	1883.	Lancaster, 1883.	Durham, 1883.
Summonses :—				
To make Infants Wards,	25	16	11	–
For the Administration of Estates,	95	82	–	16
Under the Charitable Trusts Acts,	–	–	–	–
For appointment of Guardians and maintenance of Infants,	39	43	4	–
For other purposes,	562	613	15	–
Other Summonses than to originate Proceedings,	2,013	1,872	–	141
Appointments (by Summonses, &c.), disposed of,	6,663	6,016	–	377
Orders made :—				
Of the Class drawn up by the Registrars,	1	7	6	–
Of the Class drawn up in Chambers,	1,683	1,530	–	153
Orders brought into Chamber for prosecution :—				
Other than Orders for winding up Companies,	302	296	93	–
For winding up Companies,	3	1	–	2
Number of Advertisements issued,	155	169	14	–
Receivers' Accounts passed,	21	37	6	–
Receipts therein,	£24,145	£17,163	£23,017	–
Disbursements and Allowances therein,	£25,110	£36,891	£13,111	–
Accounts passed other than Receivers' Accounts :—				
Number of Accounts,	341	316	–	25
Receipts therein,	£794,733	£628,511	–	£56,316
Disbursements and allowances therein,	£806,357	£679,123	–	£54,325

There was a decrease of 9 in Summonses for Administration of Estates, and Appointment of Guardians, from 134 in 1882, to 125 in 1883; and a decrease in Summonses other than those to originate proceedings of 141, from 2,013 in 1882 to 1,872 in 1883.

The amount of property passed in accounts decreased from £1,018,877 in 1882 to £985,676 in 1883, being a decline of £33,201.

Minor matters in Chambers

In the Lord Chancellor's, the Master of the Rolls', and the Vice-Chancellor's Chambers there were at the end of the year 451 Minor Matters, relating to 1,368 Minors. The new Matters in the year were 53, relating to 120 Minors as compared with 35 new Matters and 79 new Wards in 1882.

Clerk of Records and Writs. Table 28.

The number of actions by writ of summons was 606, showing an increase of 44 above (562) the number in 1882. The proportion of lower scale to higher scale was as 18 to 82 per cent. The originating summonses (124) are 32 more than the summonses filed (92) in 1882. In the Notice Department there were 15,255 original documents, against 10,763 in 1882, and 57,460 copies, against 40,344 in 1882.

Lord Chancellor's Secretary. Table 27.

The Lord Chancellor made 26 orders for appointments of Commissioners for administering oaths for the High Court of Justice. The warrants for Magistrates were 163, as compared with 232 in 1882; the warrants as to Coroners were 11. There were no orders on Petitions as to Notaries. The orders as to other Petitions, including Minor Matters, were 61.

Part II.
Judicial Statistics.
Central Administration of Justice.
Chancery Division.
Secretary at the Rolls. Table 37.

The return of the Secretary at the Rolls gives the particulars of 99 petitions set down for hearing before the Master of the Rolls. It appears that 38 of these were under the Trustee Acts, and 23 under the Public Works and Railway Acts.

In the Crown and Hanaper Office there were, during the year 1883, 2,663 official seals, as compared with 3,037 in 1882.

Land Judges.

Crown and Hanaper Office. Table 38.
Registrar's Returns. Table 40.

Under the Land Judges the net rental or annual value (where given) of Estates sold was £19,402, as compared with £11,895 in 1882, £19,970 in 1881, £19,598 in 1880, £45,015 in 1879, and £84,236 in 1878, and the purchase money was £233,750, as compared with £203,637 in 1882, £311,236 in 1881, £329,549 in 1880, £799,063 in 1879, and £1,317,097 in 1878. The purchase money in 1883 was equal to 11·9 years purchase on an average of all interests and all tenures. This is below 17·1 the one in 1882, 15·3 in 1881, 16·5 in 1880, 17·7 in 1879, and 18·9 in 1878, and below the average for 6 years ended 1877, which was 19·4.

The number of cases pending at the end of the year in the Chambers of Judges was 1,840, as compared with 1,811 in 1882.

Record and Affidavit Office. Table 39.

There were 308 petitions filed in 1883, against 309 in 1882, only 68 being by owners. The number of affidavits filed was 3,930, against 3,885 in 1882.

Keeper of Deeds. Table 41.

The number of abstracts of title lodged was 181, and the number of deeds and other documents lodged 6,107.

Sale of Land to Tenants. Table 40.

The sales to tenants under the Irish Land Act of 1870, in which charging orders in favour of the Board of Works for advances to enable them to purchase were made, was 38 in 1882, and 10 in 1883, for £30,221, and £13,937 respectively. Of the 10 sales in 1883, 7 were of holdings under 100 acres, including 3 of holdings under 30, 2 of which were of holdings under 10 acres; 3 were of holdings in Leinster, 3 of holdings in Munster, and the remaining 4 of holdings in Connaught.

Queen's Bench, Common Pleas, and Exchequer Divisions.

Distribution of business in Queen's Bench, Common Pleas, and Exchequer Divisions. Tables 42, 43, 44, 46, 47, and 48.

The proceedings at the Pleas side of the Queen's Bench, Common Pleas, and Exchequer Divisions are arranged in a single table for each division, although the figures have been supplied by three officers—the Clerk of Writs, the Master, and the Registrar. This has been done to produce tables comparable with those in the English returns.

The writs of summons for the Exchequer Division were 10,279 in 1882, and 7,632 in 1883; those for the Queen's Bench were 10,251 in 1882; and 7,701 in 1883; and those for the Common Pleas were in 1882, 10,249, and in 1883, 7,700.

The total number of writs of summons for these three divisions showed a decrease of 7,726 from 30,779 in 1882, to 23,033 in 1883. The number of cases which actually came to trial by jury in Dublin was 317 in 1883, as compared with 475 in 1882, being a decrease of 158; the amount of money recovered at these trials shows an increase from £25,976 in 1882, to £39,452 in 1883.

Of the other business of the Queen's Bench, Common Pleas, and Exchequer Divisions, on the Plea side, there were in the Queen's Bench 6,728 affidavits, in the Common Pleas, 7,238, and in the Exchequer 7,074, the total number being 21,040, showing a decrease of 18,609 as compared with the number for 1882.

At Chambers there were 97 summonses in the Common Pleas, 99 in the Queen's Bench, and 171 in the Exchequer Division. The motions on notice before a single Judge were, in the Queen's Bench 668, in the Common Pleas 150, and in the Exchequer Division 601. The ex-parte motions, including consent orders, granted before a single Judge, were, in the Queen's Bench 425, in the Exchequer 814, and in the Common Pleas Division 789.

The Judges for Jury trials in Dublin also hear Appeals from the Courts of the Recorder, the County Court Judge for the City and County of Dublin.

The statistics of these appeals or rehearings in 1882 and 1883 are as follows:—

Appeals (Rehearings).		Entered.	Affirmed.	Reversed.	Settled, Struck out, &c.	Remaining.
From Decree or Dismiss of Recorder of Dublin City and County Courts (including case stated),	1882,	13	3	4	3	3
	1883,	38	20	8	5	5

The proceedings as to cases to be remitted to County Courts are as follows:—

Proceedings under Stat. 40 & 41 Vic., cap. 56.	1882.	1883.	Increase, 1883.	Decrease, 1883.
Number of applications to remit to inferior Courts,	227	275	48	-
Number of applications refused,	37	34	-	3
Number of applications granted,	190	241	51	-
In Cases of Contract under £50.				
Number of applications granted,	104	132	28	-
In Cases of Tort.				
Number of applications granted under sec. 6,	86	109	23	-

It appears from this table that the number of applications to remit cases to the County Courts, was 275, showing an increase of 48 as compared with the year 1882. Of the 241 applications granted, 132 were in cases of contract and 109 in cases of tort.

Part II. Judicial Statistics. — Central Administration of Justice. — Queen's Bench, Common Pleas, and Exchequer Divisions. — Distribution of business in Queen's Bench, Common Pleas, and Exchequer Divisions, Tables 42, 43, 44, 46, 47, and 48. — Appeals heard before Judges of Consolidated Jury Trial Court, Table 49. — Cases remitted to County Courts. Table 50.

QUEEN'S BENCH DIVISION.

The Queen's Coroner, Attorney and Master on the Crown side has made his usual return of the business at the Crown side of the Queen's Bench.

Proceedings at the Crown Side, Table 51.

COMMON PLEAS DIVISION.

In 1883 there were no election petitions.

The acknowledgments by married women filed were 48, as compared with 299 in 1882.

Three acknowledgments were taken by a County Court Judge under the 65th section of the County Court and Officers' Act, 1877.

Election Petitions, Table 52. Acknowledgments by Married Women, Table 53.

PART II. Judicial Statistics. — Central Administration of Justice. — Exchequer Division.

No Perpetual Commissioners were appointed; in 1882 there were five appointments. There were 34 Special Commissions granted, as compared with 36 in 1882.

Revenue side. Tables 53 and 54.

EXCHEQUER DIVISION.

The writs issued on the Revenue side were 357, as compared with 622 in 1882. The Side Bar Rules were 34, as compared with 92 in 1882. The affidavits filed were 158, as compared with 128 in 1882; 123 Miscellaneous Records were filed.

Registry of Judgments Office. Table 55.

OFFICES OF REGISTRATION.

The number of judgments registered in the Registry of Judgments Office in 1883, as compared with the preceding year, was as follows:—

Registry of Judgments Office.	1882.	1883.	Increase, 1883.	Decrease, 1883.
Judgments of High Court of Justice registered,	7,489	4,363	–	3,126
" " re-registered,	116	158	42	–
Revivals,	–	–	–	–
Decrees, Rules, and Orders,	–	–	–	–
Lis pendens,	276	171	18	–
Judgments from Courts in England and Scotland,	26	31	5	–
Total,	8,009	4,976	–	3,033
Recognizances registered,	519	521	2	–
" re-registered,	28	15	–	8
Crown Bonds registered,	78	191	113	–
" re-registered,	38	7	–	31
Total,	659	737	78	–
Satisfactions of Judgments,	123	189	66	–
Vacates of Recognizances, and Cancellations of Crown Bonds.	91	114	23	–
Negative Searches on £1 Stamps,	–	–	–	–
" " 15s. Stamps,	1,495	1,763	268	–
" " 2s. 6d. Stamps,	193	69	–	124
Total,	1,902	2,135	233	–
Requisitions for liberty to search made by public,	9,978	6,308	–	3,670
Stamped Certificates issued,	5,768	3,015	–	2,753

The figures in the above table show a decrease in the business of the office in 1883. The number of Judgments registered has fallen from 7,489 in 1882 to 4,358 in 1883.

Of the Judgments registered, none were obtained before 15th July, 1850 (which judgments alone affect land without being registered in the Deeds Office as a Judgment Mortgage): of the 158 Judgments re-registered, 149 were obtained before 15th July, 1850, and only 9 obtained since that date.

Part II. Judicial Statistics. — Central Administration of Justice.

On comparing the number of judgments registered with the number of executions issued on Judgments in the Queen's Bench, Common Pleas, and Exchequer Divisions, it appears that, whilst 8,012 judgment executions are returned in the proceedings in Masters' Offices as entered up, 4,363 judgments were registered in the Registry of Judgments Office.

Record of Title Office. Table 38.

The total number of estates or properties, the titles to which have been recorded in the Record of Title Office since its establishment in 1865, under Stat. 28 & 29 Vict., c. 88, sec. 67, is 744. The total value is stated to be £2,388,240.

There was no application in the year to record land under the 51st section of the Act. There were only 2 new estates recorded in the Record of Title Office in 1883, and each of these was less than £1,000 in value. There were not any proceedings under the Land Debenture Act, 1865.

Bills of Sale. Table 41.

Bills of Sale are registered by the Master of the Queen's Bench Division, and included in his return of business at the Pleas side. They are grouped here with other offices of registration. The number of bills of sale was 1,391, as compared with 1,824 in 1882.

Registry of Deeds. Table 37.

The number of deeds registered in the Registry of Deeds Office in the year was 16,331, as compared with 13,397 in 1882. Judgment Mortgage Affidavits are included in this number; they amounted to 970, as compared with 940 in 1882. The searches made by the public were 5,557; those lodged for official search were 2,310, of which 1,258 were negative searches, and 1,023 common searches. The abstract book, entered up to 28th December in 1882, was, on the 31st of December, 1883, entered up to 29th of December. The lands index, which was complete to 31st of December in 1882, was completed to 19th of December in 1883. The transcription of memorials, complete to 6th of November in 1882, was completed to 6th of October in 1883. The negative searches lodged but not made were 10 in 1882, and 28 in 1883, and the common searches lodged but not made increased from 16 to 37.

The negative searches made and ready for delivery and not taken out amounted to 497, and the common searches to 45.

Taxation of Costs.

Chancery, Land Judges, Probate, Common Law. Table 33.

The Costs taxed in the Consolidated Taxing Offices and certified amounted to £215,422. The corresponding figure for 1882 was £241,326, which shows a decrease of £25,904.

Administration of Property.

Receivers under Land Judges. Table 39.

There were 151 new receivers appointed by the Land Judges, as compared with 165 in 1882, 118 in 1881, 109 in 1880, 62 in 1879, and 13 in 1878. The total number under the Land Judges at the end of the year was 939, as compared with 816 at the end of 1882.

The increase of the number of receivers appointed in the year, from 13 in 1878 to 165 in 1882, indicated a very marked increase of pressure on landed proprietors, and the number for last year shows but little diminution.

The year's rental under the Court of the receivers and guardians who passed accounts, which are filed in the Consolidated Record and Writ Office, is £278,462, of which £13,120 was in minor matters and £165,333 in other suits.

It appears that there were 420 lettings by proposal without biddings: there was not a single letting by biddings. Of the 420 lettings, 150 were for 7 years, pending the cause, and 270 were for shorter periods.

Part II. Judicial Statistics. — Central Administration of Justice. — Lunacy Department. Table 60.

The chief business in the Lunacy Department in 1883 compared with 1882 was as follows:—

Lunacy Office.	1882.	1883.	Increase, 1883.	Decrease, 1883.
Orders of the Lord Chancellor, including Fiats confirming Registrars' Reports,	365	285	–	80
Affidavits filed,	519	424	–	95
Reports of Registrar,	223	161	–	62
Accounts taken by Lord Judge,	53	43	–	10
" Registrar,	71	61	–	10
	£	£	£	£
Gross income of Lunatics,	117,000	111,269	–	5,731

This summary indicates a decrease of 80 in orders, following an increase of 5 in 1882, and a decrease of 95 in affidavits, following an increase of 66.

The number of lunatics under the control of the Lord Chancellor at the close of 1883 was 237, being 18 less than at the close of 1882.

Probate and Matrimonial Division.

Principal Registry. Table 61.

The following is a summary of the business of the Court of Probate in Ireland and the Principal Registry:—

Court of Probate—Principal Registry.	1882.	1883.	Increase, 1883.	Decrease, 1883.
Probates and administrations with Wills annexed,	1,093	1,277	184	–
Administrations without Wills,	749	797	48	–
Total probates and administrations,	1,842	2,074	232	–
Caveats,	553	499	–	54
Causes,	107	130	23	–
Trials by special jury,	12	11	–	1
Trials by common jury,	21	17	–	4
Causes heard by Judge,	31	47	16	–
Court Motions,	402	454	52	–
Petitions,	65	75	10	–
	£	£	£	£
Total amount of fees received,	8,212	8,957	745	–

From the above it appears that there was an increase of 232 in probates and letters of administration in 1883 as compared with 1882.

The petitions, as noticed last year, included those disposed of in the Registry as well as those moved in Court. The taxation of costs is now included in the returns of the Consolidated Taxing Offices.

Comptroller of Stamps' Returns as to Property under Probate, &c. Table 62.

A return received from the Comptroller of Stamp Duties shows the amount of duty paid for Grants of Probate and Administration in 1883 to be £219,162, namely, £126,668 in Dublin, and £92,494 in the country districts, as compared with £226,123, namely, £110,712 in Dublin, and £115,411 in the country districts in 1882, being a decrease of £6,961.

As to matrimonial causes and matters and proceedings under the Legitimacy Declaration Act (Ireland), 1868, it appears that there were 22 petitions filed in matrimonial causes and matters during the year; 10 citations were issued. There was one decree for divorce *a mensâ et thoro*, no decree for restitution of conjugal rights, and no decree of nullity of marriage. There were 38 motions and 4 causes heard in the year. There was no petition under the Legitimacy Act. *Part II. Judicial Statistics. — General Administration of Justice. — Jurisdiction in Matrimonial causes. Table 62.*

High Court of Admiralty.

The causes instituted in the High Court of Admiralty in Ireland in the year were 59, as compared with 55 in 1882, and 52 in 1881. There were 12 causes pending at end of 1882, making 71 in all to be disposed of. *Admiralty. Tables 64 and 65.*

The motions and summonses heard were 153, final judgments and decrees 23, and instruments, &c., prepared in the Registry 167; showing a total of 343, being considerably under the total in 1882, which amounted to 434, consisting of 184 motions and summonses, 32 judgments and decrees, and 218 instruments, &c., prepared in the Registry.

Court of Bankruptcy.

In the following summary the principal proceedings in Bankruptcy are compared with those of the preceding year:— *Bankruptcy. Table 67.*

Proceedings in Bankruptcy.	1883.	1882.	Increase, 1883.	Decrease, 1883.
Petitions of Bankruptcy:				
By Creditors,	183	171	16	–
By Debtors,	26	39	3	–
Petitions for Arrangement,	215*	219†	–	4
Sittings before the Court,	6,678	1,788	–	883
Sittings before the Chief Registrar, and the Chief Clerk,	2,867	3,020	–	563

It appears that the number of petitions of Bankruptcy in 1883 was 210, showing an increase of 21 on the number, 189, in 1882. The petitions for arrangement showed a decrease of 4.

Although Insolvency jurisdiction was abolished from 1st of January, 1873, by the Debtors (Ireland) Act of 1872, there were still, at the end of ten years, proceedings in winding up the cases previously in the Court. *Insolvency. Table 68.*

Proceedings in Insolvency.	1883.	1882.	Increase, 1883.	Decrease, 1883.
Petitions in which dividends were declared,	15	7	–	9
Sittings before the Court in Dublin for all purposes in Insolvency,	29	30	9	–
" before the First Clerk or other Officer,	63	53	–	15

Finance.

In Probate business the Accountant-General carried *over* on 1st of October £126 13s. 4d.; in 1882 the amount was £873 11s. 7d. *Accountant-General's Office. In Probate. Table 69.*

In Chancery the balance was as follows:— *In Chancery. Table 70.*

	Year ended 1st Oct., 1883.	Year ended 1st Oct., 1882.	Decrease, 1883.
Balance at the end of year,	£3,862,860	£3,683,236	£181,622

* This number includes 22 Private Arrangements turned into Bankruptcy.
† This number includes 27 do. do.

Part II. Judicial Statistics. — Central Administration of Justice. Table 71 contains particulars regarding the Receipts and Payments of the Accountant-General of the Supreme Court of Judicature in Ireland, in respect of the funds of suitors in said Court, and a statement of Liabilities and Assets in respect of such funds, also particulars of securities in Court.

Law Taxes. Table 72. A Return has been obtained from the Inland Revenue of the Law Taxes levied in connexion with High Court of Justice.

Appellate Jurisdiction.

Her Majesty's Court of Appeal, Ireland. Table 73. The Proceedings in the Supreme Courts of Appeal, in 1883, are shown in Tables 73–8.

During the year there were 37 appeals from final Judgments from Divisions of the High Court of Justice heard by Her Majesty's Court of Appeal, Ireland, 18 of which were from the Chancery Division, 3 from the Queen's Bench, 9 from the Common Pleas, 3 from the Exchequer, and 4 from the Probate and Matrimonial Causes Division. There were 31 appeals from interlocutory orders from Divisions of the High Court of Justice heard, viz.:—13 from the Chancery Division, 11 from the Queen's Bench, 3 from the Common Pleas, 3 from the Exchequer Division, and 1 from the Probate and Matrimonial Causes Division. There were also 12 original motions heard. Twelve appeals from other Judges or Courts were heard, 2 of which were from the Judges in Bankruptcy, 1 from the High Court of Admiralty, 6 were Registry of Voters Appeals, and 3 were appeals from the Irish Land Commission. The Judgments delivered were 87. In 69 of these the Judgment below was affirmed; in 15 it was reversed, in 3 reversed with declaration, direction, or finding, and in 7 cases varied.

Privy Council, Ireland. Table 76. The Privy Council in Ireland heard 1 application under the Fairs (Ireland) Act, 1868, which was granted, and 1 appeal against By-Laws and Orders made by the Inspectors of Irish Fisheries, in which case the By-Laws and Orders were confirmed.

Her Majesty in Council. Table 77. There were no appeals from Ireland to Her Majesty in Council.

House of Lords. Table 78. The number of appeals and causes in error from Ireland presented to the House of Lords in 1883 was 4. These added to 4 not disposed of in 1882 made 8 for hearing (all from the Court of Appeal); of these 1 was dismissed. Judgment was given in 5 cases: in 1 the decision below was reversed with directions. Two causes were waiting hearing at the close of the year.

Tables 74 and 75. There were 3 appeals before the Judges of the Common Law Divisions, as to Presentment for Conveyance of Prisoners. There was but one appeal before the Court for Crown Cases Reserved: the conviction was reversed.

II.—LOCAL ADMINISTRATION OF JUSTICE—LARGER DISTRICTS.

Local Administration of Justice—Larger Districts. The tables in this part are arranged chiefly according to the degree of localization carried out in the different jurisdictions.

Local Courts of Admiralty. Table 79. Admiralty jurisdiction:—In Belfast in 1883 there were 3 actions for £18 each on an average, and in Cork 23, for £93 each on an average.

Part II. Judicial Statistics. Legal Administration of Justice—Larger Districts.

In the District Registries of the Court of Probate the chief business in 1882 and 1883 was as follows:—

District Probate Registries. Table 56.

Court of Probate—District Registries.	1882.	1883.	Increase, 1883.	Decrease, 1883.
Granted in Common Form:				
Probates,	1,424	1,565	141	–
Letters of administration—(Intestate Widows' Acts)	36	15	–	21
" —others,	1,093	1,380	286	–
Letters of administration with the Will annexed,	224	315	91	–
Granted under direction of Judge:				
Probates,	20	18	–	2
Letters of administration,	8	22	14	–
Letters of administration with the Will annexed,	13	7	–	6
Granted on Decrees of County Court Judges:				
Probates,	9	12	3	–
Letters of administration,	–	6	6	–
Letters of administration with Will annexed,	2	5	3	–
Revoked or varied, or refused:				
Probates,	1	2	1	–
Letters of administration,	4	2	–	2
Total granted, &c.,	2,871	3,331	460	–
	£	£	£	£
Total amount of fees received,	8,943	9,816	873	–
Amount of duty on grants,	105,221	92,304	–	12,917

Number of probates of wills and letters of administration in Ireland.

There has been an increase of 461 in the number of wills proved and letters of administration granted, in 1883 at the District Registries, of which there are eleven. The aggregate number at both Central and District Registries (5,399) is 693 above the number (4,706) in 1882.

Proving of Wills where assets small through Officers of Inland Revenue.

The 33rd section of the Customs and Inland Revenue Act of 1881, affords local facilities for obtaining grants of probate or letters of administration, where the gross value of the personal estate of the deceased does not exceed £300. In 1883 there were in Ireland 31 towns where officers of Inland Revenue were authorized to deal with applications under this Act. These, with Dublin and the 11 District Probate Registry Towns, give 43 towns for proving wills of not more than £300 assets.

PROCEEDINGS ON CIRCUIT.

Jury Trials. Tables 61, 62, and 64.

There are six circuits in Ireland, with Assizes held in thirty-two towns. Six of these towns are counties of cities and towns with distinct Grand and Petit Juries and Officers. The Grand and Petit Jurors of the county of the town of Carrickfergus are brought to Belfast for assize purposes, but those of Drogheda are not brought to Dundalk, the county town of Louth. The causes entered for trial on circuit in 1883 were 186 as compared with 167 in 1882. The amount recovered fell from £9,146 in 1882 to £8,979 in 1883.

Appeals from County Court Judges. Table 63.

The Appeal business on circuit increased from 720 in 1882 to 1,398 in 1883.

Presentments, objections to, on Circuit. Table 61.

There were in 1883, 21 objections to Presentments heard by Judges, and 27 special directions given.

The railway traverses against the award of valuators for compensation for land, under

PART II. JUDICIAL STATISTICS. — Local Administration of Justice— Lower Courts. — Railway and other traverses on circuit. Table 84. Fines on Jurors on circuit. Table 84.

the Railways (Ireland) Act, 1851, which have been returned, were 19 in number—the amount claimed in those cases where verdicts were given (exclusive of two cases in which no specific sum was claimed), was £19,393: the amount found by verdict was £4,383. The traverses other than railway traverses in 1883, were 34 in number—£9,238 was claimed, in the cases where verdicts were given, and £1,398 found by verdict.

The memorials from persons fined for non-attendance as Jurors, after falling from 166 in 1878, to 150 in 1879, and to 137 in 1880, rose in 1881 to 163, and fell to 84 in 1882, and to 83 in 1883. The fines appealed from in cases heard rose from £398 in 1880 to £776 in 1881, fell to £166 in 1882, and rose to £304 in 1883, of which only £9 was imposed, as compared with £19 in 1882, £88 in 1881, and £99 in 1880.

COUNTY COURTS.

Table 84. Process served. Table 84.

Returns have been obtained from the Process Servers, who are appointed under statute by the County Court Judges and Recorders, and whose salary is annually voted by Parliament. Out of the entire number of 866 Process Servers, all but 40, or less than 5 per cent., have made returns.

The Civil Bill ejectments served by these officers are 22,700, as compared with 19,035 in 1882, 13,621 in 1881, 10,638 in 1880, 9,703 in 1879, and 8,881 in 1878; the number of replevins 259 as compared with 407 in 1882, 419 in 1881, 378 in 1880, 435 in 1879, and 179 in 1878; and the number of other civil bills 231,762, as compared with 220,943 in 1882, 240,366 in 1881, 289,358 in 1880, 347,909 in 1879, and 309,634 in 1878.

County Court Proceedings. Table 87.

The statistics of proceedings (other than at Equity or Land Sessions, or under Local Admiralty Jurisdiction Act) in the Courts of County Court Judges and Courts of Recorders whether ejectments, causes remitted from the Superior Courts, or other suits, have been collected into one Table.

Ejectments.

In ejectments entered there was a decrease of 2,091 in 1883, following an increase of 5,063 in 1882, and an increase of 1,916 in 1881.

	Ejectments Entered.
For 1882, . .	16,835
For 1883, . .	14,744
Decrease in 1883,	2,091

Cases Remitted.

In cases remitted from the Superior Courts which were entered below there was a decrease from 272 in 1882, to 198 in 1883; in 1881 the number was 262. In other suits there was an increase of 2,143, from 86,050 in 1882, to 88,193 in 1883, following a decrease of 6,476 between 1881 and 1882. There were only 127 cases disposed of by a jury.

Ordinary Civil Bills.

The amount decreed in the Civil Bill Courts in 1883 was £233,972 in ejectment cases, and £297,404 in other suits, making £531,376.[1] Compared with 1882, the amount decreed in ejectment cases shows a decrease of £53,536, and the amount decreed in other suits a decrease of £22,158. The costs adjudged to plaintiffs amounted to £62,706, being £9,247 under the amount in 1882. Of these costs £26,281 was in ejectment cases, and £36,425 in other suits.

Local equitable actions or proceedings. Table 88.

The Equitable Jurisdiction cases for 1883 (exclusive of Lunacy Proceedings), were 61[?] as compared with 522 cases for 1882. The aggregate amount of the subject matter in dispute, so far as returned, was £35,063 as compared with £52,484 in 1882.

County Court Lunacy Jurisdiction. Table 88.

In County Court Lunacy Cases, under the jurisdiction conferred by the Lunacy Act of 1880, there were 14 orders made. The subject matter in these orders goes to make up the £35,063 above.

[1] Including £2,771 at Land Sessions, under the Landlord and Tenant (Ireland) Act, 1870, the total was £534,147.

A classification of the ejectments executed by Sheriffs and Special Bailiffs according as they came from the High Court of Justice or the County Court, gives the following results:—

	High Court.				County Court.			
	1882.	1883.	Increase.	Decrease.	1882.	1883.	Increase.	Decrease.
Ejectments executed, .	1,107	986	-	121	5,190	3,924	-	1,266
Leinster, . . .	160	85	-	75	938	674	-	264
Munster, . . .	639	387	-	252	1,394	1,330	-	64
Ulster, . . .	135	122	-	13	1,695	1,078	-	617
Connaught, . .	173	92	-	81	1,267	946	-	321

The ejectments executed show a decrease of 1,687—from 6,597 in 1882 to 4,910 last year.

In the ejectments from the High Court which were executed there was a decrease of 121, following increases in each of the three preceding years, viz.—56 in 1882, 446 in 1881, 49 in 1880.

The County Court Ejectment Suits entered and lodged which had increased from 9,556 in 1880, to 11,772 in 1881, and to 16,835 in 1882, were last year 14,744, being a decline of 2,091, as compared with 1882.

The executions of County Court ejectments by the Sheriff show an decrease of 1,266—from 5,190 in 1882 to 3,924 in 1883.

Eleven thousand and forty-six Civil Bill decrees and dismisses are returned as executed by Sheriffs, and 6,481 by Special Bailiffs, or 17,527 in all.

The warrants to Special Bailiffs under Act 23 & 24 Vic., c. 154 (summary recovery of possession of tenements), increased from 866 in 1882, to 919 in 1883. The warrants to Special Bailiffs under 14 & 15 Vic., cap. 92, s. 15 (summary recovery of possession of tenements overheld in towns), 12,148, show a decrease of 337 from 12,485 in 1882.

The following is a Summary of the Returns of Sheriffs as to execution of ejectments, classed so as to show the proportion that were and were not for non-payment of rent:—

	Ejectments for Non-payment of Rent.				Ejectments for Other Causes.			
	1882.	1883.	Increase, 1883.	Decrease, 1883.	1882.	1883.	Increase, 1883.	Decrease, 1883.
Ireland, . .	5,447	4,099	—	1,348	1,150	811	—	339
Leinster, . .	1,087	852	—	235	299	197	—	102
Munster, . .	1,658	1,396	—	162	373	218	—	155
Ulster, . .	1,427	981	—	446	241	177	—	64
Connaught, .	1,295	990	—	305	135	118	—	17

From this Table it appears that there was a decrease of 1,348 in ejectments for non-payment of rent, and a decrease of 339 in other ejectments.

PART II. JUDICIAL STATISTICS.

Local Administration of Justice—Larger Districts.

County Courts.

Land Sessions. Table 62.

The statistics as to the proceedings under the Landlord and Tenant Act of 1870, are shown in the following table:—

CASES DISPOSED OF AT LAND SESSIONS.	1882.	1883.	Increase in 1883.	Decrease in 1883.
Total number of cases,	147	43	–	104
Confirmation of leases,	2	–	–	2
Registration of improvements,	3	3	–	–
Other cases:—	142	40	–	102
Decrees,	25	13	–	12
Dismisses,	29	12	–	17
Otherwise disposed of,	77	10	–	67
Pending at end of year,	11	5	–	6

It appears from this table that the decrease in the number of cases was 104, from 147 in 1882, to 43 in 1883. This followed a decrease of 143 in 1882, 58 in 1881, 61 in 1880, 148 in 1879, and 41 in 1878. The number of cases now is less than 6 per cent. of the number in 1878.

There were no applications in 1883 for confirmation of leases, and in the preceding year there were but 2 leases confirmed. There were 38 applications in 1878 and 35 in 1879.

The decrees in 1883, were 13, and the dismisses 12.

Decrees.

In the 13 land claim cases in which there were decrees, the total amount adjudged on the decrees was £2,271, being £3,291 less than in 1882. The following table shows the distribution of the amount in the different provinces in 1882 and 1883 for comparison:—

DECREES AT LAND SESSIONS.	Gross Amount of Decrees		Number of Decrees.		Average Gross Sum adjudged on each case.	
	1882.	1883.	1882.	1883.	1882.	1883.
Total of Ireland,	£ 5,562	£ 2,271	25	13	£ 222	£ 175
Leinster,	2,506	116	3	3	835	39
Munster,	33	605	3	2	11	301
Ulster,	2,706	279	13	7	225	40
Connaught,	857	1,243	6	1	33	1,243

It appears from this table that the average gross amount awarded, without deducting allowances for set-off to landlord, for dilapidation, rent, &c., was in all Ireland £175, as compared with £222 in 1882. In Ulster it was £40, as compared with £225 in 1882; in Leinster it was £39, as compared with £835 in 1882; in Munster it was £301, as compared with £44 in 1882; and in Connaught (where there was but one decree), £1,243 as compared with an average of £33 in 1882.

The following Table has been constructed, showing the distribution of the £5,445 claimed in cases where decrees were made, into provinces and counties, with the amount decreed in each province and county, and with the proportions for all Ireland and for each province and county of the amount decreed. There were no appeals heard during the year.

PROCEEDINGS UNDER LANDLORD AND TENANT (IRELAND) ACT, 1870.

PART II. JUDICIAL STATISTICS. — *Local Administration of Justice—Larger Districts.* — *County Courts.* — Land Sessions.

Province and County.	Amount — Claimed where Decrees made.	Amount — Decreed.	Per-centage to Amount claimed of Amount.	Province and County.	Amount — Claimed where Decrees made.	Amount — Decreed.	Per-centage of Amount claimed of Amount.
	£	£	Per cent.	MUNSTER—con.	£	£	Per cent.
IRELAND, . .	5,445	2,271	42	Limerick, . .	-	-	-
				Tipperary, . .	-	-	-
LEINSTER, . .	251	146	58	Waterford, . .	1,029	588	57
Carlow, . .	-	-	-	ULSTER, . .	1,030	279	27
Dublin, . .	-	-	-				
Kildare, . .	-	-	-	Antrim, . .	557	147	27
Kilkenny, . .	-	-	-	Armagh, . .	-	-	-
King's County, .	-	-	-	Cavan, . .	-	-	-
Longford, . .	125	125	100	Donegal, . .	-	-	-
Louth, . .	-	-	-	Down, . .	256	20	8
Meath, . .	-	-	-	Fermanagh, .	-	-	-
Queen's County,	-	-	-	Londonderry, .	217	115	53
Westmeath, .	-	-	-	Monaghan, .	-	-	-
Wexford, . .	-	-	-	Tyrone, . .	-	-	-
Wicklow, . .	126	20	16				
				CONNAUGHT, .	3,104	1,263	40
MUNSTER, .	1,059	603	57				
				Galway, . .	-	-	-
Clare, . .	30	15	50	Leitrim, . .	-	-	-
Cork, E. R., .	-	-	-	Mayo, . .	3,104	1,263	40
Cork, W. R., .	-	-	-	Roscommon, .	-	-	-
Kerry, . .	-	-	-	Sligo, . .	-	-	-

It appears from this Table that in all Ireland the amount decreed, £2,271, was 42 per cent. of the amount claimed in cases where decrees were made—£5,445. In 1882, the sum decreed was £5,562 or 31 per cent. of the amount claimed in those cases where decrees were made.

COURT OF THE IRISH LAND COMMISSION.

The Commissioners appointed under the "Land Law (Ireland) Act, 1881," have many functions of a judicial character, therefore it is necessary to refer in this Report to the judicial portion of the proceedings of the Land Commission. *Land Commission Court.*

Although not strictly in order, it is convenient here to refer to the subject as the proceedings are somewhat allied to those under the Act of 1870—dealt with above—and are mainly determined in the Courts of the Sub-Commissions which must be treated of in connexion with the local administration of justice.

It is unnecessary to give here a detailed account of the business of the Court of the Land Commission as the Reports of the Commissioners contain full information on the subject. Table 60.

Part II. Judicial Statistics. — Local Administration of Justice — Larger Districts. — Land Commission Court. — Table 90.

The following statement shows generally the extent and nature of the proceedings in connexion with the Court of the Land Commission during the year 1883:—

Nature of Proceedings.	No. of Cases.
Applications to have fair rents fixed —	
1. In court—	
Pending at beginning of year,	[illegible]
Entered and lodged during 1883,	[illegible]
Rents fixed,	[illegible]
Dismissed and struck out,	[illegible]
Withdrawn,	[illegible]
Pending at end of year	[illegible]
2. Out of court—	
Agreements fixing fair rents,	[illegible]
Applications to have leases declared void —	
Pending at beginning of year,*	[illegible]
Declared void,	[illegible]
Dismissed and struck out,	[illegible]
Withdrawn or compromised,	[illegible]
Pending at end of year,	[illegible]

Nature of Proceedings.	No. of Cases.
[illegible] —	
Pending at beginning of year,	[illegible]
Number lodged during 1883,	[illegible]
Disposed of,	[illegible]
Pending at end of year,	[illegible]
Appeals re Fair Rent, &c. —	
Pending at beginning of year,	[illegible]
Number lodged during 1883,	[illegible]
Heard,†	[illegible]
Withdrawn,‡	[illegible]
Pending at end of year,	[illegible]
Result of Appeals heard,‡	
Decisions below affirmed,	[illegible]
Do. do., [illegible]	[illegible]
Rent fixed below, increased,	[illegible]
Do. do. reduced,	[illegible]
Withdrawn or struck out,	[illegible]

The following statement shows the sums of money dealt with by the Court in fixing fair rents in the year 1883:—

Fair Rents fixed	Former Rent	Judicial Rent	Amount of Reduction	Rate per Cent
	£ s. d.	£ s. d.	£ s. d.	
In court,	[illegible]	[illegible]	[illegible]	[illegible]
Out of court,	[illegible]	[illegible]	[illegible]	[illegible]
Total,	[illegible]	[illegible]	[illegible]	[illegible]

From these statements it appears that during the year 1883 "fair rents" were fixed in 71,971 cases (37,312 in court and 34,659 out of court), the "former rent" of the holdings dealt with in these cases being in round numbers £1,282,848, and the "judicial rents" registered by the Court for these holdings being £1,046,735, showing a reduction of £236,113, or 18·4 per cent. of the "former rent." Some of the "judicial rents" included in the above are liable to variation on appeal.

The number of cases of appeal from the Land Court to the Court of Appeal, and how these were disposed of, will be found in Table 73 of Appendix, and are dealt with at page 46 under the head of Appellate Jurisdiction.

Arrears of Rent Act. Table 91.

In addition to the duties imposed upon the Land Commission under the Act of 1881, further duties were placed upon them by the Arrears of Rent (Ireland) Act, 1882.

* The time for lodging an application to have a lease declared void, expired on the 22nd February, 1882 (section 21).

† In the Report for 1882 there was an error of 11 in the number of these applications.

‡ See note (†) pages 116–7.

Table 91 sets forth the statistics of the work of this Branch of the Commission from the beginning, and includes the years 1882 and 1883. Part II. Judicial Statistics.

The number of holdings included in applications under the 1st section of the Act for free grants in discharge of antecedent arrears in cases where the Poor Law Valuation of the holding did not exceed £30 a year amounted to 133,498, and applications relating to 125,390 holdings were granted, the amount paid being £767,564 12s. 11d. One thousand and ninety tenants of holdings valued at not more than £50 applied, conjointly with their landlords, for advances to be made to the landlord under the 16th section: in 991 instances the applications were granted, the sum advanced (which became repayable by a rentcharge for thirty-five years) being £27,347 4s. 2d. The number of rentcharges payable in discharge of loans obtained under the 59th section of the Land Law Act, which were cancelled under section 15 of the Arrears of Rent Act, was 2,339, in respect of which the sum of £16,831 1s. 2d. has been, pursuant to section 15, charged upon the Irish Church Temporalities Funds. Land Administration of Justice—Larger Districts.

Proceedings of Sheriffs.

The proceedings of Sheriffs in 1883 including those having relation to Jurors summoned, and those already referred to, are set forth in detail in Tables 92 and 94. Proceedings of Sheriffs.

Jurors.

As to the revision of Jurors Lists and Books, it involved the striking off of 40,267 out of 103,033 persons, or 39 per cent.; there were only 25 persons added by Revision Court. Revision of Jurors Lists and correction of Jurors Books Table 93.

Besides those struck off on revision there were 303 exempted by Clerks of the Peace. This gives the total number of Jurors on the corrected General Jurors Books in all Ireland, 62,488. This is an increase of only 7,088, on the number (55,400) on the General Jurors Lists in 1871. 57,586 Jurors were on rated qualification, 2,434 were £10 freeholders, 2,231 were £20 leaseholders, 224 Directors or Managers of Public Companies, and 13 Harbour Commissioners.

In the case of 15,595 persons on the Special Jurors Lists, 3,669 persons were struck off by Revision Court, and 120 exempted by the Clerks of the Peace, and 335 were added, so that there was a net reduction of 3,453, or 22 per cent. The books show 12,142 Special Jurors.

Along with the jurors summoned by Sheriffs are included the jurors summoned to the Recorder's Court in the case of the boroughs of Belfast and Londonderry, which have separate Courts of Sessions of the Peace, although these are summoned by the Clerk of the Peace of the borough. Jurors Summoned. Table 94.

The total number of jurors returned as summoned in the year is 49,592, as compared with 50,903 in 1882. Of the number for 1883, 6,854 were Grand Jurors* for Assizes, Commissions, and Superior Courts; 8,607 were Grand Jurors for Quarter Sessions; 6,154* were Special Jurors for Assizes, Commissions and Superior Courts; 12,934 were Petit and Common Jurors for Assizes, Commissions and Superior Courts; 13,576 were Petit Jurors for Quarter Sessions; 1,389 were Jurors in Civil Bill cases before County Court Judges or Recorders; and 78 were jurors for other purposes.

*Special Jurors for Commissions and Superior Courts included with Grand Jurors, in the case of Dublin County and Dublin City.

Local Administration of Justice.

Appeals from Magistrates at Quarter Sessions. Table 98.

In the following summary the statistics of appeals at Quarter Sessions are compared with the figures for 1882:—

Appeals at Quarter Sessions	1882.	1883.	Increase, 1883.	Decrease, 1883.
Appeals from Magistrates—				
Affirmed, ...	234	261	–	13
Reversed, ...	161	130	–	31
Varied, ...	81	106	24	
Otherwise disposed of (including cases where there was no appearance), . . .	107	114	7	–
Total, ...	696	633	–	63

The number of appeals from Magistrates heard at Quarter Sessions, as appears from the above figures, was 63 less in 1883 than in 1882. There had been an increase of 57 in 1882, a decrease of 36 in 1881, an increase of 140 in 1880, and a decrease of 93 in 1879; the number in 1883 is 3 above that of 1878. Of the appeals heard and decided in Court during 1883, in 281 cases the previous decisions were affirmed, in 130 reversed, and in 106 varied.

Spirit Licences.

The number of licences granted at other Quarter Sessions than the annual licensing Sessions was 1,012, which, with the number granted or confirmed at the Annual Sessions (1,736), makes 2,748 in all, and of these 480 were on original application, compared with 547 in 1882.

SMALLER DISTRICT ADMINISTRATION OF JUSTICE.

Local Charter Courts. Table 97.

Local Charter Courts.

The following summary shows the business in 1883 in the eight Local Charter Courts, viz.:—Clonmel Court of Conscience, Drogheda Court of Conscience, Dublin Lord Mayor's Court, Dublin Court of Conscience, Kilkenny Court of Conscience, Limerick Court of Conscience, Londonderry Court of Conscience, and Wexford Court of Conscience. There were summonses issued, 4,998, against 4,907 in 1882; causes heard, 3,396; decisions for plaintiff, 2,494; for defendant, 681; otherwise disposed of, 221; amount recoverable, £3,111; fees collected, £393.

Petty Sessions Courts. Table 95. Civil proceedings.

Petty Sessions Courts.

Table 95 in the Appendix shows the civil business at the Courts of Petty Sessions. The summonses issued were 139,038, which shows an increase of 57 as compared with the number in 1882.

Civil cases at Petty Sessions other than proceedings against cottier and weekly tenants were disposed of as follows:—

	1883	1882	Increase in 1883	Decrease in 1883
Summonses issued, . .	113,310	111,167	[illegible]	—
Complaints heard, . .	62,902	61,556	1,333	—
Decrees made, . .	40,049	40,610	—	539
Warrants issued, . .	18,726	19,576	—	1,310

Proceedings against cottier tenants.

The table also shows the proceedings relating to cottier tenants under the Landlord and Tenant Act, 1860, (Stat. 23 & 24 Vic., c. 154,) under which cottier tenements of less than half an acre, under £5 rent, and repaired by landlord, may be summarily recovered at Petty Sessions, for waste, for non-payment of rent, or for overholding. The cases for summary recovery of tenements in towns against weekly tenants, under Stat. 14 & 15 Vic., c. 92, sec. 15, are also shown.

The proceedings against cottier and weekly tenants and against servants, herdsmen and caretakers in 1883 appear from the returns to have been as follows:— *Part II. Judicial Statistics. Local Administration of Justice—Smaller Districts. Petty Sessions Courts.*

Summary Recovery of Possession.	Summonses issued	Complaints heard	Warrants to Sheriff	Cases in which there was a stay of Execution
Cottier Tenants Under Stat. 23 & 24 Vic., c. 154.				
For Waste (sec. 84),	60	81	919	117
For Non-payment of Rent (sec. 85),	257	147		
Caretakers, Servants, and Cottier Tenants.				
For Overholding (sec. 86),	1,801	1,343		
Weekly Tenants. Under Stat. 14 & 15 Vic., c. 92.				
For Overholding in Towns (sec. 15),	22,123	16,033	12,148	107
Total,	24,576	17,481	13,067	224

The returns further indicate the number of days on which Petty Sessions were not held in consequence of the non-attendance of Magistrates. This number (792), as compared with 13,630 days on which Petty Sessions Courts other than Dublin Police Courts were held, gives a proportion of 5·8 per cent.; but this proportion is differently distributed, and reaches 13·1 per cent. in the province of Connaught, as appears from the following table:— *Number of days on which Petty Sessions not held for non-attendance of Magistrates. Table 25.*

Provinces.		Number of Days on which Petty Sessions not held for non-attendance of Magistrates	Number of Days on which Petty Sessions held	Percentage of Days when Sessions not held to Days on which Sessions held.
				Per cent.
Leinster,	162*	178	*3,493	5·1
Munster,	168	241	4,689	5·2
Ulster,	163	106	3,299	3·2
Connaught,	111	267	2,204	13·1
Total (604 Courts).*		792	*13,630	5·8

In Leinster the postponements fell from 206 in 1882 to 178 in 1883, being a decline of 28; in Munster they fell 76 or from 317 to 241; in Ulster there was an increase of 15 postponements, namely from 91 to 106, and in Connaught the number rose from 230 in 1882 to 267 in 1883, being an increase of 37. The net decrease for all Ireland was 52.

* Not including 735 days in 3 Metropolitan Police District Courts, where local Magistrates cannot act.

THOMAS W. GRIMSHAW.

APPENDIX OF TABLES.*

TABLE 1.—ESTABLISHMENTS (1).—Royal Irish Constabulary. Return of Establishment, with Population of Counties, and Counties of Cities and Counties of Towns, at last Census, and Cost under the different Heads of Service, with the Proportion paid by Her Majesty's Treasury, and also by Counties and Districts specially charged, in the Year ended 31st March, [illegible], made by the Inspector-General.

Royal Irish Constabulary.	Part I.—Establishment								Cost of Establishment										
	Inspector-General	Other Deputy Officers	County Inspectors	Sub-Inspectors*	Clerks	Constables	Messengers	Total	Salaries and Pay	Allowances and Contingent Expenses	Clothing and Accoutrements	Superannuations and Gratuities	Lodgings, Forage, &c.	Building Charges, &c.	Other Miscellaneous Charges	Total Cost	Proportion paid by Counties for unrecovered Balances of Rent	Proportion paid by Provincial Districts	Proportion paid by Her Majesty's Treasury
Head Office, Dublin Castle	[illegible]	[illegible]	[illegible]	[illegible]	[illegible]	[illegible]	[illegible]	[illegible]	£ s. d.	£ s. d.	£ s. d.	£ s. d.	£ s. d.	£ s. d.	£ s. d.	£ s. d.	£ s. d.	£ s. d.	£ s. d.
Part II (totals)									[illegible]	[illegible]	[illegible]	[illegible]	[illegible]	[illegible]	[illegible]	[illegible]	[illegible]	[illegible]	[illegible]

Part II.—Establishment excluding Depot

Inspector-General	Deputy Inspector-General and County Inspectors	Surgeon	Veterinary Surgeon	Superintendent & Store-keeper	Sub-Inspectors*	Head-Constables	Constables†	Acting-Constables‡	Sub-Constables§	Employed on special duty at Exhibition Year	Employed at ... duty Year	Total
[illegible]	[illegible]	[illegible]	[illegible]	[illegible]	[illegible]	[illegible]	[illegible]	[illegible]	[illegible]	[illegible]	[illegible]	[illegible]

a Private Secretary to the Inspector-General, included in part II. b The Detectives are of various ranks, and are included in the preceding columns.
c Employed as Clerks at Head Office, are included in part II. d Employed on special duty, included in part II. e Not included in part II.
* Designated County Inspectors from 1st October, [illegible]. † Designated Sergeants from 1st October, [illegible]. ‡ Designated Acting-Sergeants from 1st October, [illegible]. § Designated Constables from 1st October, [illegible].

Part III.—Effective Strength of the Force in Counties, and in Counties of Cities and of Towns, on the [illegible] day of September, [illegible].

Counties, and Counties of Cities and of Towns, with Riding or Division.	County Inspectors.	Sub Inspectors.	Head Constables.	Constables, Acting Constables, and Sub-Constables.	Total Effective Strength, Head Constables, Constables, Acting, and Sub-Constables.	Population according to Census of [illegible].	Number of Inhabitants to each of Force.
Antrim,	[illegible]	[illegible]	[illegible]	[illegible]	[illegible]	[illegible]	[illegible]
Armagh,	[illegible]	[illegible]	[illegible]	[illegible]	[illegible]	[illegible]	[illegible]
Carlow,	[illegible]	[illegible]	[illegible]	[illegible]	[illegible]	[illegible]	[illegible]
Cavan,	[illegible]	[illegible]	[illegible]	[illegible]	[illegible]	[illegible]	[illegible]
Clare,	[illegible]	[illegible]	[illegible]	[illegible]	[illegible]	[illegible]	[illegible]
Cork, East Riding,	[illegible]	[illegible]	[illegible]	[illegible]	[illegible]	[illegible]	[illegible]
Cork, West Riding,	[illegible]	[illegible]	[illegible]	[illegible]	[illegible]	[illegible]	[illegible]
Donegal,	[illegible]	[illegible]	[illegible]	[illegible]	[illegible]	[illegible]	[illegible]
Down,	[illegible]	[illegible]	[illegible]	[illegible]	[illegible]	[illegible]	[illegible]
Dublin,	[illegible]	[illegible]	[illegible]	[illegible]	[illegible]	[illegible]	[illegible]
Fermanagh,	[illegible]	[illegible]	[illegible]	[illegible]	[illegible]	[illegible]	[illegible]
Galway, East Riding,	[illegible]	[illegible]	[illegible]	[illegible]	[illegible]	[illegible]	[illegible]
Galway, West Riding,	[illegible]	[illegible]	[illegible]	[illegible]	[illegible]		[illegible]
Kerry,	[illegible]	[illegible]	[illegible]	[illegible]	[illegible]	[illegible]	[illegible]
Kildare,	[illegible]	[illegible]	[illegible]	[illegible]	[illegible]	[illegible]	[illegible]
Kilkenny,	[illegible]	[illegible]	[illegible]	[illegible]	[illegible]	[illegible]	[illegible]
King's,	[illegible]	[illegible]	[illegible]	[illegible]	[illegible]	[illegible]	[illegible]
Leitrim,	[illegible]	[illegible]	[illegible]	[illegible]	[illegible]	[illegible]	[illegible]
Limerick,	[illegible]	[illegible]	[illegible]	[illegible]	[illegible]	[illegible]	[illegible]
Londonderry,	[illegible]	[illegible]	[illegible]	[illegible]	[illegible]	[illegible]	[illegible]
Longford,	[illegible]	[illegible]	[illegible]	[illegible]	[illegible]	[illegible]	[illegible]
Louth,	[illegible]	[illegible]	[illegible]	[illegible]	[illegible]	[illegible]	[illegible]
Mayo,	[illegible]	[illegible]	[illegible]	[illegible]	[illegible]	[illegible]	[illegible]
Meath,	[illegible]	[illegible]	[illegible]	[illegible]	[illegible]	[illegible]	[illegible]
Monaghan,	[illegible]	[illegible]	[illegible]	[illegible]	[illegible]	[illegible]	[illegible]
Queen's,	[illegible]	[illegible]	[illegible]	[illegible]	[illegible]	[illegible]	[illegible]
Roscommon,	[illegible]	[illegible]	[illegible]	[illegible]	[illegible]	[illegible]	[illegible]
Sligo,	[illegible]	[illegible]	[illegible]	[illegible]	[illegible]	[illegible]	[illegible]
Tipperary, North Riding,	[illegible]	[illegible]	[illegible]	[illegible]	[illegible]	[illegible]	[illegible]
Tipperary, South Riding,	[illegible]	[illegible]	[illegible]	[illegible]	[illegible]	[illegible]	[illegible]
Tyrone,	[illegible]	[illegible]	[illegible]	[illegible]	[illegible]	[illegible]	[illegible]
Waterford,	[illegible]	[illegible]	[illegible]	[illegible]	[illegible]	[illegible]	[illegible]
Westmeath,	[illegible]	[illegible]	[illegible]	[illegible]	[illegible]	[illegible]	[illegible]
Wexford,	[illegible]	[illegible]	[illegible]	[illegible]	[illegible]	[illegible]	[illegible]
Wicklow,	[illegible]	[illegible]	[illegible]	[illegible]	[illegible]	[illegible]	[illegible]
Cities and Towns.							
Carrickfergus,	-	[illegible]	-	[illegible]	[illegible]	[illegible]	[illegible]
Cork,	-	[illegible]	[illegible]	[illegible]	[illegible]	[illegible]	[illegible]
Drogheda,	-	[illegible]	[illegible]	[illegible]	[illegible]	[illegible]	[illegible]
Galway,	-	[illegible]	[illegible]	[illegible]	[illegible]	[illegible]	[illegible]
Kilkenny,	-	[illegible]	[illegible]	[illegible]	[illegible]	[illegible]	[illegible]
Limerick,	-	[illegible]	[illegible]	[illegible]	[illegible]	[illegible]	[illegible]
Londonderry,	-	[illegible]	[illegible]	[illegible]	[illegible]	[illegible]	[illegible]
Waterford,	-	[illegible]	[illegible]	[illegible]	[illegible]	[illegible]	[illegible]
Total,	[illegible]	[illegible]	[illegible]	[illegible]	[illegible]	[illegible]	-
Belfast Town Force,	[illegible]	[illegible]	[illegible]	[illegible]	[illegible]	[illegible]	[illegible]
Reserve Force,	-	[illegible]	[illegible]	[illegible]	[illegible]	-	-
Depot,	[illegible]	[illegible]	[illegible]	[illegible]	[illegible]		
Total,	[illegible]	[illegible]	[illegible]	[illegible]	[illegible]	[illegible]	[illegible]

[illegible footnotes]

Part IV.—Amount Charged to Counties and Counties of Cities and of Towns for Extra Force, for the Year ended 30th September, [illegible].

Average Number of Extra Men chargeable during the Year ... [illegible]	Least Number of Extra Men chargeable in the Year ... [illegible]	Monthly average of Extra Men during the Year, ... [illegible]

Part V.—A Statement of the Cost of the Royal Irish Constabulary Force, including all items of Expenditure which have a direct bearing and reference to the Charge proper for Constabulary purposes, from 1st April, [illegible], to 31st March, [illegible].

	£	s.	d.
Superintending Officers (Salaries and Allowances),	[illegible]	[illegible]	[illegible]
Pay, Extra Pay, and Allowances,	[illegible]	[illegible]	[illegible]
Clothing,	[illegible]	[illegible]	[illegible]
Arms, Ammunition, Accoutrements, and Saddlery,	[illegible]	[illegible]	[illegible]
Horses and Forage,	[illegible]	[illegible]	[illegible]
Rent of Barracks, Barrack Furniture, Fuel, and Light,	[illegible]	[illegible]	[illegible]
Pensions and Gratuities,	[illegible]	[illegible]	[illegible]
Miscellaneous,	[illegible]	[illegible]	[illegible]
Total,	[illegible]	[illegible]	[illegible]

TABLE 9.—ESTABLISHMENTS (V.—Dublin Metropolitan Police. Return of Establishment, with Population of Divisions, and Costs under the different Heads of Service, with the Proportion paid by Her Majesty's Treasury, in the year ended 31st March, [illegible], made by the Commissioner of Police.

PART I.—Division of Commissioner of Police.

PART I.	Establishment: Commissioners 1	Other Superior Officers 2	Clerks, &c. 3	Total 4	Cost of Establishment: Salaries and Pay 5	Allowances and Contingent Expenses 6	[illegible] 7	Superannuation and Gratuities 8	Rents, [illegible] 9	Other Charges 10	Other Miscellaneous Charges 11	Total Cost 12	Proportion paid by Her Majesty's Treasury 13
					£ s. d.	£ s. d.	£ s. d.	£ s. d.	£ s. d.	£ s. d.	£ s. d.	£ s. d.	£ s. d.
Office	[illegible]	[illegible]	[illegible]	[illegible]	[illegible]	[illegible]	[illegible]	[illegible]	—	[illegible]	[illegible]	[illegible]	[illegible]

PART II.—Establishment of Dublin Metropolitan Police.

PART II.	Population, [illegible]	Number of [illegible] per 10,000 of Population	Establishment: [illegible]	[illegible]	[illegible]	[illegible]	[illegible]	[illegible]	[illegible]
Chief Superintendent	-	[illegible]		-	-	[illegible]	-	-	[illegible]
Divisions—									
1. A, City, S.W.	[illegible]	[illegible]	[illegible]	[illegible]	-	-	[illegible]	[illegible]	[illegible]
2. B, " S.E.	[illegible]	[illegible]	[illegible]	[illegible]	-	-	[illegible]	[illegible]	[illegible]
3. C, " N.E.	[illegible]	[illegible]	[illegible]	[illegible]	-	-	[illegible]	[illegible]	[illegible]
4. D, " N.W., and [illegible]*	[illegible]	[illegible]	[illegible]	[illegible]	-	-	[illegible]	[illegible]	[illegible]
5. E, " S., and [illegible]	[illegible]	[illegible]	[illegible]	[illegible]	-	-	[illegible]	[illegible]	[illegible]
6. F, " [illegible]	[illegible]	[illegible]	[illegible]	[illegible]	-	-	[illegible]	[illegible]	[illegible]
7. G	-	-	[illegible]	[illegible]	-	[illegible]	[illegible]	[illegible]	[illegible]
8. Constables employed at Public Offices	-	-	[illegible]	[illegible]	-	-	[illegible]		-
9. [illegible] paid for by parties employing them	-	-	[illegible]	[illegible]	-	-	[illegible]	[illegible]	-
10. Constables on duty at private establishments, and paid for by parties employing them	-	-	-					-	
Total	[illegible]	[illegible]	[illegible]	[illegible]		[illegible]	[illegible]	[illegible]	[illegible]

PART II.	Cost of Establishment: Salaries and Pay 1	Allowances and Contingent Expenses 2	Clothing and Accoutrements 3	Superannuation and Gratuities 4	Rents, [illegible] 5	[illegible] Charges 6	Other Miscellaneous Charges 7	Total Cost 8	Proportion paid by Her Majesty's Treasury 9
	£ s. d.	£ s. d.	£ s. d.	£ s. d.	£ s. d.	£ s. d.	£ s. d.	£ s. d.	£ s. d.
Chief Superintendent and Divisions 1–10	[illegible]	[illegible]	[illegible]	[illegible]	[illegible]	[illegible]	[illegible]	[illegible]	[illegible]
Total	[illegible]	[illegible]	[illegible]	[illegible]	[illegible]	[illegible]	[illegible]	[illegible]	[illegible]

* [illegible] † [illegible] ‡ [illegible]

§ [illegible] ‖ [illegible]

PART III.	Number of Courts.	Establishment.					Cost of Establishment.						
		Magistrates	Clerks.	Police Officers and Constables	Messengers	Total	Salaries and Pay 1	Clothing and Accoutrements 2	Fuel and Light 3	Rents, Taxes, Repairs and Incidental Charges 4	Superannuation Allowances 5	Total Cost 6	Expenses paid by Her Majesty's Treasury.
							£ s. d.	£ s. d.	£ s. d.	£ s. d.	£ s. d.	£ s. d.	£ s. d.
Police Courts,	[illegible]	[illegible]*	[illegible]	[illegible]	[illegible]	[illegible]	[illegible]	[illegible]	[illegible]	[illegible]	[illegible]	[illegible]	[illegible]

* Reduced to 4, [illegible] January, [illegible], with increased rates of Salary.—the Chief Magistrate from £[illegible] to £[illegible], and 3 Magistrates from £[illegible] to £[illegible] each.

Part IV.—A Statement of the Cost of the Dublin Metropolitan Police Force, including all those items of Expenditure which have a direct bearing and reference to the Charge proper for Police purposes, from 1st April, 18[illegible], to 31st March, 18[illegible].

	£ s. d.
1. Office Expenses, including Salaries of Commissioners' Department, Postage, Travelling Expenses, Newspapers and Advertisements, and other small Contingencies,	[illegible]
2 Law Charges,	[illegible]
3 Superintendents' Salaries,	[illegible]
4 Pay, Clothing, and Equipment of the Force,	[illegible]
5 Medical Salaries, Medicines, and Funeral Expenses,	[illegible]
6. Repairs of Premises, Rent of Premises, Rates and Taxes, Furniture and Fixtures, Cleaning Stations, [illegible] Wages, and other small Charges incidental to Premises,	[illegible]
7 Fuel and Light,	[illegible]
Total,	[illegible]

Average Cost per Man, £[illegible]

The strength of the Force (exclusive of Police employed at Police Courts) on the 31st March, 18[illegible], was [illegible].

N.B.—The amount charged for Rent is the annual sum paid, after deducting £[illegible] receipts from the Police for "Lodging Money."

The following items of Expense should be excluded in estimating the Cost per Man of the Metropolitan Police Force:—

	£ s. d.
8 Medical Attendance and Medicines for detained Prisoners,	—
9 Horses, Forage, Saddlery, &c., and Vans,	[illegible]
10 [illegible] and Purchase of [illegible],	[illegible]
11 Refreshments — [illegible], and other small Contingencies,	[illegible]
12 Extraordinary Expenses [illegible], and Conveyance of Prisoners,	[illegible]
13 Expenses and Allowances on special occasions,	[illegible]
14. Annual Allowance to Officers of Commissioners' Department, paid by the Treasury,	[illegible]
15. Police Expenditure on account of Police Courts (Pay and Cost of Clothing of [illegible] Constables),	[illegible]
Ditto Her Majesty's Yards,	—
Ditto Military Stations,	—
Ditto Dangerous Lunatics Act,	—
16 Deficiency of Police Superannuation Fund,	[illegible]
Total,	[illegible]

[illegible]

Province, County, County of City or of Town	Under 16 years M.	Under 16 years W.	16 years and above M.	16 years and above W.	Under 16 years M.	Under 16 years W.	16 years and above M.	16 years and above W.	Under 16 years M.	Under 16 years W.	16 years and above M.	16 years and above W.	Under 16 years M.	Under 16 years W.	16 years and above M.	16 years and above W.	[illegible]	[illegible]	[illegible]	[illegible]	[illegible]	Total
Leinster.																						
Carlow,	-	-	[illegible]	[illegible]	-	-	[illegible]	[illegible]	-	-	[illegible]	[illegible]	-	-	[illegible]	[illegible]	[illegible]	-	-	-	[illegible]	[illegible]
Drogheda, Town of,	-	-	-	-	-	-	-	-	-	-	11	[illegible]	-	-	[illegible]	[illegible]	-	-	-	-	[illegible]	[illegible]
Dublin County,	-	-	-	-	-	-	-	-	-	-	[illegible]	[illegible]	-	-	[illegible]	[illegible]	-	-	-	-	-	-
Dublin, City (and part of County) Metropolitan Police District—Divisions,																						
A,	-	-	[illegible]	[illegible]	-	-	[illegible]	[illegible]	[illegible]	[illegible]	[illegible]	[illegible]	[illegible]	[illegible]	[illegible]	[illegible]	[illegible]	-	-	-	[illegible]	[illegible]
B,	-	-	1	-	-	-	[illegible]	[illegible]	[illegible]	-	[illegible]	[illegible]	[illegible]	-	[illegible]	[illegible]	[illegible]	-	-	-	1	[illegible]
C,	[illegible]	-	[illegible]	17	-	-	-	[illegible]	[illegible]	-	[illegible]	[illegible]	[illegible]	-	[illegible]	[illegible]	[illegible]	-	-	-	[illegible]	[illegible]
D,	-	-	[illegible]	[illegible]	-	-	[illegible]	[illegible]	-	-	[illegible]	[illegible]	-	-	[illegible]	[illegible]	[illegible]	-	-	-	[illegible]	[illegible]
E,	-	-	[illegible]	[illegible]	-	-	-	-	-	-	[illegible]	-	-	-	[illegible]	[illegible]	-	-	-	-	-	-
F,	-	-	[illegible]	[illegible]	-	-	-	-	-	-	[illegible]	[illegible]	-	-	[illegible]	[illegible]	-	-	-	-	[illegible]	[illegible]
Total of Metropolitan Police District,	[illegible]	-	[illegible]	[illegible]	-	-	[illegible]	[illegible]	[illegible]	[illegible]	[illegible]	[illegible]	[illegible]	[illegible]	[illegible]	[illegible]	[illegible]	-	-	-	[illegible]	[illegible]
Kildare,	[illegible]	-	[illegible]	[illegible]	-	-	[illegible]	-	-	-	[illegible]	[illegible]	[illegible]	-	[illegible]	[illegible]	-	-	-	-	[illegible]	[illegible]
Kilkenny,	[illegible]	[illegible]	[illegible]	[illegible]	-	-	[illegible]	[illegible]	[illegible]	[illegible]	[illegible]	[illegible]	[illegible]	[illegible]	[illegible]	[illegible]	[illegible]	[illegible]	-	-	[illegible]	[illegible]
King's County,	-	-	[illegible]	[illegible]	-	-	-	[illegible]	[illegible]	-	[illegible]	[illegible]	[illegible]	-	[illegible]	[illegible]	[illegible]	-	-	-	[illegible]	[illegible]
Longford,	-	-	-	1	-	-	[illegible]	-	-	-	[illegible]	[illegible]	-	-	[illegible]	[illegible]	[illegible]	-	-	-	[illegible]	[illegible]
Louth,	[illegible]	-	[illegible]	[illegible]	-	-	[illegible]	-	[illegible]	-	[illegible]	[illegible]	[illegible]	-	[illegible]	[illegible]	-	-	-	-	-	-
Meath,	-	-	[illegible]	[illegible]	-	-	-	-	-	-	[illegible]	[illegible]	-	-	[illegible]	[illegible]	-	-	-	-	[illegible]	[illegible]
Queen's County,	[illegible]	-	[illegible]	-	-	-	[illegible]	[illegible]	[illegible]	-	[illegible]	[illegible]	[illegible]	-	[illegible]	[illegible]	[illegible]	-	-	-	[illegible]	[illegible]
Westmeath,	-	-	[illegible]	-	-	-	-	[illegible]	[illegible]	-	[illegible]	[illegible]	[illegible]	-	[illegible]	[illegible]	[illegible]	-	-	-	[illegible]	[illegible]
Wexford,	-	-	[illegible]	[illegible]	-	-	[illegible]	[illegible]	[illegible]	[illegible]	[illegible]	[illegible]	[illegible]	[illegible]	[illegible]	[illegible]	[illegible]	-	-	-	-	[illegible]
Wicklow,	-	-	[illegible]	[illegible]	-	-	[illegible]	[illegible]	-	-	[illegible]	[illegible]	-	-	[illegible]	[illegible]	[illegible]	-	-	-	[illegible]	[illegible]
Total of Province,	[illegible]	[illegible]	[illegible]	[illegible]	-	-	[illegible]	[illegible]	[illegible]	[illegible]	[illegible]	[illegible]	[illegible]	[illegible]	[illegible]	[illegible]	[illegible]	[illegible]	-	-	[illegible]	[illegible]

Munster:																						
Clare,	[illegible]	[illegible]	[illegible]	[illegible]	[illegible]	[illegible]	[illegible]	[illegible]	[illegible]	[illegible]	[illegible]	[illegible]	[illegible]	[illegible]	[illegible]	[illegible]	[illegible]	[illegible]	[illegible]	[illegible]	[illegible]	[illegible]
Cork, E. R.,	[illegible]	[illegible]	[illegible]	[illegible]	[illegible]	[illegible]	[illegible]	[illegible]	[illegible]	[illegible]	[illegible]	[illegible]	[illegible]	[illegible]	[illegible]	[illegible]	[illegible]	[illegible]	[illegible]	[illegible]	[illegible]	[illegible]
Cork, W. R.,	[illegible]	[illegible]	[illegible]	[illegible]	[illegible]	[illegible]	[illegible]	[illegible]	[illegible]	[illegible]	[illegible]	[illegible]	[illegible]	[illegible]	[illegible]	[illegible]	[illegible]	[illegible]	[illegible]	[illegible]	[illegible]	[illegible]
Cork City,	[illegible]	[illegible]	[illegible]	[illegible]	[illegible]	[illegible]	[illegible]	[illegible]	[illegible]	[illegible]	[illegible]	[illegible]	[illegible]	[illegible]	[illegible]	[illegible]	[illegible]	[illegible]	[illegible]	[illegible]	[illegible]	[illegible]
Kerry,	[illegible]	[illegible]	[illegible]	[illegible]	[illegible]	[illegible]	[illegible]	[illegible]	[illegible]	[illegible]	[illegible]	[illegible]	[illegible]	[illegible]	[illegible]	[illegible]	[illegible]	[illegible]	[illegible]	[illegible]	[illegible]	[illegible]
Limerick,	[illegible]	[illegible]	[illegible]	[illegible]	[illegible]	[illegible]	[illegible]	[illegible]	[illegible]	[illegible]	[illegible]	[illegible]	[illegible]	[illegible]	[illegible]	[illegible]	[illegible]	[illegible]	[illegible]	[illegible]	[illegible]	[illegible]
Limerick City,	[illegible]	[illegible]	[illegible]	[illegible]	[illegible]	[illegible]	[illegible]	[illegible]	[illegible]	[illegible]	[illegible]	[illegible]	[illegible]	[illegible]	[illegible]	[illegible]	[illegible]	[illegible]	[illegible]	[illegible]	[illegible]	[illegible]
Tipperary, N. R.,	[illegible]	[illegible]	[illegible]	[illegible]	[illegible]	[illegible]	[illegible]	[illegible]	[illegible]	[illegible]	[illegible]	[illegible]	[illegible]	[illegible]	[illegible]	[illegible]	[illegible]	[illegible]	[illegible]	[illegible]	[illegible]	[illegible]
Tipperary, S. R.,	[illegible]	[illegible]	[illegible]	[illegible]	[illegible]	[illegible]	[illegible]	[illegible]	[illegible]	[illegible]	[illegible]	[illegible]	[illegible]	[illegible]	[illegible]	[illegible]	[illegible]	[illegible]	[illegible]	[illegible]	[illegible]	[illegible]
Waterford,	[illegible]	[illegible]	[illegible]	[illegible]	[illegible]	[illegible]	[illegible]	[illegible]	[illegible]	[illegible]	[illegible]	[illegible]	[illegible]	[illegible]	[illegible]	[illegible]	[illegible]	[illegible]	[illegible]	[illegible]	[illegible]	[illegible]
Waterford City,	[illegible]	[illegible]	[illegible]	[illegible]	[illegible]	[illegible]	[illegible]	[illegible]	[illegible]	[illegible]	[illegible]	[illegible]	[illegible]	[illegible]	[illegible]	[illegible]	[illegible]	[illegible]	[illegible]	[illegible]	[illegible]	[illegible]
Total of Province,	[illegible]	[illegible]	[illegible]	[illegible]	[illegible]	[illegible]	[illegible]	[illegible]	[illegible]	[illegible]	[illegible]	[illegible]	[illegible]	[illegible]	[illegible]	[illegible]	[illegible]	[illegible]	[illegible]	[illegible]	[illegible]	[illegible]
Ulster:																						
Antrim,	[illegible]	[illegible]	[illegible]	[illegible]	[illegible]	[illegible]	[illegible]	[illegible]	[illegible]	[illegible]	[illegible]	[illegible]	[illegible]	[illegible]	[illegible]	[illegible]	[illegible]	[illegible]	[illegible]	[illegible]	[illegible]	[illegible]
Armagh,	[illegible]	[illegible]	[illegible]	[illegible]	[illegible]	[illegible]	[illegible]	[illegible]	[illegible]	[illegible]	[illegible]	[illegible]	[illegible]	[illegible]	[illegible]	[illegible]	[illegible]	[illegible]	[illegible]	[illegible]	[illegible]	[illegible]
Belfast, Town of,	[illegible]	[illegible]	[illegible]	[illegible]	[illegible]	[illegible]	[illegible]	[illegible]	[illegible]	[illegible]	[illegible]	[illegible]	[illegible]	[illegible]	[illegible]	[illegible]	[illegible]	[illegible]	[illegible]	[illegible]	[illegible]	[illegible]
Carrickfergus, Town of,	[illegible]	[illegible]	[illegible]	[illegible]	[illegible]	[illegible]	[illegible]	[illegible]	[illegible]	[illegible]	[illegible]	[illegible]	[illegible]	[illegible]	[illegible]	[illegible]	[illegible]	[illegible]	[illegible]	[illegible]	[illegible]	[illegible]
Cavan,	[illegible]	[illegible]	[illegible]	[illegible]	[illegible]	[illegible]	[illegible]	[illegible]	[illegible]	[illegible]	[illegible]	[illegible]	[illegible]	[illegible]	[illegible]	[illegible]	[illegible]	[illegible]	[illegible]	[illegible]	[illegible]	[illegible]
Donegal,	[illegible]	[illegible]	[illegible]	[illegible]	[illegible]	[illegible]	[illegible]	[illegible]	[illegible]	[illegible]	[illegible]	[illegible]	[illegible]	[illegible]	[illegible]	[illegible]	[illegible]	[illegible]	[illegible]	[illegible]	[illegible]	[illegible]
Down,	[illegible]	[illegible]	[illegible]	[illegible]	[illegible]	[illegible]	[illegible]	[illegible]	[illegible]	[illegible]	[illegible]	[illegible]	[illegible]	[illegible]	[illegible]	[illegible]	[illegible]	[illegible]	[illegible]	[illegible]	[illegible]	[illegible]
Fermanagh,	[illegible]	[illegible]	[illegible]	[illegible]	[illegible]	[illegible]	[illegible]	[illegible]	[illegible]	[illegible]	[illegible]	[illegible]	[illegible]	[illegible]	[illegible]	[illegible]	[illegible]	[illegible]	[illegible]	[illegible]	[illegible]	[illegible]
Londonderry,	[illegible]	[illegible]	[illegible]	[illegible]	[illegible]	[illegible]	[illegible]	[illegible]	[illegible]	[illegible]	[illegible]	[illegible]	[illegible]	[illegible]	[illegible]	[illegible]	[illegible]	[illegible]	[illegible]	[illegible]	[illegible]	[illegible]
Londonderry City,	[illegible]	[illegible]	[illegible]	[illegible]	[illegible]	[illegible]	[illegible]	[illegible]	[illegible]	[illegible]	[illegible]	[illegible]	[illegible]	[illegible]	[illegible]	[illegible]	[illegible]	[illegible]	[illegible]	[illegible]	[illegible]	[illegible]
Monaghan,	[illegible]	[illegible]	[illegible]	[illegible]	[illegible]	[illegible]	[illegible]	[illegible]	[illegible]	[illegible]	[illegible]	[illegible]	[illegible]	[illegible]	[illegible]	[illegible]	[illegible]	[illegible]	[illegible]	[illegible]	[illegible]	[illegible]
Tyrone,	[illegible]	[illegible]	[illegible]	[illegible]	[illegible]	[illegible]	[illegible]	[illegible]	[illegible]	[illegible]	[illegible]	[illegible]	[illegible]	[illegible]	[illegible]	[illegible]	[illegible]	[illegible]	[illegible]	[illegible]	[illegible]	[illegible]
Total of Province,	[illegible]	[illegible]	[illegible]	[illegible]	[illegible]	[illegible]	[illegible]	[illegible]	[illegible]	[illegible]	[illegible]	[illegible]	[illegible]	[illegible]	[illegible]	[illegible]	[illegible]	[illegible]	[illegible]	[illegible]	[illegible]	[illegible]
Connaught:																						
Galway, E. R.,	[illegible]	[illegible]	[illegible]	[illegible]	[illegible]	[illegible]	[illegible]	[illegible]	[illegible]	[illegible]	[illegible]	[illegible]	[illegible]	[illegible]	[illegible]	[illegible]	[illegible]	[illegible]	[illegible]	[illegible]	[illegible]	[illegible]
Galway, W. R.,	[illegible]	[illegible]	[illegible]	[illegible]	[illegible]	[illegible]	[illegible]	[illegible]	[illegible]	[illegible]	[illegible]	[illegible]	[illegible]	[illegible]	[illegible]	[illegible]	[illegible]	[illegible]	[illegible]	[illegible]	[illegible]	[illegible]
Galway, Town of,	[illegible]	[illegible]	[illegible]	[illegible]	[illegible]	[illegible]	[illegible]	[illegible]	[illegible]	[illegible]	[illegible]	[illegible]	[illegible]	[illegible]	[illegible]	[illegible]	[illegible]	[illegible]	[illegible]	[illegible]	[illegible]	[illegible]
Leitrim,	[illegible]	[illegible]	[illegible]	[illegible]	[illegible]	[illegible]	[illegible]	[illegible]	[illegible]	[illegible]	[illegible]	[illegible]	[illegible]	[illegible]	[illegible]	[illegible]	[illegible]	[illegible]	[illegible]	[illegible]	[illegible]	[illegible]
Mayo,	[illegible]	[illegible]	[illegible]	[illegible]	[illegible]	[illegible]	[illegible]	[illegible]	[illegible]	[illegible]	[illegible]	[illegible]	[illegible]	[illegible]	[illegible]	[illegible]	[illegible]	[illegible]	[illegible]	[illegible]	[illegible]	[illegible]
Roscommon,	[illegible]	[illegible]	[illegible]	[illegible]	[illegible]	[illegible]	[illegible]	[illegible]	[illegible]	[illegible]	[illegible]	[illegible]	[illegible]	[illegible]	[illegible]	[illegible]	[illegible]	[illegible]	[illegible]	[illegible]	[illegible]	[illegible]
Sligo,	[illegible]	[illegible]	[illegible]	[illegible]	[illegible]	[illegible]	[illegible]	[illegible]	[illegible]	[illegible]	[illegible]	[illegible]	[illegible]	[illegible]	[illegible]	[illegible]	[illegible]	[illegible]	[illegible]	[illegible]	[illegible]	[illegible]
Total of Province,	[illegible]	[illegible]	[illegible]	[illegible]	[illegible]	[illegible]	[illegible]	[illegible]	[illegible]	[illegible]	[illegible]	[illegible]	[illegible]	[illegible]	[illegible]	[illegible]	[illegible]	[illegible]	[illegible]	[illegible]	[illegible]	[illegible]
Total of Ireland,	[illegible]	[illegible]	[illegible]	[illegible]	[illegible]	[illegible]	[illegible]	[illegible]	[illegible]	[illegible]	[illegible]	[illegible]	[illegible]	[illegible]	[illegible]	[illegible]	[illegible]	[illegible]	[illegible]	[illegible]	[illegible]	[illegible]

TABLE 1.—RETURN OF INDICTABLE OFFENCES (not Disposed of Summarily). Number of Crimes Committed in each Police District (so far as known to the Police), the Number of Persons Apprehended, and the Disposal of the Charges against them, in the Year ended 31st December, [illegible].

Province, County, County of City or of Town.	Number of Crimes Committed: Jan. Feb. March	April, May, June	July, August, Sept.	Oct. Nov. Dec.	Total Crimes	Number of Persons Apprehended: Jan. Feb. March	April, May, June	July, August, Sept.	Oct. Nov. Dec.	Total Persons	Disposal of the Persons Apprehended: Totals M.	Totals W.	Discharged for want of Evidence M.	Discharged for want of Evidence W.	Discharged for want of Prosecution M.	Discharged for want of Prosecution W.	Bailed for Future Examination M.	Bailed for Future Examination W.	Bailed for Trial M.	Bailed for Trial W.	Committed for want of Sureties M.	Committed for want of Sureties W.	Committed for Trial M.	Committed for Trial W.
Leinster:																								
Carlow	[illegible]	[illegible]	[illegible]	[illegible]	[illegible]	[illegible]	[illegible]	[illegible]	[illegible]	[illegible]	[illegible]	[illegible]	[illegible]	[illegible]	[illegible]	[illegible]	[illegible]	[illegible]	[illegible]	[illegible]	[illegible]	[illegible]	[illegible]	[illegible]
Drogheda, Town of	[illegible]	[illegible]	[illegible]	[illegible]	[illegible]	[illegible]	[illegible]	[illegible]	[illegible]	[illegible]	[illegible]	[illegible]	[illegible]	[illegible]	[illegible]	[illegible]	[illegible]	[illegible]	[illegible]	[illegible]	[illegible]	[illegible]	[illegible]	[illegible]
Dublin County (part of)	[illegible]	[illegible]	[illegible]	[illegible]	[illegible]	[illegible]	[illegible]	[illegible]	[illegible]	[illegible]	[illegible]	[illegible]	[illegible]	[illegible]	[illegible]	[illegible]	[illegible]	[illegible]	[illegible]	[illegible]	[illegible]	[illegible]	[illegible]	[illegible]
Dublin City (and part of County) Metropolitan Police District—Divisions																								
A.	[illegible]	[illegible]	[illegible]	[illegible]	[illegible]	[illegible]	[illegible]	[illegible]	[illegible]	[illegible]	[illegible]	[illegible]	[illegible]	[illegible]	[illegible]	[illegible]	[illegible]	[illegible]	[illegible]	[illegible]	[illegible]	[illegible]	[illegible]	[illegible]
B.	[illegible]	[illegible]	[illegible]	[illegible]	[illegible]	[illegible]	[illegible]	[illegible]	[illegible]	[illegible]	[illegible]	[illegible]	[illegible]	[illegible]	[illegible]	[illegible]	[illegible]	[illegible]	[illegible]	[illegible]	[illegible]	[illegible]	[illegible]	[illegible]
C.	[illegible]	[illegible]	[illegible]	[illegible]	[illegible]	[illegible]	[illegible]	[illegible]	[illegible]	[illegible]	[illegible]	[illegible]	[illegible]	[illegible]	[illegible]	[illegible]	[illegible]	[illegible]	[illegible]	[illegible]	[illegible]	[illegible]	[illegible]	[illegible]
D.	[illegible]	[illegible]	[illegible]	[illegible]	[illegible]	[illegible]	[illegible]	[illegible]	[illegible]	[illegible]	[illegible]	[illegible]	[illegible]	[illegible]	[illegible]	[illegible]	[illegible]	[illegible]	[illegible]	[illegible]	[illegible]	[illegible]	[illegible]	[illegible]
E.	[illegible]	[illegible]	[illegible]	[illegible]	[illegible]	[illegible]	[illegible]	[illegible]	[illegible]	[illegible]	[illegible]	[illegible]	[illegible]	[illegible]	[illegible]	[illegible]	[illegible]	[illegible]	[illegible]	[illegible]	[illegible]	[illegible]	[illegible]	[illegible]
F.	[illegible]	[illegible]	[illegible]	[illegible]	[illegible]	[illegible]	[illegible]	[illegible]	[illegible]	[illegible]	[illegible]	[illegible]	[illegible]	[illegible]	[illegible]	[illegible]	[illegible]	[illegible]	[illegible]	[illegible]	[illegible]	[illegible]	[illegible]	[illegible]
Total of Met. Police District	[illegible]	[illegible]	[illegible]	[illegible]	[illegible]	[illegible]	[illegible]	[illegible]	[illegible]	[illegible]	[illegible]	[illegible]	[illegible]	[illegible]	[illegible]	[illegible]	[illegible]	[illegible]	[illegible]	[illegible]	[illegible]	[illegible]	[illegible]	[illegible]
Kildare	[illegible]	[illegible]	[illegible]	[illegible]	[illegible]	[illegible]	[illegible]	[illegible]	[illegible]	[illegible]	[illegible]	[illegible]	[illegible]	[illegible]	[illegible]	[illegible]	[illegible]	[illegible]	[illegible]	[illegible]	[illegible]	[illegible]	[illegible]	[illegible]
Kilkenny	[illegible]	[illegible]	[illegible]	[illegible]	[illegible]	[illegible]	[illegible]	[illegible]	[illegible]	[illegible]	[illegible]	[illegible]	[illegible]	[illegible]	[illegible]	[illegible]	[illegible]	[illegible]	[illegible]	[illegible]	[illegible]	[illegible]	[illegible]	[illegible]
King's County	[illegible]	[illegible]	[illegible]	[illegible]	[illegible]	[illegible]	[illegible]	[illegible]	[illegible]	[illegible]	[illegible]	[illegible]	[illegible]	[illegible]	[illegible]	[illegible]	[illegible]	[illegible]	[illegible]	[illegible]	[illegible]	[illegible]	[illegible]	[illegible]
Longford	[illegible]	[illegible]	[illegible]	[illegible]	[illegible]	[illegible]	[illegible]	[illegible]	[illegible]	[illegible]	[illegible]	[illegible]	[illegible]	[illegible]	[illegible]	[illegible]	[illegible]	[illegible]	[illegible]	[illegible]	[illegible]	[illegible]	[illegible]	[illegible]
Louth	[illegible]	[illegible]	[illegible]	[illegible]	[illegible]	[illegible]	[illegible]	[illegible]	[illegible]	[illegible]	[illegible]	[illegible]	[illegible]	[illegible]	[illegible]	[illegible]	[illegible]	[illegible]	[illegible]	[illegible]	[illegible]	[illegible]	[illegible]	[illegible]
Meath	[illegible]	[illegible]	[illegible]	[illegible]	[illegible]	[illegible]	[illegible]	[illegible]	[illegible]	[illegible]	[illegible]	[illegible]	[illegible]	[illegible]	[illegible]	[illegible]	[illegible]	[illegible]	[illegible]	[illegible]	[illegible]	[illegible]	[illegible]	[illegible]
Queen's County	[illegible]	[illegible]	[illegible]	[illegible]	[illegible]	[illegible]	[illegible]	[illegible]	[illegible]	[illegible]	[illegible]	[illegible]	[illegible]	[illegible]	[illegible]	[illegible]	[illegible]	[illegible]	[illegible]	[illegible]	[illegible]	[illegible]	[illegible]	[illegible]
Westmeath	[illegible]	[illegible]	[illegible]	[illegible]	[illegible]	[illegible]	[illegible]	[illegible]	[illegible]	[illegible]	[illegible]	[illegible]	[illegible]	[illegible]	[illegible]	[illegible]	[illegible]	[illegible]	[illegible]	[illegible]	[illegible]	[illegible]	[illegible]	[illegible]
Wexford	[illegible]	[illegible]	[illegible]	[illegible]	[illegible]	[illegible]	[illegible]	[illegible]	[illegible]	[illegible]	[illegible]	[illegible]	[illegible]	[illegible]	[illegible]	[illegible]	[illegible]	[illegible]	[illegible]	[illegible]	[illegible]	[illegible]	[illegible]	[illegible]
Wicklow	[illegible]	[illegible]	[illegible]	[illegible]	[illegible]	[illegible]	[illegible]	[illegible]	[illegible]	[illegible]	[illegible]	[illegible]	[illegible]	[illegible]	[illegible]	[illegible]	[illegible]	[illegible]	[illegible]	[illegible]	[illegible]	[illegible]	[illegible]	[illegible]
Total of Province	[illegible]	[illegible]	[illegible]	[illegible]	[illegible]	[illegible]	[illegible]	[illegible]	[illegible]	[illegible]	[illegible]	[illegible]	[illegible]	[illegible]	[illegible]	[illegible]	[illegible]	[illegible]	[illegible]	[illegible]	[illegible]	[illegible]	[illegible]	[illegible]
Munster:																								
Clare	[illegible]	[illegible]	[illegible]	[illegible]	[illegible]	[illegible]	[illegible]	[illegible]	[illegible]	[illegible]	[illegible]	[illegible]	[illegible]	[illegible]	[illegible]	[illegible]	[illegible]	[illegible]	[illegible]	[illegible]	[illegible]	[illegible]	[illegible]	[illegible]
Cork, East Riding	[illegible]	[illegible]	[illegible]	[illegible]	[illegible]	[illegible]	[illegible]	[illegible]	[illegible]	[illegible]	[illegible]	[illegible]	[illegible]	[illegible]	[illegible]	[illegible]	[illegible]	[illegible]	[illegible]	[illegible]	[illegible]	[illegible]	[illegible]	[illegible]

Cork, West Riding	[illegible]	[illegible]	[illegible]	[illegible]	[illegible]	[illegible]	[illegible]	[illegible]	[illegible]	[illegible]	[illegible]	[illegible]	[illegible]	[illegible]	[illegible]	[illegible]	[illegible]	[illegible]	[illegible]	[illegible]	[illegible]	[illegible]	[illegible]	[illegible]
Cork City	[illegible]	[illegible]	[illegible]	[illegible]	[illegible]	[illegible]	[illegible]	[illegible]	[illegible]	[illegible]	[illegible]	[illegible]	[illegible]	[illegible]	[illegible]	[illegible]	[illegible]	[illegible]	[illegible]	[illegible]	[illegible]	[illegible]	[illegible]	[illegible]
Kerry	[illegible]	[illegible]	[illegible]	[illegible]	[illegible]	[illegible]	[illegible]	[illegible]	[illegible]	[illegible]	[illegible]	[illegible]	[illegible]	[illegible]	[illegible]	[illegible]	[illegible]	[illegible]	[illegible]	[illegible]	[illegible]	[illegible]	[illegible]	[illegible]
Limerick	[illegible]	[illegible]	[illegible]	[illegible]	[illegible]	[illegible]	[illegible]	[illegible]	[illegible]	[illegible]	[illegible]	[illegible]	[illegible]	[illegible]	[illegible]	[illegible]	[illegible]	[illegible]	[illegible]	[illegible]	[illegible]	[illegible]	[illegible]	[illegible]
Limerick City	[illegible]	[illegible]	[illegible]	[illegible]	[illegible]	[illegible]	[illegible]	[illegible]	[illegible]	[illegible]	[illegible]	[illegible]	[illegible]	[illegible]	[illegible]	[illegible]	[illegible]	[illegible]	[illegible]	[illegible]	[illegible]	[illegible]	[illegible]	[illegible]
Tipperary, North Riding	[illegible]	[illegible]	[illegible]	[illegible]	[illegible]	[illegible]	[illegible]	[illegible]	[illegible]	[illegible]	[illegible]	[illegible]	[illegible]	[illegible]	[illegible]	[illegible]	[illegible]	[illegible]	[illegible]	[illegible]	[illegible]	[illegible]	[illegible]	[illegible]
Tipperary, South Riding	[illegible]	[illegible]	[illegible]	[illegible]	[illegible]	[illegible]	[illegible]	[illegible]	[illegible]	[illegible]	[illegible]	[illegible]	[illegible]	[illegible]	[illegible]	[illegible]	[illegible]	[illegible]	[illegible]	[illegible]	[illegible]	[illegible]	[illegible]	[illegible]
Waterford	[illegible]	[illegible]	[illegible]	[illegible]	[illegible]	[illegible]	[illegible]	[illegible]	[illegible]	[illegible]	[illegible]	[illegible]	[illegible]	[illegible]	[illegible]	[illegible]	[illegible]	[illegible]	[illegible]	[illegible]	[illegible]	[illegible]	[illegible]	[illegible]
Waterford City	[illegible]	[illegible]	[illegible]	[illegible]	[illegible]	[illegible]	[illegible]	[illegible]	[illegible]	[illegible]	[illegible]	[illegible]	[illegible]	[illegible]	[illegible]	[illegible]	[illegible]	[illegible]	[illegible]	[illegible]	[illegible]	[illegible]	[illegible]	[illegible]
Total of Province	[illegible]	[illegible]	[illegible]	[illegible]	[illegible]	[illegible]	[illegible]	[illegible]	[illegible]	[illegible]	[illegible]	[illegible]	[illegible]	[illegible]	[illegible]	[illegible]	[illegible]	[illegible]	[illegible]	[illegible]	[illegible]	[illegible]	[illegible]	[illegible]
Ulster:																								
Antrim	[illegible]	[illegible]	[illegible]	[illegible]	[illegible]	[illegible]	[illegible]	[illegible]	[illegible]	[illegible]	[illegible]	[illegible]	[illegible]	[illegible]	[illegible]	[illegible]	[illegible]	[illegible]	[illegible]	[illegible]	[illegible]	[illegible]	[illegible]	[illegible]
Armagh	[illegible]	[illegible]	[illegible]	[illegible]	[illegible]	[illegible]	[illegible]	[illegible]	[illegible]	[illegible]	[illegible]	[illegible]	[illegible]	[illegible]	[illegible]	[illegible]	[illegible]	[illegible]	[illegible]	[illegible]	[illegible]	[illegible]	[illegible]	[illegible]
Belfast, Town of	[illegible]	[illegible]	[illegible]	[illegible]	[illegible]	[illegible]	[illegible]	[illegible]	[illegible]	[illegible]	[illegible]	[illegible]	[illegible]	[illegible]	[illegible]	[illegible]	[illegible]	[illegible]	[illegible]	[illegible]	[illegible]	[illegible]	[illegible]	[illegible]
Carrickfergus, Town of	[illegible]	[illegible]	[illegible]	[illegible]	[illegible]	[illegible]	[illegible]	[illegible]	[illegible]	[illegible]	[illegible]	[illegible]	[illegible]	[illegible]	[illegible]	[illegible]	[illegible]	[illegible]	[illegible]	[illegible]	[illegible]	[illegible]	[illegible]	[illegible]
Cavan	[illegible]	[illegible]	[illegible]	[illegible]	[illegible]	[illegible]	[illegible]	[illegible]	[illegible]	[illegible]	[illegible]	[illegible]	[illegible]	[illegible]	[illegible]	[illegible]	[illegible]	[illegible]	[illegible]	[illegible]	[illegible]	[illegible]	[illegible]	[illegible]
Donegal	[illegible]	[illegible]	[illegible]	[illegible]	[illegible]	[illegible]	[illegible]	[illegible]	[illegible]	[illegible]	[illegible]	[illegible]	[illegible]	[illegible]	[illegible]	[illegible]	[illegible]	[illegible]	[illegible]	[illegible]	[illegible]	[illegible]	[illegible]	[illegible]
Down	[illegible]	[illegible]	[illegible]	[illegible]	[illegible]	[illegible]	[illegible]	[illegible]	[illegible]	[illegible]	[illegible]	[illegible]	[illegible]	[illegible]	[illegible]	[illegible]	[illegible]	[illegible]	[illegible]	[illegible]	[illegible]	[illegible]	[illegible]	[illegible]
Fermanagh	[illegible]	[illegible]	[illegible]	[illegible]	[illegible]	[illegible]	[illegible]	[illegible]	[illegible]	[illegible]	[illegible]	[illegible]	[illegible]	[illegible]	[illegible]	[illegible]	[illegible]	[illegible]	[illegible]	[illegible]	[illegible]	[illegible]	[illegible]	[illegible]
Londonderry	[illegible]	[illegible]	[illegible]	[illegible]	[illegible]	[illegible]	[illegible]	[illegible]	[illegible]	[illegible]	[illegible]	[illegible]	[illegible]	[illegible]	[illegible]	[illegible]	[illegible]	[illegible]	[illegible]	[illegible]	[illegible]	[illegible]	[illegible]	[illegible]
Monaghan	[illegible]	[illegible]	[illegible]	[illegible]	[illegible]	[illegible]	[illegible]	[illegible]	[illegible]	[illegible]	[illegible]	[illegible]	[illegible]	[illegible]	[illegible]	[illegible]	[illegible]	[illegible]	[illegible]	[illegible]	[illegible]	[illegible]	[illegible]	[illegible]
Tyrone	[illegible]	[illegible]	[illegible]	[illegible]	[illegible]	[illegible]	[illegible]	[illegible]	[illegible]	[illegible]	[illegible]	[illegible]	[illegible]	[illegible]	[illegible]	[illegible]	[illegible]	[illegible]	[illegible]	[illegible]	[illegible]	[illegible]	[illegible]	[illegible]
Total of Province	[illegible]	[illegible]	[illegible]	[illegible]	[illegible]	[illegible]	[illegible]	[illegible]	[illegible]	[illegible]	[illegible]	[illegible]	[illegible]	[illegible]	[illegible]	[illegible]	[illegible]	[illegible]	[illegible]	[illegible]	[illegible]	[illegible]	[illegible]	[illegible]
Connaught:																								
Galway, East Riding	[illegible]	[illegible]	[illegible]	[illegible]	[illegible]	[illegible]	[illegible]	[illegible]	[illegible]	[illegible]	[illegible]	[illegible]	[illegible]	[illegible]	[illegible]	[illegible]	[illegible]	[illegible]	[illegible]	[illegible]	[illegible]	[illegible]	[illegible]	[illegible]
Galway, West Riding	[illegible]	[illegible]	[illegible]	[illegible]	[illegible]	[illegible]	[illegible]	[illegible]	[illegible]	[illegible]	[illegible]	[illegible]	[illegible]	[illegible]	[illegible]	[illegible]	[illegible]	[illegible]	[illegible]	[illegible]	[illegible]	[illegible]	[illegible]	[illegible]
Galway, Town of	[illegible]	[illegible]	[illegible]	[illegible]	[illegible]	[illegible]	[illegible]	[illegible]	[illegible]	[illegible]	[illegible]	[illegible]	[illegible]	[illegible]	[illegible]	[illegible]	[illegible]	[illegible]	[illegible]	[illegible]	[illegible]	[illegible]	[illegible]	[illegible]
Leitrim	[illegible]	[illegible]	[illegible]	[illegible]	[illegible]	[illegible]	[illegible]	[illegible]	[illegible]	[illegible]	[illegible]	[illegible]	[illegible]	[illegible]	[illegible]	[illegible]	[illegible]	[illegible]	[illegible]	[illegible]	[illegible]	[illegible]	[illegible]	[illegible]
Mayo	[illegible]	[illegible]	[illegible]	[illegible]	[illegible]	[illegible]	[illegible]	[illegible]	[illegible]	[illegible]	[illegible]	[illegible]	[illegible]	[illegible]	[illegible]	[illegible]	[illegible]	[illegible]	[illegible]	[illegible]	[illegible]	[illegible]	[illegible]	[illegible]
Roscommon	[illegible]	[illegible]	[illegible]	[illegible]	[illegible]	[illegible]	[illegible]	[illegible]	[illegible]	[illegible]	[illegible]	[illegible]	[illegible]	[illegible]	[illegible]	[illegible]	[illegible]	[illegible]	[illegible]	[illegible]	[illegible]	[illegible]	[illegible]	[illegible]
Sligo	[illegible]	[illegible]	[illegible]	[illegible]	[illegible]	[illegible]	[illegible]	[illegible]	[illegible]	[illegible]	[illegible]	[illegible]	[illegible]	[illegible]	[illegible]	[illegible]	[illegible]	[illegible]	[illegible]	[illegible]	[illegible]	[illegible]	[illegible]	[illegible]
Total of Province	[illegible]	[illegible]	[illegible]	[illegible]	[illegible]	[illegible]	[illegible]	[illegible]	[illegible]	[illegible]	[illegible]	[illegible]	[illegible]	[illegible]	[illegible]	[illegible]	[illegible]	[illegible]	[illegible]	[illegible]	[illegible]	[illegible]	[illegible]	[illegible]
Total of Ireland	[illegible]	[illegible]	[illegible]	[illegible]	[illegible]	[illegible]	[illegible]	[illegible]	[illegible]	[illegible]	[illegible]	[illegible]	[illegible]	[illegible]	[illegible]	[illegible]	[illegible]	[illegible]	[illegible]	[illegible]	[illegible]	[illegible]	[illegible]	[illegible]

TABLE 6.—RETURN OF INDICTABLE OFFENCES (not Disposed of Summarily). TOTAL of the OFFENCES of each CLASS COMMITTED (so far as known to the Police), the NUMBER of PERSONS APPREHENDED, and the manner in which they were disposed of, in the Year ended 31st December, 18[illegible], made by the Inspector-General.

NATURE OF CRIMES.	Number of Crimes Committed: Jan. Feb. Mar.	Apr. May. June	July Aug. Sept.	Oct. Nov. Dec.	Total Crimes	Number of Persons Apprehended: Jan. Feb. Mar.	Apr. May. June	July Aug. Sept.	Oct. Nov. Dec.	Total Persons	Results: Tried M.	Tried W.	Discharged for want of Evidence M.	W.	Discharged for want of Prosecutors M.	W.	Bailed M.	W.	Traversed to next Term M.	W.	Committed for want of Sureties M.	W.	Committed for Trial M.	W.
No. 1.—Offences against the Person.																								
Murder of Infants aged one year and under,	[illegible]	[illegible]	[illegible]	[illegible]	[illegible]	[illegible]	[illegible]	[illegible]	[illegible]	[illegible]	[illegible]	[illegible]	[illegible]	[illegible]	[illegible]	[illegible]	[illegible]	[illegible]	[illegible]	[illegible]	[illegible]	[illegible]	[illegible]	[illegible]
Other Murders,	[illegible]	[illegible]	[illegible]	[illegible]	[illegible]	[illegible]	[illegible]	[illegible]	[illegible]	[illegible]	[illegible]	[illegible]	[illegible]	[illegible]	[illegible]	[illegible]	[illegible]	[illegible]	[illegible]	[illegible]	[illegible]	[illegible]	[illegible]	[illegible]
Attempts to Murder,	[illegible]	[illegible]	[illegible]	[illegible]	[illegible]	[illegible]	[illegible]	[illegible]	[illegible]	[illegible]	[illegible]	[illegible]	[illegible]	[illegible]	[illegible]	[illegible]	[illegible]	[illegible]	[illegible]	[illegible]	[illegible]	[illegible]	[illegible]	[illegible]
Shooting at, Wounding, Stabbing, &c., to do bodily harm,	[illegible]	[illegible]	[illegible]	[illegible]	[illegible]	[illegible]	[illegible]	[illegible]	[illegible]	[illegible]	[illegible]	[illegible]	[illegible]	[illegible]	[illegible]	[illegible]	[illegible]	[illegible]	[illegible]	[illegible]	[illegible]	[illegible]	[illegible]	[illegible]
Manslaughter,	[illegible]	[illegible]	[illegible]	[illegible]	[illegible]	[illegible]	[illegible]	[illegible]	[illegible]	[illegible]	[illegible]	[illegible]	[illegible]	[illegible]	[illegible]	[illegible]	[illegible]	[illegible]	[illegible]	[illegible]	[illegible]	[illegible]	[illegible]	[illegible]
Concealing the Birth of Infants,	[illegible]	[illegible]	[illegible]	[illegible]	[illegible]	[illegible]	[illegible]	[illegible]	[illegible]	[illegible]	[illegible]	[illegible]	[illegible]	[illegible]	[illegible]	[illegible]	[illegible]	[illegible]	[illegible]	[illegible]	[illegible]	[illegible]	[illegible]	[illegible]
Sodomy and Bestiality,	[illegible]	[illegible]	[illegible]	[illegible]	[illegible]	[illegible]	[illegible]	[illegible]	[illegible]	[illegible]	[illegible]	[illegible]	[illegible]	[illegible]	[illegible]	[illegible]	[illegible]	[illegible]	[illegible]	[illegible]	[illegible]	[illegible]	[illegible]	[illegible]
—— Attempts to commit, and other unnatural Misdemeanors,	[illegible]	[illegible]	[illegible]	[illegible]	[illegible]	[illegible]	[illegible]	[illegible]	[illegible]	[illegible]	[illegible]	[illegible]	[illegible]	[illegible]	[illegible]	[illegible]	[illegible]	[illegible]	[illegible]	[illegible]	[illegible]	[illegible]	[illegible]	[illegible]
Rape,	[illegible]	[illegible]	[illegible]	[illegible]	[illegible]	[illegible]	[illegible]	[illegible]	[illegible]	[illegible]	[illegible]	[illegible]	[illegible]	[illegible]	[illegible]	[illegible]	[illegible]	[illegible]	[illegible]	[illegible]	[illegible]	[illegible]	[illegible]	[illegible]
—— Assaults with intent to ravish and carnally abuse,	[illegible]	[illegible]	[illegible]	[illegible]	[illegible]	[illegible]	[illegible]	[illegible]	[illegible]	[illegible]	[illegible]	[illegible]	[illegible]	[illegible]	[illegible]	[illegible]	[illegible]	[illegible]	[illegible]	[illegible]	[illegible]	[illegible]	[illegible]	[illegible]
Bigamy,	[illegible]	[illegible]	[illegible]	[illegible]	[illegible]	[illegible]	[illegible]	[illegible]	[illegible]	[illegible]	[illegible]	[illegible]	[illegible]	[illegible]	[illegible]	[illegible]	[illegible]	[illegible]	[illegible]	[illegible]	[illegible]	[illegible]	[illegible]	[illegible]
Child Stealing,	[illegible]	[illegible]	[illegible]	[illegible]	[illegible]	[illegible]	[illegible]	[illegible]	[illegible]	[illegible]	[illegible]	[illegible]	[illegible]	[illegible]	[illegible]	[illegible]	[illegible]	[illegible]	[illegible]	[illegible]	[illegible]	[illegible]	[illegible]	[illegible]
Unlawfully abandoning Children under two years of age,	[illegible]	[illegible]	[illegible]	[illegible]	[illegible]	[illegible]	[illegible]	[illegible]	[illegible]	[illegible]	[illegible]	[illegible]	[illegible]	[illegible]	[illegible]	[illegible]	[illegible]	[illegible]	[illegible]	[illegible]	[illegible]	[illegible]	[illegible]	[illegible]
Endangering the safety of Passengers on Railways,	[illegible]	[illegible]	[illegible]	[illegible]	[illegible]	[illegible]	[illegible]	[illegible]	[illegible]	[illegible]	[illegible]	[illegible]	[illegible]	[illegible]	[illegible]	[illegible]	[illegible]	[illegible]	[illegible]	[illegible]	[illegible]	[illegible]	[illegible]	[illegible]
Assaults and inflicting bodily harm,	[illegible]	[illegible]	[illegible]	[illegible]	[illegible]	[illegible]	[illegible]	[illegible]	[illegible]	[illegible]	[illegible]	[illegible]	[illegible]	[illegible]	[illegible]	[illegible]	[illegible]	[illegible]	[illegible]	[illegible]	[illegible]	[illegible]	[illegible]	[illegible]
Assaults, common,	[illegible]	[illegible]	[illegible]	[illegible]	[illegible]	[illegible]	[illegible]	[illegible]	[illegible]	[illegible]	[illegible]	[illegible]	[illegible]	[illegible]	[illegible]	[illegible]	[illegible]	[illegible]	[illegible]	[illegible]	[illegible]	[illegible]	[illegible]	[illegible]
Assaults on Peace Officers,	[illegible]	[illegible]	[illegible]	[illegible]	[illegible]	[illegible]	[illegible]	[illegible]	[illegible]	[illegible]	[illegible]	[illegible]	[illegible]	[illegible]	[illegible]	[illegible]	[illegible]	[illegible]	[illegible]	[illegible]	[illegible]	[illegible]	[illegible]	[illegible]
Total of No. 1,	[illegible]	[illegible]	[illegible]	[illegible]	[illegible]	[illegible]	[illegible]	[illegible]	[illegible]	[illegible]	[illegible]	[illegible]	[illegible]	[illegible]	[illegible]	[illegible]	[illegible]	[illegible]	[illegible]	[illegible]	[illegible]	[illegible]	[illegible]	[illegible]
No. 2.—Offences against Property with Violence.																								
Sacrilege,	[illegible]	[illegible]	[illegible]	[illegible]	[illegible]	[illegible]	[illegible]	[illegible]	[illegible]	[illegible]	[illegible]	[illegible]	[illegible]	[illegible]	[illegible]	[illegible]	[illegible]	[illegible]	[illegible]	[illegible]	[illegible]	[illegible]	[illegible]	[illegible]
Burglary and Housebreaking,	[illegible]	[illegible]	[illegible]	[illegible]	[illegible]	[illegible]	[illegible]	[illegible]	[illegible]	[illegible]	[illegible]	[illegible]	[illegible]	[illegible]	[illegible]	[illegible]	[illegible]	[illegible]	[illegible]	[illegible]	[illegible]	[illegible]	[illegible]	[illegible]
Breaking into Shops, Warehouses, &c.,	[illegible]	[illegible]	[illegible]	[illegible]	[illegible]	[illegible]	[illegible]	[illegible]	[illegible]	[illegible]	[illegible]	[illegible]	[illegible]	[illegible]	[illegible]	[illegible]	[illegible]	[illegible]	[illegible]	[illegible]	[illegible]	[illegible]	[illegible]	[illegible]
Attempts to break into Houses, Shops, Warehouses, &c.,	[illegible]	[illegible]	[illegible]	[illegible]	[illegible]	[illegible]	[illegible]	[illegible]	[illegible]	[illegible]	[illegible]	[illegible]	[illegible]	[illegible]	[illegible]	[illegible]	[illegible]	[illegible]	[illegible]	[illegible]	[illegible]	[illegible]	[illegible]	[illegible]
Robbery,	[illegible]	[illegible]	[illegible]	[illegible]	[illegible]	[illegible]	[illegible]	[illegible]	[illegible]	[illegible]	[illegible]	[illegible]	[illegible]	[illegible]	[illegible]	[illegible]	[illegible]	[illegible]	[illegible]	[illegible]	[illegible]	[illegible]	[illegible]	[illegible]
Attempts to rob, and demanding Money by menaces,	[illegible]	[illegible]	[illegible]	[illegible]	[illegible]	[illegible]	[illegible]	[illegible]	[illegible]	[illegible]	[illegible]	[illegible]	[illegible]	[illegible]	[illegible]	[illegible]	[illegible]	[illegible]	[illegible]	[illegible]	[illegible]	[illegible]	[illegible]	[illegible]
Total of No. 2,	[illegible]	[illegible]	[illegible]	[illegible]	[illegible]	[illegible]	[illegible]	[illegible]	[illegible]	[illegible]	[illegible]	[illegible]	[illegible]	[illegible]	[illegible]	[illegible]	[illegible]	[illegible]	[illegible]	[illegible]	[illegible]	[illegible]	[illegible]	[illegible]
No. 3.—Offences against Property without Violence.																								
Cattle Stealing,	[illegible]	[illegible]	[illegible]	[illegible]	[illegible]	[illegible]	[illegible]	[illegible]	[illegible]	[illegible]	[illegible]	[illegible]	[illegible]	[illegible]	[illegible]	[illegible]	[illegible]	[illegible]	[illegible]	[illegible]	[illegible]	[illegible]	[illegible]	[illegible]
Horse Stealing,	[illegible]	[illegible]	[illegible]	[illegible]	[illegible]	[illegible]	[illegible]	[illegible]	[illegible]	[illegible]	[illegible]	[illegible]	[illegible]	[illegible]	[illegible]	[illegible]	[illegible]	[illegible]	[illegible]	[illegible]	[illegible]	[illegible]	[illegible]	[illegible]
Sheep Stealing,	[illegible]	[illegible]	[illegible]	[illegible]	[illegible]	[illegible]	[illegible]	[illegible]	[illegible]	[illegible]	[illegible]	[illegible]	[illegible]	[illegible]	[illegible]	[illegible]	[illegible]	[illegible]	[illegible]	[illegible]	[illegible]	[illegible]	[illegible]	[illegible]
Larceny to the value of £5 in Dwelling-houses,	[illegible]	[illegible]	[illegible]	[illegible]	[illegible]	[illegible]	[illegible]	[illegible]	[illegible]	[illegible]	[illegible]	[illegible]	[illegible]	[illegible]	[illegible]	[illegible]	[illegible]	[illegible]	[illegible]	[illegible]	[illegible]	[illegible]	[illegible]	[illegible]
Larceny from the Person,	[illegible]	[illegible]	[illegible]	[illegible]	[illegible]	[illegible]	[illegible]	[illegible]	[illegible]	[illegible]	[illegible]	[illegible]	[illegible]	[illegible]	[illegible]	[illegible]	[illegible]	[illegible]	[illegible]	[illegible]	[illegible]	[illegible]	[illegible]	[illegible]
Larceny by Servants,	[illegible]	[illegible]	[illegible]	[illegible]	[illegible]	[illegible]	[illegible]	[illegible]	[illegible]	[illegible]	[illegible]	[illegible]	[illegible]	[illegible]	[illegible]	[illegible]	[illegible]	[illegible]	[illegible]	[illegible]	[illegible]	[illegible]	[illegible]	[illegible]
Larceny, simple,	[illegible]	[illegible]	[illegible]	[illegible]	[illegible]	[illegible]	[illegible]	[illegible]	[illegible]	[illegible]	[illegible]	[illegible]	[illegible]	[illegible]	[illegible]	[illegible]	[illegible]	[illegible]	[illegible]	[illegible]	[illegible]	[illegible]	[illegible]	[illegible]
Larceny on Rivers, Canals, Wharfs, &c.,	[illegible]	[illegible]	[illegible]	[illegible]	[illegible]	[illegible]	[illegible]	[illegible]	[illegible]	[illegible]	[illegible]	[illegible]	[illegible]	[illegible]	[illegible]	[illegible]	[illegible]	[illegible]	[illegible]	[illegible]	[illegible]	[illegible]	[illegible]	[illegible]
Stealing Fixtures, Shrubs growing, &c.,	[illegible]	[illegible]	[illegible]	[illegible]	[illegible]	[illegible]	[illegible]	[illegible]	[illegible]	[illegible]	[illegible]	[illegible]	[illegible]	[illegible]	[illegible]	[illegible]	[illegible]	[illegible]	[illegible]	[illegible]	[illegible]	[illegible]	[illegible]	[illegible]

[illegible]	[illegible]
[illegible]	[illegible]
Larceny by Servants in the Post Office.	[illegible]
Receiving Stolen Goods.	[illegible]
Fraudulently obtaining Goods by false pretences, and attempts to defraud.	[illegible]
Total of No. 3.	[illegible]
No. 4.—Malicious Offences against Property.	
Arson and other Wilful Burning.	[illegible]
[illegible]	[illegible]
[illegible]	[illegible]
[illegible]	[illegible]
Killing and Maiming Cattle.	[illegible]
[illegible]	[illegible]
Other Wilful and Malicious Injuries to Property.	[illegible]
Total of No. 4.	[illegible]
No. 5.—Forgery and Offences against the Currency.	
Forging and uttering Forged Instruments.	[illegible]
[illegible]	[illegible]
[illegible]	[illegible]
[illegible]	[illegible]
Total of No. 5.	[illegible]
No. 6.—Offences not included in the above Classes.	
Offences against the Queen's authority and person.	[illegible]
[illegible]	[illegible]
[illegible]	[illegible]
Offences against the Game Laws.	[illegible]
[illegible]	[illegible]
Perjury, and Subornation of Perjury.	[illegible]
[illegible]	[illegible]
[illegible]	[illegible]
[illegible]	[illegible]
[illegible]	[illegible]
[illegible]	[illegible]
[illegible]	[illegible]
Total of No. 6.	[illegible]
General Total.	[illegible]

TABLE 4.—RETURN OF INDICTABLE OFFENCES (not Disposed of Summarily). Nature of the Crimes Committed ... made by the

Nature of Crimes	Total	Counties [illegible]
No. 1.—Offences against the Person.		
Murder of Infants under one year old	[illegible]	[illegible]
Other Murders	[illegible]	[illegible]
Attempts to Murder	[illegible]	[illegible]
Shooting at, Wounding, Stabbing, &c., to do bodily harm	[illegible]	[illegible]
Manslaughter	[illegible]	[illegible]
Concealing the Birth of Infants	[illegible]	[illegible]
Sodomy and Bestiality	[illegible]	[illegible]
——— Attempts [illegible]	[illegible]	[illegible]
Rape	[illegible]	[illegible]
——— Assaults, with intent to ravish and abuse	[illegible]	[illegible]
Bigamy	[illegible]	[illegible]
Child Stealing	[illegible]	[illegible]
[illegible]	[illegible]	[illegible]
[illegible]	[illegible]	[illegible]
[illegible]	[illegible]	[illegible]
Assaults [illegible]	[illegible]	[illegible]
Assaults on Peace Officers	[illegible]	[illegible]
Total of No. 1.	[illegible]	[illegible]
No. 2.—Offences against Property with Violence.		
Sacrilege	[illegible]	[illegible]
Burglary and Housebreaking	[illegible]	[illegible]
Breaking into Shops, Warehouses, &c.	[illegible]	[illegible]
Attempts to break into Houses, Shops, Warehouses, &c.	[illegible]	[illegible]
Robbery	[illegible]	[illegible]
Attempts to rob, and demanding Money by menaces	[illegible]	[illegible]
Total of No. 2.	[illegible]	[illegible]
No. 3.—Offences against Property without Violence.		
Cattle Stealing	[illegible]	[illegible]
Horse Stealing	[illegible]	[illegible]
Sheep Stealing	[illegible]	[illegible]
Larceny [illegible]	[illegible]	[illegible]
Larceny from the Person	[illegible]	[illegible]
Larceny by Servants	[illegible]	[illegible]
Larceny, Simple	[illegible]	[illegible]
[illegible]	[illegible]	[illegible]
[illegible]	[illegible]	[illegible]
Attempts to Steal	[illegible]	[illegible]
Embezzlement	[illegible]	[illegible]
[illegible]	[illegible]	[illegible]
Receiving Stolen Goods	[illegible]	[illegible]
Fraudulently obtaining Goods by false pretences, and attempts to defraud	[illegible]	[illegible]
Total of No. 3.	[illegible]	[illegible]
No. 4.—Malicious Offences against Property.		
Arson and other Wilful Burnings	[illegible]	[illegible]
[illegible]	[illegible]	[illegible]
[illegible]	[illegible]	[illegible]
[illegible]	[illegible]	[illegible]
Killing and Maiming Cattle	[illegible]	[illegible]
Malicious Injuries to Property [illegible]	[illegible]	[illegible]
Other Wilful and Malicious Injuries to Property	[illegible]	[illegible]
Total of No. 4.	[illegible]	[illegible]
No. 5.—Forgery and Offences against the Currency.		
Forgery and uttering Forged Instruments	[illegible]	[illegible]
[illegible]	[illegible]	[illegible]
Coining, and having Implements for Coining [illegible]	[illegible]	[illegible]
Uttering, [illegible] Counterfeit Coin	[illegible]	[illegible]
Total of No. 5.	[illegible]	[illegible]
No. 6.—Offences not included in the above Classes.		
Offences against the [illegible]	[illegible]	[illegible]
[illegible] by Threatening Letters [illegible]	[illegible]	[illegible]
Having Arms or Ammunition without Licence in a Proclaimed District	[illegible]	[illegible]
Being at large [illegible] Transportation or Penal Servitude	[illegible]	[illegible]
Perjury, and Subornation of Perjury	[illegible]	[illegible]
[illegible]	[illegible]	[illegible]
Unlawfully Exposing the Person	[illegible]	[illegible]
[illegible]	[illegible]	[illegible]
Other Felonies not included in the above	[illegible]	[illegible]
Other Misdemeanours not included in the above	[illegible]	[illegible]
Total of No. 6.	[illegible]	[illegible]
General Total	[illegible]	[illegible]

[illegible] each County, and County of City or of Town, so far as Known to the Police, in the Year ended 31st December, [illegible] Inspector-General.

Wexford	Wicklow	Munster: Clare	[illegible]	Cork E.R.?	Cork W.R.	Cork City	Kerry	Limerick	Limerick City	Tipperary N.R.	Tipperary S.R.	Waterford?	Waterford City	NATURE OF CRIMES.
														No. 1.—Offences against the Person.
[illegible]	[illegible]	[illegible]	[illegible]	[illegible]	[illegible]	[illegible]	[illegible]	[illegible]	[illegible]	[illegible]	[illegible]	[illegible]	[illegible]	[illegible]
[illegible]	[illegible]	[illegible]	[illegible]	[illegible]	[illegible]	[illegible]	[illegible]	[illegible]	[illegible]	[illegible]	[illegible]	[illegible]	[illegible]	Total of No. 1.
														No. 2.—Offences against Property with Violence.
[illegible]	[illegible]	[illegible]	[illegible]	[illegible]	[illegible]	[illegible]	[illegible]	[illegible]	[illegible]	[illegible]	[illegible]	[illegible]	[illegible]	[illegible]
[illegible]	[illegible]	[illegible]	[illegible]	[illegible]	[illegible]	[illegible]	[illegible]	[illegible]	[illegible]	[illegible]	[illegible]	[illegible]	[illegible]	Total of No. 2.
														No. 3.—Offences against Property without Violence.
[illegible]	[illegible]	[illegible]	[illegible]	[illegible]	[illegible]	[illegible]	[illegible]	[illegible]	[illegible]	[illegible]	[illegible]	[illegible]	[illegible]	[illegible]
[illegible]	[illegible]	[illegible]	[illegible]	[illegible]	[illegible]	[illegible]	[illegible]	[illegible]	[illegible]	[illegible]	[illegible]	[illegible]	[illegible]	Total of No. 3.
														No. 4.—Malicious Offences against Property.
[illegible]	[illegible]	[illegible]	[illegible]	[illegible]	[illegible]	[illegible]	[illegible]	[illegible]	[illegible]	[illegible]	[illegible]	[illegible]	[illegible]	[illegible]
[illegible]	[illegible]	[illegible]	[illegible]	[illegible]	[illegible]	[illegible]	[illegible]	[illegible]	[illegible]	[illegible]	[illegible]	[illegible]	[illegible]	Total of No. 4.
														No. 5.—Forgery and Offences against the Currency.
[illegible]	[illegible]	[illegible]	[illegible]	[illegible]	[illegible]	[illegible]	[illegible]	[illegible]	[illegible]	[illegible]	[illegible]	[illegible]	[illegible]	[illegible]
[illegible]	[illegible]	[illegible]	[illegible]	[illegible]	[illegible]	[illegible]	[illegible]	[illegible]	[illegible]	[illegible]	[illegible]	[illegible]	[illegible]	Total of No. 5.
														No. 6.—Offences not included in the above Classes.
[illegible]	[illegible]	[illegible]	[illegible]	[illegible]	[illegible]	[illegible]	[illegible]	[illegible]	[illegible]	[illegible]	[illegible]	[illegible]	[illegible]	[illegible]
[illegible]	[illegible]	[illegible]	[illegible]	[illegible]	[illegible]	[illegible]	[illegible]	[illegible]	[illegible]	[illegible]	[illegible]	[illegible]	[illegible]	Total of No. 6.
[illegible]	[illegible]	[illegible]	[illegible]	[illegible]	[illegible]	[illegible]	[illegible]	[illegible]	[illegible]	[illegible]	[illegible]	[illegible]	[illegible]	GENERAL TOTAL.

TABLE [illegible]—continued.—RETURN OF INDICTABLE OFFENCES [illegible]

NATURE OF OFFENCE.										
No. 1.—Offences against the Person.										
Murder of Infants [illegible]	[illegible]	[illegible]	[illegible]	[illegible]	[illegible]	[illegible]	[illegible]	[illegible]	[illegible]	[illegible]
Other Murders,	[illegible]	[illegible]	[illegible]	[illegible]	[illegible]	[illegible]	[illegible]	[illegible]	[illegible]	[illegible]
Attempts to Murder,	[illegible]	[illegible]	[illegible]	[illegible]	[illegible]	[illegible]	[illegible]	[illegible]	[illegible]	[illegible]
Shooting at, Wounding, Stabbing, &c. to do bodily harm,	[illegible]	[illegible]	[illegible]	[illegible]	[illegible]	[illegible]	[illegible]	[illegible]	[illegible]	[illegible]
Manslaughter,	[illegible]	[illegible]	[illegible]	[illegible]	[illegible]	[illegible]	[illegible]	[illegible]	[illegible]	[illegible]
Concealing the Birth of Infants,	[illegible]	[illegible]	[illegible]	[illegible]	[illegible]	[illegible]	[illegible]	[illegible]	[illegible]	[illegible]
Sodomy and Bestiality,	[illegible]	[illegible]	[illegible]	[illegible]	[illegible]	[illegible]	[illegible]	[illegible]	[illegible]	[illegible]
—— Attempts [illegible]	[illegible]	[illegible]	[illegible]	[illegible]	[illegible]	[illegible]	[illegible]	[illegible]	[illegible]	[illegible]
Rape,	[illegible]	[illegible]	[illegible]	[illegible]	[illegible]	[illegible]	[illegible]	[illegible]	[illegible]	[illegible]
—— Assaults, with intent to ravish and abuse,	[illegible]	[illegible]	[illegible]	[illegible]	[illegible]	[illegible]	[illegible]	[illegible]	[illegible]	[illegible]
Bigamy,	[illegible]	[illegible]	[illegible]	[illegible]	[illegible]	[illegible]	[illegible]	[illegible]	[illegible]	[illegible]
Child Stealing,	[illegible]	[illegible]	[illegible]	[illegible]	[illegible]	[illegible]	[illegible]	[illegible]	[illegible]	[illegible]
[illegible]	[illegible]	[illegible]	[illegible]	[illegible]	[illegible]	[illegible]	[illegible]	[illegible]	[illegible]	[illegible]
[illegible]	[illegible]	[illegible]	[illegible]	[illegible]	[illegible]	[illegible]	[illegible]	[illegible]	[illegible]	[illegible]
Assault and inflicting bodily harm,	[illegible]	[illegible]	[illegible]	[illegible]	[illegible]	[illegible]	[illegible]	[illegible]	[illegible]	[illegible]
[illegible]	[illegible]	[illegible]	[illegible]	[illegible]	[illegible]	[illegible]	[illegible]	[illegible]	[illegible]	[illegible]
Assaults on Peace Officers,	[illegible]	[illegible]	[illegible]	[illegible]	[illegible]	[illegible]	[illegible]	[illegible]	[illegible]	[illegible]
Total of No. 1,	[illegible]	[illegible]	[illegible]	[illegible]	[illegible]	[illegible]	[illegible]	[illegible]	[illegible]	[illegible]
No. 2.—Offences against Property with Violence.										
[illegible] (6 rows)	[illegible]	[illegible]	[illegible]	[illegible]	[illegible]	[illegible]	[illegible]	[illegible]	[illegible]	[illegible]
Total of No. 2,	[illegible]	[illegible]	[illegible]	[illegible]	[illegible]	[illegible]	[illegible]	[illegible]	[illegible]	[illegible]
No. 3.—Offences against Property without Violence.										
[illegible] (15 rows)	[illegible]	[illegible]	[illegible]	[illegible]	[illegible]	[illegible]	[illegible]	[illegible]	[illegible]	[illegible]
Total of No. 3,	[illegible]	[illegible]	[illegible]	[illegible]	[illegible]	[illegible]	[illegible]	[illegible]	[illegible]	[illegible]
No. 4.—Malicious Offences against Property.										
[illegible] (7 rows)	[illegible]	[illegible]	[illegible]	[illegible]	[illegible]	[illegible]	[illegible]	[illegible]	[illegible]	[illegible]
Total of No. 4,	[illegible]	[illegible]	[illegible]	[illegible]	[illegible]	[illegible]	[illegible]	[illegible]	[illegible]	[illegible]
No. 5.—Forgery and Offences against the Currency.										
[illegible] (4 rows)	[illegible]	[illegible]	[illegible]	[illegible]	[illegible]	[illegible]	[illegible]	[illegible]	[illegible]	[illegible]
Total of No. 5,	[illegible]	[illegible]	[illegible]	[illegible]	[illegible]	[illegible]	[illegible]	[illegible]	[illegible]	[illegible]
No. 6.—Offences not included in the above Classes.										
[illegible] (10 rows)	[illegible]	[illegible]	[illegible]	[illegible]	[illegible]	[illegible]	[illegible]	[illegible]	[illegible]	[illegible]
Total of No. 6,	[illegible]	[illegible]	[illegible]	[illegible]	[illegible]	[illegible]	[illegible]	[illegible]	[illegible]	[illegible]
GENERAL TOTAL,	[illegible]	[illegible]	[illegible]	[illegible]	[illegible]	[illegible]	[illegible]	[illegible]	[illegible]	[illegible]

Committed in each County, and County of City or of Town, so far as known to the Police, in the Year ended [illegible] by the Inspector-General.

[illegible]	[illegible]	Connaught. Total.	Galway, E.R.	Galway, W.R.	Galway Town.	Leitrim.	Mayo.	Roscommon.	Sligo.	NATURE OF CRIMES.
										No. 1.—Offences against the Person.
[illegible]	[illegible]	[illegible]	[illegible]	[illegible]	[illegible]	[illegible]	[illegible]	[illegible]	[illegible]	Murder of Infants aged one year and under.
[illegible]	[illegible]	[illegible]	[illegible]	[illegible]	[illegible]	[illegible]	[illegible]	[illegible]	[illegible]	Other Murders.
[illegible]	[illegible]	[illegible]	[illegible]	[illegible]	[illegible]	[illegible]	[illegible]	[illegible]	[illegible]	Attempts to Murder.
[illegible]	[illegible]	[illegible]	[illegible]	[illegible]	[illegible]	[illegible]	[illegible]	[illegible]	[illegible]	Shooting at, Wounding, Stabbing, &c., to do bodily harm.
[illegible]	[illegible]	[illegible]	[illegible]	[illegible]	[illegible]	[illegible]	[illegible]	[illegible]	[illegible]	Manslaughter.
[illegible]	[illegible]	[illegible]	[illegible]	[illegible]	[illegible]	[illegible]	[illegible]	[illegible]	[illegible]	Concealing the Birth of Infants.
[illegible]	[illegible]	[illegible]	[illegible]	[illegible]	[illegible]	[illegible]	[illegible]	[illegible]	[illegible]	Sodomy and Bestiality.
[illegible]	[illegible]	[illegible]	[illegible]	[illegible]	[illegible]	[illegible]	[illegible]	[illegible]	[illegible]	—— Attempts to commit, and other unnatural Misdemeanors.
[illegible]	[illegible]	[illegible]	[illegible]	[illegible]	[illegible]	[illegible]	[illegible]	[illegible]	[illegible]	Rape.
[illegible]	[illegible]	[illegible]	[illegible]	[illegible]	[illegible]	[illegible]	[illegible]	[illegible]	[illegible]	—— Assaults, with intent to ravish and abuse.
[illegible]	[illegible]	[illegible]	[illegible]	[illegible]	[illegible]	[illegible]	[illegible]	[illegible]	[illegible]	Bigamy.
[illegible]	[illegible]	[illegible]	[illegible]	[illegible]	[illegible]	[illegible]	[illegible]	[illegible]	[illegible]	Child Stealing.
[illegible]	[illegible]	[illegible]	[illegible]	[illegible]	[illegible]	[illegible]	[illegible]	[illegible]	[illegible]	Unlawfully abandoning Children under two years of age.
[illegible]	[illegible]	[illegible]	[illegible]	[illegible]	[illegible]	[illegible]	[illegible]	[illegible]	[illegible]	Endangering the safety of Passengers on Railways.
[illegible]	[illegible]	[illegible]	[illegible]	[illegible]	[illegible]	[illegible]	[illegible]	[illegible]	[illegible]	Assault inflicting bodily harm.
[illegible]	[illegible]	[illegible]	[illegible]	[illegible]	[illegible]	[illegible]	[illegible]	[illegible]	[illegible]	Assaults, common.
[illegible]	[illegible]	[illegible]	[illegible]	[illegible]	[illegible]	[illegible]	[illegible]	[illegible]	[illegible]	Assaults on Peace Officers.
[illegible]	[illegible]	[illegible]	[illegible]	[illegible]	[illegible]	[illegible]	[illegible]	[illegible]	[illegible]	Total of No. 1.
										No. 2.—Offences against Property with Violence.
[illegible]	[illegible]	[illegible]	[illegible]	[illegible]	[illegible]	[illegible]	[illegible]	[illegible]	[illegible]	Burglary.
[illegible]	[illegible]	[illegible]	[illegible]	[illegible]	[illegible]	[illegible]	[illegible]	[illegible]	[illegible]	Burglary and Housebreaking.
[illegible]	[illegible]	[illegible]	[illegible]	[illegible]	[illegible]	[illegible]	[illegible]	[illegible]	[illegible]	Breaking into Shops, Warehouses, &c.
[illegible]	[illegible]	[illegible]	[illegible]	[illegible]	[illegible]	[illegible]	[illegible]	[illegible]	[illegible]	Attempts to break into Houses, Shops, Warehouses, &c.
[illegible]	[illegible]	[illegible]	[illegible]	[illegible]	[illegible]	[illegible]	[illegible]	[illegible]	[illegible]	Robbery.
[illegible]	[illegible]	[illegible]	[illegible]	[illegible]	[illegible]	[illegible]	[illegible]	[illegible]	[illegible]	Attempts at rob, and demanding Money by Menaces.
[illegible]	[illegible]	[illegible]	[illegible]	[illegible]	[illegible]	[illegible]	[illegible]	[illegible]	[illegible]	Total of No. 2.
										No. 3.—Offences against Property without Violence.
[illegible]	[illegible]	[illegible]	[illegible]	[illegible]	[illegible]	[illegible]	[illegible]	[illegible]	[illegible]	Cattle Stealing.
[illegible]	[illegible]	[illegible]	[illegible]	[illegible]	[illegible]	[illegible]	[illegible]	[illegible]	[illegible]	Horse Stealing.
[illegible]	[illegible]	[illegible]	[illegible]	[illegible]	[illegible]	[illegible]	[illegible]	[illegible]	[illegible]	Sheep Stealing.
[illegible]	[illegible]	[illegible]	[illegible]	[illegible]	[illegible]	[illegible]	[illegible]	[illegible]	[illegible]	Larceny to the value of 5l. in Dwelling-houses.
[illegible]	[illegible]	[illegible]	[illegible]	[illegible]	[illegible]	[illegible]	[illegible]	[illegible]	[illegible]	Larceny from the Person.
[illegible]	[illegible]	[illegible]	[illegible]	[illegible]	[illegible]	[illegible]	[illegible]	[illegible]	[illegible]	Larceny by Servants.
[illegible]	[illegible]	[illegible]	[illegible]	[illegible]	[illegible]	[illegible]	[illegible]	[illegible]	[illegible]	Larceny, simple.
[illegible]	[illegible]	[illegible]	[illegible]	[illegible]	[illegible]	[illegible]	[illegible]	[illegible]	[illegible]	Larceny on Rivers, Canals, Wharfs, &c.
[illegible]	[illegible]	[illegible]	[illegible]	[illegible]	[illegible]	[illegible]	[illegible]	[illegible]	[illegible]	Stealing Fixtures, Shrubs growing, &c.
[illegible]	[illegible]	[illegible]	[illegible]	[illegible]	[illegible]	[illegible]	[illegible]	[illegible]	[illegible]	Attempts to Steal.
[illegible]	[illegible]	[illegible]	[illegible]	[illegible]	[illegible]	[illegible]	[illegible]	[illegible]	[illegible]	Embezzlement.
[illegible]	[illegible]	[illegible]	[illegible]	[illegible]	[illegible]	[illegible]	[illegible]	[illegible]	[illegible]	Larceny by Servants in the Post Office.
[illegible]	[illegible]	[illegible]	[illegible]	[illegible]	[illegible]	[illegible]	[illegible]	[illegible]	[illegible]	Receiving Stolen Goods.
[illegible]	[illegible]	[illegible]	[illegible]	[illegible]	[illegible]	[illegible]	[illegible]	[illegible]	[illegible]	Fraudulently obtaining Goods by false pretences, and attempts to defraud.
[illegible]	[illegible]	[illegible]	[illegible]	[illegible]	[illegible]	[illegible]	[illegible]	[illegible]	[illegible]	Total of No. 3.
										No. 4.—Malicious Offences against Property.
[illegible]	[illegible]	[illegible]	[illegible]	[illegible]	[illegible]	[illegible]	[illegible]	[illegible]	[illegible]	Arson and other Wilful Burnings.
[illegible]	[illegible]	[illegible]	[illegible]	[illegible]	[illegible]	[illegible]	[illegible]	[illegible]	[illegible]	Riotously demolishing Buildings, &c.
[illegible]	[illegible]	[illegible]	[illegible]	[illegible]	[illegible]	[illegible]	[illegible]	[illegible]	[illegible]	Destroying Goods in process of Manufacture.
[illegible]	[illegible]	[illegible]	[illegible]	[illegible]	[illegible]	[illegible]	[illegible]	[illegible]	[illegible]	Destroying Trees, Shrubs, &c., growing.
[illegible]	[illegible]	[illegible]	[illegible]	[illegible]	[illegible]	[illegible]	[illegible]	[illegible]	[illegible]	Killing and Maiming Cattle.
[illegible]	[illegible]	[illegible]	[illegible]	[illegible]	[illegible]	[illegible]	[illegible]	[illegible]	[illegible]	Malicious Injuries to Property exceeding 5l. in value.
[illegible]	[illegible]	[illegible]	[illegible]	[illegible]	[illegible]	[illegible]	[illegible]	[illegible]	[illegible]	Other Wilful and Malicious Injuries to Property.
[illegible]	[illegible]	[illegible]	[illegible]	[illegible]	[illegible]	[illegible]	[illegible]	[illegible]	[illegible]	Total of No. 4.
										No. 5.—Forgery and Offences against the Currency.
[illegible]	[illegible]	[illegible]	[illegible]	[illegible]	[illegible]	[illegible]	[illegible]	[illegible]	[illegible]	Forgery and uttering Forged Instruments.
[illegible]	[illegible]	[illegible]	[illegible]	[illegible]	[illegible]	[illegible]	[illegible]	[illegible]	[illegible]	Having in possession Forged Bank Notes.
[illegible]	[illegible]	[illegible]	[illegible]	[illegible]	[illegible]	[illegible]	[illegible]	[illegible]	[illegible]	Coining, and having Implements for Coining in possession.
[illegible]	[illegible]	[illegible]	[illegible]	[illegible]	[illegible]	[illegible]	[illegible]	[illegible]	[illegible]	Uttering, putting off, and having in possession Counterfeit Coin.
[illegible]	[illegible]	[illegible]	[illegible]	[illegible]	[illegible]	[illegible]	[illegible]	[illegible]	[illegible]	Total of No. 5.
										No. 6.—Offences not included in the above Classes.
[illegible]	[illegible]	[illegible]	[illegible]	[illegible]	[illegible]	[illegible]	[illegible]	[illegible]	[illegible]	Offences against the Queen's authority and person.
[illegible]	[illegible]	[illegible]	[illegible]	[illegible]	[illegible]	[illegible]	[illegible]	[illegible]	[illegible]	Intimidation by Threatening Letters, Notices, or otherwise.
[illegible]	[illegible]	[illegible]	[illegible]	[illegible]	[illegible]	[illegible]	[illegible]	[illegible]	[illegible]	Having Arms or Ammunition without Licence in a Proclaimed District.
[illegible]	[illegible]	[illegible]	[illegible]	[illegible]	[illegible]	[illegible]	[illegible]	[illegible]	[illegible]	Being at large under Sentence of Transportation or Penal Servitude.
[illegible]	[illegible]	[illegible]	[illegible]	[illegible]	[illegible]	[illegible]	[illegible]	[illegible]	[illegible]	Perjury and Subornation of Perjury.
[illegible]	[illegible]	[illegible]	[illegible]	[illegible]	[illegible]	[illegible]	[illegible]	[illegible]	[illegible]	Riot, Breach of the Peace, &c.
[illegible]	[illegible]	[illegible]	[illegible]	[illegible]	[illegible]	[illegible]	[illegible]	[illegible]	[illegible]	Indecently Exposing the Person.
[illegible]	[illegible]	[illegible]	[illegible]	[illegible]	[illegible]	[illegible]	[illegible]	[illegible]	[illegible]	Suicide, attempting to commit.
[illegible]	[illegible]	[illegible]	[illegible]	[illegible]	[illegible]	[illegible]	[illegible]	[illegible]	[illegible]	Other Felonies not included in the above.
[illegible]	[illegible]	[illegible]	[illegible]	[illegible]	[illegible]	[illegible]	[illegible]	[illegible]	[illegible]	Other Misdemeanors not included in the above.
[illegible]	[illegible]	[illegible]	[illegible]	[illegible]	[illegible]	[illegible]	[illegible]	[illegible]	[illegible]	Total of No. 6.
[illegible]	[illegible]	[illegible]	[illegible]	[illegible]	[illegible]	[illegible]	[illegible]	[illegible]	[illegible]	GENERAL TOTAL.

TABLE I.—RETURN OF PERSONS PROCEEDED AGAINST FOR OFFENCES DETERMINED SUMMARILY.

[illegible]

OFFENCES PUNISHABLE BY STATUTE.	[illegible]	Leinster. [illegible]
[illegible]	[illegible]	[illegible]
Total,	[illegible]	[illegible]

Total Number of Persons Proceeded against before Justices, in each County, and County of City or of Town, specifying [illegible], 18[illegible], made by the Inspector-General.

OFFENCES PUNISHABLE BY JUSTICES	Counties / Cities and Towns (figures)
Adulteration of Food, &c., Act	[illegible]
Assaults, Aggravated, on Women and Children	[illegible]
—— on Peace Officers, Resisting, Obstructing, &c.	[illegible]
—— Common	[illegible]
Bastardy Orders, disobeying	[illegible]
Breaches of the Peace, &c.	[illegible]
Cattle Plague Orders, Offences against	[illegible]
[illegible] Act, Offences against	[illegible]
Cruelty to Animals	[illegible]
[illegible]	[illegible]
Employers' and Workmen's Act, 1875	[illegible]
Fishery Acts, Offences against	[illegible]
[illegible] Acts, Offences against	[illegible]
Game Acts, Offences against, viz.:—	[illegible]
Trespassing in the day time in pursuit of Game	[illegible]
[illegible] and [illegible] Game	[illegible]
Illegally selling or buying Game	[illegible]
[illegible] Acts [illegible]	[illegible]
Other Offences against the Game Acts	[illegible]
Licensing Acts, 1872-74, Offences against, viz.:—	[illegible]
Drunkenness, and Drunk and Disorderly	[illegible]
[illegible] and [illegible] by Licensed Persons	[illegible]
Illegally selling Intoxicating Drinks	[illegible]
[illegible] Licensing [illegible]	[illegible]
[illegible] Acts, Offences against	[illegible]
Other Offences under the Licensing Acts	[illegible]
[illegible] Act, Offences against	[illegible]
Local Acts and [illegible] Bye-laws, Offences against	[illegible]
Malicious Damage to Fences, Walls, Gates, &c.	[illegible]
—— Fruit and Vegetable Productions	[illegible]
—— Trees, shrubs, &c.	[illegible]
Other Malicious and Wilful Damage, and Trespass	[illegible]
Military Acts, Offences against, viz.:—	[illegible]
Army Act	[illegible]
Navy Act	[illegible]
Militia Act	[illegible]
[illegible] Acts, Offences against	[illegible]
Nuisances, and Offences against Health, viz.:—	[illegible]
Public Health Acts	[illegible]
[illegible] Acts	[illegible]
[illegible] Acts	[illegible]
[illegible] Act	[illegible]
Common Lodging Houses Acts	[illegible]
Selling and exposing for sale unsound Food	[illegible]
Other Sanitary Offences	[illegible]
Pawnbrokers Act, Offences against, viz.:—	[illegible]
By Pawnbrokers	[illegible]
By persons unlawfully pledging or disposing	[illegible]
Other Offences	[illegible]
Police Acts, Offences against, viz.:—	[illegible]
Unlawfully possessing Goods	[illegible]
Offences [illegible]	[illegible]
[illegible]	[illegible]
Other Offences [illegible] (under other special heads)	[illegible]
[illegible] Act, [illegible]	[illegible]
Poor Law Acts, Offences against, viz.:—	[illegible]
[illegible]	[illegible]
[illegible] Conduct in Workhouse	[illegible]
[illegible] Workhouse Clothing, &c.	[illegible]
[illegible] Act	[illegible]
Revenue Laws, Offences against, viz.:—	[illegible]
Customs Acts	[illegible]
[illegible] Acts (including Hawkers and Pedlars Act)	[illegible]
[illegible] Act, Offences against	[illegible]
Stealing, or Attempts to Steal, viz.:—	[illegible]
Larceny, by offenders under 16 years (Juvenile Offenders Act)	[illegible]
Larceny, under value of 5s., and on pleading Guilty (Criminal Justice Act)	[illegible]
Larceny above value of 5s., on pleading Guilty (Criminal Justice Act)	[illegible]
Larceny or Larceny from Person, attempting to commit (Criminal Justice Act)	[illegible]
Dogs, Birds, or Beasts, &c.	[illegible]
Fruit or Vegetable Productions	[illegible]
[illegible]	[illegible]
Trees, Shrubs, &c.	[illegible]
Vagrant Act, Offences against, viz.:—	[illegible]
Prostitutes	[illegible]
Begging	[illegible]
[illegible]	[illegible]
[illegible]	[illegible]
[illegible] for unlawful purposes	[illegible]
[illegible] Public Health, &c.	[illegible]
[illegible]	[illegible]
Other Offences under Vagrant Act	[illegible]
[illegible] Acts, Offences against	[illegible]
[illegible] Acts, Offences against, viz.:—	[illegible]
[illegible] Carriage Acts	[illegible]
[illegible]	[illegible]
[illegible] Act	[illegible]
Railway Acts	[illegible]
Weights and Measures Act, Offences against	[illegible]
Other Offences not included under the above heads	[illegible]
Total	[illegible]

[illegible]
[illegible]
[illegible]
[illegible]
[illegible]
[illegible]
[illegible]

[illegible]

[illegible]	[illegible]	[illegible]	[illegible]	[illegible]	[illegible]	[illegible]	[illegible]	[illegible]	[illegible]	[illegible]
[illegible]	[illegible]	[illegible]	[illegible]	[illegible]	[illegible]	[illegible]	[illegible]	[illegible]	[illegible]	[illegible]
[illegible]	[illegible]	[illegible]	[illegible]	[illegible]	[illegible]	[illegible]	[illegible]	[illegible]	[illegible]	TOTAL.

TABLE [illegible].—OFFENCES DETERMINED SUMMARILY. [illegible] of TOTAL of PERSONS who were [illegible] against [illegible] PROCEEDINGS, made by [illegible]

OFFENCES PUNISHABLE ON [illegible].	Persons proceeded against.						
	Total.			[illegible]		[illegible]	
	M.	W.	M. & W.	M.	W.	M.	W.
[illegible]	[illegible]	[illegible]	[illegible]	[illegible]	[illegible]	[illegible]	[illegible]
TOTAL	[illegible]	[illegible]	[illegible]	[illegible]	[illegible]	[illegible]	[illegible]

...SUMMARILY before JUSTICES, for each Class of OFFENCES, in the Year ended 31st December, 18[illegible], and the Results of the Proceedings—continued.

Above Six Months (M.)	Above Six Months (W.)	Six Months and above Three (M.)	Six Months and above Three (W.)	Three Months and above One (M.)	Three Months and above One (W.)	One Month and above ... (M.)	One Month and above ... (W.)	OFFENCES PUNISHABLE BY JUSTICES
[illegible]	[illegible]	[illegible]	[illegible]	[illegible]	[illegible]	[illegible]	[illegible]	Adulteration of Food, &c., Act.
[illegible]	[illegible]	[illegible]	[illegible]	[illegible]	[illegible]	[illegible]	[illegible]	Assaults, Aggravated, on Women and Children.
[illegible]	[illegible]	[illegible]	[illegible]	[illegible]	[illegible]	[illegible]	[illegible]	——— on Peace Officers, Resisting, Obstructing, &c.
[illegible]	[illegible]	[illegible]	[illegible]	[illegible]	[illegible]	[illegible]	[illegible]	——— Common.
[illegible]	[illegible]	[illegible]	[illegible]	[illegible]	[illegible]	[illegible]	[illegible]	Bastardy Orders, Disobeying
[illegible]	[illegible]	[illegible]	[illegible]	[illegible]	[illegible]	[illegible]	[illegible]	Breaches of the Peace, want of Sureties, &c.
[illegible]	[illegible]	[illegible]	[illegible]	[illegible]	[illegible]	[illegible]	[illegible]	Cattle Plague Orders, Offences against.
[illegible]	[illegible]	[illegible]	[illegible]	[illegible]	[illegible]	[illegible]	[illegible]	Chimney Sweepers Act, Offences against.
[illegible]	[illegible]	[illegible]	[illegible]	[illegible]	[illegible]	[illegible]	[illegible]	Cruelty to Animals
[illegible]	[illegible]	[illegible]	[illegible]	[illegible]	[illegible]	[illegible]	[illegible]	Embezzlement
[illegible]	[illegible]	[illegible]	[illegible]	[illegible]	[illegible]	[illegible]	[illegible]	Employers' and Workmen's Act, 1875.
[illegible]	[illegible]	[illegible]	[illegible]	[illegible]	[illegible]	[illegible]	[illegible]	Factory Acts, Offences against
[illegible]	[illegible]	[illegible]	[illegible]	[illegible]	[illegible]	[illegible]	[illegible]	Fisheries Acts, Offences against
[illegible]	[illegible]	[illegible]	[illegible]	[illegible]	[illegible]	[illegible]	[illegible]	Game Acts, Offences against, viz.:—
[illegible]	[illegible]	[illegible]	[illegible]	[illegible]	[illegible]	[illegible]	[illegible]	Trespassing on the day-time in pursuit of Game.
[illegible]	[illegible]	[illegible]	[illegible]	[illegible]	[illegible]	[illegible]	[illegible]	Night Poaching and destroying Game.
[illegible]	[illegible]	[illegible]	[illegible]	[illegible]	[illegible]	[illegible]	[illegible]	Illegally selling or buying Game
[illegible]	[illegible]	[illegible]	[illegible]	[illegible]	[illegible]	[illegible]	[illegible]	Poaching Acts, 1862
[illegible]	[illegible]	[illegible]	[illegible]	[illegible]	[illegible]	[illegible]	[illegible]	Other Offences against the Game Acts.
[illegible]	[illegible]	[illegible]	[illegible]	[illegible]	[illegible]	[illegible]	[illegible]	Licensing Acts, 1872–74, Offences against, viz.:—
[illegible]	[illegible]	[illegible]	[illegible]	[illegible]	[illegible]	[illegible]	[illegible]	Drunkenness, and Drunk and Disorderly.
[illegible]	[illegible]	[illegible]	[illegible]	[illegible]	[illegible]	[illegible]	[illegible]	Permitting Drunkenness and Disorderly Conduct on Licensed Houses
[illegible]	[illegible]	[illegible]	[illegible]	[illegible]	[illegible]	[illegible]	[illegible]	Illegally selling Intoxicating Drinks.
[illegible]	[illegible]	[illegible]	[illegible]	[illegible]	[illegible]	[illegible]	[illegible]	Adulteration of Intoxicating Liquors
[illegible]	[illegible]	[illegible]	[illegible]	[illegible]	[illegible]	[illegible]	[illegible]	Shebeens Acts, Offences against
[illegible]	[illegible]	[illegible]	[illegible]	[illegible]	[illegible]	[illegible]	[illegible]	Other Offences under the Licensing Act
[illegible]	[illegible]	[illegible]	[illegible]	[illegible]	[illegible]	[illegible]	[illegible]	Lord's Day Act, Offences against
[illegible]	[illegible]	[illegible]	[illegible]	[illegible]	[illegible]	[illegible]	[illegible]	Local Acts and Borough Bye-Laws, Offences against.
[illegible]	[illegible]	[illegible]	[illegible]	[illegible]	[illegible]	[illegible]	[illegible]	Maliciously destroying Fences, Walls, Gates, &c.
[illegible]	[illegible]	[illegible]	[illegible]	[illegible]	[illegible]	[illegible]	[illegible]	——— ——— Fruit and Vegetable Productions.
[illegible]	[illegible]	[illegible]	[illegible]	[illegible]	[illegible]	[illegible]	[illegible]	——— ——— Trees, Shrubs, &c.
[illegible]	[illegible]	[illegible]	[illegible]	[illegible]	[illegible]	[illegible]	[illegible]	Other Malicious and Wilful Damage and Trespass.
[illegible]	[illegible]	[illegible]	[illegible]	[illegible]	[illegible]	[illegible]	[illegible]	Military Acts, Offences against, viz.:—
[illegible]	[illegible]	[illegible]	[illegible]	[illegible]	[illegible]	[illegible]	[illegible]	Army Act
[illegible]	[illegible]	[illegible]	[illegible]	[illegible]	[illegible]	[illegible]	[illegible]	Navy Act
[illegible]	[illegible]	[illegible]	[illegible]	[illegible]	[illegible]	[illegible]	[illegible]	Militia Act
[illegible]	[illegible]	[illegible]	[illegible]	[illegible]	[illegible]	[illegible]	[illegible]	Mercantile Marine Acts, Offences against
[illegible]	[illegible]	[illegible]	[illegible]	[illegible]	[illegible]	[illegible]	[illegible]	Nuisances, and Offences against Health, &c.:—
[illegible]	[illegible]	[illegible]	[illegible]	[illegible]	[illegible]	[illegible]	[illegible]	Public Health Acts
[illegible]	[illegible]	[illegible]	[illegible]	[illegible]	[illegible]	[illegible]	[illegible]	Smoke Acts
[illegible]	[illegible]	[illegible]	[illegible]	[illegible]	[illegible]	[illegible]	[illegible]	Towns Acts
[illegible]	[illegible]	[illegible]	[illegible]	[illegible]	[illegible]	[illegible]	[illegible]	Nuisances Removal Act.
[illegible]	[illegible]	[illegible]	[illegible]	[illegible]	[illegible]	[illegible]	[illegible]	Common Lodging Houses Acts.
[illegible]	[illegible]	[illegible]	[illegible]	[illegible]	[illegible]	[illegible]	[illegible]	Selling and Exposing for sale Unsound Food
[illegible]	[illegible]	[illegible]	[illegible]	[illegible]	[illegible]	[illegible]	[illegible]	Other Sanitary Offences
[illegible]	[illegible]	[illegible]	[illegible]	[illegible]	[illegible]	[illegible]	[illegible]	Pawnbrokers Act, Offences against, viz.:—
[illegible]	[illegible]	[illegible]	[illegible]	[illegible]	[illegible]	[illegible]	[illegible]	By Pawnbrokers.
[illegible]	[illegible]	[illegible]	[illegible]	[illegible]	[illegible]	[illegible]	[illegible]	By persons fraudulently pledging or disposing
[illegible]	[illegible]	[illegible]	[illegible]	[illegible]	[illegible]	[illegible]	[illegible]	Other Offences.
[illegible]	[illegible]	[illegible]	[illegible]	[illegible]	[illegible]	[illegible]	[illegible]	Police Acts, Offences against, viz.:—
[illegible]	[illegible]	[illegible]	[illegible]	[illegible]	[illegible]	[illegible]	[illegible]	Unlawfully possessing Goods.
[illegible]	[illegible]	[illegible]	[illegible]	[illegible]	[illegible]	[illegible]	[illegible]	Offences Punishable as Misdemeanours
[illegible]	[illegible]	[illegible]	[illegible]	[illegible]	[illegible]	[illegible]	[illegible]	Obstructing Street ...
[illegible]	[illegible]	[illegible]	[illegible]	[illegible]	[illegible]	[illegible]	[illegible]	Other Offences, not falling under ...
[illegible]	[illegible]	[illegible]	[illegible]	[illegible]	[illegible]	[illegible]	[illegible]	Prevention of Crime Act, 1871 ... Offences by Persons ...
[illegible]	[illegible]	[illegible]	[illegible]	[illegible]	[illegible]	[illegible]	[illegible]	Poor Law Acts, Offences against, viz.:—
[illegible]	[illegible]	[illegible]	[illegible]	[illegible]	[illegible]	[illegible]	[illegible]	Deserting or Neglecting to support Family.
[illegible]	[illegible]	[illegible]	[illegible]	[illegible]	[illegible]	[illegible]	[illegible]	Disorderly Conduct in Workhouse
[illegible]	[illegible]	[illegible]	[illegible]	[illegible]	[illegible]	[illegible]	[illegible]	Destroying Workhouse Clothing, Bedding, &c.
[illegible]	[illegible]	[illegible]	[illegible]	[illegible]	[illegible]	[illegible]	[illegible]	Refreshment Houses and Wine Licences Act
[illegible]	[illegible]	[illegible]	[illegible]	[illegible]	[illegible]	[illegible]	[illegible]	Revenue Laws, Offences against, viz.:—
[illegible]	[illegible]	[illegible]	[illegible]	[illegible]	[illegible]	[illegible]	[illegible]	Customs Acts.
[illegible]	[illegible]	[illegible]	[illegible]	[illegible]	[illegible]	[illegible]	[illegible]	Excise Acts (including Licensing and Pedlars Act)
[illegible]	[illegible]	[illegible]	[illegible]	[illegible]	[illegible]	[illegible]	[illegible]	Salmon Fisheries Act, Offences against.
[illegible]	[illegible]	[illegible]	[illegible]	[illegible]	[illegible]	[illegible]	[illegible]	Stealing, or Attempts to Steal, viz.:—
[illegible]	[illegible]	[illegible]	[illegible]	[illegible]	[illegible]	[illegible]	[illegible]	Larceny, by Children under 16 years (Juvenile Offenders Act)
[illegible]	[illegible]	[illegible]	[illegible]	[illegible]	[illegible]	[illegible]	[illegible]	Larceny, under value of 5s. and on pleading Guilty (Criminal Justice Act)
[illegible]	[illegible]	[illegible]	[illegible]	[illegible]	[illegible]	[illegible]	[illegible]	Larceny, above value of 5s., on pleading Guilty (Criminal Justice Act)
[illegible]	[illegible]	[illegible]	[illegible]	[illegible]	[illegible]	[illegible]	[illegible]	Larceny, or Larceny from Person, attempting to commit (Criminal Justice Act)
[illegible]	[illegible]	[illegible]	[illegible]	[illegible]	[illegible]	[illegible]	[illegible]	Dogs, Birds, or Beasts, &c.
[illegible]	[illegible]	[illegible]	[illegible]	[illegible]	[illegible]	[illegible]	[illegible]	Fruit or Vegetable Productions
[illegible]	[illegible]	[illegible]	[illegible]	[illegible]	[illegible]	[illegible]	[illegible]	Fences, Wood, &c.
[illegible]	[illegible]	[illegible]	[illegible]	[illegible]	[illegible]	[illegible]	[illegible]	Trees, Shrubs, &c.
[illegible]	[illegible]	[illegible]	[illegible]	[illegible]	[illegible]	[illegible]	[illegible]	Vagrant Act, Offences against, viz.:—
[illegible]	[illegible]	[illegible]	[illegible]	[illegible]	[illegible]	[illegible]	[illegible]	Prostitution.
[illegible]	[illegible]	[illegible]	[illegible]	[illegible]	[illegible]	[illegible]	[illegible]	Begging
[illegible]	[illegible]	[illegible]	[illegible]	[illegible]	[illegible]	[illegible]	[illegible]	Sleeping out, having no visible Means of Subsistence, &c.
[illegible]	[illegible]	[illegible]	[illegible]	[illegible]	[illegible]	[illegible]	[illegible]	Having Implements for Housebreaking, &c.
[illegible]	[illegible]	[illegible]	[illegible]	[illegible]	[illegible]	[illegible]	[illegible]	Found in enclosed Premises for unlawful purpose.
[illegible]	[illegible]	[illegible]	[illegible]	[illegible]	[illegible]	[illegible]	[illegible]	Frequenting Places of Public Resort, &c., to commit Felony
[illegible]	[illegible]	[illegible]	[illegible]	[illegible]	[illegible]	[illegible]	[illegible]	Incorrigible Rogues.
[illegible]	[illegible]	[illegible]	[illegible]	[illegible]	[illegible]	[illegible]	[illegible]	Other Offences under Vagrant Act.
[illegible]	[illegible]	[illegible]	[illegible]	[illegible]	[illegible]	[illegible]	[illegible]	Vaccination Acts, Offences against
[illegible]	[illegible]	[illegible]	[illegible]	[illegible]	[illegible]	[illegible]	[illegible]	Ways Acts, Offences against, viz.:—
[illegible]	[illegible]	[illegible]	[illegible]	[illegible]	[illegible]	[illegible]	[illegible]	Stage and Hackney Carriages Acts.
[illegible]	[illegible]	[illegible]	[illegible]	[illegible]	[illegible]	[illegible]	[illegible]	Highway Act (including Road Nuisances).
[illegible]	[illegible]	[illegible]	[illegible]	[illegible]	[illegible]	[illegible]	[illegible]	Tramways Act
[illegible]	[illegible]	[illegible]	[illegible]	[illegible]	[illegible]	[illegible]	[illegible]	Railway Acts.
[illegible]	[illegible]	[illegible]	[illegible]	[illegible]	[illegible]	[illegible]	[illegible]	Weights and Measures Act, Offences against.
[illegible]	[illegible]	[illegible]	[illegible]	[illegible]	[illegible]	[illegible]	[illegible]	Other Offences (not included under the above heads)
[illegible]	[illegible]	[illegible]	[illegible]	[illegible]	[illegible]	[illegible]	[illegible]	TOTAL.

TABLE 6—continued.—OFFENCES DETERMINED SUMMARILY. Return of Total of Persons who were [illegible] of the Proceedings, under

OFFENCES PUNISHABLE BY JUSTICES.	[illegible] (without [illegible] Fine or Whipping).							
	[illegible]		[illegible]		To Reformatory Schools.		To Industrial Schools.	
	M.	W.	M.	W.	M.	W.	M.	W.
Adulteration of Food, &c., Act,	.	.	.	.	.	.	.	.
Assaults, Aggravated, on Women and Children,	[illegible]	[illegible]	[illegible]	[illegible]	[illegible]	1	.	.
—— on Peace Officers, [illegible], &c.,	[illegible]	[illegible]	[illegible]	[illegible]	.	.	.	.
—— Common,	[illegible]	[illegible]	[illegible]	[illegible]	[illegible]	[illegible]	.	[illegible]
Bastardy Orders, disobeying,	1	.	.	.	.	.	.	.
Breaches of the Peace, [illegible], &c.,	[illegible]	[illegible]	[illegible]	[illegible]	.	.	.	.
Cattle [illegible] Act, Offences against,	.	.	.	.	.	.	.	.
Chimney Sweepers Act, Offences against,	.	.	.	.	.	.	.	.
Cruelty to Animals,	.	.	[illegible]	.	.	.	.	.
[illegible],	[illegible]	.	[illegible]	.	.	.	.	.
Employers' and Workmen's Act, 1875,	.	.	[illegible]	.	.	.	.	.
Factory Acts, Offences against,	.	.	.	.	.	.	.	.
Fisheries Acts, Offences against,	[illegible]	.	[illegible]	[illegible]	.	.	.	.
Game Laws, Offences against, viz.—								
Trespassing in the day-time in pursuit of Game,	[illegible]	.	[illegible]	.	.	.	.	.
Night Poaching and Destroying Game,	[illegible]	.	[illegible]	.	.	.	.	.
Illegally selling or buying Game,	.	.	.	.	.	.	.	.
Poaching Acts, 1862,	1	.	.	.	.	.	.	.
Other Offences against the Game Acts,	[illegible]	.	.	.	.	.	.	.
Licensing Acts, Offences against, viz.—								
Drunkenness, and Drunk and Disorderly,	[illegible]	[illegible]	[illegible]	[illegible]	1	1	.	.
Permitting Drunkenness and Disorderly Conduct in Licensed Houses,	.	.	.	.	.	.	.	.
Illegally selling intoxicating Liquors,	[illegible]	[illegible]	[illegible]	[illegible]	.	.	.	.
Adulteration of intoxicating Liquors,	.	.	.	.	.	.	.	.
[illegible] Acts, Offences against,	.	.	.	.	.	.	.	.
Other Offences against the Licensing Acts,	[illegible]	.	.	.	.	.	.	.
Lord's Day Act, Offences against,	.	.	1	.	.	.	.	.
Local Acts and Borough Bye-Laws, Offences against,	[illegible]	[illegible]	[illegible]	[illegible]	.	.	.	.
Wilfully Damaging Fences, Walls, Gates, &c.,	1	1	.	[illegible]	.	.	.	.
—— Fruit and Vegetable Productions,	[illegible]	.	[illegible]	.	.	.	.	.
—— Trees, Shrubs, &c.,	[illegible]	.	[illegible]	.	.	.	.	.
Other Malicious and Wilful Damage and Trespass,	[illegible]	[illegible]	[illegible]	[illegible]	[illegible]	[illegible]	1	.
Military Laws, Offences against, viz.—								
Army Act,	[illegible]	.	[illegible]	.	.	.	.	.
Navy Act,	.	.	.	.	.	.	.	.
Militia Act,	1	.	[illegible]	.	.	.	.	.
Mercantile Marine Acts, Offences against,	[illegible]	.	[illegible]	.	.	.	.	.
Nuisances, and Offences against Health, viz.—								
Public Health Acts,	.	.	.	.	.	.	.	.
Smoke Acts,	.	.	.	.	.	.	.	.
[illegible] Acts,	.	.	.	.	.	.	.	.
Nuisances Removal Act,	[illegible]	[illegible]	[illegible]	[illegible]	.	.	.	.
Common Lodging House Acts,	.	.	.	.	.	.	.	.
Selling and exposing for sale unsound Food,	[illegible]	.	.	.	.	.	.	.
Other Sanitary Offences,	.	.	.	.	.	.	.	.
Pawnbrokers' Act, Offences against, viz.—								
By Pawnbrokers,	.	.	.	.	.	.	.	.
By persons unlawfully pledging or disposing,	[illegible]	[illegible]	[illegible]	[illegible]	[illegible]	.	.	.
Other Offences,	.	.	.	.	.	.	.	.
Police Acts, Offences against, viz.—								
Unlawfully possessing Goods,	[illegible]	[illegible]	[illegible]	[illegible]	[illegible]	[illegible]	.	.
Offences [illegible] in Thoroughfares,	1	[illegible]	[illegible]	.	.	.	.	.
Constables neglecting their Duty,	.	.	.	.	.	.	.	.
Other Offences, not falling under other special heads,	[illegible]	.	[illegible]	.	.	.	.	[illegible]
Prevention of Crime Act, 1871, and Special Offences by Persons [illegible],	.	.	[illegible]	.	.	.	.	.
Poor Law Acts, Offences against, viz.—								
Deserting or Neglecting to support Family,	[illegible]	[illegible]	[illegible]	[illegible]	.	.	.	.
Disorderly Conduct in Workhouse,	[illegible]	[illegible]	[illegible]	[illegible]	.	.	.	.
Destroying Workhouse Clothing, Bedding, &c.,	[illegible]	[illegible]	[illegible]	[illegible]	.	.	.	.
[illegible] Houses and Wine Licenses Act,	.	.	.	.	.	.	.	.
Revenue Laws, Offences against, viz.—								
[illegible] Acts,	.	.	.	.	.	.	.	.
[illegible] Acts (including [illegible] Act),	[illegible]	.	[illegible]	.	.	.	.	.
Salmon Fisheries Act, Offences against,	[illegible]	.	[illegible]	.	.	.	.	.
Stealing, or Attempts to Steal, viz.—								
Larceny, by Offenders under 16 years (Juvenile Offenders Act),	[illegible]	[illegible]	[illegible]	[illegible]	[illegible]	[illegible]	[illegible]	.
Larceny, under value of 5s., and on Pleading Guilty (Criminal Justice Act),	[illegible]	[illegible]	[illegible]	[illegible]	[illegible]	[illegible]	.	.
Larceny, above value of 5s., on Pleading Guilty (Criminal Justice Act),	[illegible]	[illegible]	[illegible]	[illegible]	1	.	.	.
Larceny, or Larceny from Person, consenting to [illegible] (Criminal Justice Act),	[illegible]	[illegible]	[illegible]	[illegible]	[illegible]	.	.	.
Dogs, Birds, or Beasts, &c.,	[illegible]	[illegible]	.	[illegible]	.	.	.	.
Fruit and Vegetable Productions,	[illegible]	[illegible]	.	[illegible]	.	.	[illegible]	.
Fences, Woods, &c.,	[illegible]	.	[illegible]	[illegible]	.	.	.	.
Trees, Shrubs, &c.,	[illegible]	.	[illegible]	[illegible]	.	.	.	.
Vagrant Act, Offences against, viz.—								
Prostitution,	.	[illegible]	.	[illegible]	.	.	.	.
Begging,	[illegible]	[illegible]	[illegible]	[illegible]	.	[illegible]	[illegible]	[illegible]
Having no visible Means of Subsistence, &c.,	[illegible]	[illegible]	[illegible]	[illegible]	.	[illegible]	[illegible]	[illegible]
Having Implements for Housebreaking, &c.,	1	.	.	.	.	.	.	.
Found in enclosed Premises for unlawful purpose,	[illegible]	[illegible]	[illegible]	.	.	.	.	.
Frequenting Places of Public Resort, &c., to commit Felony,	[illegible]	.	[illegible]	[illegible]	[illegible]	.	.	.
Incorrigible Rogues,	[illegible]	[illegible]	.	.	.	.	.	.
Other Offences against Vagrant Act,	[illegible]	[illegible]	[illegible]	[illegible]	.	.	[illegible]	[illegible]
Vaccination Acts, Offences against,	.	.	.	[illegible]	.	.	.	.
[illegible] Acts, Offences against, viz.—								
Stage and Hackney Carriage Acts,	[illegible]	.	.	.	.	.	.	.
Highway Act (including [illegible]),	[illegible]	.	[illegible]	.	.	.	.	.
[illegible] Act,	.	.	.	.	.	.	.	.
Railway Acts,	[illegible]	[illegible]	[illegible]	.	.	.	.	.
Weights and Measures Act, Offences against,	.	.	.	.	.	.	.	.
Other Offences (not included under the above heads),	[illegible]	[illegible]	[illegible]	[illegible]	[illegible]	[illegible]	[illegible]	[illegible]
TOTAL,	[illegible]	[illegible]	[illegible]	[illegible]	[illegible]	[illegible]	[illegible]	[illegible]

[illegible]		Whipped.		[illegible]		[illegible]	[illegible]		[illegible]
M.	W.	M.	W.	M.	W.	M.	M.	W.	
[illegible]	[illegible]	[illegible]	[illegible]	[illegible]	[illegible]	[illegible]	[illegible]	[illegible]	TOTAL.

TABLE 8.—RETURN OF PERSONS PROCEEDED AGAINST FOR OFFENCES DETERMINED SUMMARILY. Result of the Proceedings, in each Police District against the Persons whose Cases were Determined Summarily by the Justices, in the Year ended 31st December, [illegible].

Province, County, County of City or of Town.	Number of Persons Proceeded against: Total			Discharged		Convicted		Persons Committed (with or without Fine or Whipping): [illegible]		[illegible]		[illegible]		[illegible]		[illegible]		[illegible]		[illegible]		[illegible]		Fined.		Whipped.		[illegible]		[illegible]	Other Punishments.	
	M.	W.	M. & W.	M.	W.	M.	W.	M.	W.	M.	W.	M.	W.	M.	W.	M.	W.	M.	W.	M.	W.	M.	W.	M.	W.	M.	W.	M.	W.	M.	M.	W.
Leinster:																																
Carlow	[illegible]	[illegible]	[illegible]	[illegible]	[illegible]	[illegible]	[illegible]	[illegible]	[illegible]	[illegible]	[illegible]	[illegible]	[illegible]	[illegible]	[illegible]	[illegible]	[illegible]	[illegible]	[illegible]	[illegible]	[illegible]	[illegible]	[illegible]	[illegible]	[illegible]	[illegible]	[illegible]	[illegible]	[illegible]	[illegible]	[illegible]	[illegible]
Drogheda, Town of	[illegible]	[illegible]	[illegible]	[illegible]	[illegible]	[illegible]	[illegible]	[illegible]	[illegible]	[illegible]	[illegible]	[illegible]	[illegible]	[illegible]	[illegible]	[illegible]	[illegible]	[illegible]	[illegible]	[illegible]	[illegible]	[illegible]	[illegible]	[illegible]	[illegible]	[illegible]	[illegible]	[illegible]	[illegible]	[illegible]	[illegible]	[illegible]
Dublin County	[illegible]	[illegible]	[illegible]	[illegible]	[illegible]	[illegible]	[illegible]	[illegible]	[illegible]	[illegible]	[illegible]	[illegible]	[illegible]	[illegible]	[illegible]	[illegible]	[illegible]	[illegible]	[illegible]	[illegible]	[illegible]	[illegible]	[illegible]	[illegible]	[illegible]	[illegible]	[illegible]	[illegible]	[illegible]	[illegible]	[illegible]	[illegible]
Dublin City (and part of County) Metropolitan Police District. Divisions:—																																
A.	[illegible]	[illegible]	[illegible]	[illegible]	[illegible]	[illegible]	[illegible]	[illegible]	[illegible]	[illegible]	[illegible]	[illegible]	[illegible]	[illegible]	[illegible]	[illegible]	[illegible]	[illegible]	[illegible]	[illegible]	[illegible]	[illegible]	[illegible]	[illegible]	[illegible]	[illegible]	[illegible]	[illegible]	[illegible]	[illegible]	[illegible]	[illegible]
B.	[illegible]	[illegible]	[illegible]	[illegible]	[illegible]	[illegible]	[illegible]	[illegible]	[illegible]	[illegible]	[illegible]	[illegible]	[illegible]	[illegible]	[illegible]	[illegible]	[illegible]	[illegible]	[illegible]	[illegible]	[illegible]	[illegible]	[illegible]	[illegible]	[illegible]	[illegible]	[illegible]	[illegible]	[illegible]	[illegible]	[illegible]	[illegible]
C.	[illegible]	[illegible]	[illegible]	[illegible]	[illegible]	[illegible]	[illegible]	[illegible]	[illegible]	[illegible]	[illegible]	[illegible]	[illegible]	[illegible]	[illegible]	[illegible]	[illegible]	[illegible]	[illegible]	[illegible]	[illegible]	[illegible]	[illegible]	[illegible]	[illegible]	[illegible]	[illegible]	[illegible]	[illegible]	[illegible]	[illegible]	[illegible]
D.	[illegible]	[illegible]	[illegible]	[illegible]	[illegible]	[illegible]	[illegible]	[illegible]	[illegible]	[illegible]	[illegible]	[illegible]	[illegible]	[illegible]	[illegible]	[illegible]	[illegible]	[illegible]	[illegible]	[illegible]	[illegible]	[illegible]	[illegible]	[illegible]	[illegible]	[illegible]	[illegible]	[illegible]	[illegible]	[illegible]	[illegible]	[illegible]
E.	[illegible]	[illegible]	[illegible]	[illegible]	[illegible]	[illegible]	[illegible]	[illegible]	[illegible]	[illegible]	[illegible]	[illegible]	[illegible]	[illegible]	[illegible]	[illegible]	[illegible]	[illegible]	[illegible]	[illegible]	[illegible]	[illegible]	[illegible]	[illegible]	[illegible]	[illegible]	[illegible]	[illegible]	[illegible]	[illegible]	[illegible]	[illegible]
F.	[illegible]	[illegible]	[illegible]	[illegible]	[illegible]	[illegible]	[illegible]	[illegible]	[illegible]	[illegible]	[illegible]	[illegible]	[illegible]	[illegible]	[illegible]	[illegible]	[illegible]	[illegible]	[illegible]	[illegible]	[illegible]	[illegible]	[illegible]	[illegible]	[illegible]	[illegible]	[illegible]	[illegible]	[illegible]	[illegible]	[illegible]	[illegible]
Total of Metropolitan Police District	[illegible]	[illegible]	[illegible]	[illegible]	[illegible]	[illegible]	[illegible]	[illegible]	[illegible]	[illegible]	[illegible]	[illegible]	[illegible]	[illegible]	[illegible]	[illegible]	[illegible]	[illegible]	[illegible]	[illegible]	[illegible]	[illegible]	[illegible]	[illegible]	[illegible]	[illegible]	[illegible]	[illegible]	[illegible]	[illegible]	[illegible]	[illegible]
Kildare	[illegible]	[illegible]	[illegible]	[illegible]	[illegible]	[illegible]	[illegible]	[illegible]	[illegible]	[illegible]	[illegible]	[illegible]	[illegible]	[illegible]	[illegible]	[illegible]	[illegible]	[illegible]	[illegible]	[illegible]	[illegible]	[illegible]	[illegible]	[illegible]	[illegible]	[illegible]	[illegible]	[illegible]	[illegible]	[illegible]	[illegible]	[illegible]
Kilkenny	[illegible]	[illegible]	[illegible]	[illegible]	[illegible]	[illegible]	[illegible]	[illegible]	[illegible]	[illegible]	[illegible]	[illegible]	[illegible]	[illegible]	[illegible]	[illegible]	[illegible]	[illegible]	[illegible]	[illegible]	[illegible]	[illegible]	[illegible]	[illegible]	[illegible]	[illegible]	[illegible]	[illegible]	[illegible]	[illegible]	[illegible]	[illegible]
King's County	[illegible]	[illegible]	[illegible]	[illegible]	[illegible]	[illegible]	[illegible]	[illegible]	[illegible]	[illegible]	[illegible]	[illegible]	[illegible]	[illegible]	[illegible]	[illegible]	[illegible]	[illegible]	[illegible]	[illegible]	[illegible]	[illegible]	[illegible]	[illegible]	[illegible]	[illegible]	[illegible]	[illegible]	[illegible]	[illegible]	[illegible]	[illegible]
Longford	[illegible]	[illegible]	[illegible]	[illegible]	[illegible]	[illegible]	[illegible]	[illegible]	[illegible]	[illegible]	[illegible]	[illegible]	[illegible]	[illegible]	[illegible]	[illegible]	[illegible]	[illegible]	[illegible]	[illegible]	[illegible]	[illegible]	[illegible]	[illegible]	[illegible]	[illegible]	[illegible]	[illegible]	[illegible]	[illegible]	[illegible]	[illegible]
Louth	[illegible]	[illegible]	[illegible]	[illegible]	[illegible]	[illegible]	[illegible]	[illegible]	[illegible]	[illegible]	[illegible]	[illegible]	[illegible]	[illegible]	[illegible]	[illegible]	[illegible]	[illegible]	[illegible]	[illegible]	[illegible]	[illegible]	[illegible]	[illegible]	[illegible]	[illegible]	[illegible]	[illegible]	[illegible]	[illegible]	[illegible]	[illegible]
Meath	[illegible]	[illegible]	[illegible]	[illegible]	[illegible]	[illegible]	[illegible]	[illegible]	[illegible]	[illegible]	[illegible]	[illegible]	[illegible]	[illegible]	[illegible]	[illegible]	[illegible]	[illegible]	[illegible]	[illegible]	[illegible]	[illegible]	[illegible]	[illegible]	[illegible]	[illegible]	[illegible]	[illegible]	[illegible]	[illegible]	[illegible]	[illegible]
Queen's County	[illegible]	[illegible]	[illegible]	[illegible]	[illegible]	[illegible]	[illegible]	[illegible]	[illegible]	[illegible]	[illegible]	[illegible]	[illegible]	[illegible]	[illegible]	[illegible]	[illegible]	[illegible]	[illegible]	[illegible]	[illegible]	[illegible]	[illegible]	[illegible]	[illegible]	[illegible]	[illegible]	[illegible]	[illegible]	[illegible]	[illegible]	[illegible]
Westmeath	[illegible]	[illegible]	[illegible]	[illegible]	[illegible]	[illegible]	[illegible]	[illegible]	[illegible]	[illegible]	[illegible]	[illegible]	[illegible]	[illegible]	[illegible]	[illegible]	[illegible]	[illegible]	[illegible]	[illegible]	[illegible]	[illegible]	[illegible]	[illegible]	[illegible]	[illegible]	[illegible]	[illegible]	[illegible]	[illegible]	[illegible]	[illegible]
Wexford	[illegible]	[illegible]	[illegible]	[illegible]	[illegible]	[illegible]	[illegible]	[illegible]	[illegible]	[illegible]	[illegible]	[illegible]	[illegible]	[illegible]	[illegible]	[illegible]	[illegible]	[illegible]	[illegible]	[illegible]	[illegible]	[illegible]	[illegible]	[illegible]	[illegible]	[illegible]	[illegible]	[illegible]	[illegible]	[illegible]	[illegible]	[illegible]
Wicklow	[illegible]	[illegible]	[illegible]	[illegible]	[illegible]	[illegible]	[illegible]	[illegible]	[illegible]	[illegible]	[illegible]	[illegible]	[illegible]	[illegible]	[illegible]	[illegible]	[illegible]	[illegible]	[illegible]	[illegible]	[illegible]	[illegible]	[illegible]	[illegible]	[illegible]	[illegible]	[illegible]	[illegible]	[illegible]	[illegible]	[illegible]	[illegible]
Total of Province	[illegible]	[illegible]	[illegible]	[illegible]	[illegible]	[illegible]	[illegible]	[illegible]	[illegible]	[illegible]	[illegible]	[illegible]	[illegible]	[illegible]	[illegible]	[illegible]	[illegible]	[illegible]	[illegible]	[illegible]	[illegible]	[illegible]	[illegible]	[illegible]	[illegible]	[illegible]	[illegible]	[illegible]	[illegible]	[illegible]	[illegible]	[illegible]

MUNSTER:																																				
Clare	[illegible]	[illegible]	[illegible]	[illegible]	[illegible]	[illegible]	[illegible]	[illegible]	[illegible]	[illegible]	[illegible]	[illegible]	[illegible]	[illegible]	[illegible]	[illegible]	[illegible]	[illegible]	[illegible]	[illegible]	[illegible]	[illegible]	[illegible]	[illegible]	[illegible]	[illegible]	[illegible]	[illegible]	[illegible]	[illegible]	[illegible]	[illegible]	[illegible]	[illegible]	[illegible]	[illegible]
Cork, E. R.	[illegible]	[illegible]	[illegible]	[illegible]	[illegible]	[illegible]	[illegible]	[illegible]	[illegible]	[illegible]	[illegible]	[illegible]	[illegible]	[illegible]	[illegible]	[illegible]	[illegible]	[illegible]	[illegible]	[illegible]	[illegible]	[illegible]	[illegible]	[illegible]	[illegible]	[illegible]	[illegible]	[illegible]	[illegible]	[illegible]	[illegible]	[illegible]	[illegible]	[illegible]	[illegible]	[illegible]
Cork, W. R.	[illegible]	[illegible]	[illegible]	[illegible]	[illegible]	[illegible]	[illegible]	[illegible]	[illegible]	[illegible]	[illegible]	[illegible]	[illegible]	[illegible]	[illegible]	[illegible]	[illegible]	[illegible]	[illegible]	[illegible]	[illegible]	[illegible]	[illegible]	[illegible]	[illegible]	[illegible]	[illegible]	[illegible]	[illegible]	[illegible]	[illegible]	[illegible]	[illegible]	[illegible]	[illegible]	[illegible]
Cork City	[illegible]	[illegible]	[illegible]	[illegible]	[illegible]	[illegible]	[illegible]	[illegible]	[illegible]	[illegible]	[illegible]	[illegible]	[illegible]	[illegible]	[illegible]	[illegible]	[illegible]	[illegible]	[illegible]	[illegible]	[illegible]	[illegible]	[illegible]	[illegible]	[illegible]	[illegible]	[illegible]	[illegible]	[illegible]	[illegible]	[illegible]	[illegible]	[illegible]	[illegible]	[illegible]	[illegible]
Kerry	[illegible]	[illegible]	[illegible]	[illegible]	[illegible]	[illegible]	[illegible]	[illegible]	[illegible]	[illegible]	[illegible]	[illegible]	[illegible]	[illegible]	[illegible]	[illegible]	[illegible]	[illegible]	[illegible]	[illegible]	[illegible]	[illegible]	[illegible]	[illegible]	[illegible]	[illegible]	[illegible]	[illegible]	[illegible]	[illegible]	[illegible]	[illegible]	[illegible]	[illegible]	[illegible]	[illegible]
Limerick	[illegible]	[illegible]	[illegible]	[illegible]	[illegible]	[illegible]	[illegible]	[illegible]	[illegible]	[illegible]	[illegible]	[illegible]	[illegible]	[illegible]	[illegible]	[illegible]	[illegible]	[illegible]	[illegible]	[illegible]	[illegible]	[illegible]	[illegible]	[illegible]	[illegible]	[illegible]	[illegible]	[illegible]	[illegible]	[illegible]	[illegible]	[illegible]	[illegible]	[illegible]	[illegible]	[illegible]
Limerick City	[illegible]	[illegible]	[illegible]	[illegible]	[illegible]	[illegible]	[illegible]	[illegible]	[illegible]	[illegible]	[illegible]	[illegible]	[illegible]	[illegible]	[illegible]	[illegible]	[illegible]	[illegible]	[illegible]	[illegible]	[illegible]	[illegible]	[illegible]	[illegible]	[illegible]	[illegible]	[illegible]	[illegible]	[illegible]	[illegible]	[illegible]	[illegible]	[illegible]	[illegible]	[illegible]	[illegible]
Tipperary, N. R.	[illegible]	[illegible]	[illegible]	[illegible]	[illegible]	[illegible]	[illegible]	[illegible]	[illegible]	[illegible]	[illegible]	[illegible]	[illegible]	[illegible]	[illegible]	[illegible]	[illegible]	[illegible]	[illegible]	[illegible]	[illegible]	[illegible]	[illegible]	[illegible]	[illegible]	[illegible]	[illegible]	[illegible]	[illegible]	[illegible]	[illegible]	[illegible]	[illegible]	[illegible]	[illegible]	[illegible]
Tipperary, S. R.	[illegible]	[illegible]	[illegible]	[illegible]	[illegible]	[illegible]	[illegible]	[illegible]	[illegible]	[illegible]	[illegible]	[illegible]	[illegible]	[illegible]	[illegible]	[illegible]	[illegible]	[illegible]	[illegible]	[illegible]	[illegible]	[illegible]	[illegible]	[illegible]	[illegible]	[illegible]	[illegible]	[illegible]	[illegible]	[illegible]	[illegible]	[illegible]	[illegible]	[illegible]	[illegible]	[illegible]
Waterford	[illegible]	[illegible]	[illegible]	[illegible]	[illegible]	[illegible]	[illegible]	[illegible]	[illegible]	[illegible]	[illegible]	[illegible]	[illegible]	[illegible]	[illegible]	[illegible]	[illegible]	[illegible]	[illegible]	[illegible]	[illegible]	[illegible]	[illegible]	[illegible]	[illegible]	[illegible]	[illegible]	[illegible]	[illegible]	[illegible]	[illegible]	[illegible]	[illegible]	[illegible]	[illegible]	[illegible]
Waterford City	[illegible]	[illegible]	[illegible]	[illegible]	[illegible]	[illegible]	[illegible]	[illegible]	[illegible]	[illegible]	[illegible]	[illegible]	[illegible]	[illegible]	[illegible]	[illegible]	[illegible]	[illegible]	[illegible]	[illegible]	[illegible]	[illegible]	[illegible]	[illegible]	[illegible]	[illegible]	[illegible]	[illegible]	[illegible]	[illegible]	[illegible]	[illegible]	[illegible]	[illegible]	[illegible]	[illegible]
Total of Province	[illegible]	[illegible]	[illegible]	[illegible]	[illegible]	[illegible]	[illegible]	[illegible]	[illegible]	[illegible]	[illegible]	[illegible]	[illegible]	[illegible]	[illegible]	[illegible]	[illegible]	[illegible]	[illegible]	[illegible]	[illegible]	[illegible]	[illegible]	[illegible]	[illegible]	[illegible]	[illegible]	[illegible]	[illegible]	[illegible]	[illegible]	[illegible]	[illegible]	[illegible]	[illegible]	[illegible]
ULSTER:																																				
Antrim	[illegible]	[illegible]	[illegible]	[illegible]	[illegible]	[illegible]	[illegible]	[illegible]	[illegible]	[illegible]	[illegible]	[illegible]	[illegible]	[illegible]	[illegible]	[illegible]	[illegible]	[illegible]	[illegible]	[illegible]	[illegible]	[illegible]	[illegible]	[illegible]	[illegible]	[illegible]	[illegible]	[illegible]	[illegible]	[illegible]	[illegible]	[illegible]	[illegible]	[illegible]	[illegible]	[illegible]
Armagh	[illegible]	[illegible]	[illegible]	[illegible]	[illegible]	[illegible]	[illegible]	[illegible]	[illegible]	[illegible]	[illegible]	[illegible]	[illegible]	[illegible]	[illegible]	[illegible]	[illegible]	[illegible]	[illegible]	[illegible]	[illegible]	[illegible]	[illegible]	[illegible]	[illegible]	[illegible]	[illegible]	[illegible]	[illegible]	[illegible]	[illegible]	[illegible]	[illegible]	[illegible]	[illegible]	[illegible]
Belfast, Town of	[illegible]	[illegible]	[illegible]	[illegible]	[illegible]	[illegible]	[illegible]	[illegible]	[illegible]	[illegible]	[illegible]	[illegible]	[illegible]	[illegible]	[illegible]	[illegible]	[illegible]	[illegible]	[illegible]	[illegible]	[illegible]	[illegible]	[illegible]	[illegible]	[illegible]	[illegible]	[illegible]	[illegible]	[illegible]	[illegible]	[illegible]	[illegible]	[illegible]	[illegible]	[illegible]	[illegible]
Carrickfergus, Town of	[illegible]	[illegible]	[illegible]	[illegible]	[illegible]	[illegible]	[illegible]	[illegible]	[illegible]	[illegible]	[illegible]	[illegible]	[illegible]	[illegible]	[illegible]	[illegible]	[illegible]	[illegible]	[illegible]	[illegible]	[illegible]	[illegible]	[illegible]	[illegible]	[illegible]	[illegible]	[illegible]	[illegible]	[illegible]	[illegible]	[illegible]	[illegible]	[illegible]	[illegible]	[illegible]	[illegible]
Cavan	[illegible]	[illegible]	[illegible]	[illegible]	[illegible]	[illegible]	[illegible]	[illegible]	[illegible]	[illegible]	[illegible]	[illegible]	[illegible]	[illegible]	[illegible]	[illegible]	[illegible]	[illegible]	[illegible]	[illegible]	[illegible]	[illegible]	[illegible]	[illegible]	[illegible]	[illegible]	[illegible]	[illegible]	[illegible]	[illegible]	[illegible]	[illegible]	[illegible]	[illegible]	[illegible]	[illegible]
Donegal	[illegible]	[illegible]	[illegible]	[illegible]	[illegible]	[illegible]	[illegible]	[illegible]	[illegible]	[illegible]	[illegible]	[illegible]	[illegible]	[illegible]	[illegible]	[illegible]	[illegible]	[illegible]	[illegible]	[illegible]	[illegible]	[illegible]	[illegible]	[illegible]	[illegible]	[illegible]	[illegible]	[illegible]	[illegible]	[illegible]	[illegible]	[illegible]	[illegible]	[illegible]	[illegible]	[illegible]
Down	[illegible]	[illegible]	[illegible]	[illegible]	[illegible]	[illegible]	[illegible]	[illegible]	[illegible]	[illegible]	[illegible]	[illegible]	[illegible]	[illegible]	[illegible]	[illegible]	[illegible]	[illegible]	[illegible]	[illegible]	[illegible]	[illegible]	[illegible]	[illegible]	[illegible]	[illegible]	[illegible]	[illegible]	[illegible]	[illegible]	[illegible]	[illegible]	[illegible]	[illegible]	[illegible]	[illegible]
Fermanagh	[illegible]	[illegible]	[illegible]	[illegible]	[illegible]	[illegible]	[illegible]	[illegible]	[illegible]	[illegible]	[illegible]	[illegible]	[illegible]	[illegible]	[illegible]	[illegible]	[illegible]	[illegible]	[illegible]	[illegible]	[illegible]	[illegible]	[illegible]	[illegible]	[illegible]	[illegible]	[illegible]	[illegible]	[illegible]	[illegible]	[illegible]	[illegible]	[illegible]	[illegible]	[illegible]	[illegible]
Londonderry	[illegible]	[illegible]	[illegible]	[illegible]	[illegible]	[illegible]	[illegible]	[illegible]	[illegible]	[illegible]	[illegible]	[illegible]	[illegible]	[illegible]	[illegible]	[illegible]	[illegible]	[illegible]	[illegible]	[illegible]	[illegible]	[illegible]	[illegible]	[illegible]	[illegible]	[illegible]	[illegible]	[illegible]	[illegible]	[illegible]	[illegible]	[illegible]	[illegible]	[illegible]	[illegible]	[illegible]
Monaghan	[illegible]	[illegible]	[illegible]	[illegible]	[illegible]	[illegible]	[illegible]	[illegible]	[illegible]	[illegible]	[illegible]	[illegible]	[illegible]	[illegible]	[illegible]	[illegible]	[illegible]	[illegible]	[illegible]	[illegible]	[illegible]	[illegible]	[illegible]	[illegible]	[illegible]	[illegible]	[illegible]	[illegible]	[illegible]	[illegible]	[illegible]	[illegible]	[illegible]	[illegible]	[illegible]	[illegible]
Tyrone	[illegible]	[illegible]	[illegible]	[illegible]	[illegible]	[illegible]	[illegible]	[illegible]	[illegible]	[illegible]	[illegible]	[illegible]	[illegible]	[illegible]	[illegible]	[illegible]	[illegible]	[illegible]	[illegible]	[illegible]	[illegible]	[illegible]	[illegible]	[illegible]	[illegible]	[illegible]	[illegible]	[illegible]	[illegible]	[illegible]	[illegible]	[illegible]	[illegible]	[illegible]	[illegible]	[illegible]
Total of Province	[illegible]	[illegible]	[illegible]	[illegible]	[illegible]	[illegible]	[illegible]	[illegible]	[illegible]	[illegible]	[illegible]	[illegible]	[illegible]	[illegible]	[illegible]	[illegible]	[illegible]	[illegible]	[illegible]	[illegible]	[illegible]	[illegible]	[illegible]	[illegible]	[illegible]	[illegible]	[illegible]	[illegible]	[illegible]	[illegible]	[illegible]	[illegible]	[illegible]	[illegible]	[illegible]	[illegible]
CONNAUGHT:																																				
Galway, E. R.	[illegible]	[illegible]	[illegible]	[illegible]	[illegible]	[illegible]	[illegible]	[illegible]	[illegible]	[illegible]	[illegible]	[illegible]	[illegible]	[illegible]	[illegible]	[illegible]	[illegible]	[illegible]	[illegible]	[illegible]	[illegible]	[illegible]	[illegible]	[illegible]	[illegible]	[illegible]	[illegible]	[illegible]	[illegible]	[illegible]	[illegible]	[illegible]	[illegible]	[illegible]	[illegible]	[illegible]
Galway, W. R.	[illegible]	[illegible]	[illegible]	[illegible]	[illegible]	[illegible]	[illegible]	[illegible]	[illegible]	[illegible]	[illegible]	[illegible]	[illegible]	[illegible]	[illegible]	[illegible]	[illegible]	[illegible]	[illegible]	[illegible]	[illegible]	[illegible]	[illegible]	[illegible]	[illegible]	[illegible]	[illegible]	[illegible]	[illegible]	[illegible]	[illegible]	[illegible]	[illegible]	[illegible]	[illegible]	[illegible]
Galway, Town of	[illegible]	[illegible]	[illegible]	[illegible]	[illegible]	[illegible]	[illegible]	[illegible]	[illegible]	[illegible]	[illegible]	[illegible]	[illegible]	[illegible]	[illegible]	[illegible]	[illegible]	[illegible]	[illegible]	[illegible]	[illegible]	[illegible]	[illegible]	[illegible]	[illegible]	[illegible]	[illegible]	[illegible]	[illegible]	[illegible]	[illegible]	[illegible]	[illegible]	[illegible]	[illegible]	[illegible]
Leitrim	[illegible]	[illegible]	[illegible]	[illegible]	[illegible]	[illegible]	[illegible]	[illegible]	[illegible]	[illegible]	[illegible]	[illegible]	[illegible]	[illegible]	[illegible]	[illegible]	[illegible]	[illegible]	[illegible]	[illegible]	[illegible]	[illegible]	[illegible]	[illegible]	[illegible]	[illegible]	[illegible]	[illegible]	[illegible]	[illegible]	[illegible]	[illegible]	[illegible]	[illegible]	[illegible]	[illegible]
Mayo	[illegible]	[illegible]	[illegible]	[illegible]	[illegible]	[illegible]	[illegible]	[illegible]	[illegible]	[illegible]	[illegible]	[illegible]	[illegible]	[illegible]	[illegible]	[illegible]	[illegible]	[illegible]	[illegible]	[illegible]	[illegible]	[illegible]	[illegible]	[illegible]	[illegible]	[illegible]	[illegible]	[illegible]	[illegible]	[illegible]	[illegible]	[illegible]	[illegible]	[illegible]	[illegible]	[illegible]
Roscommon	[illegible]	[illegible]	[illegible]	[illegible]	[illegible]	[illegible]	[illegible]	[illegible]	[illegible]	[illegible]	[illegible]	[illegible]	[illegible]	[illegible]	[illegible]	[illegible]	[illegible]	[illegible]	[illegible]	[illegible]	[illegible]	[illegible]	[illegible]	[illegible]	[illegible]	[illegible]	[illegible]	[illegible]	[illegible]	[illegible]	[illegible]	[illegible]	[illegible]	[illegible]	[illegible]	[illegible]
Sligo	[illegible]	[illegible]	[illegible]	[illegible]	[illegible]	[illegible]	[illegible]	[illegible]	[illegible]	[illegible]	[illegible]	[illegible]	[illegible]	[illegible]	[illegible]	[illegible]	[illegible]	[illegible]	[illegible]	[illegible]	[illegible]	[illegible]	[illegible]	[illegible]	[illegible]	[illegible]	[illegible]	[illegible]	[illegible]	[illegible]	[illegible]	[illegible]	[illegible]	[illegible]	[illegible]	[illegible]
Total of Province	[illegible]	[illegible]	[illegible]	[illegible]	[illegible]	[illegible]	[illegible]	[illegible]	[illegible]	[illegible]	[illegible]	[illegible]	[illegible]	[illegible]	[illegible]	[illegible]	[illegible]	[illegible]	[illegible]	[illegible]	[illegible]	[illegible]	[illegible]	[illegible]	[illegible]	[illegible]	[illegible]	[illegible]	[illegible]	[illegible]	[illegible]	[illegible]	[illegible]	[illegible]	[illegible]	[illegible]
Total of Ireland	[illegible]	[illegible]	[illegible]	[illegible]	[illegible]	[illegible]	[illegible]	[illegible]	[illegible]	[illegible]	[illegible]	[illegible]	[illegible]	[illegible]	[illegible]	[illegible]	[illegible]	[illegible]	[illegible]	[illegible]	[illegible]	[illegible]	[illegible]	[illegible]	[illegible]	[illegible]	[illegible]	[illegible]	[illegible]	[illegible]	[illegible]	[illegible]	[illegible]	[illegible]	[illegible]	[illegible]

IRELAND.

Cork City	[illegible]	[illegible]	[illegible]	[illegible]	[illegible]	[illegible]	[illegible]	[illegible]	[illegible]	[illegible]	[illegible]	[illegible]	[illegible]	[illegible]	[illegible]	[illegible]	[illegible]	[illegible]	[illegible]	[illegible]	[illegible]	[illegible]	[illegible]	[illegible]	[illegible]	[illegible]	[illegible]	[illegible]	[illegible]	[illegible]	[illegible]
Kerry	[illegible]	[illegible]	[illegible]	[illegible]	[illegible]	[illegible]	[illegible]	[illegible]	[illegible]	[illegible]	[illegible]	[illegible]	[illegible]	[illegible]	[illegible]	[illegible]	[illegible]	[illegible]	[illegible]	[illegible]	[illegible]	[illegible]	[illegible]	[illegible]	[illegible]	[illegible]	[illegible]	[illegible]	[illegible]	[illegible]	[illegible]
Limerick	[illegible]	[illegible]	[illegible]	[illegible]	[illegible]	[illegible]	[illegible]	[illegible]	[illegible]	[illegible]	[illegible]	[illegible]	[illegible]	[illegible]	[illegible]	[illegible]	[illegible]	[illegible]	[illegible]	[illegible]	[illegible]	[illegible]	[illegible]	[illegible]	[illegible]	[illegible]	[illegible]	[illegible]	[illegible]	[illegible]	[illegible]
Limerick City	[illegible]	[illegible]	[illegible]	[illegible]	[illegible]	[illegible]	[illegible]	[illegible]	[illegible]	[illegible]	[illegible]	[illegible]	[illegible]	[illegible]	[illegible]	[illegible]	[illegible]	[illegible]	[illegible]	[illegible]	[illegible]	[illegible]	[illegible]	[illegible]	[illegible]	[illegible]	[illegible]	[illegible]	[illegible]	[illegible]	[illegible]
Tipperary, N. Riding	[illegible]	[illegible]	[illegible]	[illegible]	[illegible]	[illegible]	[illegible]	[illegible]	[illegible]	[illegible]	[illegible]	[illegible]	[illegible]	[illegible]	[illegible]	[illegible]	[illegible]	[illegible]	[illegible]	[illegible]	[illegible]	[illegible]	[illegible]	[illegible]	[illegible]	[illegible]	[illegible]	[illegible]	[illegible]	[illegible]	[illegible]
Tipperary, S. Riding	[illegible]	[illegible]	[illegible]	[illegible]	[illegible]	[illegible]	[illegible]	[illegible]	[illegible]	[illegible]	[illegible]	[illegible]	[illegible]	[illegible]	[illegible]	[illegible]	[illegible]	[illegible]	[illegible]	[illegible]	[illegible]	[illegible]	[illegible]	[illegible]	[illegible]	[illegible]	[illegible]	[illegible]	[illegible]	[illegible]	[illegible]
Waterford	[illegible]	[illegible]	[illegible]	[illegible]	[illegible]	[illegible]	[illegible]	[illegible]	[illegible]	[illegible]	[illegible]	[illegible]	[illegible]	[illegible]	[illegible]	[illegible]	[illegible]	[illegible]	[illegible]	[illegible]	[illegible]	[illegible]	[illegible]	[illegible]	[illegible]	[illegible]	[illegible]	[illegible]	[illegible]	[illegible]	[illegible]
Waterford City	[illegible]	[illegible]	[illegible]	[illegible]	[illegible]	[illegible]	[illegible]	[illegible]	[illegible]	[illegible]	[illegible]	[illegible]	[illegible]	[illegible]	[illegible]	[illegible]	[illegible]	[illegible]	[illegible]	[illegible]	[illegible]	[illegible]	[illegible]	[illegible]	[illegible]	[illegible]	[illegible]	[illegible]	[illegible]	[illegible]	[illegible]
Total of Province	[illegible]	[illegible]	[illegible]	[illegible]	[illegible]	[illegible]	[illegible]	[illegible]	[illegible]	[illegible]	[illegible]	[illegible]	[illegible]	[illegible]	[illegible]	[illegible]	[illegible]	[illegible]	[illegible]	[illegible]	[illegible]	[illegible]	[illegible]	[illegible]	[illegible]	[illegible]	[illegible]	[illegible]	[illegible]	[illegible]	[illegible]
ULSTER:																															
Antrim	[illegible]	[illegible]	[illegible]	[illegible]	[illegible]	[illegible]	[illegible]	[illegible]	[illegible]	[illegible]	[illegible]	[illegible]	[illegible]	[illegible]	[illegible]	[illegible]	[illegible]	[illegible]	[illegible]	[illegible]	[illegible]	[illegible]	[illegible]	[illegible]	[illegible]	[illegible]	[illegible]	[illegible]	[illegible]	[illegible]	[illegible]
Armagh	[illegible]	[illegible]	[illegible]	[illegible]	[illegible]	[illegible]	[illegible]	[illegible]	[illegible]	[illegible]	[illegible]	[illegible]	[illegible]	[illegible]	[illegible]	[illegible]	[illegible]	[illegible]	[illegible]	[illegible]	[illegible]	[illegible]	[illegible]	[illegible]	[illegible]	[illegible]	[illegible]	[illegible]	[illegible]	[illegible]	[illegible]
Belfast, Town of	[illegible]	[illegible]	[illegible]	[illegible]	[illegible]	[illegible]	[illegible]	[illegible]	[illegible]	[illegible]	[illegible]	[illegible]	[illegible]	[illegible]	[illegible]	[illegible]	[illegible]	[illegible]	[illegible]	[illegible]	[illegible]	[illegible]	[illegible]	[illegible]	[illegible]	[illegible]	[illegible]	[illegible]	[illegible]	[illegible]	[illegible]
Carrickfergus, Town of	[illegible]	[illegible]	[illegible]	[illegible]	[illegible]	[illegible]	[illegible]	[illegible]	[illegible]	[illegible]	[illegible]	[illegible]	[illegible]	[illegible]	[illegible]	[illegible]	[illegible]	[illegible]	[illegible]	[illegible]	[illegible]	[illegible]	[illegible]	[illegible]	[illegible]	[illegible]	[illegible]	[illegible]	[illegible]	[illegible]	[illegible]
Cavan	[illegible]	[illegible]	[illegible]	[illegible]	[illegible]	[illegible]	[illegible]	[illegible]	[illegible]	[illegible]	[illegible]	[illegible]	[illegible]	[illegible]	[illegible]	[illegible]	[illegible]	[illegible]	[illegible]	[illegible]	[illegible]	[illegible]	[illegible]	[illegible]	[illegible]	[illegible]	[illegible]	[illegible]	[illegible]	[illegible]	[illegible]
Donegal	[illegible]	[illegible]	[illegible]	[illegible]	[illegible]	[illegible]	[illegible]	[illegible]	[illegible]	[illegible]	[illegible]	[illegible]	[illegible]	[illegible]	[illegible]	[illegible]	[illegible]	[illegible]	[illegible]	[illegible]	[illegible]	[illegible]	[illegible]	[illegible]	[illegible]	[illegible]	[illegible]	[illegible]	[illegible]	[illegible]	[illegible]
Down	[illegible]	[illegible]	[illegible]	[illegible]	[illegible]	[illegible]	[illegible]	[illegible]	[illegible]	[illegible]	[illegible]	[illegible]	[illegible]	[illegible]	[illegible]	[illegible]	[illegible]	[illegible]	[illegible]	[illegible]	[illegible]	[illegible]	[illegible]	[illegible]	[illegible]	[illegible]	[illegible]	[illegible]	[illegible]	[illegible]	[illegible]
Fermanagh	[illegible]	[illegible]	[illegible]	[illegible]	[illegible]	[illegible]	[illegible]	[illegible]	[illegible]	[illegible]	[illegible]	[illegible]	[illegible]	[illegible]	[illegible]	[illegible]	[illegible]	[illegible]	[illegible]	[illegible]	[illegible]	[illegible]	[illegible]	[illegible]	[illegible]	[illegible]	[illegible]	[illegible]	[illegible]	[illegible]	[illegible]
Londonderry	[illegible]	[illegible]	[illegible]	[illegible]	[illegible]	[illegible]	[illegible]	[illegible]	[illegible]	[illegible]	[illegible]	[illegible]	[illegible]	[illegible]	[illegible]	[illegible]	[illegible]	[illegible]	[illegible]	[illegible]	[illegible]	[illegible]	[illegible]	[illegible]	[illegible]	[illegible]	[illegible]	[illegible]	[illegible]	[illegible]	[illegible]
Monaghan	[illegible]	[illegible]	[illegible]	[illegible]	[illegible]	[illegible]	[illegible]	[illegible]	[illegible]	[illegible]	[illegible]	[illegible]	[illegible]	[illegible]	[illegible]	[illegible]	[illegible]	[illegible]	[illegible]	[illegible]	[illegible]	[illegible]	[illegible]	[illegible]	[illegible]	[illegible]	[illegible]	[illegible]	[illegible]	[illegible]	[illegible]
Tyrone	[illegible]	[illegible]	[illegible]	[illegible]	[illegible]	[illegible]	[illegible]	[illegible]	[illegible]	[illegible]	[illegible]	[illegible]	[illegible]	[illegible]	[illegible]	[illegible]	[illegible]	[illegible]	[illegible]	[illegible]	[illegible]	[illegible]	[illegible]	[illegible]	[illegible]	[illegible]	[illegible]	[illegible]	[illegible]	[illegible]	[illegible]
Total of Province	[illegible]	[illegible]	[illegible]	[illegible]	[illegible]	[illegible]	[illegible]	[illegible]	[illegible]	[illegible]	[illegible]	[illegible]	[illegible]	[illegible]	[illegible]	[illegible]	[illegible]	[illegible]	[illegible]	[illegible]	[illegible]	[illegible]	[illegible]	[illegible]	[illegible]	[illegible]	[illegible]	[illegible]	[illegible]	[illegible]	[illegible]
CONNAUGHT:																															
Galway, East Riding	[illegible]	[illegible]	[illegible]	[illegible]	[illegible]	[illegible]	[illegible]	[illegible]	[illegible]	[illegible]	[illegible]	[illegible]	[illegible]	[illegible]	[illegible]	[illegible]	[illegible]	[illegible]	[illegible]	[illegible]	[illegible]	[illegible]	[illegible]	[illegible]	[illegible]	[illegible]	[illegible]	[illegible]	[illegible]	[illegible]	[illegible]
Galway, West Riding	[illegible]	[illegible]	[illegible]	[illegible]	[illegible]	[illegible]	[illegible]	[illegible]	[illegible]	[illegible]	[illegible]	[illegible]	[illegible]	[illegible]	[illegible]	[illegible]	[illegible]	[illegible]	[illegible]	[illegible]	[illegible]	[illegible]	[illegible]	[illegible]	[illegible]	[illegible]	[illegible]	[illegible]	[illegible]	[illegible]	[illegible]
Galway, Town of	[illegible]	[illegible]	[illegible]	[illegible]	[illegible]	[illegible]	[illegible]	[illegible]	[illegible]	[illegible]	[illegible]	[illegible]	[illegible]	[illegible]	[illegible]	[illegible]	[illegible]	[illegible]	[illegible]	[illegible]	[illegible]	[illegible]	[illegible]	[illegible]	[illegible]	[illegible]	[illegible]	[illegible]	[illegible]	[illegible]	[illegible]
Leitrim	[illegible]	[illegible]	[illegible]	[illegible]	[illegible]	[illegible]	[illegible]	[illegible]	[illegible]	[illegible]	[illegible]	[illegible]	[illegible]	[illegible]	[illegible]	[illegible]	[illegible]	[illegible]	[illegible]	[illegible]	[illegible]	[illegible]	[illegible]	[illegible]	[illegible]	[illegible]	[illegible]	[illegible]	[illegible]	[illegible]	[illegible]
Mayo	[illegible]	[illegible]	[illegible]	[illegible]	[illegible]	[illegible]	[illegible]	[illegible]	[illegible]	[illegible]	[illegible]	[illegible]	[illegible]	[illegible]	[illegible]	[illegible]	[illegible]	[illegible]	[illegible]	[illegible]	[illegible]	[illegible]	[illegible]	[illegible]	[illegible]	[illegible]	[illegible]	[illegible]	[illegible]	[illegible]	[illegible]
Roscommon	[illegible]	[illegible]	[illegible]	[illegible]	[illegible]	[illegible]	[illegible]	[illegible]	[illegible]	[illegible]	[illegible]	[illegible]	[illegible]	[illegible]	[illegible]	[illegible]	[illegible]	[illegible]	[illegible]	[illegible]	[illegible]	[illegible]	[illegible]	[illegible]	[illegible]	[illegible]	[illegible]	[illegible]	[illegible]	[illegible]	[illegible]
Sligo	[illegible]	[illegible]	[illegible]	[illegible]	[illegible]	[illegible]	[illegible]	[illegible]	[illegible]	[illegible]	[illegible]	[illegible]	[illegible]	[illegible]	[illegible]	[illegible]	[illegible]	[illegible]	[illegible]	[illegible]	[illegible]	[illegible]	[illegible]	[illegible]	[illegible]	[illegible]	[illegible]	[illegible]	[illegible]	[illegible]	[illegible]
Total of Province	[illegible]	[illegible]	[illegible]	[illegible]	[illegible]	[illegible]	[illegible]	[illegible]	[illegible]	[illegible]	[illegible]	[illegible]	[illegible]	[illegible]	[illegible]	[illegible]	[illegible]	[illegible]	[illegible]	[illegible]	[illegible]	[illegible]	[illegible]	[illegible]	[illegible]	[illegible]	[illegible]	[illegible]	[illegible]	[illegible]	[illegible]
Total of Ireland	[illegible]	[illegible]	[illegible]	[illegible]	[illegible]	[illegible]	[illegible]	[illegible]	[illegible]	[illegible]	[illegible]	[illegible]	[illegible]	[illegible]	[illegible]	[illegible]	[illegible]	[illegible]	[illegible]	[illegible]	[illegible]	[illegible]	[illegible]	[illegible]	[illegible]	[illegible]	[illegible]	[illegible]	[illegible]	[illegible]	[illegible]

TABLE 11.—Return of Persons Convicted (Once, twice and upwards) of being Drunk or Drunk and Disorderly, during the year ended 31st December, 18[illegible] (so far as known to the Police).

Province, County, County of City or of Town, and Police District.	[illegible] Convicted 3 times and less than 6.	[illegible] Convicted 6 times and less than 10.	[illegible] Convicted 10 times and upwards.	Total.
LEINSTER.—				
Carlow,	[illegible]	[illegible]		[illegible]
Drogheda, Town of,	[illegible]	[illegible]	[illegible]	[illegible]
Dublin County (exclusive of part in Metropolitan Police District)	[illegible]	[illegible]	[illegible]	[illegible]
Dublin City (and part of County, Metropolitan Police District)—Divisions—				
A.	[illegible]	[illegible]	[illegible]	[illegible]
B.	[illegible]	[illegible]	[illegible]	[illegible]
C.	[illegible]	[illegible]	[illegible]	[illegible]
D.	[illegible]	[illegible]	[illegible]	[illegible]
E.	[illegible]	[illegible]		[illegible]
F.	[illegible]	[illegible]	[illegible]	[illegible]
Total of City,	[illegible]	[illegible]	[illegible]	[illegible]
Kildare,	[illegible]	[illegible]	[illegible]	[illegible]
Kilkenny,	[illegible]	[illegible]		[illegible]
King's County,	[illegible]	[illegible]		[illegible]
Longford,	[illegible]	[illegible]		[illegible]
Louth,	[illegible]	[illegible]	[illegible]	[illegible]
Meath,	[illegible]	[illegible]		[illegible]
Queen's County,	[illegible]	[illegible]		[illegible]
Westmeath,	[illegible]	[illegible]	[illegible]	[illegible]
Wexford,	[illegible]	[illegible]		[illegible]
Wicklow,	[illegible]	[illegible]	[illegible]	[illegible]
Total of Province,	[illegible]	[illegible]	[illegible]	[illegible]
MUNSTER.—				
Clare,	[illegible]	[illegible]	[illegible]	[illegible]
Cork, East Riding,	[illegible]	[illegible]	[illegible]	[illegible]
Cork, West Riding,	[illegible]	[illegible]	[illegible]	[illegible]
Cork City,	[illegible]	[illegible]	[illegible]	[illegible]
Kerry,	[illegible]	[illegible]	[illegible]	[illegible]
Limerick,	[illegible]	[illegible]	[illegible]	[illegible]
MUNSTER—continued.				
Limerick City,	[illegible]	[illegible]	[illegible]	[illegible]
Tipperary, North Riding,	[illegible]	[illegible]	[illegible]	[illegible]
Tipperary, South Riding,	[illegible]	[illegible]	[illegible]	[illegible]
Waterford,	[illegible]	[illegible]	[illegible]	[illegible]
Waterford City,	[illegible]	[illegible]	[illegible]	[illegible]
Total of Province,	[illegible]	[illegible]	[illegible]	[illegible]
ULSTER.—				
Antrim,	[illegible]	[illegible]	[illegible]	[illegible]
Armagh,	[illegible]	[illegible]	[illegible]	[illegible]
Belfast, Town of,	[illegible]	[illegible]	[illegible]	[illegible]
Carrickfergus, Town of,	[illegible]	[illegible]	[illegible]	[illegible]
Cavan,	[illegible]	[illegible]		[illegible]
Donegal,	[illegible]	[illegible]		[illegible]
Down,	[illegible]	[illegible]	[illegible]	[illegible]
Fermanagh,	[illegible]	[illegible]		[illegible]
Londonderry,	[illegible]	[illegible]	[illegible]	[illegible]
Monaghan,	[illegible]	[illegible]	[illegible]	[illegible]
Tyrone,	[illegible]	[illegible]	[illegible]	[illegible]
Total of Province,	[illegible]	[illegible]	[illegible]	[illegible]
CONNAUGHT.—				
Galway, East Riding,	[illegible]	[illegible]	[illegible]	[illegible]
Galway, West Riding,	[illegible]	[illegible]	[illegible]	[illegible]
Galway Town,	[illegible]	[illegible]	[illegible]	[illegible]
Leitrim,	[illegible]	[illegible]	[illegible]	[illegible]
Mayo,	[illegible]	[illegible]		[illegible]
Roscommon,	[illegible]	[illegible]	[illegible]	[illegible]
Sligo,	[illegible]	[illegible]	[illegible]	[illegible]
Total of Province,	[illegible]	[illegible]	[illegible]	[illegible]
Total of Ireland,	[illegible]	[illegible]	[illegible]	[illegible]

TABLE 12.—RETURN OF PERSONS PROCEEDED AGAINST FOR OFFENCES AGAINST THE [illegible] PREVENTIVE [illegible] City or of Town, qualifying the Offence.

Offence	Total of Ireland	Leinster: [illegible]	Carlow	Drogheda Town	Dublin	Dublin Metropolitan Police District	Kildare	Kilkenny	King's County	Longford	Louth	Meath	Queen's County	Westmeath	Wexford	Wicklow	Munster: [illegible]	Clare	Cork, E.R.	Cork, W.R.	Cork City	Kerry	Limerick	Limerick City
SECTION VII.																								
Intimidation,	[illegible]	[illegible]			[illegible]	[illegible]	[illegible]	[illegible]	[illegible]	[illegible]	[illegible]	[illegible]	[illegible]	[illegible]	[illegible]	[illegible]	[illegible]	[illegible]	[illegible]	[illegible]		[illegible]	[illegible]	[illegible]
SECTION VIII.																								
(a) Riot or Unlawful Assembly	[illegible]				[illegible]				[illegible]				[illegible]				[illegible]	[illegible]	[illegible]	[illegible]		[illegible]	[illegible]	[illegible]
(b) Forcible Possession,	[illegible]	[illegible]		[illegible]				[illegible]		[illegible]		[illegible]	[illegible]				[illegible]	[illegible]	[illegible]	[illegible]		[illegible]	[illegible]	
(c) Aggravated Assault or Violence against the Person	[illegible]	[illegible]			[illegible]	[illegible]		[illegible]		[illegible]	[illegible]					[illegible]	[illegible]		[illegible]	[illegible]		[illegible]	[illegible]	[illegible]
(d) Assault on Constable, Bailiff, &c., &c.	[illegible]	[illegible]			[illegible]	[illegible]	[illegible]		[illegible]			[illegible]					[illegible]	[illegible]	[illegible]			[illegible]	[illegible]	
SECTION IX.																								
Unlawful Assemblages,	[illegible]			[illegible]	[illegible]	[illegible]	[illegible]							[illegible]	[illegible]		[illegible]	[illegible]	[illegible]					
SECTION X.																								
Illegal Drilling,					[illegible]	[illegible]	[illegible]	[illegible]	[illegible]	[illegible]		[illegible]					[illegible]	[illegible]	[illegible]	[illegible]		[illegible]		
SECTION XI.																								
Found at night under Suspicious Circumstances,	[illegible]	[illegible]			[illegible]	[illegible]	[illegible]	[illegible]	[illegible]	[illegible]		[illegible]	[illegible]	[illegible]	[illegible]		[illegible]	[illegible]	[illegible]	[illegible]	[illegible]	[illegible]	[illegible]	[illegible]
SECTION XII.																								
Strangers found under Suspi-	[illegible]	[illegible]		[illegible]	[illegible]	[illegible]	[illegible]	[illegible]	[illegible]	[illegible]	[illegible]	[illegible]	[illegible]	[illegible]		[illegible]	[illegible]	[illegible]	[illegible]	[illegible]	[illegible]	[illegible]	[illegible]	[illegible]

TABLE 12.—OFFENCES AGAINST THE PREVENTION OF CRIME (IRELAND) ACT, 1882.—RETURN of TOTAL of PERSONS who were proceeded against for each CLASS of OFFENCES in the year ended 31st December, 1882.

OFFENCES.	Number of Persons proceeded against.			Sentence on Conviction.							To find Sureties	Appeals.		
	Total	Discharged	Convicted	6 Months and above	4 Months and above 3	3 Months and above 2	2 Months and above 1	1 Month and above 14 Days	14 Days and under	[illegible]	[illegible]	Affirmed	Reversed	Withdrawn
1	2	3	4	5	6	7	8	9	10	11	12	13	14	15
Section VII.														
Intimidation	[illegible]	[illegible]	[illegible]	[illegible]	[illegible]	[illegible]	[illegible]	[illegible]	[illegible]	[illegible]	[illegible]	[illegible]	[illegible]	[illegible]
Section VIII.														
(a) Riot or Unlawful Assembly	[illegible]	[illegible]	[illegible]	[illegible]	[illegible]	[illegible]	[illegible]	[illegible]	[illegible]	[illegible]			[illegible]	[illegible]
(b) Forcible Possession	[illegible]	[illegible]	[illegible]	[illegible]	[illegible]	[illegible]	[illegible]	[illegible]	[illegible]	[illegible]	[illegible]	[illegible]		[illegible]
(c) Aggravated Act of Violence against the Person	[illegible]	[illegible]	[illegible]	[illegible]	[illegible]	[illegible]	[illegible]	[illegible]	[illegible]	[illegible]	[illegible]	[illegible]	[illegible]	[illegible]
(d) Assault on Constable, Bailiff, &c. . . .	[illegible]	[illegible]	[illegible]	[illegible]	[illegible]	[illegible]	[illegible]	[illegible]	[illegible]	[illegible]	[illegible]	[illegible]	[illegible]	[illegible]
Section IX.														
Unlawful Association .	[illegible]	[illegible]		[illegible]	[illegible]	[illegible]	[illegible]		[illegible]	[illegible]		[illegible]		[illegible]
Section X.														
Illegal Meetings .	[illegible]	[illegible]		[illegible]	[illegible]	[illegible]			[illegible]	[illegible]	[illegible]	[illegible]	[illegible]	[illegible]
Section XI.														
Found at night under suspicious circumstances.	[illegible]	[illegible]	[illegible]	[illegible]	[illegible]	[illegible]	[illegible]	[illegible]	[illegible]	[illegible]	[illegible]	[illegible]	[illegible]	[illegible]
Section XII.														
Strangers found under suspicious circumstances . .	[illegible]	[illegible]	[illegible]	[illegible]	[illegible]	[illegible]		[illegible]	[illegible]		[illegible]		[illegible]	[illegible]
TOTAL .	[illegible]	[illegible]	[illegible]	[illegible]	[illegible]	[illegible]	[illegible]	[illegible]	[illegible]	[illegible]	[illegible]	[illegible]	[illegible]	[illegible]

OF CRIME (IRELAND) ACT, 1882."—TOTAL NUMBER of PERSONS PROCEEDED AGAINST in each COUNTY and COUNTY in the year ended 31st December, 1882.

Tipperary, N.R.	Tipperary, S.R.	Waterford	Waterford City	ULSTER. Total	Antrim	Armagh	Belfast Town	Carrickfergus Town	Cavan	Donegal	Down	Fermanagh	Londonderry	Londonderry City	Monaghan	Tyrone	CONNAUGHT. Total	Galway, E.R.	Galway, W.R.	Galway Town	Leitrim	Mayo	Roscommon	Sligo	OFFENCES.
																									Section VII.
[illegible]	[illegible]	[illegible]	[illegible]	[illegible]		[illegible]			[illegible]	[illegible]	[illegible]	[illegible]		[illegible]		[illegible]	[illegible]	[illegible]	[illegible]	[illegible]	[illegible]	[illegible]	[illegible]	[illegible]	Intimidation
																									Section VIII.
[illegible]	[illegible]	[illegible]	[illegible]	[illegible]	[illegible]	[illegible]	[illegible]	[illegible]	[illegible]	[illegible]	[illegible]	[illegible]	[illegible]	[illegible]	[illegible]	[illegible]	[illegible]	[illegible]	[illegible]	[illegible]	[illegible]	[illegible]	[illegible]	[illegible]	(a) Riot or Unlawful Assembly
[illegible]	[illegible]	[illegible]	[illegible]	[illegible]	[illegible]	[illegible]	[illegible]	[illegible]	[illegible]	[illegible]	[illegible]	[illegible]	[illegible]	[illegible]	[illegible]	[illegible]	[illegible]	[illegible]	[illegible]	[illegible]	[illegible]	[illegible]	[illegible]	[illegible]	(b) Forcible Possession
[illegible]	[illegible]	[illegible]	[illegible]	[illegible]	[illegible]	[illegible]	[illegible]	[illegible]	[illegible]	[illegible]	[illegible]	[illegible]	[illegible]	[illegible]	[illegible]	[illegible]	[illegible]	[illegible]	[illegible]	[illegible]	[illegible]	[illegible]	[illegible]	[illegible]	(c) Aggravated Act of Violence against the Person
[illegible]	[illegible]	[illegible]	[illegible]	[illegible]	[illegible]	[illegible]	[illegible]	[illegible]	[illegible]	[illegible]	[illegible]	[illegible]	[illegible]	[illegible]	[illegible]	[illegible]	[illegible]	[illegible]	[illegible]	[illegible]	[illegible]	[illegible]	[illegible]	[illegible]	(d) Assault on Constable, Bailiff, &c.
																									Section IX.
[illegible]		[illegible]	[illegible]	[illegible]	[illegible]	[illegible]	[illegible]	[illegible]	[illegible]	[illegible]	[illegible]	[illegible]	[illegible]	[illegible]	[illegible]	[illegible]	[illegible]	[illegible]	[illegible]	[illegible]	[illegible]	[illegible]	[illegible]	[illegible]	Unlawful Association
																									Section X.
[illegible]	[illegible]	[illegible]	[illegible]	[illegible]	[illegible]	[illegible]	[illegible]	[illegible]	[illegible]	[illegible]	[illegible]	[illegible]	[illegible]	[illegible]	[illegible]	[illegible]	[illegible]	[illegible]	[illegible]	[illegible]	[illegible]	[illegible]	[illegible]	[illegible]	Illegal Meetings
																									Section XI.
[illegible]	[illegible]	[illegible]	[illegible]	[illegible]	[illegible]	[illegible]	[illegible]	[illegible]	[illegible]	[illegible]	[illegible]	[illegible]	[illegible]	[illegible]	[illegible]	[illegible]	[illegible]	[illegible]	[illegible]	[illegible]	[illegible]	[illegible]	[illegible]	[illegible]	Found at night under suspicious circumstances
																									Section XII.
[illegible]	[illegible]	[illegible]	[illegible]	[illegible]	[illegible]	[illegible]	[illegible]	[illegible]	[illegible]	[illegible]	[illegible]	[illegible]	[illegible]	[illegible]	[illegible]	[illegible]	[illegible]	[illegible]	[illegible]	[illegible]	[illegible]	[illegible]	[illegible]	[illegible]	Strangers found under suspicious circumstances
[illegible]	[illegible]	[illegible]	[illegible]	[illegible]	[illegible]	[illegible]	[illegible]	[illegible]	[illegible]	[illegible]	[illegible]	[illegible]	[illegible]	[illegible]	[illegible]	[illegible]	[illegible]	[illegible]	[illegible]	[illegible]	[illegible]	[illegible]	[illegible]	[illegible]	TOTAL

TABLE 11.—RETURN OF PERSONS PROCEEDED AGAINST FOR OFFENCES AGAINST THE PREVENTION OF CRIME (IRELAND) ACT, 1882. RESULT of the PROCEEDINGS in each POLICE DISTRICT in the year ended 31st December, 1883.

PROVINCE, COUNTY, RIDING OF COUNTY, OR TOWN	Number of Persons proceeded against			Sentence Committed							Fined	Appeals		
	Total	Discharged	Convicted	[illegible]	[illegible]	[illegible]	[illegible]	[illegible]	[illegible]	[illegible]	[illegible]	[illegible]	[illegible]	[illegible]
LEINSTER:														
Carlow,	[illegible]	[illegible]	[illegible]	[illegible]	[illegible]	[illegible]	[illegible]	[illegible]	[illegible]	[illegible]	[illegible]	[illegible]	[illegible]	[illegible]
Drogheda Town,	[illegible]	[illegible]	[illegible]	[illegible]	[illegible]	[illegible]	[illegible]	[illegible]	[illegible]	[illegible]	[illegible]	[illegible]	[illegible]	[illegible]
Dublin County,	[illegible]	[illegible]	[illegible]	[illegible]	[illegible]	[illegible]	[illegible]	[illegible]	[illegible]	[illegible]	[illegible]	[illegible]	[illegible]	[illegible]
Dublin City (and part of the Metropolitan Police District),	[illegible]	[illegible]	[illegible]	[illegible]	[illegible]	[illegible]	[illegible]	[illegible]	[illegible]	[illegible]	[illegible]	[illegible]	[illegible]	[illegible]
Kildare,	[illegible]	[illegible]	[illegible]	[illegible]	[illegible]	[illegible]	[illegible]	[illegible]	[illegible]	[illegible]	[illegible]	[illegible]	[illegible]	[illegible]
Kilkenny,	[illegible]	[illegible]	[illegible]	[illegible]	[illegible]	[illegible]	[illegible]	[illegible]	[illegible]	[illegible]	[illegible]	[illegible]	[illegible]	[illegible]
King's County,	[illegible]	[illegible]	[illegible]	[illegible]	[illegible]	[illegible]	[illegible]	[illegible]	[illegible]	[illegible]	[illegible]	[illegible]	[illegible]	[illegible]
Longford,	[illegible]	[illegible]	[illegible]	[illegible]	[illegible]	[illegible]	[illegible]	[illegible]	[illegible]	[illegible]	[illegible]	[illegible]	[illegible]	[illegible]
Louth,	[illegible]	[illegible]	[illegible]	[illegible]	[illegible]	[illegible]	[illegible]	[illegible]	[illegible]	[illegible]	[illegible]	[illegible]	[illegible]	[illegible]
Meath,	[illegible]	[illegible]	[illegible]	[illegible]	[illegible]	[illegible]	[illegible]	[illegible]	[illegible]	[illegible]	[illegible]	[illegible]	[illegible]	[illegible]
Queen's County,	[illegible]	[illegible]	[illegible]	[illegible]	[illegible]	[illegible]	[illegible]	[illegible]	[illegible]	[illegible]	[illegible]	[illegible]	[illegible]	[illegible]
Westmeath,	[illegible]	[illegible]	[illegible]	[illegible]	[illegible]	[illegible]	[illegible]	[illegible]	[illegible]	[illegible]	[illegible]	[illegible]	[illegible]	[illegible]
Wexford,	[illegible]	[illegible]	[illegible]	[illegible]	[illegible]	[illegible]	[illegible]	[illegible]	[illegible]	[illegible]	[illegible]	[illegible]	[illegible]	[illegible]
Wicklow,	[illegible]	[illegible]	[illegible]	[illegible]	[illegible]	[illegible]	[illegible]	[illegible]	[illegible]	[illegible]	[illegible]	[illegible]	[illegible]	[illegible]
Total of Province,	[illegible]	[illegible]	[illegible]	[illegible]	[illegible]	[illegible]	[illegible]	[illegible]	[illegible]	[illegible]	[illegible]	[illegible]	[illegible]	[illegible]
MUNSTER:														
Clare,	[illegible]	[illegible]	[illegible]	[illegible]	[illegible]	[illegible]	[illegible]	[illegible]	[illegible]	[illegible]	[illegible]	[illegible]	[illegible]	[illegible]
Cork, E.R.,	[illegible]	[illegible]	[illegible]	[illegible]	[illegible]	[illegible]	[illegible]	[illegible]	[illegible]	[illegible]	[illegible]	[illegible]	[illegible]	[illegible]
Cork, W.R.,	[illegible]	[illegible]	[illegible]	[illegible]	[illegible]	[illegible]	[illegible]	[illegible]	[illegible]	[illegible]	[illegible]	[illegible]	[illegible]	[illegible]
Cork City,	[illegible]	[illegible]	[illegible]	[illegible]	[illegible]	[illegible]	[illegible]	[illegible]	[illegible]	[illegible]	[illegible]	[illegible]	[illegible]	[illegible]
Kerry,	[illegible]	[illegible]	[illegible]	[illegible]	[illegible]	[illegible]	[illegible]	[illegible]	[illegible]	[illegible]	[illegible]	[illegible]	[illegible]	[illegible]
Limerick,	[illegible]	[illegible]	[illegible]	[illegible]	[illegible]	[illegible]	[illegible]	[illegible]	[illegible]	[illegible]	[illegible]	[illegible]	[illegible]	[illegible]
Limerick City,	[illegible]	[illegible]	[illegible]	[illegible]	[illegible]	[illegible]	[illegible]	[illegible]	[illegible]	[illegible]	[illegible]	[illegible]	[illegible]	[illegible]
Tipperary, N.R.,	[illegible]	[illegible]	[illegible]	[illegible]	[illegible]	[illegible]	[illegible]	[illegible]	[illegible]	[illegible]	[illegible]	[illegible]	[illegible]	[illegible]
Tipperary, S.R.,	[illegible]	[illegible]	[illegible]	[illegible]	[illegible]	[illegible]	[illegible]	[illegible]	[illegible]	[illegible]	[illegible]	[illegible]	[illegible]	[illegible]
Waterford,	[illegible]	[illegible]	[illegible]	[illegible]	[illegible]	[illegible]	[illegible]	[illegible]	[illegible]	[illegible]	[illegible]	[illegible]	[illegible]	[illegible]
Waterford City,	[illegible]	[illegible]	[illegible]	[illegible]	[illegible]	[illegible]	[illegible]	[illegible]	[illegible]	[illegible]	[illegible]	[illegible]	[illegible]	[illegible]
Total of Province,	[illegible]	[illegible]	[illegible]	[illegible]	[illegible]	[illegible]	[illegible]	[illegible]	[illegible]	[illegible]	[illegible]	[illegible]	[illegible]	[illegible]
ULSTER:														
Antrim,	[illegible]	[illegible]	[illegible]	[illegible]	[illegible]	[illegible]	[illegible]	[illegible]	[illegible]	[illegible]	[illegible]	[illegible]	[illegible]	[illegible]
Armagh,	[illegible]	[illegible]	[illegible]	[illegible]	[illegible]	[illegible]	[illegible]	[illegible]	[illegible]	[illegible]	[illegible]	[illegible]	[illegible]	[illegible]
Belfast, Town of,	[illegible]	[illegible]	[illegible]	[illegible]	[illegible]	[illegible]	[illegible]	[illegible]	[illegible]	[illegible]	[illegible]	[illegible]	[illegible]	[illegible]
Carrickfergus, Town of,	[illegible]	[illegible]	[illegible]	[illegible]	[illegible]	[illegible]	[illegible]	[illegible]	[illegible]	[illegible]	[illegible]	[illegible]	[illegible]	[illegible]
Cavan,	[illegible]	[illegible]	[illegible]	[illegible]	[illegible]	[illegible]	[illegible]	[illegible]	[illegible]	[illegible]	[illegible]	[illegible]	[illegible]	[illegible]
Donegal,	[illegible]	[illegible]	[illegible]	[illegible]	[illegible]	[illegible]	[illegible]	[illegible]	[illegible]	[illegible]	[illegible]	[illegible]	[illegible]	[illegible]
Down,	[illegible]	[illegible]	[illegible]	[illegible]	[illegible]	[illegible]	[illegible]	[illegible]	[illegible]	[illegible]	[illegible]	[illegible]	[illegible]	[illegible]
Fermanagh,	[illegible]	[illegible]	[illegible]	[illegible]	[illegible]	[illegible]	[illegible]	[illegible]	[illegible]	[illegible]	[illegible]	[illegible]	[illegible]	[illegible]
Londonderry,	[illegible]	[illegible]	[illegible]	[illegible]	[illegible]	[illegible]	[illegible]	[illegible]	[illegible]	[illegible]	[illegible]	[illegible]	[illegible]	[illegible]
Monaghan,	[illegible]	[illegible]	[illegible]	[illegible]	[illegible]	[illegible]	[illegible]	[illegible]	[illegible]	[illegible]	[illegible]	[illegible]	[illegible]	[illegible]
Tyrone,	[illegible]	[illegible]	[illegible]	[illegible]	[illegible]	[illegible]	[illegible]	[illegible]	[illegible]	[illegible]	[illegible]	[illegible]	[illegible]	[illegible]
Total of Province,	[illegible]	[illegible]	[illegible]	[illegible]	[illegible]	[illegible]	[illegible]	[illegible]	[illegible]	[illegible]	[illegible]	[illegible]	[illegible]	[illegible]
CONNAUGHT:														
Galway, E.R.,	[illegible]	[illegible]	[illegible]	[illegible]	[illegible]	[illegible]	[illegible]	[illegible]	[illegible]	[illegible]	[illegible]	[illegible]	[illegible]	[illegible]
Galway, W.R.,	[illegible]	[illegible]	[illegible]	[illegible]	[illegible]	[illegible]	[illegible]	[illegible]	[illegible]	[illegible]	[illegible]	[illegible]	[illegible]	[illegible]
Galway, Town of,	[illegible]	[illegible]	[illegible]	[illegible]	[illegible]	[illegible]	[illegible]	[illegible]	[illegible]	[illegible]	[illegible]	[illegible]	[illegible]	[illegible]
Leitrim,	[illegible]	[illegible]	[illegible]	[illegible]	[illegible]	[illegible]	[illegible]	[illegible]	[illegible]	[illegible]	[illegible]	[illegible]	[illegible]	[illegible]
Mayo,	[illegible]	[illegible]	[illegible]	[illegible]	[illegible]	[illegible]	[illegible]	[illegible]	[illegible]	[illegible]	[illegible]	[illegible]	[illegible]	[illegible]
Roscommon,	[illegible]	[illegible]	[illegible]	[illegible]	[illegible]	[illegible]	[illegible]	[illegible]	[illegible]	[illegible]	[illegible]	[illegible]	[illegible]	[illegible]
Sligo,	[illegible]	[illegible]	[illegible]	[illegible]	[illegible]	[illegible]	[illegible]	[illegible]	[illegible]	[illegible]	[illegible]	[illegible]	[illegible]	[illegible]
Total of Province,	[illegible]	[illegible]	[illegible]	[illegible]	[illegible]	[illegible]	[illegible]	[illegible]	[illegible]	[illegible]	[illegible]	[illegible]	[illegible]	[illegible]
Total of IRELAND,	[illegible]	[illegible]	[illegible]	[illegible]	[illegible]	[illegible]	[illegible]	[illegible]	[illegible]	[illegible]	[illegible]	[illegible]	[illegible]	[illegible]

TABLES SHOWING DISTRICTS PROCLAIMED AND PRESCRIBED.

TABLE 15.—RETURN showing the several DISTRICTS which were subject to PROCLAMATIONS under 6 WM. IV., CAP. 13, on the 31st December, [illegible].

County	Proclaimed District	Date of Proclamation
Clare	The County.	17 January, [illegible]
Cork (a)	"	1 April, "
Donegal	The Baronies of East and West Inishowen.	11 December, [illegible]
	The Parish of [illegible], to the Barony of [illegible].	[illegible] May, [illegible]
Galway	The County.	1 October, [illegible]
Kerry	"	14 October, "
King's	"	9 January, [illegible]
Leitrim	"	[illegible] December, [illegible]
Limerick	"	[illegible] December, "
Limerick City	The County of the City.	[illegible] May, [illegible]
Longford	The Barony of Longford.	[illegible] January, [illegible]
Mayo	The County.	7 October, [illegible]
Roscommon (b)	"	[illegible] February, [illegible]
Sligo	The Baronies of Carbury, [illegible], Corran, and Leyney.	[illegible] January, [illegible]
	The Barony of [illegible].	12 April, "
Tipperary (c)	The County.	27 July, [illegible]
Waterford	The Baronies of [illegible] and [illegible], [illegible], [illegible], [illegible], [illegible], and [illegible].	[illegible] February, [illegible]
Westmeath	The County.	[illegible] December, [illegible]

(a) Portions of the County were proclaimed on [illegible] October, [illegible], and [illegible] March, [illegible].
(b) Ditto. ditto [illegible] January, [illegible].
(c) Ditto ditto 17th January, [illegible].

THE PEACE PRESERVATION (IRELAND) ACT.

TABLE 16.—RETURN No. 1, showing the several DISTRICTS which were under the operation of PROCLAMATIONS under the above Act, prohibiting the CARRYING OR HAVING OF ARMS, &c., on the 31st day of December, [illegible].

County, &c.	Proclaimed District	Date of Proclamation
Armagh	The Parishes of [illegible], [illegible], [illegible], [illegible], [illegible], and [illegible].	1 March, [illegible]
Carlow	The County.	27 December, [illegible]
Clare	"	1 April, "
Cork	"	" "
Cork City	The County of the City.	" "
Donegal	The Baronies of [illegible], [illegible], and [illegible] East, and the Parishes of [illegible], [illegible], [illegible] or [illegible], and [illegible] in the Barony of [illegible] West.	" "
Drogheda	The County of the Town.	27 December, "
Dublin	The County.	" "
Dublin City	The Metropolitan Police District, (a)	" "
Galway	The County.	1 April, "
Galway Town	The County of the Town.	" "
Kerry	The County.	" "
Kildare	"	27 December, "
Kilkenny	" (b)	[illegible] May, "
King's	"	1 April, "
Leitrim	"	1 April, "
Limerick	"	" "
Limerick City	The County of the City.	" "
Longford	The County.	27 December, "
Louth	"	1 April, "
Mayo	"	" "
Meath	"	27 December, "
Monaghan	The Baronies of [illegible] and [illegible], and Parish of [illegible].	1 [illegible], [illegible]
Queen's	The County.	1 April, [illegible]
Roscommon	"	" "
Sligo	"	" "
Tipperary	" (c)	27 December, "
Westmeath	"	" "
Waterford City	The County of the City.	1 April, "
Waterford	The County.	" "
Wexford	"	27 December, "
Wicklow	"	" "

(a) This District was proclaimed against the carrying of Arms, &c., on the [illegible] May, [illegible].
(b) A portion of the County was proclaimed on the [illegible] of April, [illegible].
(c) The North Riding was proclaimed against the carrying of Arms, &c., on the [illegible] April, [illegible].

TABLE [illegible].—RETURN No. [illegible], showing the several DISTRICTS which were under the operation of PROCLAMATION under the above Act, prohibiting the CARRYING OF ARMS, &c., on the 31st day of December, 1882.

County, &c.	Proclaimed District	Date of Proclamation
Armagh,	That part of the Parish of Newry in which is situate that portion of the town of Newry which is in the County Armagh, and also that part of the Barony of [illegible] which is contiguous to the aforesaid part of the Parish of Newry	[illegible]
Belfast,	The Borough,	[illegible] May, [illegible]
Cavan,	The County,	[illegible] April, "
Down,	The Barony of Lordship of Newry,	[illegible] November, [illegible]
Fermanagh,	The County,	[illegible] November, "
Londonderry City,	The Borough,	[illegible] October, [illegible]
Monaghan,	The County, [illegible]	[illegible] April, "
Tyrone,	The Baronies of Dungannon Upper and Middle,	[illegible] May, "
	The Baronies of Omagh East, Omagh West, and Clogher,	[illegible] December, [illegible]

(a) The Baronies of [illegible] and Cremorne and the Parish of [illegible] were proclaimed for having or carrying Arms, &c., on 7th August, [illegible].

THE PREVENTION OF CRIME (IRELAND) ACT, 1882.

TABLE [illegible].—RETURN showing COUNTIES and portions of COUNTIES subject to PROCLAMATIONS under the above Act, on the 31st December, 1882.

County	Proclaimed District	Sections of Act put in force *	Date of Proclamation
Armagh,	The Baronies of Tynan [illegible] and [illegible] Upper,	[illegible]	[illegible] July and October, 1882.
Cavan,	The County,	[illegible]	[illegible] July.
Clare,	Do.,	[illegible]	"
Cork,	Do.,	[illegible]	"
Cork City,	Do. of the City,	[illegible]	"
Drogheda Town,	The County of the Town,	[illegible]	"
Dublin,	The County,	[illegible]	"
Dublin City,	Do. of the City,	[illegible]	[illegible] September, "
Galway,	The County,	[illegible]	[illegible] July, "
Galway Town,	Do. of the Town,	[illegible]	"
Kerry,	The County,	[illegible]	"
Kildare,	The Baronies of [illegible] and [illegible] and West [illegible],	[illegible]	[illegible] July, "
Kilkenny,	The County,	[illegible]	[illegible] July, "
Kilkenny City,	Do. of the City,	[illegible]	"
King's,	The County,	[illegible]	[illegible] July, "
Leitrim,	Do.,	[illegible]	[illegible] July, "
Limerick,	Do.,	[illegible]	"
Limerick City,	Do. of the City,	[illegible]	"
Londonderry City,	The Borough,	[illegible]	"
Longford,	The County,	[illegible]	"
Mayo,	Do.,	[illegible]	"
Meath,	Do.,	[illegible]	[illegible] July, "
Monaghan,	The Baronies of Farney and Cremorne,	[illegible]	[illegible] July, "
Queen's,	The County,	[illegible]	[illegible] July, "
Roscommon,	Do.,	[illegible]	[illegible] July, "
Sligo,	Do.,	[illegible]	"
Tipperary,	Do.,	[illegible]	"
Waterford,	Do.,	[illegible]	"
Waterford City,	Do. of the City,	[illegible]	"
Westmeath,	The County,	[illegible]	"

* [illegible] Police and other Officers in a Proclaimed District.
Section 11 [illegible] Arrest of Persons found at night [illegible] in a Proclaimed District.
Section 12 [illegible] in a Proclaimed District.
Section 14 [illegible] Arms and Illegal Documents in a Proclaimed District.

TABLE [illegible].—STATE PRISONS.—CLASSIFICATION of ORDINARY CRIMINALS Committed during the year 1869, returned by General Prisons Board.

(a) AS TO FREQUENCY OF CONVICTIONS.	Number of First Commitments [illegible]		Number of Commitments of Ordinary Criminals other than First [illegible]		[illegible] Second		Third		Fourth		Fifth		Sixth		Seventh		Eighth		Ninth		Tenth		Eleventh		Twelfth and upwards		Number of Persons who [illegible]	
	M.	W.	M.	W.	M.	W.	M.	W.	M.	W.	M.	W.	M.	W.	M.	W.	M.	W.	M.	W.	M.	W.	M.	W.	M.	W.	M.	W.
Number in all Larger [illegible] Prisons	[illegible]	[illegible]	[illegible]	[illegible]	[illegible]	[illegible]	[illegible]	[illegible]	[illegible]	[illegible]	[illegible]	[illegible]	[illegible]	[illegible]	[illegible]	[illegible]	[illegible]	[illegible]	[illegible]	[illegible]	[illegible]	[illegible]	[illegible]	[illegible]	[illegible]	[illegible]	[illegible]	[illegible]

(b) AS TO AGE AND SEX.	Under [illegible] Years		[illegible]		[illegible]		[illegible]		[illegible]		[illegible]		[illegible]		[illegible]		Age not ascertained	
	M.	W.	M.	W.	M.	W.	M.	W.	M.	W.	M.	W.	M.	W.	M.	W.	M.	W.
Number in all Larger [illegible] Prisons	[illegible]	[illegible]	[illegible]	[illegible]	[illegible]	[illegible]	[illegible]	[illegible]	[illegible]	[illegible]	[illegible]	[illegible]	[illegible]	[illegible]	[illegible]	[illegible]	[illegible]	1

(c) AS TO BIRTHPLACE.	Ireland						England						Wales						Scotland						Colonies and East Indies						Foreign Countries						Not ascertained					
	M.	W.	M.	W.	M.	W.	M.	W.	M.	W.	M.	W.	M.	W.	M.	W.	M.	W.	M.	W.	M.	W.	M.	W.	M.	W.	M.	W.	M.	W.	M.	W.	M.	W.	M.	W.	M.	W.	M.	W.	M.	W.
Number in all Larger [illegible] Prisons	[illegible]	[illegible]	[illegible]	[illegible]	[illegible]	[illegible]	[illegible]	[illegible]	[illegible]	[illegible]	[illegible]	[illegible]	[illegible]	[illegible]	[illegible]	[illegible]	[illegible]	[illegible]	[illegible]	[illegible]	[illegible]	[illegible]	[illegible]	[illegible]	[illegible]	[illegible]	[illegible]	[illegible]	[illegible]	[illegible]	[illegible]	[illegible]	[illegible]	[illegible]	[illegible]	[illegible]	[illegible]	[illegible]	[illegible]	[illegible]	[illegible]	[illegible]

(d) AS TO DEGREE OF INSTRUCTION.	Neither Read nor Write		Read, or Read and Write Imperfectly		Read and Write Well		[illegible]		Instruction not ascertained	
	M.	W.	M.	W.	M.	W.	M.	W.	M.	W.
Number in all Larger [illegible] Prisons	[illegible]	[illegible]	[illegible]	[illegible]	[illegible]	[illegible]	[illegible]	[illegible]	[illegible]	[illegible]

(e) AS TO CLASS OF OCCUPATION.	No Occupation		Domestic Servants		[illegible]		[illegible]		[illegible]		[illegible]		[illegible]		[illegible]		[illegible]		[illegible]		[illegible]	
	M.	W.	M.	W.	M.	W.	M.	W.	M.	W.	M.	W.	M.	W.	M.	W.	M.	W.	M.	W.	M.	W.
Number in all Larger [illegible] Prisons	[illegible]	[illegible]	[illegible]	[illegible]	[illegible]	[illegible]	[illegible]	[illegible]	[illegible]	[illegible]	[illegible]	[illegible]	[illegible]	[illegible]	[illegible]	[illegible]	[illegible]	[illegible]	[illegible]	[illegible]	[illegible]	[illegible]

TABLE [illegible].—STATE PRISONS. RETURN BY GENERAL PRISONS BOARD showing [illegible] Prisoners in Central and Larger District Prisons at the end of [illegible], with the number of ordinary Criminals committed to Larger District Prisons during the Year [illegible], under and above the age of 16 years.

CENTRAL AND LARGER DISTRICT PRISONS.	Convicts in Prisons chiefly or purely for Convicts		[illegible]	Debtors and on Civil Process		Ordinary Criminals		Total in Custody		Ordinary Criminals committed during year to Larger District Prisons			
										Under 16 years of age		16 years and upwards	
	M.	F.	M.	M.	F.	M.	F.	M.	F.	M.	F.	M.	F.
Armagh,	.	.	[illegible]	.	.	[illegible]	[illegible]	[illegible]	[illegible]	[illegible]	[illegible]	[illegible]	[illegible]
Belfast,	[illegible]	.	[illegible]	[illegible]	.	[illegible]	[illegible]	[illegible]	[illegible]	[illegible]	[illegible]	[illegible]	[illegible]
Castlebar,	.	.	.	.	.	[illegible]	[illegible]	[illegible]	[illegible]	[illegible]	[illegible]	[illegible]	[illegible]
Clonmel,	.		–	–	–	[illegible]	[illegible]	[illegible]	[illegible]	[illegible]	[illegible]	[illegible]	[illegible]
Cork (for Men),	[illegible]		[illegible]	.	.	[illegible]	.	[illegible]	.	[illegible]	.	[illegible]	
" (for Women),	.	.		.	.	.	[illegible]	.	[illegible]	.	[illegible]	.	[illegible]
Downpatrick,	.	.	.	[illegible]	.	[illegible]	[illegible]	[illegible]	[illegible]	[illegible]	.	[illegible]	[illegible]
Dundalk,		.	[illegible]	–	.	[illegible]		[illegible]	–	[illegible]	.	[illegible]	.
Galway,	[illegible]	.	[illegible]	.	.	[illegible]	[illegible]	[illegible]	[illegible]	[illegible]	[illegible]	[illegible]	[illegible]
Grangegorman,	.	.	.	.	.		[illegible]	.	[illegible]	[illegible]	[illegible]	[illegible]	[illegible]
Kilkenny,	.	–	[illegible]	.		[illegible]	.	[illegible]	.	[illegible]	[illegible]	[illegible]	[illegible]
Kilmainham,	.	.	[illegible]	–	.	[illegible]	.	[illegible]	.	[illegible]	.	[illegible]	.
Limerick (for Men),	.	.	[illegible]	.	.	[illegible]	.	[illegible]	.	[illegible]	.	[illegible]	
" (for Women),	.	.	.	.	.		[illegible]	.	[illegible]	.	[illegible]	.	[illegible]
Londonderry,	.	.	[illegible]	.	.	[illegible]	[illegible]	[illegible]	[illegible]	[illegible]	[illegible]	[illegible]	[illegible]
Maryborough,	[illegible]	.	[illegible]	–	–	[illegible]	.	[illegible]	.	[illegible]	.	[illegible]	
Mullingar,	.	.	[illegible]	–	.	[illegible]	[illegible]	[illegible]	[illegible]	[illegible]	[illegible]	[illegible]	[illegible]
Naas,	.	.	[illegible]	.	.	[illegible]	[illegible]	[illegible]	[illegible]	[illegible]	[illegible]	[illegible]	[illegible]
Nenagh,	–	.			–	[illegible]	.	[illegible]	.	[illegible]	.	[illegible]	
Omagh,	.	.	[illegible]	[illegible]	.	[illegible]	[illegible]	[illegible]	[illegible]	[illegible]	[illegible]	[illegible]	[illegible]
Richmond,	.	.	[illegible]		.	[illegible]	.	[illegible]	.	[illegible]		[illegible]	.
Sligo,	.	.	.	.	.	[illegible]	[illegible]	[illegible]	[illegible]	[illegible]	[illegible]	[illegible]	[illegible]
Tralee,	[illegible]	.	[illegible]	[illegible]	.	[illegible]	[illegible]	[illegible]	[illegible]	[illegible]	[illegible]	[illegible]	[illegible]
Tullamore,	.	.	[illegible]	.	.	[illegible]	[illegible]	[illegible]	[illegible]	[illegible]	[illegible]	[illegible]	[illegible]
Waterford,	.	.	[illegible]	.	.	[illegible]	[illegible]	[illegible]	[illegible]	[illegible]	[illegible]	[illegible]	[illegible]
Wexford,	.	.	[illegible]	–	–	[illegible]	[illegible]	[illegible]	[illegible]	[illegible]	[illegible]	[illegible]	[illegible]
Mountjoy (for Men),	[illegible]	.	–	.		–	.	[illegible]	.	.		–	.
Grangegorman (for Women),	–	[illegible]	.	.		.	.		[illegible]	.	.	.	.
Lusk,	[illegible]	.	.	.		.	.	[illegible]	.	.	.	.	.
Total,	[illegible]	[illegible]	[illegible]	[illegible]		[illegible]	[illegible]	[illegible]	[illegible]	[illegible]	[illegible]	[illegible]	[illegible]

TABLE [illegible].—PRISONERS in SHORT SENTENCE PRISONS at end of [illegible] with Number Committed in [illegible].

SHORT SENTENCE PRISONS.	No. of	In custody at end of year.		[illegible]		[illegible]		Other Prisoners [illegible]	
		M.	W.	M.	W.	M.	W.	M.	W.
Totals,	[illegible]	[illegible]	[illegible]	[illegible]	[illegible]	[illegible]	[illegible]	[illegible]	[illegible]

TABLE [illegible].—Prisoners in Smaller District Prisons (Bridewells) at the end of [illegible], with the number committed to each of such Bridewells in [illegible].

Smaller District Prisons (Bridewells)		In Custody at end of [illegible]		Prisoners committed on [illegible] of Magistrates in [illegible]		Smaller District Prisons (Bridewells)		In Custody at end of [illegible]		Prisoners committed on [illegible] of Magistrates [illegible]	
Bridewells.	County.	M.	W.	M.	W.	Bridewells.	County.	M.	W.	M.	W.
[illegible]	Cavan	[illegible]	.	[illegible]	[illegible]	[illegible]	[illegible]	.	.	[illegible]	[illegible]
[illegible]	Mayo	.	.	[illegible]	[illegible]	[illegible]	Kerry	[illegible]	.	[illegible]	[illegible]
[illegible]	Galway	[illegible]	.	[illegible]	[illegible]	[illegible]	Galway	[illegible]	.	[illegible]	[illegible]
[illegible]	Mayo	.	.	[illegible]	[illegible]	[illegible]	Armagh	[illegible]	[illegible]	[illegible]	[illegible]
[illegible]	Antrim	[illegible]	.	[illegible]	[illegible]	[illegible]	Cork	[illegible]	.	[illegible]	[illegible]
[illegible]	Wexford	.	.	[illegible]	.	[illegible]	Cork	[illegible]	.	[illegible]	[illegible]
[illegible]	Cork	.	[illegible]	[illegible]	[illegible]	[illegible]	Meath	.	.	[illegible]	.
[illegible]	Kerry	.	.	[illegible]	[illegible]	[illegible]	Wexford	[illegible]	.	[illegible]	[illegible]
[illegible]	Galway	.	.	[illegible]	[illegible]	[illegible]	Down	[illegible]	[illegible]	[illegible]	[illegible]
[illegible]	Cork	[illegible]	.	[illegible]	[illegible]	[illegible]	Mayo	[illegible]	[illegible]	[illegible]	[illegible]
[illegible]	Londonderry	.	.	[illegible]	[illegible]	[illegible]	Cork	[illegible]	[illegible]	[illegible]	[illegible]
[illegible]	Kerry	.	.	[illegible]	.	[illegible]	Limerick	.	.	[illegible]	[illegible]
[illegible]	Donegal	.	.	[illegible]	[illegible]	[illegible]	Tipperary	[illegible]	.	[illegible]	[illegible]
[illegible]	Tyrone	.	.	[illegible]	[illegible]	[illegible]	Tipperary	[illegible]	[illegible]	[illegible]	[illegible]
[illegible]	Waterford	[illegible]	.	[illegible]	[illegible]	[illegible]	Galway	[illegible]	.	[illegible]	[illegible]
[illegible]	Clare	[illegible]	[illegible]	[illegible]	[illegible]	[illegible]	Cork	.	.	[illegible]	[illegible]
[illegible]	Kerry	.	.	[illegible]	[illegible]						
[illegible]	Clare	[illegible]	.	[illegible]	[illegible]	Total,		[illegible]	[illegible]	[illegible]	[illegible]

TABLE [illegible].—STAFF AND COST OF STATE PRISONS.

	Cost. £
(1) [illegible]	[illegible]
(2) [illegible]	[illegible]
(3) [illegible]	[illegible]
(4) [illegible]	[illegible]
Cost of Prisoners beyond above cost of Staff,	[illegible]
	[illegible]

TABLE [illegible].—CRIMINAL PROCEEDINGS AT ASSIZES, COMMISSION, AND QUARTER SESSIONS.—Showing the RESULT of the PROCEEDINGS—[illegible]

OFFENCES Charged in Proceedings or Indictments, and of which those Tried were Convicted or Acquitted.	Persons Convicted and Tried. Men	Women	No Bill Found. M	W	Not Guilty on Trial. M	W	Bailed and not tried. M	W	Total Acquitted and Discharged. M	W	Total Detained [illegible] M	W	No Prosecution. M	W
No. 1.—Offences against the Person.														
Murder of Infants under one year and under	[illegible]	[illegible]	[illegible]	[illegible]	[illegible]	[illegible]	[illegible]	[illegible]	[illegible]	[illegible]	[illegible]	[illegible]	[illegible]	[illegible]
Other Murders	[illegible]	[illegible]	[illegible]	[illegible]	[illegible]	[illegible]	[illegible]	[illegible]	[illegible]	[illegible]	[illegible]	[illegible]	[illegible]	[illegible]
Attempts to Murder	[illegible]	[illegible]	[illegible]	[illegible]	[illegible]	[illegible]	[illegible]	[illegible]	[illegible]	[illegible]	[illegible]	[illegible]	[illegible]	[illegible]
Shooting at, Wounding, Stabbing, &c., with intent to do bodily harm	[illegible]	[illegible]	[illegible]	[illegible]	[illegible]	[illegible]	[illegible]	[illegible]	[illegible]	[illegible]	[illegible]	[illegible]	[illegible]	[illegible]
Conspiracy to Murder	[illegible]	[illegible]	[illegible]	[illegible]	[illegible]	[illegible]	[illegible]	[illegible]	[illegible]	[illegible]	[illegible]	[illegible]	[illegible]	[illegible]
Manslaughter	[illegible]	[illegible]	[illegible]	[illegible]	[illegible]	[illegible]	[illegible]	[illegible]	[illegible]	[illegible]	[illegible]	[illegible]	[illegible]	[illegible]
Concealing the Birth of Infants	[illegible]	[illegible]	[illegible]	[illegible]	[illegible]	[illegible]	[illegible]	[illegible]	[illegible]	[illegible]	[illegible]	[illegible]	[illegible]	[illegible]
Sodomy and Bestiality	[illegible]	[illegible]	[illegible]	[illegible]	[illegible]	[illegible]	[illegible]	[illegible]	[illegible]	[illegible]	[illegible]	[illegible]	[illegible]	[illegible]
——— Attempts to Commit, and other unnatural Misdemeanours	[illegible]	[illegible]	[illegible]	[illegible]	[illegible]	[illegible]	[illegible]	[illegible]	[illegible]	[illegible]	[illegible]	[illegible]	[illegible]	[illegible]
Rape	[illegible]	[illegible]	[illegible]	[illegible]	[illegible]	[illegible]	[illegible]	[illegible]	[illegible]	[illegible]	[illegible]	[illegible]	[illegible]	[illegible]
——— Assaults, with intent to ravish and abuse	[illegible]	[illegible]	[illegible]	[illegible]	[illegible]	[illegible]	[illegible]	[illegible]	[illegible]	[illegible]	[illegible]	[illegible]	[illegible]	[illegible]
Bigamy	[illegible]	[illegible]	[illegible]	[illegible]	[illegible]	[illegible]	[illegible]	[illegible]	[illegible]	[illegible]	[illegible]	[illegible]	[illegible]	[illegible]
Child Stealing	[illegible]	[illegible]	[illegible]	[illegible]	[illegible]	[illegible]	[illegible]	[illegible]	[illegible]	[illegible]	[illegible]	[illegible]	[illegible]	[illegible]
Unlawfully abandoning Children under two years of Age	[illegible]	[illegible]	[illegible]	[illegible]	[illegible]	[illegible]	[illegible]	[illegible]	[illegible]	[illegible]	[illegible]	[illegible]	[illegible]	[illegible]
Endangering the Safety of Passengers on Railways	[illegible]	[illegible]	[illegible]	[illegible]	[illegible]	[illegible]	[illegible]	[illegible]	[illegible]	[illegible]	[illegible]	[illegible]	[illegible]	[illegible]
Assaults and inflicting bodily harm	[illegible]	[illegible]	[illegible]	[illegible]	[illegible]	[illegible]	[illegible]	[illegible]	[illegible]	[illegible]	[illegible]	[illegible]	[illegible]	[illegible]
Assaults, Common	[illegible]	[illegible]	[illegible]	[illegible]	[illegible]	[illegible]	[illegible]	[illegible]	[illegible]	[illegible]	[illegible]	[illegible]	[illegible]	[illegible]
Assaults on Peace Officers	[illegible]	[illegible]	[illegible]	[illegible]	[illegible]	[illegible]	[illegible]	[illegible]	[illegible]	[illegible]	[illegible]	[illegible]	[illegible]	[illegible]
Total of No. 1	[illegible]	[illegible]	[illegible]	[illegible]	[illegible]	[illegible]	[illegible]	[illegible]	[illegible]	[illegible]	[illegible]	[illegible]	[illegible]	[illegible]
No. 2.—Offences against Property, with Violence.														
Sacrilege	[illegible]	[illegible]	[illegible]	[illegible]	[illegible]	[illegible]	[illegible]	[illegible]	[illegible]	[illegible]	[illegible]	[illegible]	[illegible]	[illegible]
Burglary and Housebreaking	[illegible]	[illegible]	[illegible]	[illegible]	[illegible]	[illegible]	[illegible]	[illegible]	[illegible]	[illegible]	[illegible]	[illegible]	[illegible]	[illegible]
Breaking into Shops, Warehouses, &c.	[illegible]	[illegible]	[illegible]	[illegible]	[illegible]	[illegible]	[illegible]	[illegible]	[illegible]	[illegible]	[illegible]	[illegible]	[illegible]	[illegible]
Attempts to break into Houses, Shops, Warehouses, &c.	[illegible]	[illegible]	[illegible]	[illegible]	[illegible]	[illegible]	[illegible]	[illegible]	[illegible]	[illegible]	[illegible]	[illegible]	[illegible]	[illegible]
Robbery	[illegible]	[illegible]	[illegible]	[illegible]	[illegible]	[illegible]	[illegible]	[illegible]	[illegible]	[illegible]	[illegible]	[illegible]	[illegible]	[illegible]
Attempts to rob, and demanding Money by Menaces	[illegible]	[illegible]	[illegible]	[illegible]	[illegible]	[illegible]	[illegible]	[illegible]	[illegible]	[illegible]	[illegible]	[illegible]	[illegible]	[illegible]
Total of No. 2	[illegible]	[illegible]	[illegible]	[illegible]	[illegible]	[illegible]	[illegible]	[illegible]	[illegible]	[illegible]	[illegible]	[illegible]	[illegible]	[illegible]
No. 3.—Offences against Property, without Violence.														
Cattle Stealing	[illegible]	[illegible]	[illegible]	[illegible]	[illegible]	[illegible]	[illegible]	[illegible]	[illegible]	[illegible]	[illegible]	[illegible]	[illegible]	[illegible]
Horse Stealing	[illegible]	[illegible]	[illegible]	[illegible]	[illegible]	[illegible]	[illegible]	[illegible]	[illegible]	[illegible]	[illegible]	[illegible]	[illegible]	[illegible]
Sheep Stealing	[illegible]	[illegible]	[illegible]	[illegible]	[illegible]	[illegible]	[illegible]	[illegible]	[illegible]	[illegible]	[illegible]	[illegible]	[illegible]	[illegible]
Larceny, to the value of £5, in Dwelling-houses	[illegible]	[illegible]	[illegible]	[illegible]	[illegible]	[illegible]	[illegible]	[illegible]	[illegible]	[illegible]	[illegible]	[illegible]	[illegible]	[illegible]
Larceny, from the Person	[illegible]	[illegible]	[illegible]	[illegible]	[illegible]	[illegible]	[illegible]	[illegible]	[illegible]	[illegible]	[illegible]	[illegible]	[illegible]	[illegible]
Larceny, by Servants	[illegible]	[illegible]	[illegible]	[illegible]	[illegible]	[illegible]	[illegible]	[illegible]	[illegible]	[illegible]	[illegible]	[illegible]	[illegible]	[illegible]
Larceny, Simple	[illegible]	[illegible]	[illegible]	[illegible]	[illegible]	[illegible]	[illegible]	[illegible]	[illegible]	[illegible]	[illegible]	[illegible]	[illegible]	[illegible]
Larceny on Rivers, Canals, Wharfs, &c.	[illegible]	[illegible]	[illegible]	[illegible]	[illegible]	[illegible]	[illegible]	[illegible]	[illegible]	[illegible]	[illegible]	[illegible]	[illegible]	[illegible]
Stealing Fixtures, Shrubs growing, &c.	[illegible]	[illegible]	[illegible]	[illegible]	[illegible]	[illegible]	[illegible]	[illegible]	[illegible]	[illegible]	[illegible]	[illegible]	[illegible]	[illegible]
Attempts to Steal	[illegible]	[illegible]	[illegible]	[illegible]	[illegible]	[illegible]	[illegible]	[illegible]	[illegible]	[illegible]	[illegible]	[illegible]	[illegible]	[illegible]
Embezzlement	[illegible]	[illegible]	[illegible]	[illegible]	[illegible]	[illegible]	[illegible]	[illegible]	[illegible]	[illegible]	[illegible]	[illegible]	[illegible]	[illegible]
Larceny by Servants of the Post Office	[illegible]	[illegible]	[illegible]	[illegible]	[illegible]	[illegible]	[illegible]	[illegible]	[illegible]	[illegible]	[illegible]	[illegible]	[illegible]	[illegible]
Receiving Stolen Goods	[illegible]	[illegible]	[illegible]	[illegible]	[illegible]	[illegible]	[illegible]	[illegible]	[illegible]	[illegible]	[illegible]	[illegible]	[illegible]	[illegible]
Fraudulently obtaining Goods by false pretences, and attempts to defraud	[illegible]	[illegible]	[illegible]	[illegible]	[illegible]	[illegible]	[illegible]	[illegible]	[illegible]	[illegible]	[illegible]	[illegible]	[illegible]	[illegible]
Total of No. 3	[illegible]	[illegible]	[illegible]	[illegible]	[illegible]	[illegible]	[illegible]	[illegible]	[illegible]	[illegible]	[illegible]	[illegible]	[illegible]	[illegible]
No. 4.—Malicious Offences against Property.														
Arson and other Wilful Burning	[illegible]	[illegible]	[illegible]	[illegible]	[illegible]	[illegible]	[illegible]	[illegible]	[illegible]	[illegible]	[illegible]	[illegible]	[illegible]	[illegible]
Felonious Riot and demolishing Buildings, &c.	[illegible]	[illegible]	[illegible]	[illegible]	[illegible]	[illegible]	[illegible]	[illegible]	[illegible]	[illegible]	[illegible]	[illegible]	[illegible]	[illegible]
Destroying Goods in process of Manufacture	[illegible]	[illegible]	[illegible]	[illegible]	[illegible]	[illegible]	[illegible]	[illegible]	[illegible]	[illegible]	[illegible]	[illegible]	[illegible]	[illegible]
Destroying Trees, Shrubs, &c., growing	[illegible]	[illegible]	[illegible]	[illegible]	[illegible]	[illegible]	[illegible]	[illegible]	[illegible]	[illegible]	[illegible]	[illegible]	[illegible]	[illegible]
Killing and Maiming Cattle	[illegible]	[illegible]	[illegible]	[illegible]	[illegible]	[illegible]	[illegible]	[illegible]	[illegible]	[illegible]	[illegible]	[illegible]	[illegible]	[illegible]
Malicious Injuries to Property exceeding £5 in value	[illegible]	[illegible]	[illegible]	[illegible]	[illegible]	[illegible]	[illegible]	[illegible]	[illegible]	[illegible]	[illegible]	[illegible]	[illegible]	[illegible]
Other Wilful and Malicious Injuries to Property	[illegible]	[illegible]	[illegible]	[illegible]	[illegible]	[illegible]	[illegible]	[illegible]	[illegible]	[illegible]	[illegible]	[illegible]	[illegible]	[illegible]
Total of No. 4	[illegible]	[illegible]	[illegible]	[illegible]	[illegible]	[illegible]	[illegible]	[illegible]	[illegible]	[illegible]	[illegible]	[illegible]	[illegible]	[illegible]
No. 5.—Forgery and Offences against the Currency.														
Forging and uttering Forged Instruments	[illegible]	[illegible]	[illegible]	[illegible]	[illegible]	[illegible]	[illegible]	[illegible]	[illegible]	[illegible]	[illegible]	[illegible]	[illegible]	[illegible]
Having in Possession Forged Bank Notes	[illegible]	[illegible]	[illegible]	[illegible]	[illegible]	[illegible]	[illegible]	[illegible]	[illegible]	[illegible]	[illegible]	[illegible]	[illegible]	[illegible]
Coining and having in possession Instruments for Coining	[illegible]	[illegible]	[illegible]	[illegible]	[illegible]	[illegible]	[illegible]	[illegible]	[illegible]	[illegible]	[illegible]	[illegible]	[illegible]	[illegible]
Uttering, putting off, and having in possession Counterfeit Coin	[illegible]	[illegible]	[illegible]	[illegible]	[illegible]	[illegible]	[illegible]	[illegible]	[illegible]	[illegible]	[illegible]	[illegible]	[illegible]	[illegible]
Total of No. 5	[illegible]	[illegible]	[illegible]	[illegible]	[illegible]	[illegible]	[illegible]	[illegible]	[illegible]	[illegible]	[illegible]	[illegible]	[illegible]	[illegible]
No. 6.—Offences not included in the above Classes.														
Offences against the Queen's Authority and Person	[illegible]	[illegible]	[illegible]	[illegible]	[illegible]	[illegible]	[illegible]	[illegible]	[illegible]	[illegible]	[illegible]	[illegible]	[illegible]	[illegible]
Threatening by Threatening Letters, Notices or otherwise	[illegible]	[illegible]	[illegible]	[illegible]	[illegible]	[illegible]	[illegible]	[illegible]	[illegible]	[illegible]	[illegible]	[illegible]	[illegible]	[illegible]
Having Arms or Ammunition without licence in a Proclaimed District	[illegible]	[illegible]	[illegible]	[illegible]	[illegible]	[illegible]	[illegible]	[illegible]	[illegible]	[illegible]	[illegible]	[illegible]	[illegible]	[illegible]
Offences against the Game Laws	[illegible]	[illegible]	[illegible]	[illegible]	[illegible]	[illegible]	[illegible]	[illegible]	[illegible]	[illegible]	[illegible]	[illegible]	[illegible]	[illegible]
Being at large under sentence of Transportation or Penal Servitude	[illegible]	[illegible]	[illegible]	[illegible]	[illegible]	[illegible]	[illegible]	[illegible]	[illegible]	[illegible]	[illegible]	[illegible]	[illegible]	[illegible]
Perjury, and subornation of Perjury	[illegible]	[illegible]	[illegible]	[illegible]	[illegible]	[illegible]	[illegible]	[illegible]	[illegible]	[illegible]	[illegible]	[illegible]	[illegible]	[illegible]
Riot, Breach of the Peace, &c.	[illegible]	[illegible]	[illegible]	[illegible]	[illegible]	[illegible]	[illegible]	[illegible]	[illegible]	[illegible]	[illegible]	[illegible]	[illegible]	[illegible]
Keeping Disorderly Houses	[illegible]	[illegible]	[illegible]	[illegible]	[illegible]	[illegible]	[illegible]	[illegible]	[illegible]	[illegible]	[illegible]	[illegible]	[illegible]	[illegible]
Indecently Exposing the Person	[illegible]	[illegible]	[illegible]	[illegible]	[illegible]	[illegible]	[illegible]	[illegible]	[illegible]	[illegible]	[illegible]	[illegible]	[illegible]	[illegible]
Suicide, attempting to commit	[illegible]	[illegible]	[illegible]	[illegible]	[illegible]	[illegible]	[illegible]	[illegible]	[illegible]	[illegible]	[illegible]	[illegible]	[illegible]	[illegible]
Other Felonies not included in the above	[illegible]	[illegible]	[illegible]	[illegible]	[illegible]	[illegible]	[illegible]	[illegible]	[illegible]	[illegible]	[illegible]	[illegible]	[illegible]	[illegible]
Other Misdemeanours not included in the above	[illegible]	[illegible]	[illegible]	[illegible]	[illegible]	[illegible]	[illegible]	[illegible]	[illegible]	[illegible]	[illegible]	[illegible]	[illegible]	[illegible]
Total of No. 6	[illegible]	[illegible]	[illegible]	[illegible]	[illegible]	[illegible]	[illegible]	[illegible]	[illegible]	[illegible]	[illegible]	[illegible]	[illegible]	[illegible]
GRAND TOTAL	[illegible]	[illegible]	[illegible]	[illegible]	[illegible]	[illegible]	[illegible]	[illegible]	[illegible]	[illegible]	[illegible]	[illegible]	[illegible]	[illegible]

EACH OFFENCE and CLASS of OFFENCES the NUMBER of PERSONS for TRIAL in the Year [illegible], and the [illegible] by Clerks of the Crown and Clerks of the Peace.

Offences (Charged in [illegible], and of which [illegible] Convicted or Acquitted)	[illegible] M.	[illegible] F.	[illegible] M.	[illegible] F.	Death M.	Death F.	Life M.	Life F.	Above [illegible] Years M.	Above [illegible] Years F.	[illegible] Years M.	[illegible] Years F.	[illegible] Years M.	[illegible] Years F.	[illegible] Year M.	[illegible] Year F.
No. 1.—Offences against the Person.																
[illegible]	[illegible]	[illegible]	[illegible]	[illegible]	[illegible]	[illegible]	[illegible]	[illegible]	[illegible]	[illegible]	[illegible]	[illegible]	[illegible]	[illegible]	[illegible]	[illegible]
Total of No. 1.	[illegible]	[illegible]	[illegible]	[illegible]	[illegible]	[illegible]	[illegible]	[illegible]	[illegible]	[illegible]	[illegible]	[illegible]	[illegible]	[illegible]	[illegible]	[illegible]
No. 2.—Offences against Property, with Violence.																
[illegible]	[illegible]	[illegible]	[illegible]	[illegible]	[illegible]	[illegible]	[illegible]	[illegible]	[illegible]	[illegible]	[illegible]	[illegible]	[illegible]	[illegible]	[illegible]	[illegible]
Total of No. 2.	[illegible]	[illegible]	[illegible]	[illegible]	[illegible]	[illegible]	[illegible]	[illegible]	[illegible]	[illegible]	[illegible]	[illegible]	[illegible]	[illegible]	[illegible]	[illegible]
No. 3.—Offences against Property, without Violence.																
[illegible]	[illegible]	[illegible]	[illegible]	[illegible]	[illegible]	[illegible]	[illegible]	[illegible]	[illegible]	[illegible]	[illegible]	[illegible]	[illegible]	[illegible]	[illegible]	[illegible]
Total of No. 3.	[illegible]	[illegible]	[illegible]	[illegible]	[illegible]	[illegible]	[illegible]	[illegible]	[illegible]	[illegible]	[illegible]	[illegible]	[illegible]	[illegible]	[illegible]	[illegible]
No. 4.—Malicious Offences against Property.																
[illegible]	[illegible]	[illegible]	[illegible]	[illegible]	[illegible]	[illegible]	[illegible]	[illegible]	[illegible]	[illegible]	[illegible]	[illegible]	[illegible]	[illegible]	[illegible]	[illegible]
Total of No. 4.	[illegible]	[illegible]	[illegible]	[illegible]	[illegible]	[illegible]	[illegible]	[illegible]	[illegible]	[illegible]	[illegible]	[illegible]	[illegible]	[illegible]	[illegible]	[illegible]
No. 5.—Forgery and Offences against the Currency.																
[illegible]	[illegible]	[illegible]	[illegible]	[illegible]	[illegible]	[illegible]	[illegible]	[illegible]	[illegible]	[illegible]	[illegible]	[illegible]	[illegible]	[illegible]	[illegible]	[illegible]
Total of No. 5.	[illegible]	[illegible]	[illegible]	[illegible]	[illegible]	[illegible]	[illegible]	[illegible]	[illegible]	[illegible]	[illegible]	[illegible]	[illegible]	[illegible]	[illegible]	[illegible]
No. 6.—Offences not included in the above Classes.																
[illegible]	[illegible]	[illegible]	[illegible]	[illegible]	[illegible]	[illegible]	[illegible]	[illegible]	[illegible]	[illegible]	[illegible]	[illegible]	[illegible]	[illegible]	[illegible]	[illegible]
Total of No. 6.	[illegible]	[illegible]	[illegible]	[illegible]	[illegible]	[illegible]	[illegible]	[illegible]	[illegible]	[illegible]	[illegible]	[illegible]	[illegible]	[illegible]	[illegible]	[illegible]
GRAND TOTAL	[illegible]	[illegible]	[illegible]	[illegible]	[illegible]	[illegible]	[illegible]	[illegible]	[illegible]	[illegible]	[illegible]	[illegible]	[illegible]	[illegible]	[illegible]	[illegible]

[Continued on next page.

TABLE 24.—continued.—CRIMINAL PROCEEDINGS AT ASSIZES, COMMISSION, AND QUARTER SESSIONS.— and the RESULT of the PROCEEDINGS—Seven Years

OFFENCES Charged in Commitments or Indictments, and of which those Tried were Convicted or Acquitted.	CONVICTED.											
	Imprisonment, with or without Hard Labour, Whipping, Fine, &c.										Whipping, Fine, and Discharged on [illegible]	
	Above 3 Years		3 Years and above 2		2 Years and above 1		1 Year and above 6 Months		6 Months and under			
	M.	W.	M.	W.	M.	W.	M.	W.	M.	W.	M.	W.
No. 1.—Offences against the Person.												
Murder of Infants aged one year and under	[illegible]	[illegible]	[illegible]	[illegible]	[illegible]	[illegible]	[illegible]	[illegible]	[illegible]	[illegible]	[illegible]	[illegible]
Other Murders	[illegible]	[illegible]	[illegible]	[illegible]	[illegible]	[illegible]	[illegible]	[illegible]	[illegible]	[illegible]	[illegible]	[illegible]
Attempts to Murder	[illegible]	[illegible]	[illegible]	[illegible]	[illegible]	[illegible]	[illegible]	[illegible]	[illegible]	[illegible]	[illegible]	[illegible]
Shooting at, Wounding, Stabbing, &c. to do bodily harm	[illegible]	[illegible]	[illegible]	[illegible]	[illegible]	[illegible]	[illegible]	[illegible]	[illegible]	[illegible]	[illegible]	[illegible]
Conspiracy to Murder	[illegible]	[illegible]	[illegible]	[illegible]	[illegible]	[illegible]	[illegible]	[illegible]	[illegible]	[illegible]	[illegible]	[illegible]
Manslaughter	[illegible]	[illegible]	[illegible]	[illegible]	[illegible]	[illegible]	[illegible]	[illegible]	[illegible]	[illegible]	[illegible]	[illegible]
Concealing the Birth of Infants	[illegible]	[illegible]	[illegible]	[illegible]	[illegible]	[illegible]	[illegible]	[illegible]	[illegible]	[illegible]	[illegible]	[illegible]
Sodomy and Bestiality	[illegible]	[illegible]	[illegible]	[illegible]	[illegible]	[illegible]	[illegible]	[illegible]	[illegible]	[illegible]	[illegible]	[illegible]
——— Attempts to Commit, and other unnatural Misdemeanors	[illegible]	[illegible]	[illegible]	[illegible]	[illegible]	[illegible]	[illegible]	[illegible]	[illegible]	[illegible]	[illegible]	[illegible]
Rape	[illegible]	[illegible]	[illegible]	[illegible]	[illegible]	[illegible]	[illegible]	[illegible]	[illegible]	[illegible]	[illegible]	[illegible]
——— Assaults, with intent to ravish and abuse	[illegible]	[illegible]	[illegible]	[illegible]	[illegible]	[illegible]	[illegible]	[illegible]	[illegible]	[illegible]	[illegible]	[illegible]
Bigamy	[illegible]	[illegible]	[illegible]	[illegible]	[illegible]	[illegible]	[illegible]	[illegible]	[illegible]	[illegible]	[illegible]	[illegible]
Child Stealing	[illegible]	[illegible]	[illegible]	[illegible]	[illegible]	[illegible]	[illegible]	[illegible]	[illegible]	[illegible]	[illegible]	[illegible]
Unlawfully abandoning Children under two years of age	[illegible]	[illegible]	[illegible]	[illegible]	[illegible]	[illegible]	[illegible]	[illegible]	[illegible]	[illegible]	[illegible]	[illegible]
Endangering the Safety of Passengers on Railways	[illegible]	[illegible]	[illegible]	[illegible]	[illegible]	[illegible]	[illegible]	[illegible]	[illegible]	[illegible]	[illegible]	[illegible]
Assault and inflicting bodily harm	[illegible]	[illegible]	[illegible]	[illegible]	[illegible]	[illegible]	[illegible]	[illegible]	[illegible]	[illegible]	[illegible]	[illegible]
Assaults, common	[illegible]	[illegible]	[illegible]	[illegible]	[illegible]	[illegible]	[illegible]	[illegible]	[illegible]	[illegible]	[illegible]	[illegible]
Assaults on Peace Officers	[illegible]	[illegible]	[illegible]	[illegible]	[illegible]	[illegible]	[illegible]	[illegible]	[illegible]	[illegible]	[illegible]	[illegible]
Total of No. 1	[illegible]	[illegible]	[illegible]	[illegible]	[illegible]	[illegible]	[illegible]	[illegible]	[illegible]	[illegible]	[illegible]	[illegible]
No. 2.—Offences against Property, with Violence.												
Sacrilege	[illegible]	[illegible]	[illegible]	[illegible]	[illegible]	[illegible]	[illegible]	[illegible]	[illegible]	[illegible]	[illegible]	[illegible]
Burglary and Housebreaking	[illegible]	[illegible]	[illegible]	[illegible]	[illegible]	[illegible]	[illegible]	[illegible]	[illegible]	[illegible]	[illegible]	[illegible]
Breaking into Shops, Warehouses, &c.	[illegible]	[illegible]	[illegible]	[illegible]	[illegible]	[illegible]	[illegible]	[illegible]	[illegible]	[illegible]	[illegible]	[illegible]
Attempts to break into Houses, Shops, Warehouses, &c.	[illegible]	[illegible]	[illegible]	[illegible]	[illegible]	[illegible]	[illegible]	[illegible]	[illegible]	[illegible]	[illegible]	[illegible]
Robbery	[illegible]	[illegible]	[illegible]	[illegible]	[illegible]	[illegible]	[illegible]	[illegible]	[illegible]	[illegible]	[illegible]	[illegible]
Attempts to rob, and demanding Money by Menaces	[illegible]	[illegible]	[illegible]	[illegible]	[illegible]	[illegible]	[illegible]	[illegible]	[illegible]	[illegible]	[illegible]	[illegible]
Total of No. 2	[illegible]	[illegible]	[illegible]	[illegible]	[illegible]	[illegible]	[illegible]	[illegible]	[illegible]	[illegible]	[illegible]	[illegible]
No. 3.—Offences against Property, without Violence.												
Cattle Stealing	[illegible]	[illegible]	[illegible]	[illegible]	[illegible]	[illegible]	[illegible]	[illegible]	[illegible]	[illegible]	[illegible]	[illegible]
Horse Stealing	[illegible]	[illegible]	[illegible]	[illegible]	[illegible]	[illegible]	[illegible]	[illegible]	[illegible]	[illegible]	[illegible]	[illegible]
Sheep Stealing	[illegible]	[illegible]	[illegible]	[illegible]	[illegible]	[illegible]	[illegible]	[illegible]	[illegible]	[illegible]	[illegible]	[illegible]
Larceny, to the value of 5l. in Dwelling-houses	[illegible]	[illegible]	[illegible]	[illegible]	[illegible]	[illegible]	[illegible]	[illegible]	[illegible]	[illegible]	[illegible]	[illegible]
Larceny, from the Person	[illegible]	[illegible]	[illegible]	[illegible]	[illegible]	[illegible]	[illegible]	[illegible]	[illegible]	[illegible]	[illegible]	[illegible]
Larceny, by Servants	[illegible]	[illegible]	[illegible]	[illegible]	[illegible]	[illegible]	[illegible]	[illegible]	[illegible]	[illegible]	[illegible]	[illegible]
Larceny, Simple	[illegible]	[illegible]	[illegible]	[illegible]	[illegible]	[illegible]	[illegible]	[illegible]	[illegible]	[illegible]	[illegible]	[illegible]
Larceny on Rivers, Canals, Wharfs, &c.	[illegible]	[illegible]	[illegible]	[illegible]	[illegible]	[illegible]	[illegible]	[illegible]	[illegible]	[illegible]	[illegible]	[illegible]
Stealing Fixtures, Shrubs growing, &c.	[illegible]	[illegible]	[illegible]	[illegible]	[illegible]	[illegible]	[illegible]	[illegible]	[illegible]	[illegible]	[illegible]	[illegible]
Attempts at the above	[illegible]	[illegible]	[illegible]	[illegible]	[illegible]	[illegible]	[illegible]	[illegible]	[illegible]	[illegible]	[illegible]	[illegible]
Embezzlement	[illegible]	[illegible]	[illegible]	[illegible]	[illegible]	[illegible]	[illegible]	[illegible]	[illegible]	[illegible]	[illegible]	[illegible]
Larceny by Servants of the Post Office	[illegible]	[illegible]	[illegible]	[illegible]	[illegible]	[illegible]	[illegible]	[illegible]	[illegible]	[illegible]	[illegible]	[illegible]
Receiving Stolen Goods	[illegible]	[illegible]	[illegible]	[illegible]	[illegible]	[illegible]	[illegible]	[illegible]	[illegible]	[illegible]	[illegible]	[illegible]
Fraudulently obtaining Goods by false pretences and attempts to defraud	[illegible]	[illegible]	[illegible]	[illegible]	[illegible]	[illegible]	[illegible]	[illegible]	[illegible]	[illegible]	[illegible]	[illegible]
Total of No. 3	[illegible]	[illegible]	[illegible]	[illegible]	[illegible]	[illegible]	[illegible]	[illegible]	[illegible]	[illegible]	[illegible]	[illegible]
No. 4.—Malicious Offences against Property.												
Arson and other Wilful Burning	[illegible]	[illegible]	[illegible]	[illegible]	[illegible]	[illegible]	[illegible]	[illegible]	[illegible]	[illegible]	[illegible]	[illegible]
[illegible] Buildings, &c.	[illegible]	[illegible]	[illegible]	[illegible]	[illegible]	[illegible]	[illegible]	[illegible]	[illegible]	[illegible]	[illegible]	[illegible]
Destroying Goods in process of Manufacture	[illegible]	[illegible]	[illegible]	[illegible]	[illegible]	[illegible]	[illegible]	[illegible]	[illegible]	[illegible]	[illegible]	[illegible]
Destroying Trees, Shrubs, &c., growing	[illegible]	[illegible]	[illegible]	[illegible]	[illegible]	[illegible]	[illegible]	[illegible]	[illegible]	[illegible]	[illegible]	[illegible]
Killing and Maiming Cattle	[illegible]	[illegible]	[illegible]	[illegible]	[illegible]	[illegible]	[illegible]	[illegible]	[illegible]	[illegible]	[illegible]	[illegible]
Malicious Injuries to Property exceeding 5l. in value	[illegible]	[illegible]	[illegible]	[illegible]	[illegible]	[illegible]	[illegible]	[illegible]	[illegible]	[illegible]	[illegible]	[illegible]
Other Wilful and Malicious Injuries to Property	[illegible]	[illegible]	[illegible]	[illegible]	[illegible]	[illegible]	[illegible]	[illegible]	[illegible]	[illegible]	[illegible]	[illegible]
Total of No. 4	[illegible]	[illegible]	[illegible]	[illegible]	[illegible]	[illegible]	[illegible]	[illegible]	[illegible]	[illegible]	[illegible]	[illegible]
No. 5.—Forgery and Offences against the Currency.												
Forging and uttering Forged Instruments	[illegible]	[illegible]	[illegible]	[illegible]	[illegible]	[illegible]	[illegible]	[illegible]	[illegible]	[illegible]	[illegible]	[illegible]
Having in Possession Forged Bank Notes	[illegible]	[illegible]	[illegible]	[illegible]	[illegible]	[illegible]	[illegible]	[illegible]	[illegible]	[illegible]	[illegible]	[illegible]
Coining, and having in possession Implements for Coining	[illegible]	[illegible]	[illegible]	[illegible]	[illegible]	[illegible]	[illegible]	[illegible]	[illegible]	[illegible]	[illegible]	[illegible]
Uttering, putting off, and having in possession Counterfeit Coin	[illegible]	[illegible]	[illegible]	[illegible]	[illegible]	[illegible]	[illegible]	[illegible]	[illegible]	[illegible]	[illegible]	[illegible]
Total of No. 5	[illegible]	[illegible]	[illegible]	[illegible]	[illegible]	[illegible]	[illegible]	[illegible]	[illegible]	[illegible]	[illegible]	[illegible]
No. 6.—Offences not included in the above Classes.												
Offences against the Queen's Authority and Person	[illegible]	[illegible]	[illegible]	[illegible]	[illegible]	[illegible]	[illegible]	[illegible]	[illegible]	[illegible]	[illegible]	[illegible]
Intimidation by Threatening Letters, Notices, or otherwise	[illegible]	[illegible]	[illegible]	[illegible]	[illegible]	[illegible]	[illegible]	[illegible]	[illegible]	[illegible]	[illegible]	[illegible]
Having Arms or Ammunition without License in a Proclaimed District	[illegible]	[illegible]	[illegible]	[illegible]	[illegible]	[illegible]	[illegible]	[illegible]	[illegible]	[illegible]	[illegible]	[illegible]
Offences against the Game Laws	[illegible]	[illegible]	[illegible]	[illegible]	[illegible]	[illegible]	[illegible]	[illegible]	[illegible]	[illegible]	[illegible]	[illegible]
Being at large under Sentence of Transportation or Penal Servitude	[illegible]	[illegible]	[illegible]	[illegible]	[illegible]	[illegible]	[illegible]	[illegible]	[illegible]	[illegible]	[illegible]	[illegible]
Perjury, and Subornation of Perjury	[illegible]	[illegible]	[illegible]	[illegible]	[illegible]	[illegible]	[illegible]	[illegible]	[illegible]	[illegible]	[illegible]	[illegible]
Riot, Breach of the Peace, &c.	[illegible]	[illegible]	[illegible]	[illegible]	[illegible]	[illegible]	[illegible]	[illegible]	[illegible]	[illegible]	[illegible]	[illegible]
Keeping Disorderly Houses	[illegible]	[illegible]	[illegible]	[illegible]	[illegible]	[illegible]	[illegible]	[illegible]	[illegible]	[illegible]	[illegible]	[illegible]
Indecently Exposing the Person	[illegible]	[illegible]	[illegible]	[illegible]	[illegible]	[illegible]	[illegible]	[illegible]	[illegible]	[illegible]	[illegible]	[illegible]
Suicide, attempting to commit	[illegible]	[illegible]	[illegible]	[illegible]	[illegible]	[illegible]	[illegible]	[illegible]	[illegible]	[illegible]	[illegible]	[illegible]
Other Offences not included in the above	[illegible]	[illegible]	[illegible]	[illegible]	[illegible]	[illegible]	[illegible]	[illegible]	[illegible]	[illegible]	[illegible]	[illegible]
Other Misdemeanours not included in the above	[illegible]	[illegible]	[illegible]	[illegible]	[illegible]	[illegible]	[illegible]	[illegible]	[illegible]	[illegible]	[illegible]	[illegible]
Total of No. 6	[illegible]	[illegible]	[illegible]	[illegible]	[illegible]	[illegible]	[illegible]	[illegible]	[illegible]	[illegible]	[illegible]	[illegible]
Grand Total	[illegible]	[illegible]	[illegible]	[illegible]	[illegible]	[illegible]	[illegible]	[illegible]	[illegible]	[illegible]	[illegible]	[illegible]

[illegible] EACH OFFENCE and CLASS of OFFENCES the NUMBERS of PERSONS for TRIAL in the Year [illegible], made by Clerks of the Crown and Clerks of the Peace.

[illegible]		[illegible]		[illegible]		[illegible]		[illegible]		[illegible]		OFFENCES [illegible]
M.	W.	M.	W.	M.	W.	M.	W.	M.	W.	M.	W.	No. 1.—Offences against the Person.
[illegible]	[illegible]	[illegible]	[illegible]	[illegible]	[illegible]	[illegible]	[illegible]	[illegible]	[illegible]	[illegible]	[illegible]	[illegible]
[illegible]	[illegible]	[illegible]	[illegible]	[illegible]	[illegible]	[illegible]	[illegible]	[illegible]	[illegible]	[illegible]	[illegible]	Total of No. 1.
												No. 2.—Offences against Property, with Violence.
[illegible]	[illegible]	[illegible]	[illegible]	[illegible]	[illegible]	[illegible]	[illegible]	[illegible]	[illegible]	[illegible]	[illegible]	[illegible]
[illegible]	[illegible]	[illegible]	[illegible]	[illegible]	[illegible]	[illegible]	[illegible]	[illegible]	[illegible]	[illegible]	[illegible]	Total of No. 2.
												No. 3.—Offences against Property, without Violence.
[illegible]	[illegible]	[illegible]	[illegible]	[illegible]	[illegible]	[illegible]	[illegible]	[illegible]	[illegible]	[illegible]	[illegible]	[illegible]
[illegible]	[illegible]	[illegible]	[illegible]	[illegible]	[illegible]	[illegible]	[illegible]	[illegible]	[illegible]	[illegible]	[illegible]	Total of No. 3.
												No. 4.—[illegible] Offences against Property.
[illegible]	[illegible]	[illegible]	[illegible]	[illegible]	[illegible]	[illegible]	[illegible]	[illegible]	[illegible]	[illegible]	[illegible]	[illegible]
[illegible]	[illegible]	[illegible]	[illegible]	[illegible]	[illegible]	[illegible]	[illegible]	[illegible]	[illegible]	[illegible]	[illegible]	Total of No. 4.
												No. 5.—Forgery and Offences against the Currency.
[illegible]	[illegible]	[illegible]	[illegible]	[illegible]	[illegible]	[illegible]	[illegible]	[illegible]	[illegible]	[illegible]	[illegible]	[illegible]
[illegible]	[illegible]	[illegible]	[illegible]	[illegible]	[illegible]	[illegible]	[illegible]	[illegible]	[illegible]	[illegible]	[illegible]	Total of No. 5.
												No. 6.—Offences not included in the above Classes.
[illegible]	[illegible]	[illegible]	[illegible]	[illegible]	[illegible]	[illegible]	[illegible]	[illegible]	[illegible]	[illegible]	[illegible]	[illegible]
[illegible]	[illegible]	[illegible]	[illegible]	[illegible]	[illegible]	[illegible]	[illegible]	[illegible]	[illegible]	[illegible]	[illegible]	Total of No. 6.
[illegible]	[illegible]	[illegible]	[illegible]	[illegible]	[illegible]	[illegible]	[illegible]	[illegible]	[illegible]	[illegible]	[illegible]	GRAND TOTAL.

[illegible]	[illegible]	[illegible]	[illegible]	[illegible]	[illegible]	[illegible]	[illegible]	[illegible]	[illegible]	[illegible]
[illegible]	[illegible]	[illegible]	[illegible]	[illegible]	[illegible]	[illegible]	[illegible]	[illegible]	[illegible]	[illegible]
[illegible]	[illegible]	[illegible]	[illegible]	[illegible]	[illegible]	[illegible]	[illegible]	[illegible]	[illegible]	[illegible]
[illegible]	[illegible]	[illegible]	[illegible]	[illegible]	[illegible]	[illegible]		—		
[illegible]	[illegible]	[illegible]	[illegible]	—			[illegible]	[illegible]	[illegible]	[illegible]
[illegible]	[illegible]	[illegible]	[illegible]	[illegible]	[illegible]	[illegible]	[illegible]	[illegible]	[illegible]	[illegible]
[illegible]	[illegible]	[illegible]	[illegible]				[illegible]	[illegible]	[illegible]	[illegible]
[illegible]	[illegible]	[illegible]	[illegible]	[illegible]	[illegible]	[illegible]	[illegible]	[illegible]	[illegible]	[illegible]
[illegible]	[illegible]	[illegible]	[illegible]	[illegible]	[illegible]	[illegible]	[illegible]	[illegible]	[illegible]	[illegible]
	—							—		
[illegible]	[illegible]	[illegible]	[illegible]	[illegible]	[illegible]	[illegible]		[illegible]	[illegible]	[illegible]
[illegible]	[illegible]	[illegible]	[illegible]	[illegible]	[illegible]	[illegible]		—		
[illegible]	[illegible]	[illegible]	[illegible]	[illegible]	[illegible]	[illegible]	[illegible]	[illegible]	[illegible]	[illegible]
[illegible]	[illegible]	[illegible]	[illegible]				[illegible]	[illegible]	[illegible]	[illegible]
[illegible]	[illegible]	[illegible]	[illegible]	[illegible]	[illegible]	[illegible]		—		
[illegible]	[illegible]	[illegible]	[illegible]	[illegible]	[illegible]	[illegible]	[illegible]	[illegible]	[illegible]	[illegible]
[illegible]	[illegible]	[illegible]	[illegible]	[illegible]	[illegible]	[illegible]	[illegible]	[illegible]	[illegible]	[illegible]
[illegible]	[illegible]	[illegible]	[illegible]				[illegible]	[illegible]	[illegible]	[illegible]
[illegible]	[illegible]	[illegible]	[illegible]	[illegible]	[illegible]	[illegible]	[illegible]	[illegible]	[illegible]	[illegible]
[illegible]	[illegible]	[illegible]	[illegible]	[illegible]	[illegible]	[illegible]	[illegible]	[illegible]	[illegible]	[illegible]
[illegible]	[illegible]	[illegible]	[illegible]	[illegible]	[illegible]	[illegible]	[illegible]	[illegible]	[illegible]	[illegible]
[illegible]	[illegible]	[illegible]	[illegible]	[illegible]	[illegible]	[illegible]	[illegible]	[illegible]	[illegible]	[illegible]
[illegible]	[illegible]	[illegible]	[illegible]	[illegible]	[illegible]	[illegible]		—		
[illegible]	[illegible]	[illegible]	[illegible]	[illegible]	[illegible]	[illegible]	[illegible]	[illegible]	[illegible]	[illegible]
[illegible]	[illegible]	[illegible]	[illegible]	[illegible]	[illegible]	[illegible]	[illegible]	[illegible]	[illegible]	[illegible]
[illegible]	[illegible]	[illegible]	[illegible]	[illegible]	[illegible]	[illegible]	[illegible]	[illegible]	[illegible]	[illegible]
[illegible]	[illegible]	[illegible]	[illegible]	[illegible]	[illegible]	[illegible]	[illegible]	[illegible]	[illegible]	[illegible]

by Her Majesty's Treasury for Criminal Prosecutions at Assizes, the Dublin Commission Court, and Quarter Sessions [illegible] Amount of Costs under each Head, from Returns made by Crown Solicitors and County and City [illegible] Officers.

At Assizes		At Quarter Sessions		At Petty Sessions and Police Courts		Under Criminal Justice Act [illegible]		Total	Counties, and Counties of Cities and of Towns
Number of Prosecutors and Witnesses Paid	Amount Paid	Number of Prosecutors and Witnesses Paid	Amount Paid	Number of Prosecutors and Witnesses Paid	Amount Paid	Number of Prosecutors and Witnesses Paid	Amount Paid		
	£ s. d.		£ s. d.		£ s. d.		£ s. d.	£ s. d.	
[illegible]	[illegible]	[illegible]	[illegible]	[illegible]	[illegible]	.	—	[illegible]	Antrim, including Co. of Town of Carrickfergus.
[illegible]	[illegible]	[illegible]	[illegible]	[illegible]	[illegible]	.	—	[illegible]	Armagh.
[illegible]	[illegible]	[illegible]	[illegible]	[illegible]	[illegible]	.	—	[illegible]	Carlow
[illegible]	[illegible]	[illegible]	[illegible]		—	.	—	[illegible]	Cavan
[illegible]	[illegible]	[illegible]	[illegible]	[illegible]	[illegible]	.	—	[illegible]	Clare
[illegible]	[illegible]	[illegible]	[illegible]	[illegible]	[illegible]	.	—	[illegible]	Cork County.
[illegible]	[illegible]	[illegible]	[illegible]	[illegible]	[illegible]	.	—		Cork City
[illegible]	[illegible]	[illegible]	[illegible]	[illegible]	[illegible]	.	—	[illegible]	Donegal.
[illegible]	[illegible]	[illegible]	[illegible]	[illegible]	[illegible]	.	—	[illegible]	Down
[illegible]	[illegible]	[illegible]	[illegible]	[illegible]	[illegible]	.	—	[illegible]	Drogheda Town
[illegible]	[illegible]	[illegible]	[illegible]	[illegible]	[illegible]	.	—	[illegible]	Dublin County.
[illegible]	[illegible]	[illegible]	[illegible]	[illegible]	[illegible]	.	—		Dublin City.
[illegible]	[illegible]	[illegible]	[illegible]	[illegible]	[illegible]	.	—	[illegible]	Fermanagh
[illegible]	[illegible]	[illegible]	[illegible]	.	—	.	—	[illegible]	Galway County.
[illegible]	[illegible]	[illegible]	[illegible]	.	—	.	—		Galway Town
[illegible]	[illegible]	[illegible]	[illegible]	[illegible]	[illegible]	.	—	[illegible]	Kerry
[illegible]	[illegible]	[illegible]	[illegible]	[illegible]	[illegible]	.	—	[illegible]	Kildare
[illegible]	[illegible]	[illegible]	[illegible]	[illegible]	[illegible]	.	—	[illegible]	Kilkenny County.
[illegible]	[illegible]	[illegible]	[illegible]	[illegible]	[illegible]	.	—		Kilkenny City.
[illegible]	[illegible]	[illegible]	[illegible]	[illegible]	[illegible]	.	—	[illegible]	King's County.
[illegible]	[illegible]	[illegible]	[illegible]	.	—	.	—	[illegible]	Leitrim
[illegible]	[illegible]	[illegible]	[illegible]	.	—	.	—	[illegible]	Limerick County
[illegible]	[illegible]	[illegible]	[illegible]	[illegible]	[illegible]	.	—		Limerick City
[illegible]	[illegible]	[illegible]	[illegible]	[illegible]	[illegible]	.	—	[illegible]	Londonderry.
[illegible]	[illegible]	[illegible]	[illegible]	.	—	.	—	[illegible]	Longford
[illegible]	[illegible]	[illegible]	[illegible]	[illegible]	[illegible]	.	—	[illegible]	Louth
[illegible]	[illegible]	[illegible]	[illegible]	[illegible]	[illegible]	.	—	[illegible]	Mayo
[illegible]	[illegible]	[illegible]	[illegible]	[illegible]	[illegible]	.	—	[illegible]	Meath
[illegible]	[illegible]	[illegible]	[illegible]	[illegible]	[illegible]	.	—	[illegible]	Monaghan.
[illegible]	[illegible]	[illegible]	[illegible]	[illegible]	[illegible]	.	.	[illegible]	Queen's County.
[illegible]	[illegible]	[illegible]	[illegible]	.	—	.	—	[illegible]	Roscommon.
[illegible]	[illegible]	[illegible]	[illegible]	[illegible]	[illegible]	.	—	[illegible]	Sligo
[illegible]	[illegible]	[illegible]	[illegible]	.	—	.	—	[illegible]	Tipperary, North Riding.
[illegible]	[illegible]	[illegible]	[illegible]	[illegible]	[illegible]	.	—		Tipperary, South Riding.
[illegible]	[illegible]	[illegible]	[illegible]	.	—	.	—	[illegible]	Tyrone.
[illegible]	[illegible]	[illegible]	[illegible]	[illegible]	[illegible]	.	—	[illegible]	Waterford County.
[illegible]	[illegible]	[illegible]	[illegible]	[illegible]	[illegible]	.	—		Waterford City.
[illegible]	[illegible]	[illegible]	[illegible]	.	[illegible]	.	—	[illegible]	Westmeath.
[illegible]	[illegible]	[illegible]	[illegible]	[illegible]	[illegible]	.	—	[illegible]	Wexford
[illegible]	[illegible]	[illegible]	[illegible]	.	—	[illegible]	[illegible]	[illegible]	Wicklow
[illegible]	[illegible]	[illegible]	[illegible]	[illegible]	[illegible]	[illegible]	[illegible]	[illegible]	Total

[illegible]

TABLE 20.—REFORMATORY SCHOOLS.—RETURN showing AGE, STATE of INSTRUCTION, previous COMMITMENTS, and SOCIAL CONDITION of the BOYS and GIRLS received, under Sect. 21 & 22 Vic., c. [illegible], into Reformatory Schools during the Year 18[illegible], made by the Inspector of Reformatory and Industrial Schools.

SCHOOLS.	Total.	Ages when Admitted: 12 and under.	12 to 13.	13 to 14.	14 to 16.	State of Instruction on Admission: Neither read nor write.	Read or read and write imperfectly.	Read and write well.	Superior instruction.	[illegible]	Previously committed to any Prison: Once.	Twice.	Thrice and upwards.	Not previously committed.	Social Condition on Admission: Illegitimate.	Both Parents dead.	Father dead.	Mother dead.	Deserted or Parents not to be found.	One or both Parents destitute of character.	Both Parents alive, and not included in any of the foregoing.
Boys.																					
Malone, Belfast,	20	2	5	10	3	5	11	4	-	-	7	1	-	14	1	-	7	2	1	1	9
Upton, Co. Cork,	16	-	1	13	1	21	6	-	-	-	4	3	1	25	-	1	7	4	1	3	13
[illegible] place, Dublin,	5	-	-	5	-	3	2	1	-	-	-	-	-	4	-	1	-	-	-	1	2
Philipstown, King's Co.,	43	6	17	19	10	20	11	3	-	-	5	5	-	27	4	1	5	6	2	10	13
Glencree, Co. Wicklow,	50	4	13	16	16	29	20	16	-	-	6	6	-	27	3	10	9	3	5	13	16
Total,	130	13	31	45	30	21	50	24	-	-	14	6	1	111	10	10	15	22	17	24	56
Girls.																					
[illegible], Dublin,	3	-	-	3	-	1	-	-	-	-	-	-	-	3	-	-	-	-	-	3	-
High Park, Dublin,	20	-	3	11	1	17	4	1	-	-	-	-	-	10	-	1	1	5	1	1	10
Ballinasloe,	8	1	5	-	-	1	5	-	-	-	-	-	-	3	-	-	-	-	-	5	6
Limerick,	8	-	5	1	6	7	3	5	-	-	-	-	-	6	-	-	-	-	2	-	6
Monaghan,	15	-	4	1	1	10	2	-	-	-	1	-	-	11	-	-	3	-	1	7	6
Total,	45	1	9	25	10	20	14	16	-	-	1	-	-	44	-	1	1	1	4	13	28
Total Boys and Girls,	175	14	40	[illegible]	[illegible]	[illegible]	[illegible]	[illegible]	-	-	15	6	1	[illegible]	10	[illegible]	16	23	21	37	[illegible]

TABLE 31.—REFORMATORY SCHOOLS.—RETURN showing the NUMBER of BOYS and GIRLS UNDER DETENTION, COMMITTED, DISCHARGED, and REMOVED in the Year [illegible], made by the Inspector of Reformatory and Industrial Schools.

Certified Schools, to which the Committals were made, with the Date of Certificate, and Religion of Children received in School.	Under Detention at Commencement of Year: In School	On Licence	In Prison	Absconded	Removed to Industrial School	Total	Admitted in Year: Committed	Recommitted	Discharged or Removed during Year: Transferred to other Schools	Discharged	Dead	Total Discharged or Removed	Under Detention at End of Year: In School	On Licence	In Prison	Absconded	Removed	Total	Average number of Inmates	Weekly Cost	Expenses in: Imperial Funds	Local Taxes	Other Sources
Boys.																				£ s. d.	£ s. d.	£ s. d.	£ s. d.
Malone, Belfast, County Antrim, [illegible] (Protestant).	[illegible]	[illegible]	[illegible]	[illegible]	–	[illegible]	[illegible]	–	–	[illegible]	–	[illegible]	[illegible]	[illegible]	[illegible]	[illegible]	–	[illegible]	[illegible]	[illegible]	[illegible]	[illegible]	[illegible]
St. Patrick's, Upton, County Cork, 4th July, [illegible] (Roman Catholic).	[illegible]	[illegible]	–	–	–	[illegible]	[illegible]	–	–	[illegible]	[illegible]	[illegible]	[illegible]	[illegible]	–	–	[illegible]	[illegible]	[illegible]	[illegible]	[illegible]	[illegible]	[illegible]
[illegible] place, Dublin, [illegible] November, [illegible] (Protestant).	[illegible]	–	–	–	[illegible]	[illegible]	[illegible]	–	–	[illegible]	–	[illegible]	[illegible]	[illegible]	–	[illegible]	[illegible]	[illegible]	[illegible]	[illegible]	[illegible]	[illegible]	[illegible]
King's County Reformatory School, Philipstown, [illegible] December, [illegible] (Roman Catholic).	[illegible]	[illegible]	[illegible]	[illegible]	–	[illegible]	[illegible]	–	–	[illegible]	–	[illegible]	[illegible]	[illegible]	–	[illegible]	–	[illegible]	[illegible]	[illegible]	[illegible]	[illegible]	[illegible]
St. Kevin's, Glencree, County Wicklow, [illegible] April, [illegible] (Roman Catholic).	[illegible]	[illegible]	–	[illegible]	–	[illegible]	[illegible]	–	–	[illegible]	[illegible]	[illegible]	[illegible]	[illegible]	[illegible]	–	–	[illegible]	[illegible]	[illegible]	[illegible]	[illegible]	[illegible]
Total Boys	[illegible]	[illegible]	[illegible]	[illegible]	[illegible]	[illegible]	[illegible]	–	–	[illegible]	[illegible]	[illegible]	[illegible]	[illegible]	[illegible]	[illegible]	[illegible]	[illegible]	[illegible]	[illegible]	[illegible]	[illegible]	[illegible]
Girls.																							
[illegible], Dublin, [illegible] April, [illegible] (Protestant).	[illegible]	–	–	–	–	[illegible]	[illegible]	–	–	[illegible]	–	[illegible]	[illegible]	[illegible]	–	–	–	[illegible]	[illegible]	[illegible]	[illegible]	[illegible]	[illegible]
High Park, Drumcondra, County Dublin, [illegible] (Roman Catholic).	[illegible]	[illegible]	–	–	[illegible]	[illegible]	[illegible]	[illegible]	[illegible]	[illegible]	–	[illegible]	[illegible]	–	–	–	–	[illegible]	[illegible]	[illegible]	[illegible]	[illegible]	[illegible]
St. Joseph's, Ballinasloe, County Galway, [illegible] (Roman Catholic).	[illegible]	[illegible]	–	–	[illegible]	[illegible]	[illegible]	–	[illegible]	[illegible]	[illegible]	[illegible]	[illegible]	–	–	–	–	[illegible]	[illegible]	[illegible]	[illegible]	[illegible]	[illegible]
St. Joseph's, Limerick, [illegible] January, [illegible] (Roman Catholic).	[illegible]	–	–	–	–	[illegible]	[illegible]	–	–	[illegible]	–	[illegible]	[illegible]	–	–	–	–	[illegible]	[illegible]	[illegible]	[illegible]	[illegible]	[illegible]
Spark's Lake, Monaghan, [illegible] July, [illegible] (Roman Catholic).	[illegible]	[illegible]	–	–	[illegible]	[illegible]	[illegible]	[illegible]	–	[illegible]	[illegible]	[illegible]	[illegible]	–	–	–	–	[illegible]	[illegible]	[illegible]	[illegible]	[illegible]	[illegible]
Total Girls	[illegible]	[illegible]	–	–	[illegible]	[illegible]	[illegible]	[illegible]	[illegible]	[illegible]	[illegible]	[illegible]	[illegible]	[illegible]	–	–	–	[illegible]	[illegible]	[illegible]	[illegible]	[illegible]	[illegible]
Total Boys and Girls	[illegible]	[illegible]	[illegible]	[illegible]	[illegible]	[illegible]	[illegible]	[illegible]	[illegible]	[illegible]	[illegible]	[illegible]	[illegible]	[illegible]	[illegible]	[illegible]	[illegible]	[illegible]	[illegible]	[illegible]	[illegible]	[illegible]	[illegible]

* These were not under Order of Detention, but were received with their own consent and provided with employment.

TABLE [illegible].—REFORMATORY SCHOOLS.—RETURN showing OCCASION of COMMITTALS and SENTENCES passed upon BOYS and GIRLS RECEIVED during the Year [illegible]. Made by the Inspector of Reformatories and Industrial Schools.

Reformatory Schools, in which the Commitments were made, with the Date of Certificate, and the Names of Children received in each School.	Commitments on Indictment and Summarily: On Indictment, by Judges of Assize Courts, Chairmen at Quarter Sessions, or Recorders	Summarily by Divisional Magistrates of Police, by Justices at Petty Sessions	Total Committed on Indictment and Summarily	Sentences: Previous Imprisonment: 14 Days	1 Month and above 14 Days	2 Months and above 1	6 Months and above 2	Above 6 Months	Term of Detention in Reformatory Schools: 3 Years	[illegible]	[illegible]	[illegible]
Boys.												
Malone, Belfast, [illegible] (Protestant),	[illegible]	[illegible]	[illegible]	[illegible]	[illegible]	[illegible]	[illegible]	[illegible]	[illegible]	[illegible]	[illegible]	[illegible]
St. Patrick's, Upton, County Cork, [illegible] July, [illegible] (Roman Catholic),	[illegible]	[illegible]	[illegible]	[illegible]	[illegible]	[illegible]	[illegible]	[illegible]	[illegible]	[illegible]	[illegible]	[illegible]
[illegible], Dublin, [illegible] (Protestant),	[illegible]	[illegible]	[illegible]	[illegible]	[illegible]	[illegible]	[illegible]	[illegible]	[illegible]	[illegible]	[illegible]	[illegible]
[illegible], King's County, [illegible] December, [illegible] (Roman Catholic),	[illegible]	[illegible]	[illegible]	[illegible]	[illegible]	[illegible]	[illegible]	[illegible]	[illegible]	[illegible]	[illegible]	[illegible]
St. Kevin's, Glencree, [illegible] April, [illegible] (Roman Catholic),	[illegible]	[illegible]	[illegible]	[illegible]	[illegible]	[illegible]	[illegible]	[illegible]	[illegible]	[illegible]	[illegible]	[illegible]
Total Boys,	[illegible]	[illegible]	[illegible]	[illegible]	[illegible]	[illegible]	[illegible]	[illegible]	[illegible]	[illegible]	[illegible]	[illegible]
Girls.												
[illegible], Dublin, [illegible] April, [illegible] (Protestant),	[illegible]	[illegible]	[illegible]	[illegible]	[illegible]	[illegible]	[illegible]	[illegible]	[illegible]	[illegible]	[illegible]	[illegible]
[illegible] Park, Drumcondra, County Dublin, [illegible] December, [illegible] (Roman Catholic),	[illegible]	[illegible]	[illegible]	[illegible]	[illegible]	[illegible]	[illegible]	[illegible]	[illegible]	[illegible]	[illegible]	[illegible]
St. Joseph's, Ballinasloe, [illegible] December, [illegible] (Roman Catholic),	[illegible]	[illegible]	[illegible]	[illegible]	[illegible]	[illegible]	[illegible]	[illegible]	[illegible]	[illegible]	[illegible]	[illegible]
St. Joseph's, Limerick, [illegible] (Roman Catholic),	[illegible]	[illegible]	[illegible]	[illegible]	[illegible]	[illegible]	[illegible]	[illegible]	[illegible]	[illegible]	[illegible]	[illegible]
[illegible], Monaghan, [illegible] July, [illegible] (Roman Catholic),	[illegible]	[illegible]	[illegible]	[illegible]	[illegible]	[illegible]	[illegible]	[illegible]	[illegible]	[illegible]	[illegible]	[illegible]
Total Girls,	[illegible]	[illegible]	[illegible]	[illegible]	[illegible]	[illegible]	[illegible]	[illegible]	[illegible]	[illegible]	[illegible]	[illegible]
Total Boys and Girls,	[illegible]	[illegible]	[illegible]	[illegible]	[illegible]	[illegible]	[illegible]	[illegible]	[illegible]	[illegible]	[illegible]	[illegible]
Total Roman Catholics,	[illegible]	[illegible]	[illegible]	[illegible]	[illegible]	[illegible]	[illegible]	[illegible]	[illegible]	[illegible]	[illegible]	[illegible]
Total Protestants,	[illegible]	[illegible]	[illegible]	[illegible]	[illegible]	[illegible]	[illegible]	[illegible]	[illegible]	[illegible]	[illegible]	[illegible]

TABLE [illegible].—REFORMATORY SCHOOLS.—RETURN of OFFENCES of which the BOYS and GIRLS were CONVICTED, who were RECEIVED under Sect. [illegible] Vic., c. [illegible], into REFORMATORY SCHOOLS during the Year [illegible]. Made by the Inspector of Reformatories and Industrial Schools.

OFFENCES.	Boys: [illegible]	[illegible]	[illegible]	[illegible]	[illegible]	Girls: [illegible]	[illegible]	[illegible]	[illegible]	[illegible]	Total Committed in [illegible]: B.	G.	B. & G.
Larceny and Petty Theft,	[illegible]	[illegible]	[illegible]	[illegible]	[illegible]	[illegible]	[illegible]	[illegible]	[illegible]	[illegible]	[illegible]	[illegible]	[illegible]
" [illegible],	[illegible]	[illegible]	[illegible]	[illegible]	[illegible]	[illegible]	[illegible]	[illegible]	[illegible]	[illegible]	[illegible]	[illegible]	[illegible]
" by Servants,	[illegible]	[illegible]	[illegible]	[illegible]	[illegible]	[illegible]	[illegible]	[illegible]	[illegible]	[illegible]	[illegible]	[illegible]	[illegible]
" from Person,	[illegible]	[illegible]	[illegible]	[illegible]	[illegible]	[illegible]	[illegible]	[illegible]	[illegible]	[illegible]	[illegible]	[illegible]	[illegible]
" in Dwelling-house,	[illegible]	[illegible]	[illegible]	[illegible]	[illegible]	[illegible]	[illegible]	[illegible]	[illegible]	[illegible]	[illegible]	[illegible]	[illegible]
Attempt to Steal,	[illegible]	[illegible]	[illegible]	[illegible]	[illegible]	[illegible]	[illegible]	[illegible]	[illegible]	[illegible]	[illegible]	[illegible]	[illegible]
Unlawful Possession of Goods,	[illegible]	[illegible]	[illegible]	[illegible]	[illegible]	[illegible]	[illegible]	[illegible]	[illegible]	[illegible]	[illegible]	[illegible]	[illegible]
Receiving Stolen Goods,	[illegible]	[illegible]	[illegible]	[illegible]	[illegible]	[illegible]	[illegible]	[illegible]	[illegible]	[illegible]	[illegible]	[illegible]	[illegible]
Fraudulent Offences,	[illegible]	[illegible]	[illegible]	[illegible]	[illegible]	[illegible]	[illegible]	[illegible]	[illegible]	[illegible]	[illegible]	[illegible]	[illegible]
Embezzlement,	[illegible]	[illegible]	[illegible]	[illegible]	[illegible]	[illegible]	[illegible]	[illegible]	[illegible]	[illegible]	[illegible]	[illegible]	[illegible]
Horse Stealing,	[illegible]	[illegible]	[illegible]	[illegible]	[illegible]	[illegible]	[illegible]	[illegible]	[illegible]	[illegible]	[illegible]	[illegible]	[illegible]
Sheep Stealing,	[illegible]	[illegible]	[illegible]	[illegible]	[illegible]	[illegible]	[illegible]	[illegible]	[illegible]	[illegible]	[illegible]	[illegible]	[illegible]
Cattle Stealing,	[illegible]	[illegible]	[illegible]	[illegible]	[illegible]	[illegible]	[illegible]	[illegible]	[illegible]	[illegible]	[illegible]	[illegible]	[illegible]
Housebreaking, Shopbreaking, &c.,	[illegible]	[illegible]	[illegible]	[illegible]	[illegible]	[illegible]	[illegible]	[illegible]	[illegible]	[illegible]	[illegible]	[illegible]	[illegible]
Burglary,	[illegible]	[illegible]	[illegible]	[illegible]	[illegible]	[illegible]	[illegible]	[illegible]	[illegible]	[illegible]	[illegible]	[illegible]	[illegible]
Robbery on the Highway,	[illegible]	[illegible]	[illegible]	[illegible]	[illegible]	[illegible]	[illegible]	[illegible]	[illegible]	[illegible]	[illegible]	[illegible]	[illegible]
Attempt to Break into Houses, &c.,	[illegible]	[illegible]	[illegible]	[illegible]	[illegible]	[illegible]	[illegible]	[illegible]	[illegible]	[illegible]	[illegible]	[illegible]	[illegible]
Arson and Wilful Burning,	[illegible]	[illegible]	[illegible]	[illegible]	[illegible]	[illegible]	[illegible]	[illegible]	[illegible]	[illegible]	[illegible]	[illegible]	[illegible]
Wilful Damage and other Malicious Offences,	[illegible]	[illegible]	[illegible]	[illegible]	[illegible]	[illegible]	[illegible]	[illegible]	[illegible]	[illegible]	[illegible]	[illegible]	[illegible]
Assaults,	[illegible]	[illegible]	[illegible]	[illegible]	[illegible]	[illegible]	[illegible]	[illegible]	[illegible]	[illegible]	[illegible]	[illegible]	[illegible]
Assault with intent to Ravish,	[illegible]	[illegible]	[illegible]	[illegible]	[illegible]	[illegible]	[illegible]	[illegible]	[illegible]	[illegible]	[illegible]	[illegible]	[illegible]
Forgery,	[illegible]	[illegible]	[illegible]	[illegible]	[illegible]	[illegible]	[illegible]	[illegible]	[illegible]	[illegible]	[illegible]	[illegible]	[illegible]
Uttering Counterfeit Coin,	[illegible]	[illegible]	[illegible]	[illegible]	[illegible]	[illegible]	[illegible]	[illegible]	[illegible]	[illegible]	[illegible]	[illegible]	[illegible]
Vagrancy,	[illegible]	[illegible]	[illegible]	[illegible]	[illegible]	[illegible]	[illegible]	[illegible]	[illegible]	[illegible]	[illegible]	[illegible]	[illegible]
Other Offences,	[illegible]	[illegible]	[illegible]	[illegible]	[illegible]	[illegible]	[illegible]	[illegible]	[illegible]	[illegible]	[illegible]	[illegible]	[illegible]
Total,	[illegible]	[illegible]	[illegible]	[illegible]	[illegible]	[illegible]	[illegible]	[illegible]	[illegible]	[illegible]	[illegible]	[illegible]	[illegible]

INDUSTRIAL SCHOOLS, ARRANGED IN COUNTIES.	[illegible]					[illegible]			[illegible]					[illegible]					[illegible]					[illegible]				Total Cost.	[illegible]		
	In School	On Licence	Absconded	[illegible]	Total	[illegible]	[illegible]	[illegible]	[illegible]	[illegible]	[illegible]	[illegible]	[illegible]	In School	On Licence	Absconded	[illegible]	Total	[illegible]	[illegible]	[illegible]	[illegible]	[illegible]	[illegible]	[illegible]	[illegible]	[illegible]		Treasury	Local Taxes	Other Sources
GIRLS.																															
Antrim.																															
[illegible] Home (Protestant)	[illegible]	[illegible]	[illegible]	[illegible]	[illegible]	[illegible]	[illegible]	[illegible]	[illegible]	[illegible]	[illegible]	[illegible]	[illegible]	[illegible]	[illegible]	[illegible]	[illegible]	[illegible]	[illegible]	[illegible]	[illegible]	[illegible]	[illegible]	[illegible]	[illegible]	[illegible]	[illegible]	[illegible]	[illegible]	[illegible]	[illegible]
St. Patrick's (R.C.)	[illegible]	[illegible]	[illegible]	[illegible]	[illegible]	[illegible]	[illegible]	[illegible]	[illegible]	[illegible]	[illegible]	[illegible]	[illegible]	[illegible]	[illegible]	[illegible]	[illegible]	[illegible]	[illegible]	[illegible]	[illegible]	[illegible]	[illegible]	[illegible]	[illegible]	[illegible]	[illegible]	[illegible]	[illegible]	[illegible]	[illegible]
Armagh.																															
[illegible] (R.C.)	[illegible]	[illegible]	[illegible]	[illegible]	[illegible]	[illegible]	[illegible]	[illegible]	[illegible]	[illegible]	[illegible]	[illegible]	[illegible]	[illegible]	[illegible]	[illegible]	[illegible]	[illegible]	[illegible]	[illegible]	[illegible]	[illegible]	[illegible]	[illegible]	[illegible]	[illegible]	[illegible]	[illegible]	[illegible]	[illegible]	[illegible]
Cavan.																															
St. Joseph's Convent (R.C.)	[illegible]	[illegible]	[illegible]	[illegible]	[illegible]	[illegible]	[illegible]	[illegible]	[illegible]	[illegible]	[illegible]	[illegible]	[illegible]	[illegible]	[illegible]	[illegible]	[illegible]	[illegible]	[illegible]	[illegible]	[illegible]	[illegible]	[illegible]	[illegible]	[illegible]	[illegible]	[illegible]	[illegible]	[illegible]	[illegible]	[illegible]
Clare.																															
[illegible]	[illegible]	[illegible]	[illegible]	[illegible]	[illegible]	[illegible]	[illegible]	[illegible]	[illegible]	[illegible]	[illegible]	[illegible]	[illegible]	[illegible]	[illegible]	[illegible]	[illegible]	[illegible]	[illegible]	[illegible]	[illegible]	[illegible]	[illegible]	[illegible]	[illegible]	[illegible]	[illegible]	[illegible]	[illegible]	[illegible]	[illegible]
Cork.																															
St. [illegible] (R.C.)	[illegible]	[illegible]	[illegible]	[illegible]	[illegible]	[illegible]	[illegible]	[illegible]	[illegible]	[illegible]	[illegible]	[illegible]	[illegible]	[illegible]	[illegible]	[illegible]	[illegible]	[illegible]	[illegible]	[illegible]	[illegible]	[illegible]	[illegible]	[illegible]	[illegible]	[illegible]	[illegible]	[illegible]	[illegible]	[illegible]	[illegible]
St. [illegible], Queenstown (R.C.)	[illegible]	[illegible]	[illegible]	[illegible]	[illegible]	[illegible]	[illegible]	[illegible]	[illegible]	[illegible]	[illegible]	[illegible]	[illegible]	[illegible]	[illegible]	[illegible]	[illegible]	[illegible]	[illegible]	[illegible]	[illegible]	[illegible]	[illegible]	[illegible]	[illegible]	[illegible]	[illegible]	[illegible]	[illegible]	[illegible]	[illegible]
Our Lady of [illegible] (R.C.)	[illegible]	[illegible]	[illegible]	[illegible]	[illegible]	[illegible]	[illegible]	[illegible]	[illegible]	[illegible]	[illegible]	[illegible]	[illegible]	[illegible]	[illegible]	[illegible]	[illegible]	[illegible]	[illegible]	[illegible]	[illegible]	[illegible]	[illegible]	[illegible]	[illegible]	[illegible]	[illegible]	[illegible]	[illegible]	[illegible]	[illegible]
[illegible] Home, [illegible] (Protestant)	[illegible]	[illegible]	[illegible]	[illegible]	[illegible]	[illegible]	[illegible]	[illegible]	[illegible]	[illegible]	[illegible]	[illegible]	[illegible]	[illegible]	[illegible]	[illegible]	[illegible]	[illegible]	[illegible]	[illegible]	[illegible]	[illegible]	[illegible]	[illegible]	[illegible]	[illegible]	[illegible]	[illegible]	[illegible]	[illegible]	[illegible]
[illegible]	[illegible]	[illegible]	[illegible]	[illegible]	[illegible]	[illegible]	[illegible]	[illegible]	[illegible]	[illegible]	[illegible]	[illegible]	[illegible]	[illegible]	[illegible]	[illegible]	[illegible]	[illegible]	[illegible]	[illegible]	[illegible]	[illegible]	[illegible]	[illegible]	[illegible]	[illegible]	[illegible]	[illegible]	[illegible]	[illegible]	[illegible]
St. [illegible], Cork (R.C.)	[illegible]	[illegible]	[illegible]	[illegible]	[illegible]	[illegible]	[illegible]	[illegible]	[illegible]	[illegible]	[illegible]	[illegible]	[illegible]	[illegible]	[illegible]	[illegible]	[illegible]	[illegible]	[illegible]	[illegible]	[illegible]	[illegible]	[illegible]	[illegible]	[illegible]	[illegible]	[illegible]	[illegible]	[illegible]	[illegible]	[illegible]
[illegible] Home, Cork (Protestant)	[illegible]	[illegible]	[illegible]	[illegible]	[illegible]	[illegible]	[illegible]	[illegible]	[illegible]	[illegible]	[illegible]	[illegible]	[illegible]	[illegible]	[illegible]	[illegible]	[illegible]	[illegible]	[illegible]	[illegible]	[illegible]	[illegible]	[illegible]	[illegible]	[illegible]	[illegible]	[illegible]	[illegible]	[illegible]	[illegible]	[illegible]
Dublin.																															
[illegible] (R.C.)	[illegible]	[illegible]	[illegible]	[illegible]	[illegible]	[illegible]	[illegible]	[illegible]	[illegible]	[illegible]	[illegible]	[illegible]	[illegible]	[illegible]	[illegible]	[illegible]	[illegible]	[illegible]	[illegible]	[illegible]	[illegible]	[illegible]	[illegible]	[illegible]	[illegible]	[illegible]	[illegible]	[illegible]	[illegible]	[illegible]	[illegible]
Golden Bridge	[illegible]	[illegible]	[illegible]	[illegible]	[illegible]	[illegible]	[illegible]	[illegible]	[illegible]	[illegible]	[illegible]	[illegible]	[illegible]	[illegible]	[illegible]	[illegible]	[illegible]	[illegible]	[illegible]	[illegible]	[illegible]	[illegible]	[illegible]	[illegible]	[illegible]	[illegible]	[illegible]	[illegible]	[illegible]	[illegible]	[illegible]
[illegible] (R.C.)	[illegible]	[illegible]	[illegible]	[illegible]	[illegible]	[illegible]	[illegible]	[illegible]	[illegible]	[illegible]	[illegible]	[illegible]	[illegible]	[illegible]	[illegible]	[illegible]	[illegible]	[illegible]	[illegible]	[illegible]	[illegible]	[illegible]	[illegible]	[illegible]	[illegible]	[illegible]	[illegible]	[illegible]	[illegible]	[illegible]	[illegible]
[illegible] (R.C.)	[illegible]	[illegible]	[illegible]	[illegible]	[illegible]	[illegible]	[illegible]	[illegible]	[illegible]	[illegible]	[illegible]	[illegible]	[illegible]	[illegible]	[illegible]	[illegible]	[illegible]	[illegible]	[illegible]	[illegible]	[illegible]	[illegible]	[illegible]	[illegible]	[illegible]	[illegible]	[illegible]	[illegible]	[illegible]	[illegible]	[illegible]
[illegible] of Dublin (Protestant)	[illegible]	[illegible]	[illegible]	[illegible]	[illegible]	[illegible]	[illegible]	[illegible]	[illegible]	[illegible]	[illegible]	[illegible]	[illegible]	[illegible]	[illegible]	[illegible]	[illegible]	[illegible]	[illegible]	[illegible]	[illegible]	[illegible]	[illegible]	[illegible]	[illegible]	[illegible]	[illegible]	[illegible]	[illegible]	[illegible]	[illegible]
Galway.																															
[illegible] (R.C.)	[illegible]	[illegible]	[illegible]	[illegible]	[illegible]	[illegible]	[illegible]	[illegible]	[illegible]	[illegible]	[illegible]	[illegible]	[illegible]	[illegible]	[illegible]	[illegible]	[illegible]	[illegible]	[illegible]	[illegible]	[illegible]	[illegible]	[illegible]	[illegible]	[illegible]	[illegible]	[illegible]	[illegible]	[illegible]	[illegible]	[illegible]
Clifden (R.C.)	[illegible]	[illegible]	[illegible]	[illegible]	[illegible]	[illegible]	[illegible]	[illegible]	[illegible]	[illegible]	[illegible]	[illegible]	[illegible]	[illegible]	[illegible]	[illegible]	[illegible]	[illegible]	[illegible]	[illegible]	[illegible]	[illegible]	[illegible]	[illegible]	[illegible]	[illegible]	[illegible]	[illegible]	[illegible]	[illegible]	[illegible]
[illegible] (R.C.)	[illegible]	[illegible]	[illegible]	[illegible]	[illegible]	[illegible]	[illegible]	[illegible]	[illegible]	[illegible]	[illegible]	[illegible]	[illegible]	[illegible]	[illegible]	[illegible]	[illegible]	[illegible]	[illegible]	[illegible]	[illegible]	[illegible]	[illegible]	[illegible]	[illegible]	[illegible]	[illegible]	[illegible]	[illegible]	[illegible]	[illegible]
St. Anne's, Galway (R.C.)	[illegible]	[illegible]	[illegible]	[illegible]	[illegible]	[illegible]	[illegible]	[illegible]	[illegible]	[illegible]	[illegible]	[illegible]	[illegible]	[illegible]	[illegible]	[illegible]	[illegible]	[illegible]	[illegible]	[illegible]	[illegible]	[illegible]	[illegible]	[illegible]	[illegible]	[illegible]	[illegible]	[illegible]	[illegible]	[illegible]	[illegible]

* [illegible]

† [illegible]

TABLE 6a.—INDUSTRIAL SCHOOLS.—RETURN showing the NUMBER under DETENTION, COMMITTED, DISCHARGED, REMOVED, or TRANSFERRED in the year [illegible], with the COSTS, under Stat. 31 Vict. c. 25—concluded.

INDUSTRIAL SCHOOLS, ARRANGED IN COUNTIES	Under detention at beginning of year: In School	On Licence	Absconded	Removed to School [illegible]	Total	Admitted in [illegible]: Committed during the year	Received from other Industrial Schools	Recommitted	Discharges, Removals, etc.: Discharged on expiration of [illegible]	Transferred to other Schools [illegible]	Committed to Reformatories	Died	Total Discharged [illegible]	Under detention at close of year: In School	On Licence	Absconded	Removed to School [illegible]	Total	[illegible]	[illegible]	[illegible]	[illegible]	[illegible]	[illegible]	[illegible]	[illegible]	[illegible]	Total Costs	Contributed by: Imperial Taxes	Local Taxes	Other Sources
GIRLS—continued.																												£	£	£	£
Kerry:																															
Killarney (R.C.)	[illegible]	[illegible]	[illegible]	[illegible]	[illegible]	[illegible]	[illegible]	[illegible]	[illegible]	[illegible]	[illegible]	[illegible]	[illegible]	[illegible]	[illegible]	[illegible]	[illegible]	[illegible]	[illegible]	[illegible]	[illegible]	[illegible]	[illegible]	[illegible]	[illegible]	[illegible]	[illegible]	[illegible]	[illegible]	[illegible]	[illegible]
Pembroke Alms (R.C.)	[illegible]	[illegible]	[illegible]	[illegible]	[illegible]	[illegible]	[illegible]	[illegible]	[illegible]	[illegible]	[illegible]	[illegible]	[illegible]	[illegible]	[illegible]	[illegible]	[illegible]	[illegible]	[illegible]	[illegible]	[illegible]	[illegible]	[illegible]	[illegible]	[illegible]	[illegible]	[illegible]	[illegible]	[illegible]	[illegible]	[illegible]
Kilkenny:																															
Kilkenny (R.C.)	[illegible]	[illegible]	[illegible]	[illegible]	[illegible]	[illegible]	[illegible]	[illegible]	[illegible]	[illegible]	[illegible]	[illegible]	[illegible]	[illegible]	[illegible]	[illegible]	[illegible]	[illegible]	[illegible]	[illegible]	[illegible]	[illegible]	[illegible]	[illegible]	[illegible]	[illegible]	[illegible]	[illegible]	[illegible]	[illegible]	[illegible]
King's County:																															
Parsonstown (R.C.)	[illegible]	[illegible]	[illegible]	[illegible]	[illegible]	[illegible]	[illegible]	[illegible]	[illegible]	[illegible]	[illegible]	[illegible]	[illegible]	[illegible]	[illegible]	[illegible]	[illegible]	[illegible]	[illegible]	[illegible]	[illegible]	[illegible]	[illegible]	[illegible]	[illegible]	[illegible]	[illegible]	[illegible]	[illegible]	[illegible]	[illegible]
Limerick:																															
St. George's, Limerick (R.C.)	[illegible]	[illegible]	[illegible]	[illegible]	[illegible]	[illegible]	[illegible]	[illegible]	[illegible]	[illegible]	[illegible]	[illegible]	[illegible]	[illegible]	[illegible]	[illegible]	[illegible]	[illegible]	[illegible]	[illegible]	[illegible]	[illegible]	[illegible]	[illegible]	[illegible]	[illegible]	[illegible]	[illegible]	[illegible]	[illegible]	[illegible]
St. Vincent's — (R.C.)	[illegible]	[illegible]	[illegible]	[illegible]	[illegible]	[illegible]	[illegible]	[illegible]	[illegible]	[illegible]	[illegible]	[illegible]	[illegible]	[illegible]	[illegible]	[illegible]	[illegible]	[illegible]	[illegible]	[illegible]	[illegible]	[illegible]	[illegible]	[illegible]	[illegible]	[illegible]	[illegible]	[illegible]	[illegible]	[illegible]	[illegible]
Longford:																															
Newtownforbes (R.C.)	[illegible]	[illegible]	[illegible]	[illegible]	[illegible]	[illegible]	[illegible]	[illegible]	[illegible]	[illegible]	[illegible]	[illegible]	[illegible]	[illegible]	[illegible]	[illegible]	[illegible]	[illegible]	[illegible]	[illegible]	[illegible]	[illegible]	[illegible]	[illegible]	[illegible]	[illegible]	[illegible]	[illegible]	[illegible]	[illegible]	[illegible]
Louth:																															
Dundalk (R.C.)	[illegible]	[illegible]	[illegible]	[illegible]	[illegible]	[illegible]	[illegible]	[illegible]	[illegible]	[illegible]	[illegible]	[illegible]	[illegible]	[illegible]	[illegible]	[illegible]	[illegible]	[illegible]	[illegible]	[illegible]	[illegible]	[illegible]	[illegible]	[illegible]	[illegible]	[illegible]	[illegible]	[illegible]	[illegible]	[illegible]	[illegible]
Mayo:																															
Westport (R.C.)	[illegible]	[illegible]	[illegible]	[illegible]	[illegible]	[illegible]	[illegible]	[illegible]	[illegible]	[illegible]	[illegible]	[illegible]	[illegible]	[illegible]	[illegible]	[illegible]	[illegible]	[illegible]	[illegible]	[illegible]	[illegible]	[illegible]	[illegible]	[illegible]	[illegible]	[illegible]	[illegible]	[illegible]	[illegible]	[illegible]	[illegible]
Monaghan:																															
Monaghan (R.C.)	[illegible]	[illegible]	[illegible]	[illegible]	[illegible]	[illegible]	[illegible]	[illegible]	[illegible]	[illegible]	[illegible]	[illegible]	[illegible]	[illegible]	[illegible]	[illegible]	[illegible]	[illegible]	[illegible]	[illegible]	[illegible]	[illegible]	[illegible]	[illegible]	[illegible]	[illegible]	[illegible]	[illegible]	[illegible]	[illegible]	[illegible]
Roscommon:																															
Roscommon (R.C.)	[illegible]	[illegible]	[illegible]	[illegible]	[illegible]	[illegible]	[illegible]	[illegible]	[illegible]	[illegible]	[illegible]	[illegible]	[illegible]	[illegible]	[illegible]	[illegible]	[illegible]	[illegible]	[illegible]	[illegible]	[illegible]	[illegible]	[illegible]	[illegible]	[illegible]	[illegible]	[illegible]	[illegible]	[illegible]	[illegible]	[illegible]
Summerhill, Athlone (R.C.)	[illegible]	[illegible]	[illegible]	[illegible]	[illegible]	[illegible]	[illegible]	[illegible]	[illegible]	[illegible]	[illegible]	[illegible]	[illegible]	[illegible]	[illegible]	[illegible]	[illegible]	[illegible]	[illegible]	[illegible]	[illegible]	[illegible]	[illegible]	[illegible]	[illegible]	[illegible]	[illegible]	[illegible]	[illegible]	[illegible]	[illegible]
Sligo:																															
Benada Abbey (R.C.)	[illegible]	[illegible]	[illegible]	[illegible]	[illegible]	[illegible]	[illegible]	[illegible]	[illegible]	[illegible]	[illegible]	[illegible]	[illegible]	[illegible]	[illegible]	[illegible]	[illegible]	[illegible]	[illegible]	[illegible]	[illegible]	[illegible]	[illegible]	[illegible]	[illegible]	[illegible]	[illegible]	[illegible]	[illegible]	[illegible]	[illegible]
Sligo (R.C.)	[illegible]	[illegible]	[illegible]	[illegible]	[illegible]	[illegible]	[illegible]	[illegible]	[illegible]	[illegible]	[illegible]	[illegible]	[illegible]	[illegible]	[illegible]	[illegible]	[illegible]	[illegible]	[illegible]	[illegible]	[illegible]	[illegible]	[illegible]	[illegible]	[illegible]	[illegible]	[illegible]	[illegible]	[illegible]	[illegible]	[illegible]
Tipperary:																															
Templemore (R.C.)	[illegible]	[illegible]	[illegible]	[illegible]	[illegible]	[illegible]	[illegible]	[illegible]	[illegible]	[illegible]	[illegible]	[illegible]	[illegible]	[illegible]	[illegible]	[illegible]	[illegible]	[illegible]	[illegible]	[illegible]	[illegible]	[illegible]	[illegible]	[illegible]	[illegible]	[illegible]	[illegible]	[illegible]	[illegible]	[illegible]	[illegible]
Cashel (R.C.)	[illegible]	[illegible]	[illegible]	[illegible]	[illegible]	[illegible]	[illegible]	[illegible]	[illegible]	[illegible]	[illegible]	[illegible]	[illegible]	[illegible]	[illegible]	[illegible]	[illegible]	[illegible]	[illegible]	[illegible]	[illegible]	[illegible]	[illegible]	[illegible]	[illegible]	[illegible]	[illegible]	[illegible]	[illegible]	[illegible]	[illegible]

TABLE XI.—LUNATIC ASYLUMS. AS TO CRIMINAL LUNATICS and DANGEROUS LUNATICS CHARGED WITH INTENT TO COMMIT A CRIME.—1. RETURN showing Number undergoing Detention, Committed, and Discharged or Removed in the Year [illegible]. Made by the Inspectors of Lunatic Asylums.

Asylums in which Detained	Total Received	Discharged, Removed, or Died during the Year	Total remaining	Total Cost	Daily Average Number	Average Annual Cost per Head
Armagh	[illegible]	[illegible]	[illegible]	[illegible]	[illegible]	[illegible]
Ballinasloe	[illegible]	[illegible]	[illegible]	[illegible]	[illegible]	[illegible]
Belfast	[illegible]	[illegible]	[illegible]	[illegible]	[illegible]	[illegible]
Carlow	[illegible]	[illegible]	[illegible]	[illegible]	[illegible]	[illegible]
Castlebar	[illegible]	[illegible]	[illegible]	[illegible]	[illegible]	[illegible]
Clonmel	[illegible]	[illegible]	[illegible]	[illegible]	[illegible]	[illegible]
Cork	[illegible]	[illegible]	[illegible]	[illegible]	[illegible]	[illegible]
Ennis	[illegible]	[illegible]	[illegible]	[illegible]	[illegible]	[illegible]
[illegible]	[illegible]	[illegible]	[illegible]	[illegible]	[illegible]	[illegible]
[illegible]	[illegible]	[illegible]	[illegible]	[illegible]	[illegible]	[illegible]
Enniscorthy	[illegible]	[illegible]	[illegible]	[illegible]	[illegible]	[illegible]
Killarney	[illegible]	[illegible]	[illegible]	[illegible]	[illegible]	[illegible]
Kilkenny	[illegible]	[illegible]	[illegible]	[illegible]	[illegible]	[illegible]
Letterkenny	[illegible]	[illegible]	[illegible]	[illegible]	[illegible]	[illegible]
Limerick	[illegible]	[illegible]	[illegible]	[illegible]	[illegible]	[illegible]
Londonderry	[illegible]	[illegible]	[illegible]	[illegible]	[illegible]	[illegible]
Maryborough	[illegible]	[illegible]	[illegible]	[illegible]	[illegible]	[illegible]
Monaghan	[illegible]	[illegible]	[illegible]	[illegible]	[illegible]	[illegible]
Mullingar	[illegible]	[illegible]	[illegible]	[illegible]	[illegible]	[illegible]
Omagh	[illegible]	[illegible]	[illegible]	[illegible]	[illegible]	[illegible]
Richmond	[illegible]	[illegible]	[illegible]	[illegible]	[illegible]	[illegible]
Sligo	[illegible]	[illegible]	[illegible]	[illegible]	[illegible]	[illegible]
Waterford	[illegible]	[illegible]	[illegible]	[illegible]	[illegible]	[illegible]
Total	[illegible]	[illegible]	[illegible]	[illegible]	[illegible]	[illegible]

[illegible]

[illegible]	Total.			[illegible]		[illegible]		[illegible]		[illegible]		[illegible]		[illegible]	
	M.&W.	M.	W.	M.	W.	M.	W.	M.	W.	M.	W.	M.	W.	M.	W.
Part I.—[illegible]															
[illegible]	[illegible]	[illegible]	[illegible]	[illegible]	[illegible]	[illegible]	[illegible]	[illegible]	[illegible]	[illegible]	[illegible]	[illegible]	[illegible]	[illegible]	[illegible]
Part II.—[illegible]															
[illegible]	[illegible]	[illegible]	[illegible]	[illegible]	[illegible]	[illegible]	[illegible]	[illegible]	[illegible]	[illegible]	[illegible]	[illegible]	[illegible]	[illegible]	[illegible]
Part III.—[illegible]															
[illegible]	[illegible]	[illegible]	[illegible]	[illegible]	[illegible]	[illegible]	[illegible]	[illegible]	[illegible]	[illegible]	[illegible]	[illegible]	[illegible]	[illegible]	[illegible]

TABLE [illegible].—CRIMINAL LUNATICS IN ASYLUMS.—Showing for each Asylum—1. The Number of those under

	Cork. — County and City of Cork.		Derry. — County of Derry.		Dundrum, or Central — Dublin Criminal for Ireland.		Ennis. — County of Clare.		Enniscorthy. — County of Wexford.		Kilkenny. — County and City of Kilkenny.		Killarney. — County of Kerry.		Letterkenny. — County of Donegal.	
	M.	W.	M.	W.	M.	W.	M.	W.	M.	W.	M.	W.	M.	W.	M.	W.
PART I.—AUTHORITY FOR CONFINEMENT OF THOSE IN CONFINEMENT AT THE END OF THE YEAR [illegible].																
Total number in confinement at end of year [illegible].	[illegible]	[illegible]	[illegible]	[illegible]	[illegible]	[illegible]	[illegible]	[illegible]	[illegible]	[illegible]	[illegible]	[illegible]	[illegible]	[illegible]	[illegible]	[illegible]
Those insane committed by Juries,	[illegible]	[illegible]	[illegible]	[illegible]	.		[illegible]	[illegible]	[illegible]	[illegible]	[illegible]	[illegible]	[illegible]	[illegible]	[illegible]	[illegible]
Those insane held in confinement by Warrant of Lord Lieutenant.	[illegible]	[illegible]	[illegible]	[illegible]	[illegible]	[illegible]	[illegible]	[illegible]	[illegible]	[illegible]	[illegible]	[illegible]	[illegible]	[illegible]	[illegible]	[illegible]
PART II.—PERIOD OF DETENTION IN ASYLUM OF THOSE OF WHOM THERE WERE REMAINING AT END OF THE YEAR [illegible].																
Number who have been detained in Asylums—																
One year and under,	[illegible]	[illegible]	[illegible]	[illegible]	[illegible]	[illegible]	[illegible]	[illegible]	[illegible]	[illegible]	[illegible]	[illegible]	[illegible]	[illegible]	[illegible]	[illegible]
Two years and above one,	[illegible]	[illegible]	[illegible]	[illegible]	[illegible]	[illegible]	[illegible]	[illegible]	[illegible]	[illegible]	[illegible]	[illegible]	[illegible]	[illegible]	[illegible]	[illegible]
Three years and above two,	[illegible]	[illegible]	[illegible]	[illegible]	[illegible]	[illegible]	[illegible]	[illegible]	[illegible]	[illegible]	[illegible]	[illegible]	[illegible]	[illegible]	[illegible]	[illegible]
Five years and above three,	[illegible]	[illegible]	[illegible]	[illegible]	[illegible]	[illegible]	[illegible]	[illegible]	[illegible]	[illegible]	[illegible]	[illegible]	[illegible]	[illegible]	[illegible]	[illegible]
Ten years and above five,	[illegible]	[illegible]	[illegible]	[illegible]	[illegible]	[illegible]	[illegible]	[illegible]	[illegible]	[illegible]	[illegible]	[illegible]	[illegible]	[illegible]	[illegible]	[illegible]
Fifteen years and above ten,	[illegible]	[illegible]	[illegible]	[illegible]	[illegible]	[illegible]	[illegible]	[illegible]	[illegible]	[illegible]	[illegible]	[illegible]	[illegible]	[illegible]	[illegible]	[illegible]
Twenty years and above fifteen,	[illegible]	[illegible]	[illegible]	[illegible]	[illegible]	[illegible]	[illegible]	[illegible]	[illegible]	[illegible]	[illegible]	[illegible]	[illegible]	[illegible]	[illegible]	[illegible]
Above twenty years,	[illegible]	[illegible]	[illegible]	[illegible]	[illegible]	[illegible]	[illegible]	[illegible]	[illegible]	[illegible]	[illegible]	[illegible]	[illegible]	[illegible]	[illegible]	[illegible]
Total in confinement at end of year [illegible].	[illegible]	[illegible]	[illegible]	[illegible]	[illegible]	[illegible]	[illegible]	[illegible]	[illegible]	[illegible]	[illegible]	[illegible]	[illegible]	[illegible]	[illegible]	[illegible]
PART III.—OFFENCES OF LUNATICS COMMITTED TO ASYLUMS DURING THE YEAR [illegible].																
[illegible] (rows of offences)	[illegible]	[illegible]	[illegible]	[illegible]	[illegible]	[illegible]	[illegible]	[illegible]	[illegible]	[illegible]	[illegible]	[illegible]	[illegible]	[illegible]	[illegible]	[illegible]
Total number committed during the year [illegible].	[illegible]	[illegible]	[illegible]	[illegible]	[illegible]	[illegible]	[illegible]	[illegible]	[illegible]	[illegible]	[illegible]	[illegible]	[illegible]	[illegible]	[illegible]	[illegible]
PART IV.—AUTHORITY UNDER WHICH LUNATICS COMMITTED TO ASYLUMS DURING THE YEAR [illegible].																
Transmitted from Gaols by Lord Lieutenant's Warrant—																
[illegible]	[illegible]	[illegible]	[illegible]	[illegible]	[illegible]	[illegible]	[illegible]	[illegible]	[illegible]	[illegible]	[illegible]	[illegible]	[illegible]	[illegible]	[illegible]	[illegible]
Committed to Asylums by Justices as Dangerous, under Stat. [illegible]	[illegible]	[illegible]	[illegible]	[illegible]	–	–	[illegible]	[illegible]	[illegible]	[illegible]	[illegible]	[illegible]	[illegible]	[illegible]	[illegible]	[illegible]
Total number committed during the year [illegible].	[illegible]	[illegible]	[illegible]	[illegible]	[illegible]	[illegible]	[illegible]	[illegible]	[illegible]	[illegible]	[illegible]	[illegible]	[illegible]	[illegible]	[illegible]	[illegible]

* Including one transfer.

[illegible]

TABLE [illegible].—HIGH COURT OF JUSTICE.—CHANCERY DIVISION.—RETURN of PROCEEDINGS in the OFFICE of the REGISTRARS, in the Year 18[illegible], made by the REGISTRARS.

NATURE OF PROCEEDINGS.	Total.	[illegible]	[illegible]	[illegible]	[illegible]	NATURE OF PROCEEDINGS.	Total.	[illegible]	[illegible]	[illegible]	[illegible]
[illegible]	[illegible]	[illegible]	[illegible]	[illegible]	[illegible]	[illegible]	[illegible]	[illegible]	[illegible]	[illegible]	[illegible]

[illegible]

TABLE [illegible].—HIGH COURT OF JUSTICE.—CHANCERY DIVISION.—RETURN of APPEALS from COUNTY COURTS in EQUITY, CIVIL BILLS, and PROCEEDINGS in the year 18[illegible], by the proper officer under Order XVII., Rule [illegible], of County Courts (Ireland) Rules, [illegible].

[illegible]	Number
[illegible]	[illegible]

TABLE [illegible].—HIGH COURT OF JUSTICE.—CHANCERY DIVISION.—RETURN of PROCEEDINGS in the CHAMBERS of the LORD CHANCELLOR, MASTER of the ROLLS, and VICE-CHANCELLOR, for the year [illegible] made by the Chief Clerks to the Judges.

NATURE OF PROCEEDINGS.	Total.		Lord Chancellor.		Master of the Rolls.		Vice-Chancellor.	
	No.	Amount.	No.	Amount.	No.	Amount.	No.	Amount.
Number issued of Summonses to commence Proceedings, &c.:—		£ s. d.		£ s. d.		£ s. d.		£ s. d.
To make Infants Wards,	[illegible]	—	[illegible]	—	[illegible]	—	[illegible]	—
For the Administration of Estates,	[illegible]	—	[illegible]	—	[illegible]	—	[illegible]	—
Under the Chancery Trusts Act	[illegible]	—	[illegible]	—	[illegible]	—	[illegible]	—
For the Appointment of Guardians and Maintenance of Infants,	[illegible]	—	[illegible]	—	[illegible]	—	[illegible]	—
For other purposes,	[illegible]	—	[illegible]	—	[illegible]	—	[illegible]	—
Number issued of Summonses [illegible] in original Proceedings,	[illegible]	—	[illegible]	—	[illegible]	—	[illegible]	—
Number of Orders made, viz.:—								
Of the class drawn up by the Registrar,	[illegible]	—	[illegible]	—	[illegible]	—	[illegible]	—
Of the class drawn up in Chambers,	[illegible]	—	[illegible]	—	[illegible]	—	[illegible]	—
Number of Orders brought into Chambers [illegible], other than Orders for winding up Companies,	[illegible]	—	[illegible]	—	[illegible]	—	[illegible]	—
Number of Orders brought into Chambers for winding up Companies,	[illegible]	—	[illegible]	—	[illegible]	—	[illegible]	—
Number of Adjournments [illegible],	[illegible]	—	[illegible]	—	[illegible]	—	[illegible]	—
Number of Debts claimed and adjudicated on,	[illegible]	—	[illegible]	—	[illegible]	—	[illegible]	—
Amount of Debts proved,		[illegible]	[illegible]	—		[illegible]		[illegible]
Number of Contributories [illegible] on Lists of Contributories,	[illegible]	—	[illegible]	—	[illegible]	—	[illegible]	—
Number of Contributories [illegible] from Lists of Contributories	[illegible]	—	[illegible]	—	[illegible]	—	[illegible]	—
Amount of Calls made under Orders for winding up Companies,	[illegible]	—	[illegible]	—	[illegible]	—	[illegible]	—
Amount of Dividends ordered to be paid to Creditors,	[illegible]	—	[illegible]	—	[illegible]	—	[illegible]	—
Amount ordered to be refunded to Contributories,	[illegible]	—	[illegible]	—	[illegible]	—	[illegible]	—
Number of Accounts passed, other than Receivers' Accounts,	[illegible]	—	[illegible]	—	[illegible]	—	[illegible]	—
Amount of Receipts thereon,		[illegible]		[illegible]		[illegible]		[illegible]
Amount of Disbursements and Allowances thereon,		[illegible]		[illegible]		[illegible]		[illegible]
Number of Receivers' Accounts passed,	[illegible]	—	[illegible]	—	[illegible]	—	[illegible]	—
Amount of Receipts thereon,		[illegible]		[illegible]		[illegible]		[illegible]
Amount of Disbursements and Allowances thereon,		[illegible]		[illegible]		[illegible]		[illegible]
Number of [illegible] and other Accounts referred to [illegible] Judge,	[illegible]	—	[illegible]	—	[illegible]	—	[illegible]	—
Number of Sales of [illegible] under Orders of Court,	[illegible]	—	[illegible]	—	[illegible]	—	[illegible]	—
Amount realised by Sales of [illegible],		[illegible]		[illegible]		—		[illegible]
Number of Purchases of [illegible] under Orders of Court,	[illegible]	—	[illegible]	—	[illegible]	—	[illegible]	—
Number of Certificates filed,	[illegible]	—	[illegible]	—	[illegible]	—	[illegible]	—
Number of Appointments for Attendances, &c. [illegible] before Lord Chancellor,	[illegible]	—	[illegible]	—	[illegible]	—	[illegible]	—
Number of Orders under which Accounts and Inquiries were pending on 1st January, [illegible]	[illegible]	—	[illegible]	—	[illegible]	—	[illegible]	—
Number of Orders for Winding up Companies [illegible]	[illegible]	—	[illegible]	—	[illegible]	—	[illegible]	—
Amount of Fees [illegible] in Chambers by Stamps,		[illegible]		[illegible]		[illegible]		[illegible]
Number of Days Chief Clerks sitting in Court or Judges' Chambers [illegible],	[illegible]	—	[illegible]	—	[illegible]	—	[illegible]	—
Number of new Minor or Lunacy Matters,	[illegible]	—	[illegible]	—	[illegible]	—	[illegible]	—
Number of new Wards in Lunacy Matters,	[illegible]	—	[illegible]	—	[illegible]	—	[illegible]	—
Number of [illegible] transferred to Lord Chancellor's Chambers from [illegible] Offices,	[illegible]	—	[illegible]	—	[illegible]	—		—
Number of Marriage Settlements and other Deeds approved,	[illegible]	—	[illegible]	—	[illegible]	—	[illegible]	—
Number of Minor Matters at end of year,	[illegible]	—	[illegible]	—	[illegible]	—	[illegible]	—
Number of Wards of Court at end of year,	[illegible]	—	[illegible]	—	[illegible]	—	[illegible]	—
Number of Bills of Costs taxed at Chambers,	[illegible]	—	[illegible]	—	[illegible]	—	[illegible]	—
Amount of Costs taxed,		[illegible]		[illegible]		—		[illegible]
Petitions under Leinster Estate Act,	[illegible]	—	[illegible]	—	[illegible]	—	[illegible]	—
Petitions under Settled Estates Act, [illegible]	[illegible]	—	[illegible]	—	[illegible]	—	[illegible]	—
Petitions under Building Leases,	[illegible]	—	[illegible]	—	[illegible]	—	[illegible]	—

TABLE 61.—HIGH COURT OF JUSTICE—CHANCERY DIVISION.—RETURN of PROCEEDINGS in the OFFICE of the CLERK of RECORDS and WRITS, for the Year 1884, including Stamps on Writs issued in Writ and Seal Office, Consolidated Record and Writ Office, for the Common Law Division, made by the Clerk of Records and Writs.

NATURE OF PROCEEDINGS	High Court	Chancery	General Offices			Fees.	NATURE OF PROCEEDINGS	Number.
			The Land Commission	The Master of the Rolls	The Vice Chancellor			
[illegible]	[illegible]	[illegible]	[illegible]	[illegible]	[illegible]	[illegible]	[illegible]	[illegible]
Total,	[illegible]	[illegible]	[illegible]	[illegible]	[illegible]	[illegible]	Total,	[illegible]

TABLE 57.—HIGH COURT OF JUSTICE.—CHANCERY DIVISION.—RETURN of PROCEEDINGS in the OFFICE of the LORD CHANCELLOR'S SECRETARY, made by the LORD CHANCELLOR'S SECRETARY, and in the OFFICE of the SECRETARY of the RULES, made by the SECRETARY of the RULES, in the Year 188[illegible].

Proceedings in the Office of the Lord Chancellor's Secretary.	Number.	Proceedings in the Office of the Secretary of the Rules.	Number.
		Petitions set down for Hearing:	
		In Minor Matters,	[illegible]
		Under Acts relating to Public Charities,	[illegible]
		Under [illegible] Acts, [illegible],	[illegible]
Orders on Petitions as to Minors,	[illegible]	Under Trustee Relief Act [illegible],	[illegible]
Orders on Petitions as to Commissioners for Administering Oaths for High Court of Justice,	[illegible]	Under Trustee Relief Act [illegible],	[illegible]
		Under Leases and Sales of Settled Estates Act, [illegible],	[illegible]
Orders on other Petitions referred to Lord Chancellor, including Minor Petitions,	[illegible]	Under Public Works and Railway Acts,	[illegible]
		Under [illegible] Act,	[illegible]
		Under Winding up Acts,	[illegible]
Total Number of Orders,	[illegible]	Under Infants' [illegible] Acts [illegible], and [illegible],	[illegible]
		Under [illegible], for Charity Orders,	[illegible]
		Under [illegible] Act [illegible],	[illegible]
		For [illegible] under [illegible] Act [illegible],	[illegible]
		For [illegible] under [illegible] and Public Works Act,	[illegible]
		Under Parliamentary Deposit Act [illegible],	[illegible]
		In Solicitors' Matters,	[illegible]
Warrants for Commissions of the Peace,	[illegible]	In other Matters,	[illegible]
Warrants as to Coroners,	[illegible]		
Other Warrants in the [illegible] Office,	[illegible]	Total Number of Petitions set down for Hearing,	
		Viz.—On the Higher Scale, . . . [illegible]	[illegible]
		On the Lower Scale, . . . [illegible]	
Total Number of Warrants,	[illegible]		

TABLE 58.—HIGH COURT OF JUSTICE.—CHANCERY DIVISION.—RETURN of PROCEEDINGS in the CROWN and HANAPER OFFICE for the Year 188[illegible], made by the CLERK of the CROWN and HANAPER.

Proceedings.	Number.	Proceedings.	Number.
Fiats for appointment of Peers,		Writs for the Election of Members of Parliament,	[illegible]
Fiats for appointment of [illegible] Lords Justices [illegible] Lord Lieutenant,	[illegible]	Writs for the Election of Representative Peers,	[illegible]
Patents connected with the appointment of the Lord Chancellor, Judges, Law Officers, &c.,	[illegible]	[illegible] of Orders to Lord Chancellor of England,	[illegible]
Patents appointing Lieutenant and Custos Rotulorum for the several Counties in Ireland,	[illegible]	[illegible] for the Election of Representative Peers,	[illegible]
Patents [illegible] Fairs and [illegible]	[illegible]	[illegible] to Queen's Bench, &c.,	[illegible]
		[illegible] of persons to whom Oaths were administered by the Clerk of the Crown and Hanaper, before Lord Chancellor,	[illegible]
Commissions of Assize and Oyer and Terminer [illegible],	[illegible]	[illegible] Rules and Orders in [illegible] Proceedings at the Petty Bag Side of the Chancery Division,	[illegible]
Commissions of Lunacy,	[illegible]	[illegible] and other [illegible],	[illegible]
Commissions appointing Commissioners for administering Oaths,	[illegible]	[illegible] and [illegible],	[illegible]
		[illegible],	[illegible]
Commissions connected with the appointment of Justices of the Peace,	[illegible]	[illegible] Judgments,	[illegible]
		[illegible] of Lunacy,	[illegible]
Writs to supersede Justices of the Peace,	[illegible]	Special Commissions of Oyer and Terminer,	[illegible]
[illegible] Justices of the Peace, &c.,	[illegible]	[illegible] Notaries Public,	[illegible]
Attested Copies of all Documents [illegible] in Office,	[illegible]	Total,	[illegible]
Writs of [illegible], and other Writs,	[illegible]		
Writs for the Election of Coroners,	[illegible]	Amount of [illegible] by means of Stamps, [illegible]	

TABLE 59.—HIGH COURT OF JUSTICE.—CHANCERY DIVISION.—LAND JUDGES.—RETURN of PROCEEDINGS in the RECORD and AFFIDAVIT OFFICE, for the Year ended 31st October, 188[illegible], made by the CLERK OF RECORDS AND AFFIDAVITS.

Proceedings.	Number.	Proceedings.	Number.
Petitions filed—		Fiats entered,	[illegible]
By Owners,	[illegible]	Solicitors' Copies,	[illegible]
By other Petitioners,	[illegible]	[illegible] of Landed or Farm Act,	[illegible]
Final Schedule of Incumbrances,	[illegible]	[illegible] Landlord and Tenant Act, [illegible]	[illegible]
Objections to [illegible],	[illegible]		
Claims,	[illegible]	[illegible] Landlord and Tenant Act, [illegible]	[illegible]
Trustees' Objections,	[illegible]		
Miscellaneous Documents,	[illegible]	[illegible] Act, 187[illegible],	[illegible]
Affidavits filed,	[illegible]	Reports [illegible],	[illegible]
Appearances entered,	[illegible]		

TABLE 44.—HIGH COURT OF JUSTICE.—CHANCERY DIVISION.—LAND JUDGES.—RETURN of JUDICIAL PROCEEDINGS in the Year ended 31st December, 1883 [illegible].

PROCEEDINGS.	Total.	Judge [illegible]	Judge [illegible]
Number of Cases pending in Chambers of Judges—			
— at commencement of year,	[illegible]	[illegible]	[illegible]
— at end of year,	[illegible]	[illegible]	[illegible]
— referred to Chambers of Judges,	[illegible]	[illegible]	[illegible]
— for Sale of Encumbered Estates (of which include also applications for Partition),	[illegible]	[illegible]	[illegible]
— for Sale of Unencumbered Estates,	[illegible]	[illegible]	[illegible]
— Settled Estates,	[illegible]	[illegible]	[illegible]
— Investigation of Title,	[illegible]	[illegible]	[illegible]
— Partitions,	[illegible]	[illegible]	[illegible]
— [illegible] on Renewed Leases,	[illegible]	[illegible]	[illegible]
— Apportionment of Rent,	[illegible]	[illegible]	[illegible]
— Specific performance of Contracts of Sale,	[illegible]	[illegible]	[illegible]
— Appointments of New Trustees,	[illegible]	[illegible]	[illegible]
— Orders for Sale by Church Temporalities Commissioners,	[illegible]	[illegible]	[illegible]
Agreements under Landlord and Tenant Act, 1870, Part II,	[illegible]	[illegible]	[illegible]
Building Leases approved,	[illegible]	[illegible]	[illegible]
Petitions [illegible]	[illegible]	[illegible]	[illegible]
Cases in which Titles approved of,	[illegible]	[illegible]	[illegible]
[illegible]	[illegible]	[illegible]	[illegible]
Cases in which Final Schedules have been settled,	[illegible]	[illegible]	[illegible]
Conveyances [illegible] of Title executed,	[illegible]	[illegible]	[illegible]
Petitions dismissed,	[illegible]	[illegible]	[illegible]
Proceedings under Tenure and Improvement of Land (Ireland) Act, [illegible]—			
Number of [illegible]	[illegible]	[illegible]	[illegible]
Number of Orders [illegible]	[illegible]	[illegible]	[illegible]
Number of Orders made on such Petitions,	[illegible]	[illegible]	[illegible]

PARTICULARS.	Total.	Judge [illegible]	Judge [illegible]
	£ s. d.	£ s. d.	£ s. d.
Amount of duty paid in respect of [illegible] Court during the year,	[illegible]	[illegible]	[illegible]
Amount of money paid out during the year,	[illegible]	[illegible]	[illegible]
Amount of Value of Estates whose Title declared,	[illegible]	[illegible]	[illegible]
Net Rental, or Annual Value [illegible] sold,	[illegible]	[illegible]	[illegible]
Amount of the Purchase-money,	[illegible]	[illegible]	[illegible]
Sales to Tenants under Part III of the Land Act, 1870— Amount of Purchase money [illegible] in the years [illegible]	[illegible]	[illegible]	[illegible]
In Cases of Sales of Land in Ulster,	[illegible]	[illegible]	[illegible]
— Munster,	[illegible]	[illegible]	[illegible]
— Leinster,	[illegible]	[illegible]	[illegible]
— Connaught,	[illegible]	[illegible]	[illegible]
Number of Tenant Purchasers in such Sales—			
In those of Land in Ulster,	[illegible]	[illegible]	[illegible]
— Munster,	[illegible]	[illegible]	[illegible]
— Leinster,	[illegible]	[illegible]	[illegible]
— Connaught,	[illegible]	[illegible]	[illegible]
Area of Holdings so Sold to Tenant Purchasers—			
Holdings under [illegible] Acres,	[illegible]	[illegible]	[illegible]
— [illegible]	[illegible]	[illegible]	[illegible]
— [illegible]	[illegible]	[illegible]	[illegible]
— [illegible]	[illegible]	[illegible]	[illegible]
— [illegible]	[illegible]	[illegible]	[illegible]
— [illegible]	[illegible]	[illegible]	[illegible]
— [illegible] Acres and upwards,	[illegible]	[illegible]	[illegible]

TABLE 12.—HIGH COURT OF JUSTICE.—QUEEN'S BENCH DIVISION.—Return of the Proceedings of the Court on the Plea Side in the Year [illegible], made by the Masters of the Court, the Registrar, and the Clerk of Writs.

PROCEEDINGS	Total.		Quarter ending 31st March.		Quarter ending 30th June.		Quarter ending 30th September.		Quarter ending 31st December.	
	No.	Matters Heard in Banco	No.	Matters Heard in Banco	No.	Matters Heard in Banco	No.	Matters Heard in Banco	No.	Matters Heard in Banco
Recorded by Clerk of Writs.										
Writs of Summons issued,	[illegible]	-	[illegible]	-	[illegible]	-	[illegible]	-	[illegible]	-
Writs of Error,	1	-	-	-	-	-	-	-	1	-
Writs of [illegible],	-	-	-	-	-	-	-	-	-	-
[illegible], &c.,	-	-	-	-	-	-	-	-	-	-
[illegible] and Records under Old System,	-	-	-	-	-	-	-	-	-	-
Recorded by Masters.										
Appearances entered,	[illegible]	-	[illegible]	[illegible]	[illegible]	-	[illegible]	-	[illegible]	-
Judgments entered:										
On Affidavit of Service on default of Appearance,	[illegible]	-	[illegible]	[illegible]	[illegible]	-	[illegible]	-	[illegible]	-
By default after default of Appearance—for Plaintiff,	[illegible]	-	[illegible]	-	[illegible]	-	[illegible]	-	[illegible]	-
On Judge's Order, for substituted Service,	[illegible]	-	[illegible]		[illegible]	-	[illegible]	-	[illegible]	-
(Summary) under Order 14, Rule 1,	[illegible]	-	[illegible]	-	[illegible]	-	[illegible]	-	[illegible]	-
On Demurrer, for Plaintiff,	-	-	-	-	-	-	-	-	-	-
On Demurrer, for Defendant,	-	-	-	-	-	-	-	-	-	-
For Plaintiff on Verdict, or Writ of Inquiry,	[illegible]	[illegible]	[illegible]	-	[illegible]	-	[illegible]	-	[illegible]	-
For Defendant on Verdict, or Nonsuit,	[illegible]	-	[illegible]	-	[illegible]	-	[illegible]	-	[illegible]	-
For Defendant on Counter Claim,	[illegible]	-	[illegible]	-	[illegible]	-	-	-	[illegible]	-
Of [illegible],	[illegible]	-	[illegible]	-	-	-	-	-	[illegible]	-
On Special Case for Plaintiff,	-	-	-	-	-	-	-	-	-	-
On Special Case for Defendant,	-	-	-	-	-	-	-	-	-	-
On Judges' orders to stay Proceedings,	-	-	-	-	-	-	-	-	-	-
On Warrants of Attorney,	[illegible]	-	[illegible]	-	[illegible]	-	[illegible]	-	[illegible]	-
On Certificates of Master,	[illegible]	-	[illegible]	-	[illegible]	-	[illegible]	-	[illegible]	-
Other Judgments entered,	[illegible]	-	[illegible]	-	[illegible]	-	[illegible]	-	[illegible]	[illegible]
Executions.										
Writs of Fieri Facias,	[illegible]	-	[illegible]	-	[illegible]	-	[illegible]	-	[illegible]	-
Writs of Possession,	[illegible]	-	[illegible]	-	[illegible]	-	[illegible]	-	[illegible]	-
Writs of [illegible],	-	-	-	-	-	-	-	-	-	-
Recorded by the Registrar.										
Motions for New Trial, or to enter Judgment (Heard):										
Refused,	-	[illegible]	-	[illegible]	-	-	-	-	-	[illegible]
Rules Nisi granted,	-	[illegible]	-	[illegible]	-	[illegible]	-	-	-	[illegible]
Rules Absolute,	-	[illegible]	-	[illegible]	-	[illegible]	-	-	-	[illegible]
Rules Discharged,	-	[illegible]	-	[illegible]	-	[illegible]	-	-	-	[illegible]
Other Motions (Heard):										
Refused,	-	-	-	-	-	-	-	-	-	-
Granted,	-	-	-	-	-	-	-	-	-	[illegible]
Special Cases (Heard):										
Judgment for Plaintiff,	-	[illegible]	[illegible]	-	-	[illegible]	-	-	-	[illegible]
Judgment for Defendant,	-	-	-	-	-	-	-	-	-	-
Demurrers (Heard):										
Judgment for Plaintiff,	-	[illegible]	[illegible]	-	-	[illegible]	-	-	-	-
Judgment for Defendant,	-	[illegible]	-	-	-	[illegible]	-	-	-	[illegible]
Side Bar Rules,	[illegible]	-	[illegible]	-	[illegible]	[illegible]	[illegible]	-	[illegible]	-
Matters heard on which the Court divided,	[illegible]	[illegible]	-	-	-	[illegible]	-	-	-	-
Other Proceedings,	-	-	-	-	-	[illegible]	-	-	[illegible]	-
Recorded by the Master.										
Causes referred to Masters under Common Law Procedure Acts, [illegible] and [illegible], and in other Matters,	[illegible]	-	[illegible]	-	[illegible]	[illegible]	[illegible]	-	[illegible]	-
Bills of Sale,	[illegible]	-	[illegible]	-	[illegible]	-	[illegible]	-	[illegible]	-
Affidavits filed,	[illegible]	-	[illegible]	-	[illegible]	-	[illegible]	-	[illegible]	-

TABLE [illegible].—HIGH COURT OF JUSTICE.—COMMON PLEAS DIVISION.—Return of the Proceedings of the Court on the [illegible] Side in the Year [illegible], made by the Master of the Court, the Registrar, and the Clerk of Writs.

PROCEEDINGS	Total. No.	Total. Matters Heard in Banc	Quarter ending 31st March. No.	Quarter ending 31st March. Matters Heard in Banc	Quarter ending 30th June. No.	Quarter ending 30th June. Matters Heard in Banc	Quarter ending 30th September. No.	Quarter ending 30th September. Matters Heard in Banc	Quarter ending 31st December. No.	Quarter ending 31st December. Matters Heard in Banc
Issued by Clerk of Writs.										
Writs of Summons issued	[illegible]		[illegible]	-	[illegible]	-	[illegible]	-	[illegible]	
Writs of Revivor	[illegible]	.	[illegible]	.	.	.	.	.	[illegible]	
Writs of Replevin	.	.	.	.	.	.	.	.	.	.
Injunction, Certiorari, &c.	.	.	.	.	.	.	-	.	.	.
Executions and Records under Old System	.		.	.	.	.	.		.	.
Issued by Master.										
Appearances entered	[illegible]		[illegible]	.	[illegible]	.	[illegible]	.	[illegible]	
Judgments entered: On Affidavit of Service on default of Appearance	.	.	.		.	.	.	.	.	
By default [illegible] Appearance for Plaintiff	[illegible]	.	[illegible]	.	[illegible]	.	[illegible]	.	[illegible]	.
On Judge's Order, for substituted Service	[illegible]	.	[illegible]	.	[illegible]	.	[illegible]	.	.	
(Summary) under Order [illegible], Rule [illegible]	[illegible]	.	[illegible]	.	[illegible]	.	[illegible]	.	[illegible]	.
On Demurrer for Plaintiff		.	.	.		.		.	.	.
On Demurrer for Defendant		.	.	.	.	.		.	.	
For Plaintiff on Verdict, or Writ of Inquiry	[illegible]	.	[illegible]	.	[illegible]	.	[illegible]	.	[illegible]	
For Defendant on Verdict, or Nonsuit	[illegible]		[illegible]	-	[illegible]	.	[illegible]	-	[illegible]	.
For Defendant on [illegible]		.		.		.		.		
Of Nonpros, for Defendant	[illegible]	.	[illegible]	.	[illegible]	.	[illegible]	.	[illegible]	
On Special Case for Plaintiff		.	.	.	.	.	.	.		
On Special Case for Defendant		.	.	.	.	.	.	.		
On Judges' Orders in any Proceedings		.	.	.	.	.	.	.		.
On Warrants of Attorney	[illegible]	.	[illegible]	.	[illegible]	.	[illegible]	.	[illegible]	
On [illegible]	[illegible]	.	[illegible]	.	[illegible]	.	[illegible]	.	[illegible]	.
Other Judgments, entered	[illegible]	.	[illegible]	.	[illegible]	.	[illegible]	.	[illegible]	
Executions: Writs of Fieri Facias	[illegible]	.	[illegible]	.	[illegible]	.	[illegible]		[illegible]	
Writs of Possession	[illegible]	.	[illegible]	.	[illegible]	.	[illegible]		[illegible]	.
Writs of Elegit	.	.	.	.	.	.	.	.	.	.
Entered by the Registrar.										
Motions for New Trial, or to enter Judgment [illegible]: Refused	.	[illegible]	.	[illegible]	.	.	.			[illegible]
Rule Nisi granted	.	[illegible]	.	[illegible]	.	[illegible]	.			[illegible]
Rule made Absolute	.	[illegible]	.	[illegible]	.	[illegible]	.			[illegible]
Rule Discharged	.	[illegible]	.	[illegible]	.	[illegible]	.	.		[illegible]
Other Motions (Heard): Refused	.	[illegible]	.	[illegible]	.	[illegible]	.	.		[illegible]
Granted	.	[illegible]	.	[illegible]	.	[illegible]	.	.		[illegible]
Special Cases (Heard): Judgment for Plaintiff	.	[illegible]	.	.	.	[illegible]	.	.		.
Judgment for Defendant	.	.	.	.	.	.	.	.		.
Other Special Cases (Heard)	.	.	.	.	.	.	.	.	.	.
Demurrers (Heard): Judgment for Plaintiff	.	[illegible]	.	[illegible]	.	[illegible]	.	.	.	.
Judgment for Defendant	.	[illegible]	.	[illegible]	.	.	.	.	.	.
Other Demurrers (Heard)	.	.	.	.	.	.	.	.	.	.
Appeals Decided	.	[illegible]	.	.	.	[illegible]	.	.	.	.
[illegible]	[illegible]	.	[illegible]	.	[illegible]	.	[illegible]	.	[illegible]	.
Matters heard in which the Court divided	[illegible]	.	[illegible]	.	.	.	.	.	[illegible]	.
Other Proceedings: Cases Referred to Master	.	[illegible]	.	[illegible]	.	[illegible]	.	.	.	[illegible]
Jurors' Fines and Appeals	.	[illegible]	.	[illegible]	.	.	.	.	.	.
Returned by the Master.										
Causes referred to Master under Common Law Procedure Acts, [illegible] and [illegible], and on other questions	[illegible]	.	[illegible]	.	[illegible]	.	[illegible]	.	[illegible]	.
Number of [illegible]	[illegible]	.	[illegible]	.	[illegible]	-	[illegible]	.	[illegible]	.
Affidavits filed	[illegible]	.	[illegible]	.	[illegible]		[illegible]	.	[illegible]	.
Mortgage Affidavits	[illegible]	.	[illegible]	-	[illegible]	.	[illegible]	.	[illegible]	.

a [illegible]

TABLE 44.—HIGH COURT OF JUSTICE.—EXCHEQUER DIVISION.—Returns of the Proceedings of the Court on the Plea Side in the Year [illegible], made by the Master of the Court, the Registrar, and the Clerk of Writs.

PROCEEDINGS	Total No.	Total Motions Heard or Taken	Quarter ending 31st March No.	Motions Heard or Taken	Quarter ending 30th June No.	Motions Heard or Taken	Quarter ending 30th September No.	Motions Heard or Taken	Quarter ending 31st December No.	Motions Heard or Taken
Entered by Clerk of Writs.										
Writs of Summons issued,	[illegible]	.	[illegible]	.	[illegible]	.	[illegible]		[illegible]	.
Writs of Revivor,	[illegible]	.	[illegible]	.	.	.	[illegible]	.	.	.
Writs of Replevin,	.	.	.	.	.	.	.	.	.	.
Enquiries, Suggestions, &c.,	1	.	.	.	.	.	.	.	[illegible]	.
[illegible] under Old System,	.	.	.	.	.	.	.	.	.	.
Entered by Master.										
Appearances entered,	[illegible]	.	[illegible]	.	[illegible]	.	[illegible]	.	[illegible]	
Judgments entered:— On Affidavit of Service for default of Appearance or Defence,	[illegible]	.	[illegible]	.	[illegible]		[illegible]	.	[illegible]	
By default after [illegible] of Appearance for Plaintiff	.	.	.	.	.		.	.	.	.
On Judge's Order, for [illegible] Service, (Summary) under Order [illegible]	[illegible]	.	[illegible]	.	[illegible]	.	[illegible]	.	[illegible]	
On Demurrer, for Plaintiff,	.	.	.	.		.	.	.	.	.
On Demurrer, for Defendant,	.	.		.	.	.	.	.		
For Plaintiff on Verdict, or Writ of Enquiry,	[illegible]	.	[illegible]	.	[illegible]	.	[illegible]	.	[illegible]	.
For Defendant on Verdict, or Nonsuit,	[illegible]	.	[illegible]	.	[illegible]	.	[illegible]	.	7	.
For Defendant on Common Claim,	.	.	.	.	.		.	.		.
On Demurrer, for Defendant,	.	.	.	.		.		.	.	.
On Special Case for Plaintiff,	.	.	.	.	.		.	.		.
On Special Case for Defendant,	.	.	.	.	.		.	.	.	.
On Judges' Orders in other Proceedings,	.	.	.	.	.		.		.	.
On Warrants of Attorney,	[illegible]	.	[illegible]	.	[illegible]		[illegible]	.	[illegible]	.
*On Certificate of Master	[illegible]	.	[illegible]	.	[illegible]	.	1		[illegible]	.
Other Judgments entered,	[illegible]	.	[illegible]	.	[illegible]		[illegible]	.	[illegible]	.
Executions:— Writs of Fieri Facias,	[illegible]	.	[illegible]	.	[illegible]	.	[illegible]		[illegible]	.
Writs of Possession,	[illegible]	.	[illegible]	.	[illegible]		[illegible]	.	[illegible]	.
Writs of [illegible],	.	.	.	.	.	.		.	.	
Entered by the Registrar.										
Motions for New Trial, or to enter Judgment (Heard):— Refused,	.	[illegible]	.	.	.	[illegible]	.			[illegible]
Rules Nisi granted,	.	[illegible]	.	.	.	[illegible]	.	.		[illegible]
Rules Absolute,	.	[illegible]	.	.	.	[illegible]	.	.	.	[illegible]
Rules Discharged,	.	[illegible]	.	[illegible]	.	[illegible]	.	.	.	[illegible]
Other Motions (Heard):— Refused,	.	[illegible]	.	[illegible]	.	[illegible]	.	[illegible]	.	[illegible]
Granted,	.	[illegible]	.	[illegible]	.	[illegible]	.	[illegible]	.	[illegible]
Special Case (Heard):— Judgment for Plaintiff,	.	[illegible]	.	.	.	1	.	.		1
Judgment for Defendant,	.	1	.	.	.	1	.	.	.	.
Demurrers (Heard):— Judgment for Plaintiff,	.	[illegible]	.	[illegible]	.	[illegible]	.	.	.	.
Judgment for Defendant,	.	[illegible]	.	[illegible]	.	[illegible]	.	.	.	
Side Bar Rules,	[illegible]	.	[illegible]	.	[illegible]	.	[illegible]	.	[illegible]	.
Matters heard in which the Court divided,	.	.	.	.	.			.	.	.
Other Proceedings,	.	.	.	.	.			.	.	.
Entered by Master.										
Causes referred to Master under Common Law Procedure Acts, 1853 and 1856, and on other Matters,	[illegible]		[illegible]	.	[illegible]	.	[illegible]	.	[illegible]	.
Affidavits filed,	[illegible]	.	[illegible]	.	[illegible]	.	[illegible]	.	[illegible]	.
Other Documents filed (and all [illegible] entered herein),	.	.	.	.	.	.	.	.	.	.

* Judgment is rarely entered on the [illegible] [illegible] generally paid [illegible].

TABLE [illegible].—HIGH COURT OF JUSTICE.—QUEEN'S BENCH, COMMON PLEAS, AND EXCHEQUER DIVISIONS.—RETURN of BUSINESS at CHAMBERS and Before a SINGLE JUDGE in COURT in the Year [illegible], made by the Registrars.

PROCEEDINGS.	Total in all Divisions	Queen's Bench Division: Total in Year	Quarters ending 31st March	30th June	30th Sept	31st Dec	Common Pleas Division: Total in Year	Quarters ending 31st March	30th June	30th Sept	31st Dec	Exchequer Division: Total in Year	Quarters ending 31st March	30th June	30th Sept	31st Dec
At Chambers																
Summonses,	[illegible]	[illegible]	[illegible]	[illegible]	[illegible]	[illegible]	[illegible]	[illegible]	[illegible]	[illegible]	[illegible]	[illegible]	[illegible]	[illegible]	[illegible]	[illegible]
Before a Single Judge in Court or at Chambers																
Ex parte Motions concerning Common Orders, Lapsed,	[illegible]	[illegible]	[illegible]	[illegible]	[illegible]	[illegible]	[illegible]	[illegible]	[illegible]	[illegible]	[illegible]	[illegible]	[illegible]	[illegible]	[illegible]	[illegible]
Motions on Notice:																
Granted,	[illegible]	[illegible]	[illegible]	[illegible]	[illegible]	[illegible]	[illegible]	[illegible]	[illegible]	[illegible]	[illegible]	[illegible]	[illegible]	[illegible]	[illegible]	[illegible]
Refused, or no Rule,	[illegible]	[illegible]	[illegible]	[illegible]	[illegible]	[illegible]	[illegible]	[illegible]	[illegible]	[illegible]	[illegible]	[illegible]	[illegible]	[illegible]	[illegible]	[illegible]
Discharged,	[illegible]	[illegible]	[illegible]	–	–	[illegible]	[illegible]	[illegible]	[illegible]	[illegible]	[illegible]	[illegible]	[illegible]	[illegible]	[illegible]	[illegible]
Referred to Master,	[illegible]	[illegible]	[illegible]	[illegible]	[illegible]	[illegible]	[illegible]	–	[illegible]	[illegible]	[illegible]	[illegible]	[illegible]	[illegible]	[illegible]	[illegible]

TABLE [illegible].—HIGH COURT OF JUSTICE.—QUEEN'S BENCH, COMMON PLEAS AND EXCHEQUER DIVISIONS.—Return of Proceedings and State of the Business as to Actions entered for Jury Trial at the Courts in the Year [illegible], made by the Registrars.

PARTICULARS	Total	Hilary Sittings, ending 1st April	Easter Sittings, ending 16th May	Trinity Sittings, ending 12th August	Michaelmas Sittings, ending 21st December
Number of New Actions entered for Trial, including Remanets from previous Sittings,	[illegible]	[illegible]	[illegible]	[illegible]	[illegible]
Number of Trials determined before a Special Jury [illegible], before a Common Jury [illegible], before a Judge without a Jury [illegible],	[illegible]	[illegible]	[illegible]	[illegible]	[illegible]
Number of Trials undetermined before a Special Jury [illegible], before a Common Jury [illegible],	[illegible]	[illegible]	[illegible]	[illegible]	[illegible]
Referred to Master,	–	–	–	–	–
Referred to Arbitration,	[illegible]	[illegible]	[illegible]	–	–
Number of Remanets by order, &c.,	[illegible]	[illegible]	[illegible]	[illegible]	[illegible]
Number of Remanets for want of time to try,					
Number of Causes withdrawn,	[illegible]	–	[illegible]	[illegible]	–
Number of Actions struck out, &c.,	[illegible]	[illegible]	[illegible]	[illegible]	[illegible]
Venue changed,	[illegible]	[illegible]	–	[illegible]	[illegible]

TABLE 4A.—HIGH COURT OF JUSTICE.—QUEEN'S BENCH, COMMON PLEAS AND EXCHEQUER DIVISIONS.—Return of the Nature and Results of the Actions Tried or otherwise Disposed of in Court, in the Year [illegible], made by the Registrars.

NATURE OF THE SUITS TRIED OR OTHERWISE DISPOSED OF IN COURT.	Total.	Total Amount Recovered.
On Promissory Notes, Bills of Exchange, &c.	[illegible]	[illegible]
On Bonds,	[illegible]	[illegible]
For Goods sold and delivered, and bargained and sold,	[illegible]	[illegible]
For Work and Labour done,	[illegible]	[illegible]
For Money paid, advanced, lent, or received,	[illegible]	[illegible]
For Compensation for Personal Injuries, and Compensation under Lord Campbell's Act,	[illegible]	[illegible]
Against Professional Men for Negligence,	[illegible]	[illegible]
For Compensation for other Injuries from Negligence,	[illegible]	[illegible]
Actions in respect of Distress,	[illegible]	[illegible]
Actions of Trover or Detinue,	[illegible]	[illegible]
For Breach of Contract,	[illegible]	[illegible]
For Breach of Warranty,	[illegible]	[illegible]
For Recovery of Land (Ejectment),	[illegible]	[illegible]
Trespass to Land, Houses, &c.	[illegible]	[illegible]
For Breach of Promise of Marriage,	[illegible]	[illegible]
Seduction,	[illegible]	[illegible]
Criminal Conversation with Wife,	[illegible]	[illegible]
Libel,	[illegible]	[illegible]
Slander,	[illegible]	[illegible]
Malicious Prosecution,	[illegible]	[illegible]
False Imprisonment,	[illegible]	[illegible]
Assault,	[illegible]	[illegible]
Interpleader Issues,	[illegible]	[illegible]
For Breach of Covenant,	[illegible]	[illegible]
For Recovery of Rent, and Use and Occupation,	[illegible]	[illegible]
On Life, Fire, and Marine Policies,	[illegible]	[illegible]
Fraudulent Misrepresentation,	[illegible]	[illegible]
Calls on Shares,	[illegible]	[illegible]
Wrongful Dismissal,	[illegible]	[illegible]
Other Suits,	[illegible]	[illegible]
TOTAL,	[illegible]	[illegible]

TABLE 19.—DUBLIN COUNTY COURT APPEALS.—RETURN of NUMBER of APPEALS entered for hearing before a Single Judge of Superior Courts in the Year 1882, from the Recorder of the City, and County Court Judge of the County of Dublin, made by the Registrar [illegible] (Sec. [illegible] Vic. c. [illegible], and [illegible] Vic. c. [illegible])

APPEALS	Total	Hilary Sittings				Easter Sittings				Trinity Sittings				Michaelmas Sittings			
		Entered	Affirmed	Reversed	Settled, Struck out, or Withdrawn	Entered	Affirmed	Reversed	Settled, Struck out, or Withdrawn	Entered	Affirmed	Reversed	Settled, Struck out, or Withdrawn	Entered	Affirmed	Reversed	Settled, Struck out, or Withdrawn
Equity																	
From Recorder, City of Dublin	[illegible]	[illegible]	[illegible]	[illegible]	[illegible]	[illegible]	[illegible]	[illegible]	[illegible]	[illegible]	[illegible]	[illegible]	[illegible]	[illegible]	[illegible]	[illegible]	[illegible]
From County Court Judge, County of Dublin	[illegible]	[illegible]	[illegible]	[illegible]	[illegible]	[illegible]	[illegible]	[illegible]	[illegible]	[illegible]	[illegible]	[illegible]	[illegible]	[illegible]	[illegible]	[illegible]	[illegible]
Civil																	
From Recorder, City of Dublin	[illegible]	[illegible]	[illegible]	[illegible]	[illegible]	[illegible]	[illegible]	[illegible]	[illegible]	[illegible]	[illegible]	[illegible]	[illegible]	[illegible]	[illegible]	[illegible]	[illegible]
From County Court Judge, County of Dublin	[illegible]	[illegible]	[illegible]	[illegible]	[illegible]	[illegible]	[illegible]	[illegible]	[illegible]	[illegible]	[illegible]	[illegible]	[illegible]	[illegible]	[illegible]	[illegible]	[illegible]
Case Stated																	
From Recorder, City of Dublin	[illegible]	[illegible]	[illegible]	[illegible]	[illegible]	[illegible]	[illegible]	[illegible]	[illegible]	[illegible]	[illegible]	[illegible]	[illegible]	[illegible]	[illegible]	[illegible]	[illegible]
From County Court Judge, County of Dublin	[illegible]	[illegible]	[illegible]	[illegible]	[illegible]	[illegible]	[illegible]	[illegible]	[illegible]	[illegible]	[illegible]	[illegible]	[illegible]	[illegible]	[illegible]	[illegible]	[illegible]
Total Number of Appeals entered	[illegible]	[illegible]	[illegible]	[illegible]	[illegible]	[illegible]	[illegible]	[illegible]	[illegible]	[illegible]	[illegible]	[illegible]	[illegible]	[illegible]	[illegible]	[illegible]	[illegible]

a [illegible] b [illegible] c [illegible]

TABLE 20.—QUEEN'S BENCH, COMMON PLEAS, AND EXCHEQUER DIVISIONS OF THE HIGH COURT OF JUSTICE.—RETURN of CASES of [illegible] remitted to Civil Bill Courts, under [illegible] Vic., cap. [illegible], secs. [illegible] and [illegible], for the year 1882 made by the Registrars.

PROCEEDINGS UNDER STAT. [illegible] VIC., CAP. [illegible]	Queen's Bench		Common Pleas		Exchequer		[illegible]		
	[illegible]	[illegible]	[illegible]	[illegible]	[illegible]	[illegible]	[illegible]	[illegible]	Total
Number of Applications to refer Cases of Contract to County Court (sec. [illegible])	[illegible]	[illegible]	[illegible]	[illegible]	[illegible]	[illegible]	[illegible]	[illegible]	[illegible]
Applications granted	[illegible]	[illegible]	[illegible]	[illegible]	[illegible]	[illegible]	[illegible]	[illegible]	[illegible]
" refused	[illegible]	[illegible]	[illegible]	[illegible]	[illegible]	[illegible]	[illegible]	[illegible]	[illegible]
Number of Applications to refer cases of Tort to County Court (sec. [illegible])	[illegible]	[illegible]	[illegible]	[illegible]	[illegible]	[illegible]	[illegible]	[illegible]	[illegible]
Applications refused	[illegible]	[illegible]	[illegible]	[illegible]	[illegible]	[illegible]	[illegible]	[illegible]	[illegible]
" granted	[illegible]	[illegible]	[illegible]	[illegible]	[illegible]	[illegible]	[illegible]	[illegible]	[illegible]
" [illegible] Security for costs, and [illegible] in Superior Court	[illegible]	[illegible]	[illegible]	[illegible]	[illegible]	[illegible]	[illegible]	[illegible]	[illegible]
" [illegible] to give Security, and so remitted	[illegible]	[illegible]	[illegible]	[illegible]	[illegible]	[illegible]	[illegible]	[illegible]	[illegible]

* The Registrars of the Queen's Bench and Exchequer Divisions [illegible] that the number of these applications is not known to them.

TABLE 5.—HIGH COURT OF JUSTICE, QUEEN'S BENCH DIVISION. CROWN SIDE.—(a) Proceedings other than Causes entered for Jury Trial.—Return of Queen's Coroner, Attorney, and Master on the Crown Side, for the Year [illegible].

Proceedings in [illegible]	Number	Proceedings [illegible]	Number	Amount [illegible] £ s. d.
Writs or Rules applied for, viz.—		[illegible]		
[illegible]	[illegible]	[illegible]—City of Dublin,	[illegible]	[illegible]
Attachment,	[illegible]	County of Dublin,	[illegible]	[illegible]
Mandamus,	[illegible]	[illegible]		
Quo Warranto,	[illegible]	[illegible]	[illegible]	—
Habeas Corpus ad Subjiciendum,	[illegible]	[illegible]	[illegible]	—
Prohibition,	[illegible]	[illegible]		
Certiorari including Orders of Sessions and Special Cases removed,	[illegible]	Allowed,		—
Error,	[illegible]	Disallowed,		—
Jury Process,	[illegible]	[illegible]		
Other Special Rules,	[illegible]	Allowed,	[illegible]	
Total Writs or Rules applied for,	[illegible]	Disallowed,	[illegible]	
[illegible] Grand Jury [illegible]	[illegible]	[illegible]	[illegible]	
Applications to quash Grand Jury [illegible]		Allowed,		
Grand Jury under the [illegible]	[illegible]	Disallowed,		
Informations—(1) Filed ex officio,	[illegible]			
(2) Leave to file, applied for,	[illegible]	Proceedings in Banco.		
Trial by Jury—Criminal Cases—at Bar,	[illegible]	Special [illegible]—Granted,	[illegible]	—
by Single Judge,	[illegible]	[illegible]	[illegible]	—
[illegible]	[illegible]	[illegible]—[illegible]	[illegible]	—
Number of [illegible]	[illegible]	[illegible]	[illegible]	—
Affidavits filed,	[illegible]	[illegible]		—
[illegible]		[illegible]		—
Grounded on Affidavits,	[illegible]	[illegible]—Allowed,		—
Not so grounded,	[illegible]	Overruled,		—
Quo Warranto Informations filed,	[illegible]	[illegible]—Allowed,		—
Writs of [illegible] issued,	[illegible]	[illegible]		—
[illegible]		[illegible]	[illegible]	—
[illegible]	[illegible]	[illegible]		—
[illegible]	[illegible]	[illegible]		—
[illegible]	[illegible]	[illegible]	[illegible]	—
[illegible]	[illegible]	[illegible]	[illegible]	—
[illegible]	[illegible]	[illegible]	[illegible]	—

* [illegible]

(b.) Nature of the Causes entered for Trial, and Results of the Causes Tried at Court, together with the Amount [illegible] by Traversers and the Number of each Class of Amount.

Nature of the Causes Entered for Trial.	[illegible]	[illegible]										[illegible]											[illegible]
[illegible]	[illegible]	[illegible]	[illegible]	[illegible]	[illegible]	[illegible]	[illegible]	[illegible]	[illegible]	[illegible]	[illegible]	[illegible]	[illegible]	[illegible]	[illegible]	[illegible]	[illegible]	[illegible]	[illegible]	[illegible]	[illegible]	[illegible]	[illegible]
Total,	[illegible]	[illegible]	[illegible]	[illegible]	[illegible]	[illegible]	[illegible]	[illegible]	[illegible]	[illegible]	[illegible]	[illegible]	[illegible]	[illegible]	[illegible]	[illegible]	[illegible]	[illegible]	[illegible]	[illegible]	[illegible]	[illegible]	[illegible]

	Number
[illegible]	[illegible]
[illegible]	[illegible]
[illegible]	[illegible]
[illegible]	[illegible]
[illegible]	[illegible]
[illegible]	[illegible]
[illegible]	[illegible]
[illegible]	[illegible]
[illegible]	[illegible]
	[illegible]

Note.—This Return is made subject to the General Observations [illegible] to Crown Office Returns, Criminal and Judicial Statistics, [illegible], page [illegible]

TABLE [illegible].—PROCEEDINGS as to ELECTION PETITIONS. Return of Petitions lodged in 1883, made by the Master of the Common Pleas Division of the High Court of Justice.

Number of each Petition lodged	County or Borough in which the Election took place	Grounds of Petition	Decision of Judge		Petition withdrawn	Petition abated	Costs of Petitioner	Costs of Respondent	General Observations
			For Petitioner	For Respondent					
							£ s. d.	£ s. d.	
	—	—	—	—	—	—	—	—	—

TABLE [illegible].—HIGH COURT OF JUSTICE, COMMON PLEAS DIVISION.—Return of Proceedings relating to the Acknowledgments of Deeds by Married Women, in the year 1883, made by the Registrar of Certificates and Affidavits of Acknowledgments, under 3 and 4 Wm. IV., cap. 92.

PROCEEDINGS	Number
Acknowledgments filed, total number,	[illegible]
Number Acknowledged before Perpetual Commissioners,	[illegible]
" " Special Commissioners,	[illegible]
" " Judges of High Court of Justice,	[illegible]
" " County Court Judges and Chairman ... Act, 1877,	[illegible]
Perpetual Commissioners appointed,	[illegible]
Special Commissions granted,	[illegible]
Searches for Acknowledgments,	[illegible]

TABLE [illegible].—HIGH COURT OF JUSTICE, EXCHEQUER DIVISION.—REVENUE SIDE.—Return of Proceedings in the year 1883, made by the Master of the Division.

PROCEEDINGS	Number
Equity—	
Informations filed,	[illegible]
[illegible]	[illegible]
[illegible]	[illegible]
[illegible]	[illegible]
[illegible]	[illegible]
[illegible]	[illegible]
[illegible]	[illegible]
[illegible]	[illegible]
[illegible]	[illegible]
[illegible]	[illegible]
[illegible]	[illegible]
[illegible] (Crown Bonds, and Recognizances),	[illegible]
Affidavits filed,	[illegible]
Writs and Fiants filed,	[illegible]
[illegible]	[illegible]
[illegible]	[illegible]
[illegible]	[illegible]
Warrants,	[illegible]
[illegible]	[illegible]
Powers of Attorney,	[illegible]
[illegible]	[illegible]
Appointments of [illegible] ordered,	[illegible]
Warrants of Appointment by Lord Lieutenant of Sheriffs,	[illegible]
[illegible]	[illegible]
[illegible]	[illegible]

TABLE [illegible].—REGISTRY OF JUDGMENTS.—Return of Proceedings in the Office for the Year 1883, made by the Registrar of Judgments.

PROCEEDINGS	Registered	Re-registered	Total	PROCEEDINGS	Registered	Re-registered	Total
Judgments of Superior Courts obtained before 16th July, 1850,	[illegible]	[illegible]	[illegible]	Recognizances,	[illegible]	[illegible]	[illegible]
Judgments of Superior Courts obtained since 16th July, 1850,	[illegible]	[illegible]	[illegible]	Crown Bonds,	[illegible]	[illegible]	[illegible]
Revivals,	[illegible]	[illegible]	[illegible]	Judgments at Suit of Crown,	[illegible]	[illegible]	[illegible]
Decrees, Rules, and Orders,	[illegible]	[illegible]	[illegible]	[illegible]	[illegible]	[illegible]	[illegible]
Lis pendens,	[illegible]	[illegible]	[illegible]	Inquisitions,	[illegible]	[illegible]	[illegible]
Civil Bill Decrees [illegible],	[illegible]	[illegible]	[illegible]	Acceptances of Office,	[illegible]	[illegible]	[illegible]
Judgments from Courts in England and Scotland,	[illegible]	[illegible]	[illegible]				
Total,	[illegible]	[illegible]	[illegible]	Total,	[illegible]	[illegible]	[illegible]

Satisfactions of Judgments,	[illegible]	Negative Searches on the [illegible] Stamps made,	[illegible]
Vacates of Recognizances,	[illegible]	Do. do. [illegible] do.	[illegible]
Cancellations of Crown Bonds,	[illegible]	[illegible] Searches made by Public,	[illegible]
Negative Searches on [illegible] Stamps made,	[illegible]	Duplicate [illegible] issued,	[illegible]

Number of [illegible] Certificates issued upon which the Registrar, pursuant to [illegible] Vic., c. [illegible], received fees, . . . [illegible]

TABLE [illegible].—HIGH COURT OF JUSTICE—CHANCERY DIVISION—LAND JUDGES.—RETURN of PROCEEDINGS in the RECORD of TITLE OFFICE for the Year ended [illegible] November, [illegible], made by the [illegible].

—	[illegible]			[illegible]		
	Number	Value [illegible]	Amount of [illegible]	Number	Value [illegible]	Amount of [illegible]
		£ s. d.	£ s. d.		£ s. d.	£ s. d.
[illegible] of Title.	[illegible]	[illegible]	[illegible]	[illegible]	[illegible]	[illegible]
Number of [illegible]	[illegible]	—	—	[illegible]	—	—
Number of [illegible]	[illegible]	—	—	[illegible]	—	—
Number of [illegible]	—	—	—	[illegible]	—	—
[illegible] Estates.	[illegible]	—	—	[illegible]	—	—
Applications under [illegible] of Act.	—	—	—	[illegible]	—	—
[illegible] of Title [illegible] in such Applications.	—	—	—	[illegible]	—	—
Proceedings under "Land [illegible] Act"—						
Certificates [illegible] by the Court [illegible]	None.					
[illegible] actually issued,						

TABLE [illegible].—REGISTRY OF DEEDS, IRELAND.—RETURN showing STATE of BUSINESS in [illegible], made by the [illegible]

—	Number	—	At Commencement of Year.	At End of Year.
Number of [illegible]	[illegible]	Dates up to which [illegible]	[illegible]	[illegible]
[illegible]	[illegible]	[illegible]	[illegible]	[illegible]
[illegible]	[illegible]	[illegible]	[illegible]	[illegible]
[illegible]	[illegible]	[illegible]	[illegible]	[illegible]
[illegible]	[illegible]	Number of [illegible]	[illegible]	[illegible]
[illegible]	[illegible]	[illegible]	[illegible]	[illegible]
Number of [illegible]				[illegible]
[illegible]				[illegible]

TABLE [illegible].—HIGH COURT OF JUSTICE—CONSOLIDATED TAXING OFFICE.—[illegible] in the [illegible] for the Year [illegible], made by the [illegible].

NATURE OF PROCEEDINGS.	Number [illegible]	Number of [illegible]	Number of [illegible]	Amount of [illegible]	Amount of [illegible]	Amount [illegible]
Chancery Division				£ s. d.	£ s. d.	£ s. d.
[illegible]	[illegible]	[illegible]	[illegible]	[illegible]	[illegible]	[illegible]
Land Judges [illegible]	[illegible]	[illegible]	[illegible]	—	[illegible]	[illegible]
Probate and Matrimonial Division,	[illegible]	[illegible]	[illegible]	[illegible]	[illegible]	[illegible]
Common Law [illegible]	[illegible]	[illegible]	[illegible]	[illegible]	[illegible]	[illegible]
Total [illegible] all Divisions.	[illegible]	[illegible]	[illegible]	[illegible]	[illegible]	[illegible]
[illegible] Bills [illegible]	[illegible]	[illegible]	[illegible]	[illegible]	[illegible]	—
[illegible] Bills [illegible]	[illegible]	[illegible]	[illegible]	[illegible]	[illegible]	—

(a) [illegible]

[illegible]

TABLE [illegible].—HIGH COURT OF JUSTICE—CHANCERY DIVISION.—(a.) RECEIVERS' OFFICE OF LAND JUDGES.—RETURN for the Year [illegible], made by the Examiner.

Number of Receivers appointed by Land Judges during [illegible],	[illegible]	
" " " by other Judges of the High Court of Justice during [illegible], but attending before Land Judges,	[illegible]	[illegible]
" " previously appointed, still under Land Judges,	[illegible]	
Total number of Receivers under Land Judges at end of [illegible],	[illegible]	
Number of Lodgings for [illegible] years, pending the Cause,	[illegible]	
" " for shorter periods,	[illegible]	
" " by lodgings,	[illegible]	
" " by [illegible] without lodgings,	[illegible]	
" Affidavits filed,	[illegible]	
" Summonses issued,	[illegible]	
" [illegible] in writing of Receivers,	[illegible]	
" Leases,	[illegible]	
" Agreements for Lettings of Land,	[illegible]	
" Directions or Adjudications of Land Judges,	[illegible]	
" Orders of Land Judges,	[illegible]	

* Including directions and [illegible] of Examiner under General Orders [illegible].

(b.) Receivers' and Guardians' Accounts passed, which are filed in Consolidated Receipts and Writ Office, by Class of Receipts and Writs.

—	Number of Accounts passed in [illegible]	Receipt of each Account.
By Guardians or Receivers in Minor Matters,	[illegible]	[illegible]
By Receivers in other Actions and Suits,	[illegible]	[illegible]
Total,	[illegible]	[illegible]

TABLE [illegible].—LUNACY DEPARTMENT.—Return of Proceedings in the Office of the Registrar in Lunacy for the Year ended 31st December, [illegible], made by the Chief Clerk.

PROCEEDINGS	Number	PROCEEDINGS	Number
Number of Lunatics under Court, 31st December, [illegible],	[illegible]	Number of Medical Visitors' Reports received, [illegible]	[illegible]
Orders for Commission of Lunacy,	[illegible]	Number of Medical Visitors' Reports received under [illegible], [illegible]	
[illegible] of Lunacy in lieu of Commissions, and Declarations that persons are [illegible] under the third [illegible] of the Lunacy Regulation (Ireland) Act [illegible],	[illegible]	Certificates of Medical Visitors' Fees issued,	[illegible]
Reports made to the Lord Chancellor by the Registrar in Lunacy as to Property, [illegible] and Maintenance, of Lunatics and their families, and Appointment of new Persons and Estates [illegible], and for [illegible] or varying Maintenance or [illegible] of Lunatics, and as to granting Leases, and for [illegible] of Lunatics' Estates, and other Miscellaneous Matters,	[illegible]	Reports received from Clerks of [illegible] as to Dangerous Lunatics,	[illegible]
Orders by Lord Chancellor, including [illegible] confirming Registrar's Reports,	[illegible]	Reports received from [illegible] of Lunatic Asylums as to Persons admitted into Private Lunatic Asylums,	[illegible]
Affidavits filed,	[illegible]	Returns received from [illegible] Private Lunatic Asylums,	[illegible]
Petitions of Applications for Commission of Persons for Estates,	[illegible]	Receipts of Orders of [illegible],	[illegible]
[illegible] issued from Committee of Persons,	[illegible]	Copies issued,	[illegible]
Number of Applications to Committee of Estates for Returns,	[illegible]	Attested Copies of other Documents issued,	[illegible]
Returns sent and [illegible] Committee of Estate,	[illegible]	Number of Lunatics under Court, 31st December, [illegible],	[illegible]
Notices of Appointments for [illegible] of Medical Visitors, [illegible]		Number of Lunacy Matters under Court, 31st December, [illegible],	[illegible]
Number of Appointments for Reports of Medical Visitors, under section [illegible] of Lunacy Regulation (Ireland) Act, [illegible], [illegible]	[illegible]	Accounts and Affidavits of Committees and Receivers taken and passed by the Lord Judge, [illegible]	
		Accounts passed by the Registrar in Lunacy, [illegible]	[illegible]
		Gross Annual Rentals of Lunatics under Control of the Lord Chancellor, [illegible] by the Committee [illegible] with the [illegible] of [illegible], or of [illegible] on 31st December, [illegible], £[illegible]	

TABLE [illegible].—PROBATE AND MATRIMONIAL DIVISION OF THE HIGH COURT OF JUSTICE.—MATRIMONIAL BUSINESS. RETURN of PROCEEDINGS in [illegible] under "The Legitimacy Declaration Act (Ireland), [illegible]," during the Year [illegible], and for Matrimonial Causes and Matters, under [illegible] Vict., c. [illegible].

PROCEEDINGS.	Number	PROCEEDINGS.	Number.
Petitions filed—		[illegible]	[illegible]
In [illegible] Pauperis,	[illegible]	[illegible] before Judge [illegible]	[illegible]
For Divorce a mensa et thoro,	[illegible]	[illegible]	[illegible]
For Nullity of Marriage,	[illegible]	[illegible] and Special Jury,	[illegible]
For Restitution of Conjugal Rights,	[illegible]	[illegible] and Common Jury,	[illegible]
[illegible] of Marriage,	[illegible]	Decrees for Divorce a mensa et thoro,	[illegible]
Declaration under Legitimacy Declaration Act,	[illegible]	[illegible] Nullity of Marriage,	[illegible]
For alimony, pendente lite,	[illegible]	[illegible] Restitution of Conjugal Rights,	[illegible]
For Alimony, permanent,	[illegible]	[illegible] of Marriage,	[illegible]
Citations [illegible],	[illegible]	[illegible] Legitimacy Declaration Act,	[illegible]
Appearances entered,	[illegible]	Applications for new Trial,	[illegible]
[illegible] filed,	[illegible]	Appeals to H. M. Court of Appeal,	[illegible]
Replies filed by Petitioners,	[illegible]	Dismissal of Petitions,	[illegible]
Rejoinders by Respondents,	[illegible]	Other [illegible] by the Principal Registrar, and not included in the above return.	[illegible]

Total amount of Fees received (Matrimonial Causes), £ [illegible] s. [illegible] d. [illegible]

TABLE [illegible].—AFFIDAVIT DUTY FOR GRANTS OF PROBATE AND ADMINISTRATION.—RETURN by the COMPTROLLER of STAMPS AND TAXES.

—	[illegible]	[illegible]*	[illegible]	Property upon which payable, [illegible]*
	£	£	£	£
Received at Dublin,	[illegible]	—	[illegible]	—
" [illegible] country,	[illegible]	—	[illegible]	—
Total,	[illegible]	—	[illegible]	

* The Comptroller of Stamps and Taxes states that it is not [illegible] in his power to give this information.

TABLE [illegible].—HIGH COURT OF ADMIRALTY.—RETURN of PROCEEDINGS in the HIGH COURT of ADMIRALTY of IRELAND for the Year ended 31st December, [illegible], made by the [illegible].

CAUSES INSTITUTED DURING YEAR.	Number	Amount.
		£ s. d.
Salvage,	[illegible]	[illegible]
Damage by Collision,	[illegible]	[illegible]
Bottomry,	[illegible]	[illegible]
Possession,	[illegible]	[illegible]
Towage,	[illegible]	[illegible]
Seamen's Wages,	[illegible]	[illegible]
Masters' Wages and Disbursements,	[illegible]	[illegible]
Damage to Cargo,	[illegible]	—
Co-ownership,	[illegible]	[illegible]
Use or Hire of Ship, Carriage of Goods, &c., and in respect of Goods,	[illegible]	[illegible]
Other Causes,	[illegible]	[illegible]
Total Causes during year,	[illegible]	[illegible]
Causes pending [illegible] of year,	[illegible]	[illegible]
Total Causes,	[illegible]	[illegible]
Causes transferred to Local Courts,	—	—
Causes transferred from Local Courts,	[illegible]	[illegible]
Warrants—		
I. In Court—		
(1.) Opposed,	[illegible]	—
(2.) Unopposed,	[illegible]	—
II. In Chambers,	[illegible]	—
Total,	[illegible]	—
Summonses issued,	[illegible]	—
Final Judgments and Decrees—		
I. After Appearance—		
(1.) For Plaintiff,	[illegible]	[illegible]
(2.) For Defendant,	[illegible]	[illegible]
II. By consent,	[illegible]	[illegible]
III. In default,	[illegible]	—
Total,	[illegible]	[illegible]

CAUSES INSTITUTED DURING YEAR.	Number	Amount.
Taxation of Costs—continued.		£ s. d.
III. Defendants' Costs in contested Causes— Amount of Plaintiffs' and Defendants' Bills submitted for Taxation,	[illegible]	[illegible]
Disallowed,	[illegible]	[illegible]
Reported due,	—	[illegible]
IV. Costs in default Causes— Amount of Proctors' and Solicitors' Bills submitted for Taxation,	—	—
Disallowed,	—	—
Reported due,	—	—
V. Marshal's Bills— Amount claimed,	[illegible]	[illegible]
Disallowed,	[illegible]	[illegible]
Reported due,	—	[illegible]
VI. Court Charges in all cases [illegible],	—	—
Disallowed,	—	—
Reported due,	[illegible]	—
VII. Total Amount of Costs and Charges submitted for Taxation,	[illegible]	[illegible]
Disallowed,	[illegible]	[illegible]
Reported due,	—	[illegible]
Appeals from Local Courts heard—		
Affirmed,	—	—
Varied or Reversed,	—	—
[illegible]—		
(1.) Actions [illegible] of a Warrant,	[illegible]	—
(2.) Against the sale or [illegible] of Property,	[illegible]	—
(3.) Actions [illegible] of the Registry,	[illegible]	—
Total,	[illegible]	—

TABLE 6.—HIGH COURT OF ADMIRALTY.—3. RETURN of PROCEEDINGS in the HIGH COURT of ADMIRALTY of IRELAND for the Year ended 31st December, [illegible], made by the Registrar.

NATURE OF PROCEEDINGS.	Totals.	Salvage.	Damage.	Bottomry.	Possession.	Towage.	Seamen's Wages.	Master's Wages and Disbursements.	Damage to Cargo.	Ownership.	*Use or Hire of Ships, Carriage, or Tort in respect of Goods.	Other Causes.
Instruments executed, viz.:—												
Warrants,	[illegible]	[illegible]	[illegible]	[illegible]	[illegible]	[illegible]	[illegible]	[illegible]	[illegible]	[illegible]	[illegible]	[illegible]
Citations in rem,	[illegible]	[illegible]	[illegible]	[illegible]	[illegible]	[illegible]	[illegible]	[illegible]	[illegible]	[illegible]	[illegible]	[illegible]
Citations in personam,	[illegible]	[illegible]	[illegible]	[illegible]	[illegible]	[illegible]	[illegible]	[illegible]	[illegible]	[illegible]	[illegible]	[illegible]
Monitions for different purposes,	[illegible]	[illegible]	[illegible]	[illegible]	[illegible]	[illegible]	[illegible]	[illegible]	[illegible]	[illegible]	[illegible]	[illegible]
Attachments,	[illegible]	[illegible]	[illegible]	[illegible]	[illegible]	[illegible]	[illegible]	[illegible]	[illegible]	[illegible]	[illegible]	[illegible]
Subpoenas,	[illegible]	[illegible]	[illegible]	[illegible]	[illegible]	[illegible]	[illegible]	[illegible]	[illegible]	[illegible]	[illegible]	[illegible]
Decrees of Possession,	[illegible]	[illegible]	[illegible]	[illegible]	[illegible]	[illegible]	[illegible]	[illegible]	[illegible]	[illegible]	[illegible]	[illegible]
Releases,	[illegible]	[illegible]	[illegible]	[illegible]	[illegible]	[illegible]	[illegible]	[illegible]	[illegible]	[illegible]	[illegible]	[illegible]
Commissions of Appraisement,	[illegible]	[illegible]	[illegible]	[illegible]	[illegible]	[illegible]	[illegible]	[illegible]	[illegible]	[illegible]	[illegible]	[illegible]
" of Appraisement and Sale,	[illegible]	[illegible]	[illegible]	[illegible]	[illegible]	[illegible]	[illegible]	[illegible]	[illegible]	[illegible]	[illegible]	[illegible]
" of Removal,	[illegible]	[illegible]	[illegible]	[illegible]	[illegible]	[illegible]	[illegible]	[illegible]	[illegible]	[illegible]	[illegible]	[illegible]
Total,	[illegible]	[illegible]	[illegible]	[illegible]	[illegible]	[illegible]	[illegible]	[illegible]	[illegible]	[illegible]	[illegible]	[illegible]
[illegible] Sales of Ships,	[illegible]	[illegible]	[illegible]	[illegible]	[illegible]	[illegible]	[illegible]	[illegible]	[illegible]	[illegible]	[illegible]	[illegible]
" of Ships and Cargoes,	[illegible]	[illegible]	[illegible]	[illegible]	[illegible]	[illegible]	[illegible]	[illegible]	[illegible]	[illegible]	[illegible]	[illegible]
" of Ships and Freights,	[illegible]	[illegible]	[illegible]	[illegible]	[illegible]	[illegible]	[illegible]	[illegible]	[illegible]	[illegible]	[illegible]	[illegible]
" of Ships, Cargoes, and Freights,	[illegible]	[illegible]	[illegible]	[illegible]	[illegible]	[illegible]	[illegible]	[illegible]	[illegible]	[illegible]	[illegible]	[illegible]
" of Cargoes and Freights,	[illegible]	[illegible]	[illegible]	[illegible]	[illegible]	[illegible]	[illegible]	[illegible]	[illegible]	[illegible]	[illegible]	[illegible]
" of Cargoes only,	[illegible]	[illegible]	[illegible]	[illegible]	[illegible]	[illegible]	[illegible]	[illegible]	[illegible]	[illegible]	[illegible]	[illegible]
" of Freights only,	[illegible]	[illegible]	[illegible]	[illegible]	[illegible]	[illegible]	[illegible]	[illegible]	[illegible]	[illegible]	[illegible]	[illegible]
" of Stores, &c.,	[illegible]	[illegible]	[illegible]	[illegible]	[illegible]	[illegible]	[illegible]	[illegible]	[illegible]	[illegible]	[illegible]	[illegible]
" of Proceeds in Registry,	[illegible]	[illegible]	[illegible]	[illegible]	[illegible]	[illegible]	[illegible]	[illegible]	[illegible]	[illegible]	[illegible]	[illegible]
Total,	[illegible]	[illegible]	[illegible]	[illegible]	[illegible]	[illegible]	[illegible]	[illegible]	[illegible]	[illegible]	[illegible]	[illegible]
Notices of Bail,	[illegible]	[illegible]	[illegible]	[illegible]	[illegible]	[illegible]	[illegible]	[illegible]	[illegible]	[illegible]	[illegible]	[illegible]
Reports as to sufficiency of Bail,	[illegible]	[illegible]	[illegible]	[illegible]	[illegible]	[illegible]	[illegible]	[illegible]	[illegible]	[illegible]	[illegible]	[illegible]
Total,	[illegible]	[illegible]	[illegible]	[illegible]	[illegible]	[illegible]	[illegible]	[illegible]	[illegible]	[illegible]	[illegible]	[illegible]
	£ s. d.	£ s. d.	£ s. d.	£ s. d.	£ s. d.	£ s. d.	£ s. d.	£ s. d.	£ s. d.	£ s. d.	£ s. d.	£ s. d.
Amount of Bail received,	[illegible]	[illegible]	[illegible]	[illegible]	[illegible]	[illegible]	[illegible]	[illegible]	[illegible]	[illegible]	[illegible]	[illegible]
Amount of Proceeds paid into Registry:—												
Of Ships only,	[illegible]	[illegible]	[illegible]	[illegible]	[illegible]	[illegible]	[illegible]	[illegible]	[illegible]	[illegible]	[illegible]	[illegible]
Of Cargoes only,	[illegible]	[illegible]	[illegible]	[illegible]	[illegible]	[illegible]	[illegible]	[illegible]	[illegible]	[illegible]	[illegible]	[illegible]
Total,	[illegible]	[illegible]	[illegible]	[illegible]	[illegible]	[illegible]	[illegible]	[illegible]	[illegible]	[illegible]	[illegible]	[illegible]

* Court of Admiralty, Ireland, Amendment Act, [illegible]

[illegible]

	£ s. d.	£ s. d.
Balances in hand at the beginning of the year:—		
[illegible] Admiralty Court Deposit Fund,	—	—
[illegible] of Ireland,	—	[illegible]
Received during the year:—		
[illegible]	[illegible]	
[illegible]	[illegible]	
Deposits [illegible]	[illegible]	
Other receipts,	[illegible]	[illegible]
[illegible]	[illegible]	
[illegible]	—	
[illegible]	[illegible]	[illegible]
Total,		[illegible]

	£ s. d.	£ s. d.
Paid during the year:—		
[illegible]	[illegible]	
[illegible]	[illegible]	
[illegible]	—	
[illegible]	—	
[illegible]	—	
[illegible]	[illegible]	
[illegible]	[illegible]	
[illegible]	[illegible]	
[illegible]	—	
[illegible]	—	
[illegible]	—	
[illegible]	[illegible]	
[illegible]	—	
[illegible]	—	
[illegible]	[illegible]	
[illegible]	[illegible]	
[illegible]	[illegible]	
[illegible]	[illegible]	[illegible]
Balances in hand at the end of the year:—		
[illegible] Admiralty Court Deposit Fund,	—	—
[illegible] of Ireland,	—	[illegible]
[illegible]	[illegible]	
[illegible]	[illegible]	[illegible]
Total,		[illegible]

General Business of the Court.

	No.
Number of Days on which the Court sat [illegible]	[illegible]
[illegible]	[illegible]
Commissions, &c., [illegible]:—	
[illegible]	—
[illegible]	—
[illegible]	—

	No.	Amount £ s. d.
[illegible]	—	—
[illegible]	[illegible]	[illegible]
[illegible]	[illegible]	—
[illegible]	[illegible]	—
[illegible]	—	—
[illegible]	[illegible]	—
[illegible]	—	[illegible]
[illegible]	—	[illegible]
[illegible]	—	[illegible]

TABLE [illegible].—COURT OF BANKRUPTCY IN IRELAND.—TABLE [illegible] OFFICIAL ASSIGNEES to PARLIAMENT, under IRISH BANKRUPTCY and INSOLVENCY ACT, [illegible], for the Year [illegible].

	[illegible]					[illegible]	[illegible]	[illegible]	[illegible]	[illegible]	[illegible]	[illegible]
[illegible]	[illegible]	[illegible]	[illegible]	[illegible]	[illegible]	[illegible]	[illegible]	[illegible]	[illegible]	[illegible]	[illegible]	[illegible]
Total	[illegible]	[illegible]	[illegible]	[illegible]	[illegible]	[illegible]	[illegible]	[illegible]	[illegible]	[illegible]	[illegible]	[illegible]
[illegible]	[illegible]	[illegible]	[illegible]	[illegible]	[illegible]	[illegible]	[illegible]	[illegible]	[illegible]	[illegible]	[illegible]	[illegible]
Total	[illegible]	[illegible]	[illegible]	[illegible]	[illegible]	[illegible]	[illegible]	[illegible]	[illegible]	[illegible]	[illegible]	[illegible]
General Total	[illegible]	[illegible]	[illegible]	[illegible]	[illegible]	[illegible]	[illegible]	[illegible]	[illegible]	[illegible]	[illegible]	[illegible]

	[illegible]	[illegible]	[illegible]	[illegible]	[illegible]	[illegible]	[illegible]	[illegible]			
[illegible]	[illegible]	[illegible]	[illegible]	[illegible]	[illegible]	[illegible]	[illegible]	[illegible]	[illegible]	[illegible]	[illegible]
Total	[illegible]	[illegible]	[illegible]	[illegible]	[illegible]	[illegible]	[illegible]	[illegible]	[illegible]	[illegible]	[illegible]
[illegible]	[illegible]	[illegible]	[illegible]	[illegible]	[illegible]	[illegible]	[illegible]	[illegible]	[illegible]	[illegible]	[illegible]
Total	[illegible]	[illegible]	[illegible]	[illegible]	[illegible]	[illegible]	[illegible]	[illegible]	[illegible]	[illegible]	[illegible]
General Total	[illegible]	[illegible]	[illegible]	[illegible]	[illegible]	[illegible]	[illegible]	[illegible]	[illegible]	[illegible]	[illegible]

TABLE [illegible].—THE COURT OF BANKRUPTCY IN IRELAND.—RETURN of PROCEEDINGS in BANKRUPTCY for the Year [illegible], made by the [illegible].

PROCEEDINGS IN BANKRUPTCY	Number	Amount
		£ s. d.
[illegible] —		
By [illegible], [illegible]		
By [illegible], [illegible]	[illegible]	—
[illegible] Arrangements turned into Bankruptcy, [illegible]		
Petitions by Debtors for [illegible] Arrangements under the control of the Court,	[illegible]	—
[illegible]	[illegible]	—
Sittings before the Judges of the Court,	[illegible]	—
Sittings before the [illegible] and the Chief Clerk,	[illegible]	—
Number of Bills of Costs [illegible],	[illegible]	—
Number of [illegible],	[illegible]	—
Amount of Costs on [illegible],	-	[illegible]
[illegible] on [illegible],	-	[illegible]
Amount as [illegible],	-	[illegible]
Number of [illegible] who entered [illegible] to practise in the Court,	[illegible]	—
Amount of Government Stock standing to the credit of the [illegible] Account on the Bank of Ireland, with [illegible] of Chief [illegible], [illegible] December, [illegible],	-	—
Amount of Cash at the Account,	-	[illegible]
Number of cases of Bankruptcy referred to Chairmen of Quarter Sessions,	-	—
Number of Warrants issued for [illegible] of [illegible] Debtors,	[illegible]	—
Number of [illegible] for [illegible] up [illegible] by Trustees	-	—

* The [illegible] private arrangements turned into bankruptcy are included herein.

TABLE [illegible].—THE COURT OF BANKRUPTCY IN IRELAND.—RETURN of PROCEEDINGS in INSOLVENCY in the Year [illegible], made by the First Clerk in Insolvency.

PROCEEDINGS IN INSOLVENCY.	Number	Amount
		£ s. d.
[illegible]	[illegible]	—
Amount of Dividends [illegible],	-	[illegible]
Amount of Debts upon which Dividends declared,	-	[illegible]
Average Dividend in the £1,	-	[illegible]
Amount of [illegible] allowed to the Official Assignees on the above sums of Dividend,	-	[illegible]
Amount of Law Costs of the Assignees on the above sums of Dividend, being the Law Expenses of [illegible] and distribution,	-	[illegible]
Average Cost of [illegible],	-	[illegible]
Amount of [illegible] allowed to Official Assignees on other [illegible],	-	[illegible]
Sittings before the Court in Dublin for all purposes in [illegible],	[illegible]	—
Sittings before the First Clerk or other Officer for all purposes in Insolvency,	[illegible]	—
Bills of Costs Taxed,	[illegible]	—
Number of [illegible],	[illegible]	—
Amount [illegible],	-	[illegible]
[illegible] on [illegible],	-	[illegible]
Amount as [illegible],	-	[illegible]

TABLE [illegible].—HIGH COURT OF JUSTICE.—PROBATE AND MATRIMONIAL DIVISION.—RETURN of PROCEEDINGS in the Office of the ACCOUNTANT-GENERAL for the Year ended 1st October, [illegible], made by the ACCOUNTANT-GENERAL.

Cash, Securities, and other Effects Paid and Transferred.	Into Court.	Out of Court.	Other Proceedings in the Office.	No.	Amount.
	£ s. d.	£ s. d.			£ s. d.
Cash,	[illegible]	[illegible]	Total Cheques signed,	[illegible]	—
[illegible] per cent. Annuities,	—	—	Amount of Cash, Securities, and other effects [illegible] in the Accountant-General's books, [illegible] —		
[illegible] Annuities,	—	—	Cash, [illegible]		[illegible]
Government [illegible] per cent. Stock,	—	[illegible]	Stock, [illegible]		
[illegible]	—	—	[illegible]		
[illegible]	—	—	[illegible]	-	—
[illegible]	—	—	[illegible]	-	—
[illegible]	—	—	[illegible]	-	—
Cash, Securities, and Effects,	—	—	Total Number of Accounts,	-	—
			Amount of Fees [illegible],	-	—

TABLE [illegible].—HIGH COURT OF JUSTICE.—CHANCERY DIVISION.—RETURN of PROCEEDINGS in the Office of the ACCOUNTANT-GENERAL for the Year ended 1st October, [illegible], made by the ACCOUNTANT-GENERAL.

Cash, Securities, and other Effects paid and transferred.	Into Court.	Out of Court.	Other Proceedings in the Office.	No.	Amount.
	£ s. d.	£ s. d.			£ s. d.
Cash,	[illegible]	[illegible]	Total Cheques signed,	[illegible]	—
Government [illegible] per cent. Stock,	[illegible]	[illegible]	Amount of Cash, Securities, and other effects [illegible] in the Accountant-General's books, being the balance of year ended 1st October, [illegible] —		
Government [illegible] per cent. Consols,	[illegible]	[illegible]	Cash, [illegible]		[illegible]
Bank of Ireland Stock,	[illegible]	[illegible]	[illegible]		
Government [illegible] per cent. Reduced Annuities,	—	—	[illegible]	[illegible]	—
[illegible] Bills,	—	—	[illegible]		—
			Total number of Accounts,	[illegible]	—
Amount of Fees collected, [illegible]					

TABLE 71.—SUPREME COURT OF JUDICATURE, IRELAND.—(1) Account of the Receipts and Payments of the Accountant-General of the Supreme Court of Judicature in Ireland, in respect of the Funds of Suitors in the said Court, in the Year to 30th September, 1883, prepared in pursuance of Rules of Court made under the provisions of the Supreme Court of Judicature Act (Ireland) 1877.

—	£ s. d.	Cash. £ s. d.	Securities. £ s. d.
Balance of Cash standing in the name of the account of "the Accountant-General of the Court of Chancery" at the Bank of Ireland, on 30th September, 1882, viz.:—			
Chancery, &c., Division	[illegible]		
Land Judges	[illegible]	[illegible]	—
Amount of Government and other Securities standing in the name of "the Accountant-General of the Court of Chancery," on the books of the Bank of Ireland, and of other Companies, on the same date, viz.:—			
Chancery, &c., Division	[illegible]		
Land Judges	[illegible]	—	[illegible]
Receipts and transfers into Court in the Year to 30th September, 1883, viz.:—			
Chancery and Common Law Divisions.			
[illegible]	[illegible]		
Cash proceeds of sale of Securities in Court [illegible]	[illegible]		
Other Cash [illegible] into Court	[illegible]	[illegible]	—
Securities purchased with money in Court	[illegible]		
Other Securities brought into Court	[illegible]	—	[illegible]
Land Judges' Division.			
Dividends on Securities in Court	[illegible]		
Cash proceeds of sale of Securities in Court [illegible]	[illegible]		
Other Cash brought into Court	[illegible]	[illegible]	—
Securities purchased with money in Court	[illegible]		
Other Securities brought into Court	[illegible]	—	[illegible]
		[illegible]	[illegible]

—	£ s. d.	Cash. £ s. d.	Securities. £ s. d.
Payments and transfers out of Court in the Year to 30th September, 1883, viz.:—			
Chancery and Common Law Divisions.			
Cash paid for securities purchased (as per contra)	[illegible]		
Other Cash paid out of Court	[illegible]	[illegible]	—
Securities sold	[illegible]		
Other Securities transferred out of Court	[illegible]	—	[illegible]
Land Judges' Division.			
Cash paid for Securities purchased (as per contra)	[illegible]		
Other Cash paid out of Court	[illegible]	[illegible]	—
Securities sold	[illegible]		
Other Securities transferred out of Court	[illegible]	—	[illegible]
Balance of Cash and Securities standing in the name of the Accountant-General of the Supreme Court of Judicature in Ireland, on 30th September, 1883, viz.:—			
Cash (Bank of Ireland): Chancery, &c., Division	[illegible]		
Cash (Bank of Ireland): Land Judges' Division	[illegible]	[illegible]	—
Securities*: Chancery, &c., Division	[illegible]		
Securities*: Land Judges' Division	[illegible]	—	[illegible]
		[illegible]	[illegible]

* Particulars of the Securities are appended (page 130).

(7.) Statement of Liabilities and Assets in respect of the Funds of Suitors in the Supreme Court of Judicature in Ireland, on the [illegible] September, 18[illegible].

Liabilities.	Cash.	Securities.	Assets.	Cash.	Securities.
	£ s. d.	£ s. d.		£ s. d.	£ s. d.
Amounts of Cash and Securities standing to the credit of the accounts of suitors in the books of the Accountant-General of the Supreme Court of Judicature in Ireland, viz.:—			Amounts of Cash held by the Bank of Ireland, and of Government and other Securities standing in the name of the Accountant-General of the Supreme Court of Judicature in Ireland, in the books of the Bank of Ireland, and of other Companies, viz.:—		
Chancery and Common Law Division Accounts,	[illegible]	[illegible]	Chancery and Common Law Division Accounts,	[illegible]	[illegible]
Land Judges' Division Accounts,	[illegible]	[illegible]	Land Judges' Division Accounts,	[illegible]	[illegible]
			Deficiency of Cash Balances, in respect of Suitors' Cash, which the Consolidated Fund is liable to make good (as referred to in Note.)*	[illegible]	—
			Suspense Account, being Deficiency of Cash Balance of [illegible] Division.†	[illegible]	—
	[illegible]	[illegible]		[illegible]	[illegible]

* [illegible]

† This deficiency, which is [illegible]

(8.) Particulars of Securities appearing by the Books of the Accountant-General to be in Court on the [illegible] September, 18[illegible].

—	Chancery Division.	Land Judges' Division.	—	Chancery Division.	Land Judges' Division.
	£ s. d.	£ s. d.		£ s. d.	£ s. d.
New 3 per cent. Annuities,	[illegible]	[illegible]	[illegible] Shares,	[illegible]	
Consols,	[illegible]	[illegible]	[illegible] Civil Service Permanent Building Society Shares,	[illegible]	—
Reduced 3 per cent. Annuities,	[illegible]	—	Londonderry and Enniskillen Railway Stock,	[illegible]	—
[illegible] per cent. Stock,	[illegible]	[illegible]	London and North-Western Railway Stock,	[illegible]	—
India [illegible] per cent. Stock,	[illegible]	[illegible]	London and South-Western Railway Stock,	[illegible]	—
Bank of Ireland Stock,	[illegible]	[illegible]	[illegible] and District [illegible] Shares,	[illegible]	—
[illegible] Debentures,	[illegible]	—	Midland Great Western Railway Stock,	[illegible]	—
Belfast, Holywood, and Bangor Railway Stock,	[illegible]	—	Mining Company of Ireland Shares,	[illegible]	—
[illegible] Railway Stock,	[illegible]	—	[illegible] and Co. Debentures,	[illegible]	—
City Debentures,	[illegible]	—	National Bank Shares,	[illegible]	—
City of Dublin Steam Packet Company Stock,	[illegible]	—	National Building and Land Investment Company Shares,	[illegible]	—
Cork and Bandon Railway Stock,	[illegible]	—	[illegible] Railway Stock,	[illegible]	[illegible]
Dublin and Kingstown Railway Stock,	[illegible]	—	[illegible] Company Shares,	[illegible]	[illegible]
Dublin, Wicklow, and Wexford Railway Stock,	[illegible]	—	[illegible] Steam Packet Company Shares,	[illegible]	—
East Indian Railway Stock,	[illegible]	—	Pipe Water Debentures,	[illegible]	—
Egyptian Bonds,	[illegible]	—	[illegible] Stock,	[illegible]	—
Grand Canal Stock,	[illegible]	—	Waterford, Dungarvan, and Lismore Railway Shares,	[illegible]	—
Great Northern Railway (Ireland) Stock,	[illegible]	—	Waterford and Limerick Railway Shares,	[illegible]	—
Great Northern Railway (England) Stock,	[illegible]	—		[illegible]	[illegible]
Great Southern and Western Railway Stock,	[illegible]	—			
Great Western Railway (England) Stock,	[illegible]	—			

TABLE 17.—HIGH COURT OF JUSTICE.—STAMPS AND TAXES.—(a.) A RETURN showing the Amount received in respect of the following denominations of Stamps for the year ended 31st Dec., 188[illegible], viz., Judicature, Judgment Registry, Registry of Deeds, Admiralty Court, Bankruptcy, and Chancery Fund in Lunacy Matters, by COMMISSIONERS of STAMPS and TAXES.

DENOMINATION	Gross Amount	Discount	Net Amount
	£ s. d.	£ s. d.	£ s. d.
1. Judicature (including Probate Courts),	[illegible]	[illegible]	[illegible]
2. Judgment Registry,	[illegible]	[illegible]	[illegible]
3. Registry of Deeds,	[illegible]	[illegible]	[illegible]
4. Admiralty Court,	[illegible]	—	[illegible]
5. Bankruptcy Fund,	[illegible]	—	[illegible]
6. Chancery Fund (Lunacy),	[illegible]	[illegible]	[illegible]

(b.) RETURN BY ACCOUNTANT-GENERAL.

Amount of percentage on Legatees' Results in Year 188[illegible]—	£ s. d.
Cash,	[illegible]
Government New 3 per cent. Stock,	[illegible]

TABLE 18.—SUPREME COURTS OF APPEAL.—HER MAJESTY'S COURT OF APPEAL, IRELAND.—RETURN of PROCEEDINGS for the Year 188[illegible], made by the REGISTRAR of the CHANCERY DIVISION.

I. APPEALS FROM DIVISIONS OF HIGH COURT OF JUSTICE.

NATURE OF PROCEEDINGS.	Totals	Chancery Division	Queen's Bench Division	Common Pleas Division	Exchequer Division	Probate and Matrimonial Division	[illegible]
1. *Appeals from final Judgments.*							
Awaiting Judgment,	[illegible]	[illegible]					
Awaiting a hearing at commencement of year,	[illegible]	[illegible]	[illegible]	[illegible]	[illegible]		
Set down during the year,	[illegible]	[illegible]	[illegible]	[illegible]	[illegible]	[illegible]	
Heard, and Judgment delivered during the year,	[illegible]	[illegible]	[illegible]	[illegible]	[illegible]	[illegible]	
Otherwise disposed of,	[illegible]		[illegible]	[illegible]	[illegible]		
Awaiting a hearing at end of year,	[illegible]	[illegible]		[illegible]	[illegible]		
Awaiting Judgment,							
2. *Appeals from Interlocutory Orders*							
Awaiting Judgment at commencement of year,	[illegible]				[illegible]		
Awaiting a hearing at commencement of year,	[illegible]	[illegible]					
Set down during the year,	[illegible]	[illegible]	[illegible]	[illegible]	[illegible]	[illegible]	
Heard during the year,	[illegible]	[illegible]	[illegible]	[illegible]	[illegible]	[illegible]	
Otherwise disposed of,	[illegible]	[illegible]	[illegible]		[illegible]		
Awaiting a hearing at end of year,	[illegible]	[illegible]	[illegible]	[illegible]			
Made ex parte,	[illegible]		[illegible]				
3. *Original Matters*							
Awaiting a hearing at commencement of year,	[illegible]				[illegible]		
Heard during the year,	[illegible]	[illegible]	[illegible]	[illegible]	[illegible]	[illegible]	[illegible]
Otherwise disposed of,							
Awaiting a hearing at end of year,							

II. APPEALS FROM OTHER JUDGES OR COURTS.

NATURE OF PROCEEDINGS.	Totals.	Judge in Bankruptcy	High Court of Admiralty	Registry of Tenure Appeals	Land Commission	Irish Land Commission
1. *Appeals*						
Awaiting Judgment at commencement of year,	[illegible]	[illegible]				[illegible]
Awaiting a hearing at commencement of year,	[illegible]		[illegible]			[illegible]
Set down during the year,	[illegible]	[illegible]	[illegible]	[illegible]		[illegible]
Heard during the year,	[illegible]	[illegible]	[illegible]	[illegible]		[illegible]
Otherwise disposed of,	[illegible]	[illegible]				[illegible]
Awaiting a hearing at end of year,	[illegible]					[illegible]
Awaiting Judgment,	[illegible]					[illegible]

III. RESULTS OF APPEALS.

DIVISION OR COURT FROM WHICH APPEAL BROUGHT.	Judgments below affirmed	Judgments below reversed	Judgments below varied	Judgments below [illegible]	Cases remitted for further inquiry	Judgment below [illegible]
1. Chancery Division,	[illegible]	[illegible]	[illegible]	[illegible]		[illegible]
Queen's Bench Division,	[illegible]	[illegible]	[illegible]	[illegible]		
Common Pleas Division,	[illegible]	[illegible]	[illegible]	[illegible]		
Exchequer Division,	[illegible]	[illegible]				
Probate and Matrimonial Division,	[illegible]	[illegible]		[illegible]		
Judge in Bankruptcy,	[illegible]	[illegible]	[illegible]			
High Court of Admiralty,	[illegible]	[illegible]				
Registry of Tenure Appeals,	[illegible]	[illegible]		[illegible]		
Land Cases Reserved,						
Irish Land Commission,	[illegible]	[illegible]		[illegible]		[illegible]
Total disposed,	[illegible]	[illegible]	[illegible]	[illegible]		[illegible]

4. Number of Days on which Court of Appeal sat, ... [illegible]

TABLE 74.—SUPREME COURTS OF APPEAL.—COURT FOR CROWN CASES RESERVED.—RETURN showing CASES reserved for the consideration of the Court in the Year 1883, the COURT before which the Case stood for Trial, the OFFENCES CHARGED, and JUDGMENT of the Court in each Case. By the Master of the Crown Office, Queen's Bench Division.

No.	Court before which case stood for Trial.	Offence charged.	Judgment of the Court.	Observations.
1	County Court Judge and Chairman of Down, ...	Common Assault, ...	Conviction affirmed	

TABLE 75.—SUPREME COURTS OF APPEAL.—CASES RESERVED for the JUDGES of QUEEN'S BENCH, COMMON PLEAS, and EXCHEQUER DIVISIONS as to PRESENTMENT and other CASES not within the 11 & 12 Vic., c. 78, in the Year 1883, by the Master of the Crown Office, Queen's Bench Division.

No.	Name of Case.	Question arising under	Observations.
1	County Cork Summer Assizes, 1883—Presentment for Conveyance of Prisoners.	"The General Prisons (Ireland) Act, 1877," and [illegible]	"An opinion was given by their Lordships, by consent of the Solicitor-General on the part of the Crown, and of the Counsel for the Grand Jury of Cork County, [illegible] Judge.
2	County Galway Spring Assizes 1883—Presentment for Conveyance of Prisoners	Same Act, ...	Not considered necessary to argue the case. Referred to as [illegible] "observations."

TABLE 76.—SUPREME COURTS OF APPEAL.—PRIVY COUNCIL IN IRELAND.—RETURN of JUDICIAL PROCEEDINGS of the PRIVY COUNCIL in the Year 1883.

NATURE OF PROCEEDINGS.	No.	[illegible] from 1882	Result. Applications to Appeal: Granted	Refused	Withdrawn	Appeal: By-law, Order, &c., Confirmed	By-law, Order, &c., Quashed or Varied	Pending at end of Year
Appeals against By-laws and Orders made by the Inspectors of Irish Fisheries, .	1	.	.	.	.	1	.	
Applications for Orders in Council under The [illegible] (Ireland) Act, [illegible] . . .	.	1	1	.	.	.	.	

TABLE 77.—SUPREME COURTS OF APPEAL.—APPEALS BEFORE HER MAJESTY IN COUNCIL.—RETURN of the PROCEEDINGS of the JUDICIAL COMMITTEE of PRIVY COUNCIL in the Year 1883, made by the [illegible] of the Privy Council.

Cases.	Pending [illegible]	Referred by.	Court Appealed from.	How disposed of.
None, .	—	—	—	—

TABLE 78.—SUPREME COURTS OF APPEAL.—HOUSE OF LORDS.—RETURN of APPEALS and CAUSES in [illegible] from IRELAND for the Year [illegible], made by the [illegible] of the PARLIAMENTS.

—	Total	Court of Bankruptcy Chancery	Court of Appeal
Number of Causes presented,	[illegible]	[illegible]	[illegible]
Do. withdrawn,	[illegible]	[illegible]	[illegible]
Do. dismissed,	[illegible]	[illegible]	[illegible]
Number of Judgments,	[illegible]	[illegible]	[illegible]
Reversed with directions,	[illegible]	[illegible]	[illegible]
Causes waiting for the same,	[illegible]	[illegible]	[illegible]
Total Amount of Fees,	£ s. d. 197 [illegible] [illegible]	£ s. d. [illegible]	£ s. d. [illegible] [illegible] [illegible]

TABLE 79.—LOCAL COURTS OF ADMIRALTY.—PROCEEDINGS in the Year [illegible], from Returns made by the Registrars.

PLACE WHERE COURT HELD	Total Number of Admiralty Actions of Proceedings	Arrests of Vessels	Part Shares	Amount of Claims	Amount of Solicitors' Costs allowed	Suitors' Moneys, Paid under Order of Court	Suitors' Moneys, In Bank under Order at end of year	Instruments Deposited	Number of Bail
				£ s. d.	£ s. d.	£ s. d.	£ s. d.		
1. Belfast,	[illegible]	[illegible]	[illegible]	[illegible]	[illegible]	[illegible]	[illegible]	[illegible]	[illegible]
2. Cork,	[illegible]	72	[illegible]	[illegible]	[illegible]	[illegible]	[illegible]	[illegible]	[illegible]

TABLE 80.—HIGH COURT OF JUSTICE.—PROBATE AND MATRIMONIAL DIVISION.—LOCAL PROBATE BUSINESS.—TABLE of PROCEEDINGS before the DISTRICT REGISTRARS in the Year [illegible], and of the AMOUNT of PROBATE DUTY received, from Returns made by the DISTRICT REGISTRARS.

DISTRICT REGISTRIES.	Total Number of Grants issued in Year	Granted in Common Form, Probates	Granted in Common Form, Letters of Administration (with the Will annexed)	Granted in Common Form, Letters of Administration, [illegible]	Granted in Common Form, Letters of Administration, Others	Granted under direction of Judge, Probates	Granted under direction of Judge, Letters of Administration with the Will annexed	Granted under direction of Judge, Letters of Administration	Refused under directions of Judge, Probates	Refused under directions of Judge, Letters of Administration
Armagh,	[illegible]	[illegible]	[illegible]	[illegible]	[illegible]	[illegible]	[illegible]	[illegible]	[illegible]	[illegible]
Ballina,	[illegible]	[illegible]	[illegible]	[illegible]	[illegible]	[illegible]	[illegible]	[illegible]	[illegible]	[illegible]
Belfast,	[illegible]	[illegible]	[illegible]	[illegible]	[illegible]	[illegible]	[illegible]	[illegible]	[illegible]	[illegible]
Cavan,	[illegible]	[illegible]	[illegible]	[illegible]	[illegible]	[illegible]	[illegible]	[illegible]	[illegible]	[illegible]
Cork,	[illegible]	[illegible]	[illegible]	[illegible]	[illegible]	[illegible]	[illegible]	[illegible]	[illegible]	[illegible]
Kilkenny,	[illegible]	[illegible]	[illegible]	[illegible]	[illegible]	[illegible]	[illegible]	[illegible]	[illegible]	[illegible]
Limerick,	[illegible]	[illegible]	[illegible]	[illegible]	[illegible]	[illegible]	[illegible]	[illegible]	[illegible]	[illegible]
Londonderry,	[illegible]	[illegible]	[illegible]	[illegible]	[illegible]	[illegible]	[illegible]	[illegible]	[illegible]	[illegible]
Mullingar,	[illegible]	[illegible]	[illegible]	[illegible]	[illegible]	[illegible]	[illegible]	[illegible]	[illegible]	[illegible]
Tuam,	[illegible]	[illegible]	[illegible]	[illegible]	[illegible]	[illegible]	[illegible]	[illegible]	[illegible]	[illegible]
Waterford,	[illegible]	[illegible]	[illegible]	[illegible]	[illegible]	[illegible]	[illegible]	[illegible]	[illegible]	[illegible]
Total,	[illegible]	[illegible]	[illegible]	[illegible]	[illegible]	[illegible]	[illegible]	[illegible]	[illegible]	[illegible]

DISTRICT REGISTRIES.	Granted on Decree of County Court Judge, Probates	Granted on Decree of County Court Judge, Letters of Administration with the Will annexed	Granted on Decree of County Court Judge, Letters of Administration	Revoked or Impaired, Probates	Revoked or Impaired, Letters of Administration	Caveats entered against Probates and Letters of Administration	Amount of Fees received on Intestates	Fees on [illegible]	Total of all Fees received in Registry	Amount of Duty on Affidavits [illegible]
							£ s. d.	£ s. d.	£ s. d.	£ s. d.
Armagh,	[illegible]	[illegible]	[illegible]	[illegible]	[illegible]	[illegible]	[illegible]	[illegible]	[illegible]	[illegible]
Ballina,	[illegible]	[illegible]	[illegible]	[illegible]	[illegible]	[illegible]	[illegible]	[illegible]	[illegible]	[illegible]
Belfast,	[illegible]	[illegible]	[illegible]	[illegible]	[illegible]	[illegible]	[illegible]	[illegible]	[illegible]	[illegible]
Cavan,	[illegible]	[illegible]	[illegible]	[illegible]	[illegible]	[illegible]	[illegible]	[illegible]	[illegible]	[illegible]
Cork,	[illegible]	[illegible]	[illegible]	[illegible]	[illegible]	[illegible]	[illegible]	[illegible]	[illegible]	[illegible]
Kilkenny,	[illegible]	[illegible]	[illegible]	[illegible]	[illegible]	[illegible]	[illegible]	[illegible]	[illegible]	[illegible]
Limerick,	[illegible]	[illegible]	[illegible]	[illegible]	[illegible]	[illegible]	[illegible]	[illegible]	[illegible]	[illegible]
Londonderry,	[illegible]	[illegible]	[illegible]	[illegible]	[illegible]	[illegible]	[illegible]	[illegible]	[illegible]	[illegible]
Mullingar,	[illegible]	[illegible]	[illegible]	[illegible]	[illegible]	[illegible]	[illegible]	[illegible]	[illegible]	[illegible]
Tuam,	[illegible]	[illegible]	[illegible]	[illegible]	[illegible]	[illegible]	[illegible]	[illegible]	[illegible]	[illegible]
Waterford,	[illegible]	[illegible]	[illegible]	[illegible]	[illegible]	[illegible]	[illegible]	[illegible]	[illegible]	[illegible]
Total,	[illegible]	1	[illegible]	[illegible]	4	[illegible]	[illegible]	[illegible]	[illegible]	[illegible]

TABLE [illegible].—HIGH COURT OF JUSTICE.—PROCEEDINGS ON CIRCUIT.—Proceedings in Causes entered for Trial at the [illegible], Queen's Bench, Common Pleas, [illegible], and Probate Divisions, on Circuit, in the Year 1883, from Returns made by Judges' [illegible].

Counties and Counties of Cities and of Towns arranged in Circuits	Total Causes Entered for Trial	Causes Tried: [illegible]	Causes Tried: [illegible]	[illegible]	[illegible]	[illegible]	[illegible]	Causes Withdrawn	[illegible]
Home Circuit.									
Carlow,	-	-	-	-	-	-	-	-	-
Kildare,	1	2	-	-	-	-	-	-	-
King's County,	2	2	-	-	-	-	-	-	-
Meath,	-	-	-	-	-	-	-	-	-
Queen's County,	5	5	-	-	-	-	-	-	-
Westmeath,	-	-	-	-	-	-	-	-	-
Total,	9	9	-	-	-	-	-	-	-
Leinster Circuit.									
Kilkenny,	-	-	-	-	-	-	-	-	-
Kilkenny City,	-	-	-	-	-	-	-	-	-
Tipperary, N. R.,	3	1	-	-	-	-	-	-	-
Tipperary, S. R.,	4	4	-	-	-	-	-	-	-
Waterford,	-	-	-	-	-	-	-	-	-
Waterford City,	3	1	-	-	-	-	-	-	-
Wexford,	2	3	-	-	-	-	-	-	-
Wicklow,	4	3	-	1	-	-	-	-	-
Total,	16	14		1	-	-	-	-	[illegible]
Munster Circuit.									
Clare,	6	3	-	-	-	-	-	-	2
Cork,	4	4	-	-	-	-	-	1	1
Cork City,	16	21	3	-	-	-	-	1	-
Kerry,	4	4	-	-	-	-	-	-	-
Limerick,	9	4	-	1	-	-	-	-	2
Limerick City,	4	3	-	-	-	-	-	1	-
Total,	41	41	3	1	-	-	-	3	4

Counties and Counties of Cities and of Towns arranged in Circuits	Total Causes Entered for Trial	Causes Tried: [illegible]	Causes Tried: [illegible]	[illegible]	[illegible]	[illegible]	Causes Withdrawn	[illegible]
North-East Circuit.								
Antrim,	31	24	4	-	-	-	8	1
Armagh,	9	9	-	-	-	-	-	-
Carrickfergus Town,	-	-	-	-	-	-	-	-
Down,	3	3	2	-	-	-	-	-
Louth,	5	3	-	-	-	-	-	-
Drogheda Town,	2	2	2	-	-	-	-	-
Monaghan,	4	5	2	1	-	-	1	-
Total,	44	26	8	1	-	-	4	1
North-West Circuit.								
Cavan,	3	5	-	-	-	-	-	-
Donegal,	5	3	-	-	-	-	-	-
Fermanagh,	6	6	-	-	-	1	-	-
Londonderry, County and City,	10	14	1	-	-	-	2	-
Longford,	-	-	-	-	-	-	-	-
Tyrone,	4	3	-	-	-	-	1	-
Total,	30	30	1	-	-	1	3	-
Connaught Circuit.								
Galway,	4	5	-	-	-	-	7	-
Galway Town,	-	-	-	-	-	-	-	-
Leitrim,	2	3	-	-	-	-	-	-
Mayo,	4	1	-	-	-	-	-	-
Roscommon,	1	1	-	-	-	-	-	-
Sligo,	4	6	-	-	-	-	-	-
Total,	15	16		-	-	-	8	-
Total of Ireland,	[illegible]	114	15	3	-	3	37	7

TABLE 61.—HIGH COURT OF JUSTICE.—PROCEEDINGS ON CIRCUIT.—NATURE and RESULT of the CAUSES TRIED or otherwise disposed of on CIRCUIT in the Year [illegible], from Returns made by Judges' Registrars.

NATURE OF THE SUITS ENTERED FOR TRIAL AND ACCOUNTED FOR IN THIS RETURN	Total Entered and Disposed of	Divisions from which Causes accounted for in this Return were sent for Trial: No Division given in Returns	Chancery	Queen's Bench	Common Pleas	Exchequer	Probate and Matrimonial	Results of Causes Tried and Disposed of on Trial: Total Actions Tried	Verdict for Plaintiff	Verdict for Plaintiff reduced by Special Case	Verdict by Consent with Reference	Nonsuit	Verdict for Defendant	Jury Discharged without Verdict	Juror withdrawn	Not Proceeded
On Promissory Notes, Bills of Exchange, &c.	[illegible]	[illegible]	[illegible]	[illegible]	[illegible]	[illegible]	[illegible]	[illegible]	[illegible]	[illegible]	[illegible]	[illegible]	[illegible]	[illegible]	[illegible]	[illegible]
On Bonds,	[illegible]	[illegible]	[illegible]	[illegible]	[illegible]	[illegible]	[illegible]	[illegible]	[illegible]	[illegible]	[illegible]	[illegible]	[illegible]	[illegible]	[illegible]	[illegible]
For Goods sold and delivered,	[illegible]	[illegible]	[illegible]	[illegible]	[illegible]	[illegible]	[illegible]	[illegible]	[illegible]	[illegible]	[illegible]	[illegible]	[illegible]	[illegible]	[illegible]	[illegible]
For Work and Labour done,	[illegible]	[illegible]	[illegible]	[illegible]	[illegible]	[illegible]	[illegible]	[illegible]	[illegible]	[illegible]	[illegible]	[illegible]	[illegible]	[illegible]	[illegible]	[illegible]
For Money paid, laid out, or lent,	[illegible]	[illegible]	[illegible]	[illegible]	[illegible]	[illegible]	[illegible]	[illegible]	[illegible]	[illegible]	[illegible]	[illegible]	[illegible]	[illegible]	[illegible]	[illegible]
For Money received,	[illegible]	[illegible]	[illegible]	[illegible]	[illegible]	[illegible]	[illegible]	[illegible]	[illegible]	[illegible]	[illegible]	[illegible]	[illegible]	[illegible]	[illegible]	[illegible]
For Compensation for Personal Injuries and Compensation under Lord Campbell's Act,	[illegible]	[illegible]	[illegible]	[illegible]	[illegible]	[illegible]	[illegible]	[illegible]	[illegible]	[illegible]	[illegible]	[illegible]	[illegible]	[illegible]	[illegible]	[illegible]
Against Carriers for Negligence,	[illegible]	[illegible]	[illegible]	[illegible]	[illegible]	[illegible]	[illegible]	[illegible]	[illegible]	[illegible]	[illegible]	[illegible]	[illegible]	[illegible]	[illegible]	[illegible]
Against Professional Men for Negligence,	[illegible]	[illegible]	[illegible]	[illegible]	[illegible]	[illegible]	[illegible]	[illegible]	[illegible]	[illegible]	[illegible]	[illegible]	[illegible]	[illegible]	[illegible]	[illegible]
For Compensation for other Injury—from Negligence,	[illegible]	[illegible]	[illegible]	[illegible]	[illegible]	[illegible]	[illegible]	[illegible]	[illegible]	[illegible]	[illegible]	[illegible]	[illegible]	[illegible]	[illegible]	[illegible]
Replevin or Actions in respect of Distress,	[illegible]	[illegible]	[illegible]	[illegible]	[illegible]	[illegible]	[illegible]	[illegible]	[illegible]	[illegible]	[illegible]	[illegible]	[illegible]	[illegible]	[illegible]	[illegible]
Actions in Questions of [illegible],	[illegible]	[illegible]	[illegible]	[illegible]	[illegible]	[illegible]	[illegible]	[illegible]	[illegible]	[illegible]	[illegible]	[illegible]	[illegible]	[illegible]	[illegible]	[illegible]
For Breach of Contract,	[illegible]	[illegible]	[illegible]	[illegible]	[illegible]	[illegible]	[illegible]	[illegible]	[illegible]	[illegible]	[illegible]	[illegible]	[illegible]	[illegible]	[illegible]	[illegible]
For Breach of Warranty,	[illegible]	[illegible]	[illegible]	[illegible]	[illegible]	[illegible]	[illegible]	[illegible]	[illegible]	[illegible]	[illegible]	[illegible]	[illegible]	[illegible]	[illegible]	[illegible]
For Infringement of Patents,	[illegible]	[illegible]	[illegible]	[illegible]	[illegible]	[illegible]	[illegible]	[illegible]	[illegible]	[illegible]	[illegible]	[illegible]	[illegible]	[illegible]	[illegible]	[illegible]
For Recovery of Land (Ejectment),	[illegible]	[illegible]	[illegible]	[illegible]	[illegible]	[illegible]	[illegible]	[illegible]	[illegible]	[illegible]	[illegible]	[illegible]	[illegible]	[illegible]	[illegible]	[illegible]
Trespass relative to Land, Houses, &c.	[illegible]	[illegible]	[illegible]	[illegible]	[illegible]	[illegible]	[illegible]	[illegible]	[illegible]	[illegible]	[illegible]	[illegible]	[illegible]	[illegible]	[illegible]	[illegible]
For Breach of Promise of Marriage,	[illegible]	[illegible]	[illegible]	[illegible]	[illegible]	[illegible]	[illegible]	[illegible]	[illegible]	[illegible]	[illegible]	[illegible]	[illegible]	[illegible]	[illegible]	[illegible]
Seduction,	[illegible]	[illegible]	[illegible]	[illegible]	[illegible]	[illegible]	[illegible]	[illegible]	[illegible]	[illegible]	[illegible]	[illegible]	[illegible]	[illegible]	[illegible]	[illegible]
Libel,	[illegible]	[illegible]	[illegible]	[illegible]	[illegible]	[illegible]	[illegible]	[illegible]	[illegible]	[illegible]	[illegible]	[illegible]	[illegible]	[illegible]	[illegible]	[illegible]
Slander,	[illegible]	[illegible]	[illegible]	[illegible]	[illegible]	[illegible]	[illegible]	[illegible]	[illegible]	[illegible]	[illegible]	[illegible]	[illegible]	[illegible]	[illegible]	[illegible]
Malicious Prosecution,	[illegible]	[illegible]	[illegible]	[illegible]	[illegible]	[illegible]	[illegible]	[illegible]	[illegible]	[illegible]	[illegible]	[illegible]	[illegible]	[illegible]	[illegible]	[illegible]
False Imprisonment,	[illegible]	[illegible]	[illegible]	[illegible]	[illegible]	[illegible]	[illegible]	[illegible]	[illegible]	[illegible]	[illegible]	[illegible]	[illegible]	[illegible]	[illegible]	[illegible]
Assault,	[illegible]	[illegible]	[illegible]	[illegible]	[illegible]	[illegible]	[illegible]	[illegible]	[illegible]	[illegible]	[illegible]	[illegible]	[illegible]	[illegible]	[illegible]	[illegible]
Interpleader Issues,	[illegible]	[illegible]	[illegible]	[illegible]	[illegible]	[illegible]	[illegible]	[illegible]	[illegible]	[illegible]	[illegible]	[illegible]	[illegible]	[illegible]	[illegible]	[illegible]
Issues from Courts of Equity,	[illegible]	[illegible]	[illegible]	[illegible]	[illegible]	[illegible]	[illegible]	[illegible]	[illegible]	[illegible]	[illegible]	[illegible]	[illegible]	[illegible]	[illegible]	[illegible]
[illegible]	[illegible]	[illegible]	[illegible]	[illegible]	[illegible]	[illegible]	[illegible]	[illegible]	[illegible]	[illegible]	[illegible]	[illegible]	[illegible]	[illegible]	[illegible]	[illegible]
For Breach of Covenant,	[illegible]	[illegible]	[illegible]	[illegible]	[illegible]	[illegible]	[illegible]	[illegible]	[illegible]	[illegible]	[illegible]	[illegible]	[illegible]	[illegible]	[illegible]	[illegible]
For Recovery of Rent,	[illegible]	[illegible]	[illegible]	[illegible]	[illegible]	[illegible]	[illegible]	[illegible]	[illegible]	[illegible]	[illegible]	[illegible]	[illegible]	[illegible]	[illegible]	[illegible]
On Life and Fire Policies,	[illegible]	[illegible]	[illegible]	[illegible]	[illegible]	[illegible]	[illegible]	[illegible]	[illegible]	[illegible]	[illegible]	[illegible]	[illegible]	[illegible]	[illegible]	[illegible]
Fraudulent Representations,	[illegible]	[illegible]	[illegible]	[illegible]	[illegible]	[illegible]	[illegible]	[illegible]	[illegible]	[illegible]	[illegible]	[illegible]	[illegible]	[illegible]	[illegible]	[illegible]
Calls on Shares,	[illegible]	[illegible]	[illegible]	[illegible]	[illegible]	[illegible]	[illegible]	[illegible]	[illegible]	[illegible]	[illegible]	[illegible]	[illegible]	[illegible]	[illegible]	[illegible]
Wrongful Dismissal,	[illegible]	[illegible]	[illegible]	[illegible]	[illegible]	[illegible]	[illegible]	[illegible]	[illegible]	[illegible]	[illegible]	[illegible]	[illegible]	[illegible]	[illegible]	[illegible]
Other Actions,	[illegible]	[illegible]	[illegible]	[illegible]	[illegible]	[illegible]	[illegible]	[illegible]	[illegible]	[illegible]	[illegible]	[illegible]	[illegible]	[illegible]	[illegible]	[illegible]
Totals,	[illegible]	[illegible]	[illegible]	[illegible]	[illegible]	[illegible]	[illegible]	[illegible]	[illegible]	[illegible]	[illegible]	[illegible]	[illegible]	[illegible]	[illegible]	[illegible]

TABLE 45.—HIGH COURT OF JUSTICE.—PROCEEDINGS ON CIRCUIT.—NATURE of the CAUSES TRIED on CIRCUIT, and the Class of Amounts, and Total Amount recovered, in the Year [illegible], from Returns made by Judges' Registrars.

Nature of the Suits tried or otherwise disposed of in Court	Total Number of Verdicts for Plaintiff	Number of each Class of Amounts Recovered by Verdict: [illegible]	[illegible]	[illegible]	[illegible]	[illegible]	[illegible]	[illegible]	[illegible]	[illegible]	[illegible]	[illegible]	No Amount, but Verdict [illegible]	Total Amount Recovered by Verdicts
On Promissory Notes, Bills of Exchange, &c.	[illegible]	[illegible]	[illegible]	[illegible]	[illegible]	[illegible]	[illegible]	[illegible]	[illegible]	[illegible]	[illegible]	[illegible]	[illegible]	[illegible]
On Bonds,	[illegible]	[illegible]	[illegible]	[illegible]	[illegible]	[illegible]	[illegible]	[illegible]	[illegible]	[illegible]	[illegible]	[illegible]	[illegible]	[illegible]
For Goods sold and delivered,	[illegible]	[illegible]	[illegible]	[illegible]	[illegible]	[illegible]	[illegible]	[illegible]	[illegible]	[illegible]	[illegible]	[illegible]	[illegible]	[illegible]
For Work and Labour done,	[illegible]	[illegible]	[illegible]	[illegible]	[illegible]	[illegible]	[illegible]	[illegible]	[illegible]	[illegible]	[illegible]	[illegible]	[illegible]	[illegible]
For Money paid, [illegible]	[illegible]	[illegible]	[illegible]	[illegible]	[illegible]	[illegible]	[illegible]	[illegible]	[illegible]	[illegible]	[illegible]	[illegible]	[illegible]	[illegible]
For Money received,	[illegible]	[illegible]	[illegible]	[illegible]	[illegible]	[illegible]	[illegible]	[illegible]	[illegible]	[illegible]	[illegible]	[illegible]	[illegible]	[illegible]
For Compensation for Personal Injuries and Compensation under Lord Campbell's Act,	[illegible]	[illegible]	[illegible]	[illegible]	[illegible]	[illegible]	[illegible]	[illegible]	[illegible]	[illegible]	[illegible]	[illegible]	[illegible]	[illegible]
Against Carriers for Negligence,	[illegible]	[illegible]	[illegible]	[illegible]	[illegible]	[illegible]	[illegible]	[illegible]	[illegible]	[illegible]	[illegible]	[illegible]	[illegible]	[illegible]
Against Professional Men for Negligence,	[illegible]	[illegible]	[illegible]	[illegible]	[illegible]	[illegible]	[illegible]	[illegible]	[illegible]	[illegible]	[illegible]	[illegible]	[illegible]	[illegible]
For Compensation for other Injuries from Negligence,	[illegible]	[illegible]	[illegible]	[illegible]	[illegible]	[illegible]	[illegible]	[illegible]	[illegible]	[illegible]	[illegible]	[illegible]	[illegible]	[illegible]
Replevin or Actions in respect of Distress,	[illegible]	[illegible]	[illegible]	[illegible]	[illegible]	[illegible]	[illegible]	[illegible]	[illegible]	[illegible]	[illegible]	[illegible]	[illegible]	[illegible]
Actions in the Nature of Actions of Trover or Detinue,	[illegible]	[illegible]	[illegible]	[illegible]	[illegible]	[illegible]	[illegible]	[illegible]	[illegible]	[illegible]	[illegible]	[illegible]	[illegible]	[illegible]
For Breach of Contract,	[illegible]	[illegible]	[illegible]	[illegible]	[illegible]	[illegible]	[illegible]	[illegible]	[illegible]	[illegible]	[illegible]	[illegible]	[illegible]	[illegible]
For Breach of Warranty,	[illegible]	[illegible]	[illegible]	[illegible]	[illegible]	[illegible]	[illegible]	[illegible]	[illegible]	[illegible]	[illegible]	[illegible]	[illegible]	[illegible]
For Infringement of Patents,	[illegible]	[illegible]	[illegible]	[illegible]	[illegible]	[illegible]	[illegible]	[illegible]	[illegible]	[illegible]	[illegible]	[illegible]	[illegible]	[illegible]
For Recovery of Land (Ejectment),	[illegible]	[illegible]	[illegible]	[illegible]	[illegible]	[illegible]	[illegible]	[illegible]	[illegible]	[illegible]	[illegible]	[illegible]	[illegible]	[illegible]
Trespass to Land, Houses, &c.	[illegible]	[illegible]	[illegible]	[illegible]	[illegible]	[illegible]	[illegible]	[illegible]	[illegible]	[illegible]	[illegible]	[illegible]	[illegible]	[illegible]
For Breach of Promise of Marriage,	[illegible]	[illegible]	[illegible]	[illegible]	[illegible]	[illegible]	[illegible]	[illegible]	[illegible]	[illegible]	[illegible]	[illegible]	[illegible]	[illegible]
Seduction,	[illegible]	[illegible]	[illegible]	[illegible]	[illegible]	[illegible]	[illegible]	[illegible]	[illegible]	[illegible]	[illegible]	[illegible]	[illegible]	[illegible]
Libel,	[illegible]	[illegible]	[illegible]	[illegible]	[illegible]	[illegible]	[illegible]	[illegible]	[illegible]	[illegible]	[illegible]	[illegible]	[illegible]	[illegible]
Slander,	[illegible]	[illegible]	[illegible]	[illegible]	[illegible]	[illegible]	[illegible]	[illegible]	[illegible]	[illegible]	[illegible]	[illegible]	[illegible]	[illegible]
Malicious Prosecution,	[illegible]	[illegible]	[illegible]	[illegible]	[illegible]	[illegible]	[illegible]	[illegible]	[illegible]	[illegible]	[illegible]	[illegible]	[illegible]	[illegible]
False Imprisonment,	[illegible]	[illegible]	[illegible]	[illegible]	[illegible]	[illegible]	[illegible]	[illegible]	[illegible]	[illegible]	[illegible]	[illegible]	[illegible]	[illegible]
Assault,	[illegible]	[illegible]	[illegible]	[illegible]	[illegible]	[illegible]	[illegible]	[illegible]	[illegible]	[illegible]	[illegible]	[illegible]	[illegible]	[illegible]
Interpleader Issues,	[illegible]	[illegible]	[illegible]	[illegible]	[illegible]	[illegible]	[illegible]	[illegible]	[illegible]	[illegible]	[illegible]	[illegible]	[illegible]	[illegible]
Issues from Courts of Equity,	[illegible]	[illegible]	[illegible]	[illegible]	[illegible]	[illegible]	[illegible]	[illegible]	[illegible]	[illegible]	[illegible]	[illegible]	[illegible]	[illegible]
Nuisance,	[illegible]	[illegible]	[illegible]	[illegible]	[illegible]	[illegible]	[illegible]	[illegible]	[illegible]	[illegible]	[illegible]	[illegible]	[illegible]	[illegible]
For Breach of Covenant,	[illegible]	[illegible]	[illegible]	[illegible]	[illegible]	[illegible]	[illegible]	[illegible]	[illegible]	[illegible]	[illegible]	[illegible]	[illegible]	[illegible]
For Recovery of Rent,	[illegible]	[illegible]	[illegible]	[illegible]	[illegible]	[illegible]	[illegible]	[illegible]	[illegible]	[illegible]	[illegible]	[illegible]	[illegible]	[illegible]
On Life and Fire Policies,	[illegible]	[illegible]	[illegible]	[illegible]	[illegible]	[illegible]	[illegible]	[illegible]	[illegible]	[illegible]	[illegible]	[illegible]	[illegible]	[illegible]
Fraudulent Representation,	[illegible]	[illegible]	[illegible]	[illegible]	[illegible]	[illegible]	[illegible]	[illegible]	[illegible]	[illegible]	[illegible]	[illegible]	[illegible]	[illegible]
Calls on Shares,	[illegible]	[illegible]	[illegible]	[illegible]	[illegible]	[illegible]	[illegible]	[illegible]	[illegible]	[illegible]	[illegible]	[illegible]	[illegible]	[illegible]
Wrongful Dismissal,	[illegible]	[illegible]	[illegible]	[illegible]	[illegible]	[illegible]	[illegible]	[illegible]	[illegible]	[illegible]	[illegible]	[illegible]	[illegible]	[illegible]
Other Actions,	[illegible]	[illegible]	[illegible]	[illegible]	[illegible]	[illegible]	[illegible]	[illegible]	[illegible]	[illegible]	[illegible]	[illegible]	[illegible]	[illegible]
Total,	[illegible]	[illegible]	[illegible]	[illegible]	[illegible]	[illegible]	[illegible]	[illegible]	[illegible]	[illegible]	[illegible]	[illegible]	[illegible]	[illegible]

TABLE 64.—HIGH COURT OF JUSTICE.—PROCEEDINGS ON CIRCUIT.—PROCEEDINGS in regard to TRAVERSERS, and APPEALS from Poor Rate for Non-Attendance as JURORS, and FISCAL PRESENTMENTS, from Returns made by Clerks of the Crown, for the Year 1880.

COUNTIES AND COUNTIES OF CITIES AND TOWNS, ARRANGED BY CIRCUITS	[illegible]						[illegible]						[illegible]					[illegible]	
	Spring Assizes			Summer Assizes			Spring Assizes			Summer Assizes			[illegible]						
	Number	Amount claimed	Amount fixed	Number	Amount claimed	Amount fixed	Number	Amount claimed	Amount fixed	Number	Amount claimed	Amount fixed	Lodged	Heard	[illegible]	[illegible]	[illegible]	[illegible]	[illegible]
		£ s. d.	£ s. d.		£ s. d.	£ s. d.		£ s. d.	£ s. d.		£ s. d.	£ s. d.				£ s. d.	£ s. d.		
HOME CIRCUIT:																			
Meath,	[illegible]	[illegible]	[illegible]	[illegible]	[illegible]	[illegible]	[illegible]	[illegible]	[illegible]	[illegible]	[illegible]	[illegible]	[illegible]	[illegible]	[illegible]	[illegible]	[illegible]	[illegible]	[illegible]
Westmeath,	[illegible]	[illegible]	[illegible]	[illegible]	[illegible]	[illegible]	[illegible]	[illegible]	[illegible]	[illegible]	[illegible]	[illegible]	[illegible]	[illegible]	[illegible]	[illegible]	[illegible]	[illegible]	[illegible]
King's County,	[illegible]	[illegible]	[illegible]	[illegible]	[illegible]	[illegible]	[illegible]	[illegible]	[illegible]	[illegible]	[illegible]	[illegible]	[illegible]	[illegible]	[illegible]	[illegible]	[illegible]	[illegible]	[illegible]
Queen's County,	[illegible]	[illegible]	[illegible]	[illegible]	[illegible]	[illegible]	[illegible]	[illegible]	[illegible]	[illegible]	[illegible]	[illegible]	[illegible]	[illegible]	[illegible]	[illegible]	[illegible]	[illegible]	[illegible]
Carlow,	[illegible]	[illegible]	[illegible]	[illegible]	[illegible]	[illegible]	[illegible]	[illegible]	[illegible]	[illegible]	[illegible]	[illegible]	[illegible]	[illegible]	[illegible]	[illegible]	[illegible]	[illegible]	[illegible]
Kildare,	[illegible]	[illegible]	[illegible]	[illegible]	[illegible]	[illegible]	[illegible]	[illegible]	[illegible]	[illegible]	[illegible]	[illegible]	[illegible]	[illegible]	[illegible]	[illegible]	[illegible]	[illegible]	[illegible]
LEINSTER CIRCUIT:																			
Tipperary, N.R.,	[illegible]	[illegible]	[illegible]	[illegible]	[illegible]	[illegible]	[illegible]	[illegible]	[illegible]	[illegible]	[illegible]	[illegible]	[illegible]	[illegible]	[illegible]	[illegible]	[illegible]	[illegible]	[illegible]
Kilkenny County,	[illegible]	[illegible]	[illegible]	[illegible]	[illegible]	[illegible]	[illegible]	[illegible]	[illegible]	[illegible]	[illegible]	[illegible]	[illegible]	[illegible]	[illegible]	[illegible]	[illegible]	[illegible]	[illegible]
Kilkenny City,	[illegible]	[illegible]	[illegible]	[illegible]	[illegible]	[illegible]	[illegible]	[illegible]	[illegible]	[illegible]	[illegible]	[illegible]	[illegible]	[illegible]	[illegible]	[illegible]	[illegible]	[illegible]	[illegible]
Tipperary, S.R.,	[illegible]	[illegible]	[illegible]	[illegible]	[illegible]	[illegible]	[illegible]	[illegible]	[illegible]	[illegible]	[illegible]	[illegible]	[illegible]	[illegible]	[illegible]	[illegible]	[illegible]	[illegible]	[illegible]
Waterford County,	[illegible]	[illegible]	[illegible]	[illegible]	[illegible]	[illegible]	[illegible]	[illegible]	[illegible]	[illegible]	[illegible]	[illegible]	[illegible]	[illegible]	[illegible]	[illegible]	[illegible]	[illegible]	[illegible]
Waterford City,	[illegible]	[illegible]	[illegible]	[illegible]	[illegible]	[illegible]	[illegible]	[illegible]	[illegible]	[illegible]	[illegible]	[illegible]	[illegible]	[illegible]	[illegible]	[illegible]	[illegible]	[illegible]	[illegible]
Wexford,	[illegible]	[illegible]	[illegible]	[illegible]	[illegible]	[illegible]	[illegible]	[illegible]	[illegible]	[illegible]	[illegible]	[illegible]	[illegible]	[illegible]	[illegible]	[illegible]	[illegible]	[illegible]	[illegible]
Wicklow,	[illegible]	[illegible]	[illegible]	[illegible]	[illegible]	[illegible]	[illegible]	[illegible]	[illegible]	[illegible]	[illegible]	[illegible]	[illegible]	[illegible]	[illegible]	[illegible]	[illegible]	[illegible]	[illegible]
MUNSTER CIRCUIT:																			
Clare,	[illegible]	[illegible]	[illegible]	[illegible]	[illegible]	[illegible]	[illegible]	[illegible]	[illegible]	[illegible]	[illegible]	[illegible]	[illegible]	[illegible]	[illegible]	[illegible]	[illegible]	[illegible]	[illegible]
Limerick County,	[illegible]	[illegible]	[illegible]	[illegible]	[illegible]	[illegible]	[illegible]	[illegible]	[illegible]	[illegible]	[illegible]	[illegible]	[illegible]	[illegible]	[illegible]	[illegible]	[illegible]	[illegible]	[illegible]
Limerick City,	[illegible]	[illegible]	[illegible]	[illegible]	[illegible]	[illegible]	[illegible]	[illegible]	[illegible]	[illegible]	[illegible]	[illegible]	[illegible]	[illegible]	[illegible]	[illegible]	[illegible]	[illegible]	[illegible]
Kerry,	[illegible]	[illegible]	[illegible]	[illegible]	[illegible]	[illegible]	[illegible]	[illegible]	[illegible]	[illegible]	[illegible]	[illegible]	[illegible]	[illegible]	[illegible]	[illegible]	[illegible]	[illegible]	[illegible]
Cork County,	[illegible]	[illegible]	[illegible]	[illegible]	[illegible]	[illegible]	[illegible]	[illegible]	[illegible]	[illegible]	[illegible]	[illegible]	[illegible]	[illegible]	[illegible]	[illegible]	[illegible]	[illegible]	[illegible]
Cork City,	[illegible]	[illegible]	[illegible]	[illegible]	[illegible]	[illegible]	[illegible]	[illegible]	[illegible]	[illegible]	[illegible]	[illegible]	[illegible]	[illegible]	[illegible]	[illegible]	[illegible]	[illegible]	[illegible]
NORTH-EAST CIRCUIT:																			
Drogheda Town,	[illegible]	[illegible]	[illegible]	[illegible]	[illegible]	[illegible]	[illegible]	[illegible]	[illegible]	[illegible]	[illegible]	[illegible]	[illegible]	[illegible]	[illegible]	[illegible]	[illegible]	[illegible]	[illegible]
Louth,	[illegible]	[illegible]	[illegible]	[illegible]	[illegible]	[illegible]	[illegible]	[illegible]	[illegible]	[illegible]	[illegible]	[illegible]	[illegible]	[illegible]	[illegible]	[illegible]	[illegible]	[illegible]	[illegible]
Monaghan,	[illegible]	[illegible]	[illegible]	[illegible]	[illegible]	[illegible]	[illegible]	[illegible]	[illegible]	[illegible]	[illegible]	[illegible]	[illegible]	[illegible]	[illegible]	[illegible]	[illegible]	[illegible]	[illegible]
Armagh,	[illegible]	[illegible]	[illegible]	[illegible]	[illegible]	[illegible]	[illegible]	[illegible]	[illegible]	[illegible]	[illegible]	[illegible]	[illegible]	[illegible]	[illegible]	[illegible]	[illegible]	[illegible]	[illegible]
Down,	[illegible]	[illegible]	[illegible]	[illegible]	[illegible]	[illegible]	[illegible]	[illegible]	[illegible]	[illegible]	[illegible]	[illegible]	[illegible]	[illegible]	[illegible]	[illegible]	[illegible]	[illegible]	[illegible]
Antrim,	[illegible]	[illegible]	[illegible]	[illegible]	[illegible]	[illegible]	[illegible]	[illegible]	[illegible]	[illegible]	[illegible]	[illegible]	[illegible]	[illegible]	[illegible]	[illegible]	[illegible]	[illegible]	[illegible]
Carrickfergus Town,	[illegible]	[illegible]	[illegible]	[illegible]	[illegible]	[illegible]	[illegible]	[illegible]	[illegible]	[illegible]	[illegible]	[illegible]	[illegible]	[illegible]	[illegible]	[illegible]	[illegible]	[illegible]	[illegible]
NORTH-WEST CIRCUIT:																			
Longford,	[illegible]	[illegible]	[illegible]	[illegible]	[illegible]	[illegible]	[illegible]	[illegible]	[illegible]	[illegible]	[illegible]	[illegible]	[illegible]	[illegible]	[illegible]	[illegible]	[illegible]	[illegible]	[illegible]
Cavan,	[illegible]	[illegible]	[illegible]	[illegible]	[illegible]	[illegible]	[illegible]	[illegible]	[illegible]	[illegible]	[illegible]	[illegible]	[illegible]	[illegible]	[illegible]	[illegible]	[illegible]	[illegible]	[illegible]
Fermanagh,	[illegible]	[illegible]	[illegible]	[illegible]	[illegible]	[illegible]	[illegible]	[illegible]	[illegible]	[illegible]	[illegible]	[illegible]	[illegible]	[illegible]	[illegible]	[illegible]	[illegible]	[illegible]	[illegible]
Tyrone,	[illegible]	[illegible]	[illegible]	[illegible]	[illegible]	[illegible]	[illegible]	[illegible]	[illegible]	[illegible]	[illegible]	[illegible]	[illegible]	[illegible]	[illegible]	[illegible]	[illegible]	[illegible]	[illegible]
Donegal,	[illegible]	[illegible]	[illegible]	[illegible]	[illegible]	[illegible]	[illegible]	[illegible]	[illegible]	[illegible]	[illegible]	[illegible]	[illegible]	[illegible]	[illegible]	[illegible]	[illegible]	[illegible]	[illegible]
Londonderry,	[illegible]	[illegible]	[illegible]	[illegible]	[illegible]	[illegible]	[illegible]	[illegible]	[illegible]	[illegible]	[illegible]	[illegible]	[illegible]	[illegible]	[illegible]	[illegible]	[illegible]	[illegible]	[illegible]
CONNAUGHT CIRCUIT:																			
Leitrim,	[illegible]	[illegible]	[illegible]	[illegible]	[illegible]	[illegible]	[illegible]	[illegible]	[illegible]	[illegible]	[illegible]	[illegible]	[illegible]	[illegible]	[illegible]	[illegible]	[illegible]	[illegible]	[illegible]
Sligo,	[illegible]	[illegible]	[illegible]	[illegible]	[illegible]	[illegible]	[illegible]	[illegible]	[illegible]	[illegible]	[illegible]	[illegible]	[illegible]	[illegible]	[illegible]	[illegible]	[illegible]	[illegible]	[illegible]
Roscommon,	[illegible]	[illegible]	[illegible]	[illegible]	[illegible]	[illegible]	[illegible]	[illegible]	[illegible]	[illegible]	[illegible]	[illegible]	[illegible]	[illegible]	[illegible]	[illegible]	[illegible]	[illegible]	[illegible]
Mayo,	[illegible]	[illegible]	[illegible]	[illegible]	[illegible]	[illegible]	[illegible]	[illegible]	[illegible]	[illegible]	[illegible]	[illegible]	[illegible]	[illegible]	[illegible]	[illegible]	[illegible]	[illegible]	[illegible]
Galway,	[illegible]	[illegible]	[illegible]	[illegible]	[illegible]	[illegible]	[illegible]	[illegible]	[illegible]	[illegible]	[illegible]	[illegible]	[illegible]	[illegible]	[illegible]	[illegible]	[illegible]	[illegible]	[illegible]
Galway Town,	[illegible]	[illegible]	[illegible]	[illegible]	[illegible]	[illegible]	[illegible]	[illegible]	[illegible]	[illegible]	[illegible]	[illegible]	[illegible]	[illegible]	[illegible]	[illegible]	[illegible]	[illegible]	[illegible]
Total,	[illegible]	[illegible]	[illegible]	[illegible]	[illegible]	[illegible]	[illegible]	[illegible]	[illegible]	[illegible]	[illegible]	[illegible]	[illegible]	[illegible]	[illegible]	[illegible]	[illegible]	[illegible]	[illegible]

[illegible]

TABLE [illegible].—HIGH COURT OF JUSTICE.—PROCEEDINGS ON CIRCUIT.—APPEALS from COUNTY COURT JUDGES and RECORDERS in 18[illegible], from Returns made by Clerks of the Peace and Registrars of Recorders.

Counties and Counties of Cities and of Towns, arranged in Circuits	Appeals from County Court Judges and Recorders: Entered	Heard: Affirmed	Heard: Varied or Reversed	Struck out, Withdrawn, Respited, &c.
Home Circuit:				
Carlow,	[illegible]	[illegible]	[illegible]	[illegible]
Kildare,	[illegible]	[illegible]	[illegible]	[illegible]
King's County,	[illegible]	[illegible]	[illegible]	[illegible]
Meath,	[illegible]	[illegible]	[illegible]	[illegible]
Queen's County,	[illegible]	[illegible]	[illegible]	[illegible]
Westmeath,	[illegible]	[illegible]	[illegible]	[illegible]
Total,	[illegible]	[illegible]	[illegible]	[illegible]
Leinster Circuit:				
Kilkenny,	[illegible]	[illegible]	[illegible]	[illegible]
Tipperary, North Riding,	[illegible]	[illegible]	[illegible]	[illegible]
Tipperary, South Riding,	[illegible]	[illegible]	[illegible]	[illegible]
Waterford,	[illegible]	[illegible]	[illegible]	[illegible]
Wexford,	[illegible]	[illegible]	[illegible]	[illegible]
Wicklow,	[illegible]	[illegible]	[illegible]	[illegible]
Total,	[illegible]	[illegible]	[illegible]	[illegible]
Munster Circuit:				
Clare,	[illegible]	[illegible]	[illegible]	[illegible]
Cork, East Riding,	[illegible]	[illegible]	[illegible]	[illegible]
Cork, West Riding,	[illegible]	[illegible]	[illegible]	[illegible]
Kerry,	[illegible]	[illegible]	[illegible]	[illegible]
Limerick,	[illegible]	[illegible]	[illegible]	[illegible]
Total,	[illegible]	[illegible]	[illegible]	[illegible]
North-East Circuit:				
Antrim,	[illegible]	[illegible]	[illegible]	[illegible]
Armagh,	[illegible]	[illegible]	[illegible]	[illegible]
Down,	[illegible]	[illegible]	[illegible]	[illegible]
Louth,	[illegible]	[illegible]	[illegible]	[illegible]
Monaghan,	[illegible]	[illegible]	[illegible]	[illegible]
Total,	[illegible]	[illegible]	[illegible]	[illegible]
North-West Circuit:				
Cavan,	[illegible]	[illegible]	[illegible]	[illegible]
Donegal,	[illegible]	[illegible]	[illegible]	[illegible]
Fermanagh,	[illegible]	[illegible]	[illegible]	[illegible]
Londonderry,	[illegible]	[illegible]	[illegible]	[illegible]
Longford,	[illegible]	[illegible]	[illegible]	[illegible]
Tyrone,	[illegible]	[illegible]	[illegible]	[illegible]
Total,	[illegible]	[illegible]	[illegible]	[illegible]
Connaught Circuit:				
Galway,	[illegible]	[illegible]	[illegible]	[illegible]
Leitrim,	[illegible]	[illegible]	[illegible]	[illegible]
Mayo,	[illegible]	[illegible]	[illegible]	[illegible]
Roscommon,	[illegible]	[illegible]	[illegible]	[illegible]
Sligo,	[illegible]	[illegible]	[illegible]	[illegible]
Total,	[illegible]	[illegible]	[illegible]	[illegible]
Belfast, Recorder's Court,	[illegible]	[illegible]	[illegible]	[illegible]
Cork City, Recorder's Court,	[illegible]	[illegible]	[illegible]	[illegible]
Galway Town, Commissioners' Court,	[illegible]	[illegible]	[illegible]	[illegible]
Londonderry City, Recorder's Court,	[illegible]	[illegible]	[illegible]	[illegible]
Total,	[illegible]	[illegible]	[illegible]	[illegible]
Total of Ireland,	[illegible]	[illegible]	[illegible]	[illegible]

TABLE [illegible].—COUNTY COURTS AND RECORDERS' COURTS.—CIVIL BILL EJECTMENTS, REPLEVINS, and other CIVIL BILLS Served in 18[illegible], from Returns made by Process Servers appointed by COUNTY COURT JUDGES and RECORDERS.

Counties, and Counties of Cities or of Towns	Number of Process Servers appointed	Number of Process Servers who have made Returns	Number of Process Servers who have not made Returns	Number of Processes Served: Civil Bill Ejectments	Replevins	Other Civil Bills
Leinster.						
Carlow,	[illegible]	[illegible]	[illegible]	[illegible]	[illegible]	[illegible]
Dublin,	[illegible]	[illegible]	[illegible]	[illegible]	[illegible]	[illegible]
Dublin City,	[illegible]	[illegible]	[illegible]	[illegible]	[illegible]	[illegible]
Kildare,	[illegible]	[illegible]	[illegible]	[illegible]	[illegible]	[illegible]
Kilkenny, and City,	[illegible]	[illegible]	[illegible]	[illegible]	[illegible]	[illegible]
King's County,	[illegible]	[illegible]	[illegible]	[illegible]	[illegible]	[illegible]
Longford,	[illegible]	[illegible]	[illegible]	[illegible]	[illegible]	[illegible]
Louth, and Drogheda Town,	[illegible]	[illegible]	[illegible]	[illegible]	[illegible]	[illegible]
Meath,	[illegible]	[illegible]	[illegible]	[illegible]	[illegible]	[illegible]
Queen's County,	[illegible]	[illegible]	[illegible]	[illegible]	[illegible]	[illegible]
Westmeath,	[illegible]	[illegible]	[illegible]	[illegible]	[illegible]	[illegible]
Wexford,	[illegible]	[illegible]	[illegible]	[illegible]	[illegible]	[illegible]
Wicklow,	[illegible]	[illegible]	[illegible]	[illegible]	[illegible]	[illegible]
Total of Province,	[illegible]	[illegible]	[illegible]	[illegible]	[illegible]	[illegible]
Munster.						
Clare,	[illegible]	[illegible]	[illegible]	[illegible]	[illegible]	[illegible]
Cork, East Riding,	[illegible]	[illegible]	[illegible]	[illegible]	[illegible]	[illegible]
Cork, West Riding,	[illegible]	[illegible]	[illegible]	[illegible]	[illegible]	[illegible]
Cork City (Recorder's Court),	[illegible]	[illegible]	[illegible]	[illegible]	[illegible]	[illegible]
Kerry,	[illegible]	[illegible]	[illegible]	[illegible]	[illegible]	[illegible]
Limerick, and City,	[illegible]	[illegible]	[illegible]	[illegible]	[illegible]	[illegible]
Tipperary,	[illegible]	[illegible]	[illegible]	[illegible]	[illegible]	[illegible]
Waterford, and City,	[illegible]	[illegible]	[illegible]	[illegible]	[illegible]	[illegible]
Total of Province,	[illegible]	[illegible]	[illegible]	[illegible]	[illegible]	[illegible]
Ulster.						
Antrim (including Carrickfergus),	[illegible]	[illegible]	[illegible]	[illegible]	[illegible]	[illegible]
Armagh,	[illegible]	[illegible]	[illegible]	[illegible]	[illegible]	[illegible]
Cavan,	[illegible]	[illegible]	[illegible]	[illegible]	[illegible]	[illegible]
Donegal,	[illegible]	[illegible]	[illegible]	[illegible]	[illegible]	[illegible]
Down,	[illegible]	[illegible]	[illegible]	[illegible]	[illegible]	[illegible]
Fermanagh,	[illegible]	[illegible]	[illegible]	[illegible]	[illegible]	[illegible]
Londonderry,	[illegible]	[illegible]	[illegible]	[illegible]	[illegible]	[illegible]
Monaghan,	[illegible]	[illegible]	[illegible]	[illegible]	[illegible]	[illegible]
Tyrone,	[illegible]	[illegible]	[illegible]	[illegible]	[illegible]	[illegible]
Total of Province,	[illegible]	[illegible]	[illegible]	[illegible]	[illegible]	[illegible]
Connaught.						
Galway, and Town,	[illegible]	[illegible]	[illegible]	[illegible]	[illegible]	[illegible]
Leitrim,	[illegible]	[illegible]	[illegible]	[illegible]	[illegible]	[illegible]
Mayo,	[illegible]	[illegible]	[illegible]	[illegible]	[illegible]	[illegible]
Roscommon,	[illegible]	[illegible]	[illegible]	[illegible]	[illegible]	[illegible]
Sligo,	[illegible]	[illegible]	[illegible]	[illegible]	[illegible]	[illegible]

TABLE [illegible].—COUNTY COURTS AND RECORDERS' COURTS.—PROCEEDINGS in all SUITS (except [illegible]) Returns made by Clerks of the Peace

COUNTIES	[illegible]	[illegible]	[illegible]	[illegible]	[illegible]	[illegible]	[illegible]	[illegible]	[illegible]	[illegible]	[illegible]	[illegible]	[illegible]	[illegible]
Leinster.														
Carlow,	[illegible]	[illegible]	[illegible]	[illegible]	[illegible]	[illegible]	[illegible]	[illegible]	[illegible]	[illegible]	[illegible]	[illegible]	[illegible]	[illegible]
Dublin,	[illegible]	[illegible]	[illegible]	[illegible]	[illegible]	[illegible]	[illegible]	[illegible]	[illegible]	[illegible]	[illegible]	[illegible]	[illegible]	[illegible]
Dublin City (Recorder's Court)	[illegible]	[illegible]	[illegible]	[illegible]	[illegible]	[illegible]	[illegible]	[illegible]	[illegible]	[illegible]	[illegible]	[illegible]	[illegible]	[illegible]
Kildare,	[illegible]	[illegible]	[illegible]	[illegible]	[illegible]	[illegible]	[illegible]	[illegible]	[illegible]	[illegible]	[illegible]	[illegible]	[illegible]	[illegible]
Kilkenny,	[illegible]	[illegible]	[illegible]	[illegible]	[illegible]	[illegible]	[illegible]	[illegible]	[illegible]	[illegible]	[illegible]	[illegible]	[illegible]	[illegible]
King's County,	[illegible]	[illegible]	[illegible]	[illegible]	[illegible]	[illegible]	[illegible]	[illegible]	[illegible]	[illegible]	[illegible]	[illegible]	[illegible]	[illegible]
Longford,	[illegible]	[illegible]	[illegible]	[illegible]	[illegible]	[illegible]	[illegible]	[illegible]	[illegible]	[illegible]	[illegible]	[illegible]	[illegible]	[illegible]
Louth,	[illegible]	[illegible]	[illegible]	[illegible]	[illegible]	[illegible]	[illegible]	[illegible]	[illegible]	[illegible]	[illegible]	[illegible]	[illegible]	[illegible]
Meath,	[illegible]	[illegible]	[illegible]	[illegible]	[illegible]	[illegible]	[illegible]	[illegible]	[illegible]	[illegible]	[illegible]	[illegible]	[illegible]	[illegible]
Queen's County,	[illegible]	[illegible]	[illegible]	[illegible]	[illegible]	[illegible]	[illegible]	[illegible]	[illegible]	[illegible]	[illegible]	[illegible]	[illegible]	[illegible]
Westmeath,	[illegible]	[illegible]	[illegible]	[illegible]	[illegible]	[illegible]	[illegible]	[illegible]	[illegible]	[illegible]	[illegible]	[illegible]	[illegible]	[illegible]
Wexford,	[illegible]	[illegible]	[illegible]	[illegible]	[illegible]	[illegible]	[illegible]	[illegible]	[illegible]	[illegible]	[illegible]	[illegible]	[illegible]	[illegible]
Wicklow,	[illegible]	[illegible]	[illegible]	[illegible]	[illegible]	[illegible]	[illegible]	[illegible]	[illegible]	[illegible]	[illegible]	[illegible]	[illegible]	[illegible]
Total of Leinster,	[illegible]	[illegible]	[illegible]	[illegible]	[illegible]	[illegible]	[illegible]	[illegible]	[illegible]	[illegible]	[illegible]	[illegible]	[illegible]	[illegible]
Munster.														
Clare,	[illegible]	[illegible]	[illegible]	[illegible]	[illegible]	[illegible]	[illegible]	[illegible]	[illegible]	[illegible]	[illegible]	[illegible]	[illegible]	[illegible]
Cork, E.R.,	[illegible]	[illegible]	[illegible]	[illegible]	[illegible]	[illegible]	[illegible]	[illegible]	[illegible]	[illegible]	[illegible]	[illegible]	[illegible]	[illegible]
Cork, W.R.,	[illegible]	[illegible]	[illegible]	[illegible]	[illegible]	[illegible]	[illegible]	[illegible]	[illegible]	[illegible]	[illegible]	[illegible]	[illegible]	[illegible]
Cork City (Recorder's Court)	[illegible]	[illegible]	[illegible]	[illegible]	[illegible]	[illegible]	[illegible]	[illegible]	[illegible]	[illegible]	[illegible]	[illegible]	[illegible]	[illegible]
Kerry,	[illegible]	[illegible]	[illegible]	[illegible]	[illegible]	[illegible]	[illegible]	[illegible]	[illegible]	[illegible]	[illegible]	[illegible]	[illegible]	[illegible]
Limerick,	[illegible]	[illegible]	[illegible]	[illegible]	[illegible]	[illegible]	[illegible]	[illegible]	[illegible]	[illegible]	[illegible]	[illegible]	[illegible]	[illegible]
Tipperary,	[illegible]	[illegible]	[illegible]	[illegible]	[illegible]	[illegible]	[illegible]	[illegible]	[illegible]	[illegible]	[illegible]	[illegible]	[illegible]	[illegible]
Waterford,	[illegible]	[illegible]	[illegible]	[illegible]	[illegible]	[illegible]	[illegible]	[illegible]	[illegible]	[illegible]	[illegible]	[illegible]	[illegible]	[illegible]
Total of Munster,	[illegible]	[illegible]	[illegible]	[illegible]	[illegible]	[illegible]	[illegible]	[illegible]	[illegible]	[illegible]	[illegible]	[illegible]	[illegible]	[illegible]
Ulster.														
Antrim,	[illegible]	[illegible]	[illegible]	[illegible]	[illegible]	[illegible]	[illegible]	[illegible]	[illegible]	[illegible]	[illegible]	[illegible]	[illegible]	[illegible]
Armagh,	[illegible]	[illegible]	[illegible]	[illegible]	[illegible]	[illegible]	[illegible]	[illegible]	[illegible]	[illegible]	[illegible]	[illegible]	[illegible]	[illegible]
Belfast (Recorder's Court)	[illegible]	[illegible]	[illegible]	[illegible]	[illegible]	[illegible]	[illegible]	[illegible]	[illegible]	[illegible]	[illegible]	[illegible]	[illegible]	[illegible]
Cavan,	[illegible]	[illegible]	[illegible]	[illegible]	[illegible]	[illegible]	[illegible]	[illegible]	[illegible]	[illegible]	[illegible]	[illegible]	[illegible]	[illegible]
Donegal,	[illegible]	[illegible]	[illegible]	[illegible]	[illegible]	[illegible]	[illegible]	[illegible]	[illegible]	[illegible]	[illegible]	[illegible]	[illegible]	[illegible]
Down,	[illegible]	[illegible]	[illegible]	[illegible]	[illegible]	[illegible]	[illegible]	[illegible]	[illegible]	[illegible]	[illegible]	[illegible]	[illegible]	[illegible]
Fermanagh,	[illegible]	[illegible]	[illegible]	[illegible]	[illegible]	[illegible]	[illegible]	[illegible]	[illegible]	[illegible]	[illegible]	[illegible]	[illegible]	[illegible]
Londonderry City (Recorder's Court)	[illegible]	[illegible]	[illegible]	[illegible]	[illegible]	[illegible]	[illegible]	[illegible]	[illegible]	[illegible]	[illegible]	[illegible]	[illegible]	[illegible]
Londonderry,	[illegible]	[illegible]	[illegible]	[illegible]	[illegible]	[illegible]	[illegible]	[illegible]	[illegible]	[illegible]	[illegible]	[illegible]	[illegible]	[illegible]
Monaghan,	[illegible]	[illegible]	[illegible]	[illegible]	[illegible]	[illegible]	[illegible]	[illegible]	[illegible]	[illegible]	[illegible]	[illegible]	[illegible]	[illegible]
Tyrone,	[illegible]	[illegible]	[illegible]	[illegible]	[illegible]	[illegible]	[illegible]	[illegible]	[illegible]	[illegible]	[illegible]	[illegible]	[illegible]	[illegible]
Total of Ulster,	[illegible]	[illegible]	[illegible]	[illegible]	[illegible]	[illegible]	[illegible]	[illegible]	[illegible]	[illegible]	[illegible]	[illegible]	[illegible]	[illegible]
Connaught.														
Galway,	[illegible]	[illegible]	[illegible]	[illegible]	[illegible]	[illegible]	[illegible]	[illegible]	[illegible]	[illegible]	[illegible]	[illegible]	[illegible]	[illegible]
Galway Town (Recorder's Court)	[illegible]	[illegible]	[illegible]	[illegible]	[illegible]	[illegible]	[illegible]	[illegible]	[illegible]	[illegible]	[illegible]	[illegible]	[illegible]	[illegible]
Leitrim,	[illegible]	[illegible]	[illegible]	[illegible]	[illegible]	[illegible]	[illegible]	[illegible]	[illegible]	[illegible]	[illegible]	[illegible]	[illegible]	[illegible]
Mayo,	[illegible]	[illegible]	[illegible]	[illegible]	[illegible]	[illegible]	[illegible]	[illegible]	[illegible]	[illegible]	[illegible]	[illegible]	[illegible]	[illegible]
Roscommon,	[illegible]	[illegible]	[illegible]	[illegible]	[illegible]	[illegible]	[illegible]	[illegible]	[illegible]	[illegible]	[illegible]	[illegible]	[illegible]	[illegible]
Sligo,	[illegible]	[illegible]	[illegible]	[illegible]	[illegible]	[illegible]	[illegible]	[illegible]	[illegible]	[illegible]	[illegible]	[illegible]	[illegible]	[illegible]
Total of Connaught,	[illegible]	[illegible]	[illegible]	[illegible]	[illegible]	[illegible]	[illegible]	[illegible]	[illegible]	[illegible]	[illegible]	[illegible]	[illegible]	[illegible]
Total of Ireland,	[illegible]	[illegible]	[illegible]	[illegible]	[illegible]	[illegible]	[illegible]	[illegible]	[illegible]	[illegible]	[illegible]	[illegible]	[illegible]	[illegible]

[illegible]

[illegible] Local Admiralty Jurisdiction Act) in the Year [illegible]

[illegible]						[illegible]												COUNTIES
[illegible]		[illegible]		[illegible]		[illegible]		[illegible]		[illegible]		[illegible]						
[illegible]	[illegible]	[illegible]	[illegible]	[illegible]	[illegible]	[illegible]	[illegible]	[illegible]	[illegible]	[illegible]	[illegible]	[illegible]	[illegible]					
																		LEINSTER:
[illegible]	[illegible]	[illegible]	[illegible]	[illegible]	[illegible]	[illegible]	[illegible]	[illegible]	[illegible]	[illegible]	[illegible]	[illegible]	[illegible]					Carlow.
[illegible]	[illegible]	[illegible]	[illegible]	[illegible]	[illegible]	[illegible]	[illegible]	[illegible]	[illegible]	[illegible]	[illegible]	[illegible]	[illegible]					Dublin
[illegible]	[illegible]	[illegible]	[illegible]	[illegible]	[illegible]	[illegible]	[illegible]	[illegible]	[illegible]	[illegible]	[illegible]	[illegible]	[illegible]					Dublin City (Recorder's Court).
[illegible]	[illegible]	[illegible]	[illegible]	[illegible]	[illegible]	[illegible]	[illegible]	[illegible]	[illegible]	[illegible]	[illegible]	[illegible]	[illegible]					Kildare
[illegible]	[illegible]	[illegible]	[illegible]	[illegible]	[illegible]	[illegible]	[illegible]	[illegible]	[illegible]	[illegible]	[illegible]	[illegible]	[illegible]					Kilkenny.
[illegible]	[illegible]	[illegible]	[illegible]	[illegible]	[illegible]	[illegible]	[illegible]	[illegible]	[illegible]	[illegible]	[illegible]	[illegible]	[illegible]					King's County
[illegible]	[illegible]	[illegible]	[illegible]	[illegible]	[illegible]	[illegible]	[illegible]	[illegible]	[illegible]	[illegible]	[illegible]	[illegible]	[illegible]					Longford.
[illegible]	[illegible]	[illegible]	[illegible]	[illegible]	[illegible]	[illegible]	[illegible]	[illegible]	[illegible]	[illegible]	[illegible]	[illegible]	[illegible]					Louth
[illegible]	[illegible]	[illegible]	[illegible]	[illegible]	[illegible]	[illegible]	[illegible]	[illegible]	[illegible]	[illegible]	[illegible]	[illegible]	[illegible]					Meath
[illegible]	[illegible]	[illegible]	[illegible]	[illegible]	[illegible]	[illegible]	[illegible]	[illegible]	[illegible]	[illegible]	[illegible]	[illegible]	[illegible]					Queen's County.
[illegible]	[illegible]	[illegible]	[illegible]	[illegible]	[illegible]	[illegible]	[illegible]	[illegible]	[illegible]	[illegible]	[illegible]	[illegible]	[illegible]					Westmeath
[illegible]	[illegible]	[illegible]	[illegible]	[illegible]	[illegible]	[illegible]	[illegible]	[illegible]	[illegible]	[illegible]	[illegible]	[illegible]	[illegible]					Wexford.
[illegible]	[illegible]	[illegible]	[illegible]	[illegible]	[illegible]	[illegible]	[illegible]	[illegible]	[illegible]	[illegible]	[illegible]	[illegible]	[illegible]					Wicklow.
[illegible]	[illegible]	[illegible]	[illegible]	[illegible]	[illegible]	[illegible]	[illegible]	[illegible]	[illegible]	[illegible]	[illegible]	[illegible]	[illegible]					Total of Leinster
																		MUNSTER:
[illegible]	[illegible]	[illegible]	[illegible]	[illegible]	[illegible]	[illegible]	[illegible]	[illegible]	[illegible]	[illegible]	[illegible]	[illegible]	[illegible]					Clare
[illegible]	[illegible]	[illegible]	[illegible]	[illegible]	[illegible]	[illegible]	[illegible]	[illegible]	[illegible]	[illegible]	[illegible]	[illegible]	[illegible]					Cork, E.R.
[illegible]	[illegible]	[illegible]	[illegible]	[illegible]	[illegible]	[illegible]	[illegible]	[illegible]	[illegible]	[illegible]	[illegible]	[illegible]	[illegible]					Cork, W.R.
[illegible]	[illegible]	[illegible]	[illegible]	[illegible]	[illegible]	[illegible]	[illegible]	[illegible]	[illegible]	[illegible]	[illegible]	[illegible]	[illegible]					Cork City (Recorder's Court)
[illegible]	[illegible]	[illegible]	[illegible]	[illegible]	[illegible]	[illegible]	[illegible]	[illegible]	[illegible]	[illegible]	[illegible]	[illegible]	[illegible]					Kerry
[illegible]	[illegible]	[illegible]	[illegible]	[illegible]	[illegible]	[illegible]	[illegible]	[illegible]	[illegible]	[illegible]	[illegible]	[illegible]	[illegible]					Limerick
[illegible]	[illegible]	[illegible]	[illegible]	[illegible]	[illegible]	[illegible]	[illegible]	[illegible]	[illegible]	[illegible]	[illegible]	[illegible]	[illegible]					Tipperary
[illegible]	[illegible]	[illegible]	[illegible]	[illegible]	[illegible]	[illegible]	[illegible]	[illegible]	[illegible]	[illegible]	[illegible]	[illegible]	[illegible]					Waterford
[illegible]	[illegible]	[illegible]	[illegible]	[illegible]	[illegible]	[illegible]	[illegible]	[illegible]	[illegible]	[illegible]	[illegible]	[illegible]	[illegible]					Total of Munster.
																		ULSTER:
[illegible]	[illegible]	[illegible]	[illegible]	[illegible]	[illegible]	[illegible]	[illegible]	[illegible]	[illegible]	[illegible]	[illegible]	[illegible]	[illegible]					Antrim
[illegible]	[illegible]	[illegible]	[illegible]	[illegible]	[illegible]	[illegible]	[illegible]	[illegible]	[illegible]	[illegible]	[illegible]	[illegible]	[illegible]					Armagh
[illegible]	[illegible]	[illegible]	[illegible]	[illegible]	[illegible]	[illegible]	[illegible]	[illegible]	[illegible]	[illegible]	[illegible]	[illegible]	[illegible]					Belfast (Recorder's Court)
[illegible]	[illegible]	[illegible]	[illegible]	[illegible]	[illegible]	[illegible]	[illegible]	[illegible]	[illegible]	[illegible]	[illegible]	[illegible]	[illegible]					Cavan
[illegible]	[illegible]	[illegible]	[illegible]	[illegible]	[illegible]	[illegible]	[illegible]	[illegible]	[illegible]	[illegible]	[illegible]	[illegible]	[illegible]					Donegal
[illegible]	[illegible]	[illegible]	[illegible]	[illegible]	[illegible]	[illegible]	[illegible]	[illegible]	[illegible]	[illegible]	[illegible]	[illegible]	[illegible]					Down
[illegible]	[illegible]	[illegible]	[illegible]	[illegible]	[illegible]	[illegible]	[illegible]	[illegible]	[illegible]	[illegible]	[illegible]	[illegible]	[illegible]					Fermanagh
[illegible]	[illegible]	[illegible]	[illegible]	[illegible]	[illegible]	[illegible]	[illegible]	[illegible]	[illegible]	[illegible]	[illegible]	[illegible]	[illegible]					Londonderry City (Recorder's Court)
[illegible]	[illegible]	[illegible]	[illegible]	[illegible]	[illegible]	[illegible]	[illegible]	[illegible]	[illegible]	[illegible]	[illegible]	[illegible]	[illegible]					Londonderry
[illegible]	[illegible]	[illegible]	[illegible]	[illegible]	[illegible]	[illegible]	[illegible]	[illegible]	[illegible]	[illegible]	[illegible]	[illegible]	[illegible]					Monaghan
[illegible]	[illegible]	[illegible]	[illegible]	[illegible]	[illegible]	[illegible]	[illegible]	[illegible]	[illegible]	[illegible]	[illegible]	[illegible]	[illegible]					Tyrone
[illegible]	[illegible]	[illegible]	[illegible]	[illegible]	[illegible]	[illegible]	[illegible]	[illegible]	[illegible]	[illegible]	[illegible]	[illegible]	[illegible]					Total of Ulster.
																		CONNAUGHT:
[illegible]	[illegible]	[illegible]	[illegible]	[illegible]	[illegible]	[illegible]	[illegible]	[illegible]	[illegible]	[illegible]	[illegible]	[illegible]	[illegible]					Galway.
[illegible]	[illegible]	[illegible]	[illegible]	[illegible]	[illegible]	[illegible]	[illegible]	[illegible]	[illegible]	[illegible]	[illegible]	[illegible]	[illegible]					Galway Town (Recorder's Court).
[illegible]	[illegible]	[illegible]	[illegible]	[illegible]	[illegible]	[illegible]	[illegible]	[illegible]	[illegible]	[illegible]	[illegible]	[illegible]	[illegible]					Leitrim.
[illegible]	[illegible]	[illegible]	[illegible]	[illegible]	[illegible]	[illegible]	[illegible]	[illegible]	[illegible]	[illegible]	[illegible]	[illegible]	[illegible]					Mayo
[illegible]	[illegible]	[illegible]	[illegible]	[illegible]	[illegible]	[illegible]	[illegible]	[illegible]	[illegible]	[illegible]	[illegible]	[illegible]	[illegible]					Roscommon
[illegible]	[illegible]	[illegible]	[illegible]	[illegible]	[illegible]	[illegible]	[illegible]	[illegible]	[illegible]	[illegible]	[illegible]	[illegible]	[illegible]					Sligo.
[illegible]	[illegible]	[illegible]	[illegible]	[illegible]	[illegible]	[illegible]	[illegible]	[illegible]	[illegible]	[illegible]	[illegible]	[illegible]	[illegible]					Total of Connaught.
[illegible]	[illegible]	[illegible]	[illegible]	[illegible]	[illegible]	[illegible]	[illegible]	[illegible]	[illegible]	[illegible]	[illegible]	[illegible]	[illegible]					Total of Ireland

BILLS of PROCEEDINGS in the Year [illegible], from Returns made by the Clerks of the Peace.

Proceedings. [illegible]	[illegible]	[illegible]	[illegible]	[illegible]	[illegible]	[illegible]	[illegible]	[illegible]	[illegible]	[illegible]	COUNTIES.
	£ s. d.			£ s. d.	£ s. d.						LEINSTER:
.	—	.	.	—	—	.	.	–	.	.	Carlow.
.	—	[illegible]	.	—	—	[illegible]	[illegible]	.	–	.	Dublin.
.	[illegible]	[illegible]	.	[illegible] —	[illegible] —	.	.	–	.	.	Dublin City.
.	—	.	.	[illegible]	[illegible]	[illegible]	[illegible]	.	.	.	Kildare.
.	—	.	.	—	[illegible]	.	.	.	.	.	Kilkenny.
.	—	–	.	. –		[illegible]	.	.	.	.	King's County.
.	—	.	.	[illegible]	—	[illegible]	.	.	.	.	Longford.
.	—	.	.	[illegible]	[illegible]	[illegible]	[illegible]	.	.	.	Louth.
.	—	.	.	[illegible]	—	[illegible]	.	.	.	.	Meath.
.	—	[illegible]	.	[illegible]	[illegible]	[illegible]	.	.	.	.	Queen's County.
.	—	.	.	—	—	[illegible]	.	.	.	.	Westmeath.
[illegible]	—	.	.	—	[illegible]	[illegible]	.	.	.	.	Wexford.
.	—	.	.	[illegible]	[illegible]	[illegible]	.	.	[illegible]	.	Wicklow.
[illegible]	[illegible]	[illegible]	.	[illegible]	[illegible]	[illegible]	[illegible]	.	[illegible]	.	Total
											MUNSTER:
.	—	.	.	[illegible]	. —	[illegible]	.	.	.	.	Clare.
.	—	.	.	[illegible]	[illegible] —	[illegible]	[illegible]	.	.	.	Cork, East Riding.
.	—	.	[illegible]	—	—	.	.	.	.	.	Cork, West Riding.
.	—	[illegible]	.	[illegible]	[illegible]	[illegible]	[illegible]	.	.	[illegible]	Kerry.
[illegible]	[illegible]	[illegible]	.	[illegible]	[illegible]	[illegible]	[illegible]	.	[illegible]	.	Limerick.
.	[illegible] —	[illegible]	.	[illegible]	[illegible]	[illegible]	.	.	.	.	Tipperary.
.	—	.	.	[illegible]	[illegible]	[illegible]	.	.	.	.	Waterford.
[illegible]	[illegible]	[illegible]	[illegible]	[illegible]	[illegible]	[illegible]	[illegible]	.	[illegible]	[illegible]	Total
											ULSTER:
.	—	.	[illegible]	[illegible] —	[illegible]	[illegible]	[illegible]	.	[illegible]	.	Antrim.
.	—	.	.	[illegible]	[illegible]	[illegible]	.	.	.	.	Armagh.
.	—	.	.	[illegible]	[illegible]	[illegible]	[illegible]	.	.	.	Cavan.
.	—	.	.	[illegible]	[illegible]	[illegible]	.	.	.	.	Donegal.
.	—	.	.	[illegible]	[illegible]	[illegible]	[illegible]	.	.	.	Down.
.	—	.	.	[illegible]	[illegible]	[illegible]	.	.	.	.	Fermanagh.
.	—	.	.	[illegible]	[illegible]	[illegible]	[illegible]	[illegible]	[illegible]	.	Londonderry.
.	—	.	.	[illegible]	[illegible]	[illegible]	[illegible]	.	.	.	Monaghan.
.	—	.	[illegible]	[illegible]	[illegible]	[illegible]	[illegible]	.	.	[illegible]	Tyrone.
.	—	[illegible]	[illegible]	[illegible]	[illegible]	[illegible]	.	[illegible]	.	[illegible]	Total
											CONNAUGHT:
.	[illegible]	[illegible]	.	[illegible]	[illegible]	.	—	.	.	.	Galway.
.	—	.	.	[illegible]	—	[illegible]	.	.	.	.	Leitrim.
.	—	.	.	[illegible]	[illegible]	[illegible]	.	.	.	.	Mayo.
.	—	.	[illegible]	—	—	[illegible]	.	.	.	.	Roscommon.
.	—	.	.	[illegible]	[illegible]	[illegible]	.	.	.	.	Sligo.
.	[illegible]	[illegible]	[illegible]	[illegible]	[illegible]	[illegible]	.	.	.	.	Total
[illegible]	[illegible]	[illegible]	[illegible]	[illegible]	[illegible]	[illegible]	[illegible]	[illegible]	.	.	Total of Ireland.

(a) Besides this number, there were [illegible] cases from the previous year.
(b) [illegible]
(c) [illegible]

TABLE [illegible].—COUNTY COURTS.—LAND SESSIONS—PROCEEDINGS in the year 18[illegible], under the

COUNTIES, ARRANGED IN PROVINCES.	[illegible]	Land Sessions														Appeals			Result of Appeals			
		Land Claims [illegible]						Applications of Tenants [illegible]				Applications of Tenants [illegible]										
		[illegible]	[illegible]	[illegible]	[illegible]	[illegible]	[illegible]	[illegible]	[illegible]	[illegible]	[illegible]	[illegible]	[illegible]	[illegible]	[illegible]	[illegible]	[illegible]	[illegible]	[illegible]	[illegible]	[illegible]	[illegible]
LEINSTER:																						
Carlow,	.	.	.	.	.	.	.	.	.	.	.	.	.	.	.	.	.	.	.	.	.	.
Dublin,	.	.	.	.	.	.	.	.	.	.	.	.	.	.	.	.	.	.	.	.	.	.
Kildare,	.	.	.	.	.	.	.	.	.	.	.	.	.	.	.	.	.	.	.	.	.	.
Kilkenny,	.	.	.	.	.	.	.	.	.	.	.	.	.	.	.	.	.	.	.	.	.	.
King's County,	.	.	.	.	.	.	.	.	.	.	.	.	.	.	.	.	.	.	.	.	.	.
Longford,	[illegible]	[illegible]	[illegible]	[illegible]	[illegible]	.	.	.	.	.	.	.	.	.	.	[illegible]	[illegible]	.	.	.	.	.
Louth,	[illegible]	[illegible]	.	[illegible]	.	.	.	.	.	.	.	.	.	.	.	.	.	.	.	.	.	.
Meath,	[illegible]	[illegible]	.	.	.	[illegible]	.	.	.	.	[illegible]	[illegible]	.	.	.	.	.	.	.	.	.	.
Queen's County,	[illegible]	[illegible]	.	[illegible]	.	.	.	.	.	.	.	.	.	.	.	.	.	.	.	.	.	.
Westmeath,	.	.	.	.	.	.	.	.	.	.	.	.	.	.	.	.	.	.	.	.	.	.
Wexford,	.	.	.	.	.	.	.	.	.	.	.	.	.	.	.	.	.	.	.	.	.	.
Wicklow,	[illegible]	[illegible]	[illegible]	[illegible]	.	[illegible]	.	.	.	.	.	.	.	.	.	.	.	.	.	.	.	.
Total of Leinster,	[illegible]	[illegible]	[illegible]	[illegible]	[illegible]	[illegible]	.	.	.	.	[illegible]	[illegible]	.	.	[illegible]	[illegible]	.	.	.	.	.	.
MUNSTER:																						
Clare,	[illegible]	[illegible]	[illegible]	[illegible]	[illegible]	.	.	.	.	.	[illegible]	.	.	[illegible]	.	.	.	.	.	.	.	.
Cork, E. R.,	[illegible]	[illegible]	.	[illegible]	[illegible]	.	.	.	.	.	.	.	.	.	[illegible]	[illegible]	.	.	.	.	.	.
Cork, W. R.,	[illegible]	[illegible]	.	[illegible]	.	.	.	.	.	.	.	.	.	.	.	.	.	.	.	.	.	.
Kerry,	.	.	.	.	.	.	.	.	.	.	.	.	.	.	.	.	.	.	.	.	.	.
Limerick,	[illegible]	[illegible]	.	.	[illegible]	[illegible]	.	.	.	.	.	.	.	.	.	.	.	.	.	.	.	.
Tipperary,	.	.	.	.	.	.	.	.	.	.	[illegible]	.	.	[illegible]	.	.	.	.	.	.	.	.
Waterford,	[illegible]	[illegible]	[illegible]	.	.	.	.	.	.	.	.	.	.	.	[illegible]	[illegible]	.	.	.	.	.	.
Total of Munster,	[illegible]	[illegible]	[illegible]	.	[illegible]	[illegible]	.	.	.	.	[illegible]	.	.	[illegible]	[illegible]	[illegible]	.	.	.	.	.	.
ULSTER:																						
Antrim,	[illegible]	[illegible]	[illegible]	[illegible]	[illegible]	.	.	.	.	.	.	.	.	.	.	.	.	.	.	.	.	.
Armagh,	.	.	.	.	.	.	.	.	.	.	.	.	.	.	.	.	.	.	.	.	.	.
Cavan,	.	.	.	.	.	.	.	.	.	.	.	.	.	.	.	.	.	.	.	.	.	.
Donegal,	.	.	.	.	.	.	.	.	.	.	.	.	.	.	.	.	.	.	.	.	.	.
Down,	[illegible]	[illegible]	[illegible]	[illegible]	[illegible]	.	.	.	.	.	.	.	.	.	.	.	.	.	.	.	.	.
Fermanagh,	[illegible]	[illegible]	.	.	.	[illegible]	.	.	.	.	.	.	.	.	.	.	.	.	.	.	.	.
Londonderry,	[illegible]	[illegible]	[illegible]	[illegible]	[illegible]	.	.	.	.	.	.	.	.	.	[illegible]	[illegible]	.	.	.	.	.	.
Monaghan,	.	.	.	.	.	.	.	.	.	.	.	.	.	.	.	.	.	.	.	.	.	.
Tyrone,	.	.	.	.	.	.	.	.	.	.	.	.	.	.	.	.	.	.	.	.	.	.
Total of Ulster,	[illegible]	[illegible]	[illegible]	[illegible]	[illegible]	[illegible]	.	.	.	.	.	.	.	.	[illegible]	[illegible]	.	.	.	.	.	.
CONNAUGHT:																						
Galway,	[illegible]	[illegible]	.	.	[illegible]	[illegible]	.	.	.	.	.	.	.	.	.	.	.	.	.	.	.	.
Leitrim,	.	.	.	.	.	.	.	.	.	.	.	.	.	.	.	.	.	.	.	.	.	.
Mayo,	[illegible]	[illegible]	[illegible]	.	.	.	.	.	.	.	.	.	.	.	.	.	.	.	.	.	.	.
Roscommon,	[illegible]	.	.	.	.	.	.	.	.	.	.	.	.	.	.	.	.	.	.	.	.	.
Sligo,	.	.	.	.	.	.	.	.	.	.	.	.	.	.	.	.	.	.	.	.	.	.
Total of Connaught,	[illegible]	[illegible]	[illegible]	.	[illegible]	[illegible]	.	.	.	.	.	.	.	.	.	.	.	.	.	.	.	.
Total of Ireland,	[illegible]	[illegible]	[illegible]	[illegible]	[illegible]	[illegible]	.	.	.	.	[illegible]	[illegible]	.	[illegible]	[illegible]	[illegible]	.	.	.	.	.	.

Landlord and Tenant (Ireland) Act, 1870, from Returns made by the Clerks of the Peace.

Amount Claimed.					Amount Awarded, and Costs.					[illegible]						Counties, arranged in Provinces.
[illegible]	[illegible]	[illegible]	[illegible]	[illegible]	[illegible]	[illegible]	[illegible]	[illegible]	[illegible]	[illegible]	[illegible]	[illegible]	[illegible]	[illegible]	[illegible]	
£	£	£	£	£	£	£	£	£	£	£	£	£	£	£	£	Leinster:-
-	-	-	-	-	-	-	-	-	-	-	-	-	-	-	-	Carlow.
-	-	-	-	-	-	-	-	-	-	-	-	-	-	-	-	Dublin.
-	-	-	-	-	-	-	-	-	-	-	-	-	-	-	-	Kildare.
-	-	-	-	-	-	-	-	-	-	-	-	-	-	-	-	Kilkenny.
-	-	-	-	-	-	-	-	-	-	-	-	-	-	-	-	King's County.
[illegible]	[illegible]	[illegible]	[illegible]	-	[illegible]	[illegible]	[illegible]	[illegible]	[illegible]	[illegible]	[illegible]	[illegible]	[illegible]	-	[illegible]	Longford.
[illegible]	-	-	[illegible]	-	-	-	-	-	-	[illegible]		-	[illegible]	-	-	Louth.
[illegible]	-	-	-	[illegible]	-	-	-	-	-	-	-	-	-	-	-	Meath.
[illegible]	-	-	[illegible]	-	-	-	-	-	-	-	-	-	-	-	-	Queen's County.
-	-	-	-	-	-	-	-	-	-	-	-	-	-	-	-	Westmeath.
-	-	-	-	-	-	-	-	-	-	-	-	-	-	-	-	Wexford.
[illegible]	-	[illegible]	[illegible]	[illegible]	[illegible]	[illegible]	[illegible]	[illegible]	[illegible]	-	-	-	-	-	-	Wicklow.
[illegible]	[illegible]	[illegible]	[illegible]	[illegible]	[illegible]	[illegible]	[illegible]	[illegible]	[illegible]	[illegible]	[illegible]	[illegible]	[illegible]	-	[illegible]	Total of Leinster.
																Munster:-
[illegible]	[illegible]	[illegible]	[illegible]	-	[illegible]	-	[illegible]	-	-	-	-	-	-	-	-	Clare.
[illegible]	[illegible]	-	[illegible]	-	-	-	-	-	-	-	-	-	-	-	-	Cork, E.R.
[illegible]	-	-	[illegible]	-	-	-	-	-	-	[illegible]	-	-	[illegible]	-	-	Cork, W.R.
-	-	-	-	-	-	-	-	-	-	-	-	-	-	-	-	Kerry.
[illegible]	[illegible]	-	-	[illegible]	-	-	-	-	-	[illegible]	[illegible]	-	-	-	-	Limerick.
-	-	-	-	-	-	-	-	-	-	-	-	-	-	-	-	Tipperary.
[illegible]	-	[illegible]	-	-	[illegible]	[illegible]	[illegible]	[illegible]	-	-	-	-	-	-	-	Waterford.
[illegible]	[illegible]	[illegible]	[illegible]	[illegible]	[illegible]	[illegible]	[illegible]	[illegible]	-	[illegible]	[illegible]	-	[illegible]	-	-	Total of Munster.
																Ulster:-
[illegible]	[illegible]	[illegible]	[illegible]	-	[illegible]	[illegible]	[illegible]	[illegible]	[illegible]	-	-	-	-	-	-	Antrim.
-	-	-	-	-	-	-	-	-	-	-	-	-	-	-	-	Armagh.
-	-	-	-	-	-	-	-	-	-	-	-	-	-	-	-	Cavan.
-	-	-	-	-	-	-	-	-	-	-	-	-	-	-	-	Donegal.
[illegible]	[illegible]	[illegible]	[illegible]	-	[illegible]	[illegible]	[illegible]	[illegible]	[illegible]	[illegible]	[illegible]	-	-	-	-	Down.
[illegible]	-	-	-	[illegible]	-	-	-	-	-	[illegible]	-	-	-	[illegible]	-	Fermanagh.
[illegible]	[illegible]	[illegible]	[illegible]	-	[illegible]	[illegible]	[illegible]	[illegible]	[illegible]	[illegible]	[illegible]	[illegible]	[illegible]	-	[illegible]	Londonderry.
-	-	-	-	-	-	-	-	-	-	-	-	-	-	-	-	Monaghan.
-	-	-	-	-	-	-	-	-	-	-	-	-	-	-	-	Tyrone.
[illegible]	[illegible]	[illegible]	[illegible]	[illegible]	[illegible]	[illegible]	[illegible]	[illegible]	[illegible]	[illegible]	[illegible]	[illegible]	[illegible]	[illegible]	[illegible]	Total of Ulster.
																Connaught:-
[illegible]	[illegible]	-	-	[illegible]	-	-	-	-	-	[illegible]	[illegible]	-	-	[illegible]	-	Galway.
-	-	-	-	-	-	-	-	-	-	-	-	-	-	-	-	Leitrim.
[illegible]	-	[illegible]	-	-	[illegible]	[illegible]	[illegible]	-	-	-	-	-	-	-	-	Mayo.
-	-	-	-	-	-	-	-	-	-	-	-	-	-	-	-	Roscommon.
-	-	-	-	-	-	-	-	-	-	-	-	-	-	-	-	Sligo.
[illegible]	[illegible]	[illegible]	-	[illegible]	[illegible]	[illegible]	[illegible]	-	-	[illegible]	[illegible]	-	-	[illegible]	-	Total of Connaught.
[illegible]	[illegible]	[illegible]	[illegible]	[illegible]	[illegible]	[illegible]	[illegible]	[illegible]	[illegible]	[illegible]	[illegible]	[illegible]	[illegible]	[illegible]	[illegible]	Total of Ireland.

COUNTIES, ARRANGED IN PROVINCES.	[illegible]	[illegible]	[illegible]	[illegible]	[illegible]	[illegible]	[illegible]	[illegible]	[illegible]	[illegible]	[illegible]	[illegible]	[illegible]	[illegible]	[illegible]	[illegible]	[illegible]
Leinster:	£	£	£	£	£	£	£	£	£	£	£	£	£	£	£	£	£
Carlow	-	-	-	-	-	-	-	-	-	-	-	-	-	-	-	-	-
Dublin	-	-	-	-	-	-	-	-	-	-	-	-	-	-	-	-	-
Kildare	-	-	-	-	-	-	-	-	-	-	-	-	-	-	-	-	-
Kilkenny	-	-	-	-	-	-	-	-	-	-	-	-	-	-	-	-	-
King's County	-	-	-	-	-	-	-	-	-	-	-	-	-	-	-	-	-
Longford	[illegible]	-	-	[illegible]	-	-	-	-	-	-	-	-	-	-	-	-	-
Louth	[illegible]	-	-	-	[illegible]	-	-	-	-	-	-	-	-	-	-	-	-
Meath	[illegible]	-	-	-	[illegible]	-	-	-	-	-	-	-	-	-	-	-	-
Queen's County	[illegible]	-	-	[illegible]	-	-	-	-	-	-	-	-	-	-	-	-	-
Westmeath	-	-	-	-	-	-	-	-	-	-	-	-	-	-	-	-	-
Wexford	-	-	-	-	-	-	-	-	-	-	-	-	-	-	-	-	-
Wicklow	[illegible]	-	[illegible]	[illegible]	[illegible]	[illegible]	-	-	-	-	-	-	-	-	-	-	-
Total of Leinster	[illegible]	-	[illegible]	[illegible]	[illegible]	[illegible]	-	-	-	-	-	-	-	-	-	-	-
Munster:																	
Clare	[illegible]	-	[illegible]	[illegible]	-	[illegible]	[illegible]	[illegible]	-	-	-	-	-	-	-	-	-
Cork, E.R.	[illegible]	[illegible]	-	[illegible]	-	-	-	-	-	-	-	-	-	-	-	-	-
Cork, W.R.	[illegible]	-	-	[illegible]	-	-	-	-	-	-	-	-	-	-	-	-	-
Kerry	-	-	-	-	-	-	-	-	-	-	-	-	-	-	-	-	-
Limerick	[illegible]	-	-	-	[illegible]	-	-	-	-	-	-	-	-	-	-	-	-
Tipperary	-	-	-	-	-	-	-	-	-	-	-	-	-	-	-	-	-
Waterford	[illegible]	-	[illegible]	-	-	[illegible]	-	-	-	-	-	-	-	-	-	-	-
Total of Munster	[illegible]	[illegible]	[illegible]	[illegible]	[illegible]	[illegible]	[illegible]	[illegible]	-	-	-	-	-	-	-	-	-
Ulster:																	
Antrim	-	-	-	-	-	-	[illegible]	[illegible]	[illegible]	[illegible]	-	[illegible]	-	-	-	-	-
Armagh	-	-	-	-	-	-	-	-	-	-	-	-	-	-	-	-	-
Cavan	-	-	-	-	-	-	-	-	-	-	-	-	-	-	-	-	-
Donegal	-	-	-	-	-	-	-	-	-	-	-	-	-	-	-	-	-
Down	[illegible]	[illegible]	[illegible]	[illegible]	-	-	-	-	-	-	-	-	[illegible]	-	[illegible]	[illegible]	-
Fermanagh	-	-	-	-	-	-	-	-	-	-	-	-	-	-	-	-	-
Londonderry	[illegible]	[illegible]	[illegible]	[illegible]	-	[illegible]	-	-	-	-	-	-	[illegible]	[illegible]	[illegible]	[illegible]	-
Monaghan	-	-	-	-	-	-	-	-	-	-	-	-	-	-	-	-	-
Tyrone	-	-	-	-	-	-	-	-	-	-	-	-	-	-	-	-	-
Total of Ulster	[illegible]	[illegible]	[illegible]	[illegible]	-	[illegible]	[illegible]	[illegible]	[illegible]	[illegible]	-	[illegible]	[illegible]	[illegible]	[illegible]	[illegible]	-
Connaught:																	
Galway	[illegible]	[illegible]	-	-	-	-	-	-	-	-	-	-	-	-	-	-	-
Leitrim	-	-	-	-	-	-	-	-	-	-	-	-	-	-	-	-	-
Mayo	[illegible]	-	[illegible]	-	-	[illegible]	-	-	-	-	-	-	-	-	-	-	-
Roscommon	-	-	-	-	-	-	-	-	-	-	-	-	-	-	-	-	-
Sligo	-	-	-	-	-	-	-	-	-	-	-	-	-	-	-	-	-
Total of Connaught	[illegible]	[illegible]	[illegible]	-	-	[illegible]	-	-	-	-	-	-	-	-	-	-	-

[illegible] Landlord and Tenant (Ireland) Act, 1870, from Returns made by the Clerks of the Peace.

[illegible]	[illegible]	[illegible]	[illegible]	[illegible]	[illegible]	[illegible]	[illegible]	[illegible]	[illegible]	[illegible]	[illegible]	[illegible]	[illegible]	[illegible]	COUNTIES, ARRANGED IN PROVINCES.
															LEINSTER.
-	-	-	-	-	-	-	-	-	-	-	-	-	-	-	Carlow
-	-	-	-	-	-	-	-	-	-	-	-	-	-	-	Dublin
-	-	-	-	-	-	-	-	-	-	-	-	-	-	-	Kildare
-	-	-	-	-	-	-	-	-	-	-	-	-	-	-	Kilkenny
-	-	-	-	-	-	-	-	-	-	-	-	-	-	-	King's County.
120	-	-	-	-	-	-	-	-	-	-	-	-	-	-	Longford.
-	-	-	-	-	-	-	-	-	-	-	-	-	-	-	Louth.
-	-	-	-	-	-	-	-	-	-	-	-	-	-	-	Meath
-	-	-	-	-	-	-	-	-	-	-	-	-	-	-	Queen's County.
-	-	-	-	-	-	-	-	-	-	-	-	-	-	-	Westmeath.
-	-	-	-	-	-	-	-	-	-	-	-	-	-	-	Wexford.
-	-	-	-	-	-	-	-	-	-	-	-	-	-	-	Wicklow
[illegible]	-	-	-	-	-	-	-	-	-	-	-	-	-	-	Total of Leinster.
															MUNSTER.
-	-	-	-	-	-	-	-	-	-	-	-	-	-	-	Clare.
-	-	-	-	-	-	-	-	-	-	-	-	-	-	-	Cork, E.R.
-	-	-	-	-	-	-	-	-	-	-	-	-	-	-	Cork, W.R.
-	-	-	-	-	-	-	-	-	-	-	-	-	-	-	Kerry.
-	-	-	-	-	-	-	-	-	-	-	-	-	-	-	Limerick
-	-	-	-	-	-	-	-	-	-	-	-	-	-	-	Tipperary
[illegible]	-	-	-	-	-	-	-	-	-	-	-	-	-	-	Waterford.
[illegible]	-	-	-	-	-	-	-	-	-	-	-	-	-	-	Total of Munster.
															ULSTER.
-	-	-	-	-	-	-	-	-	-	-	-	-	-	-	Antrim.
-	-	-	-	-	-	-	-	-	-	-	-	-	-	-	Armagh
-	-	-	-	-	-	-	-	-	-	-	-	-	-	-	Cavan.
-	-	-	-	-	-	-	-	-	-	-	-	-	-	-	Donegal.
-	-	-	-	-	-	-	-	-	-	-	-	-	-	-	Down.
-	-	-	-	-	-	-	-	-	-	-	-	-	-	-	Fermanagh.
[illegible]	-	-	-	-	-	-	-	-	-	-	-	-	-	-	Londonderry.
-	-	-	-	-	-	-	-	-	-	-	-	-	-	-	Monaghan.
-	-	-	-	-	-	-	-	-	-	-	-	-	-	-	Tyrone.
[illegible]	-	-	-	-	-	-	-	-	-	-	-	-	-	-	Total of Ulster.
															CONNAUGHT.
-	-	-	-	-	-	-	-	-	-	-	-	-	-	-	Galway
-	-	-	-	-	-	-	-	-	-	-	-	-	-	-	Leitrim.
-	-	-	-	-	-	-	-	-	-	-	-	-	-	-	Mayo
-	-	-	-	-	-	-	-	-	-	-	-	-	-	-	Roscommon.
-	-	-	-	-	-	-	-	-	-	-	-	-	-	-	Sligo
-	-	-	-	-	-	-	-	-	-	-	-	-	-	-	Total of Connaught.
[illegible]	-	-	-	-	-	-	-	-	-	-	-	-	-	-	Total of Ireland.

TABLE ..—RETURN of PROCEEDINGS under the Land Law (Ireland)

COUNTIES ARRANGED IN PROVINCES	Applications to have Fair Rent Fixed: In Court					Out of Court	Total Number of Fair Rents fixed in Court and out of Court	[illegible]				[illegible]			Appeals re Fair Rent, &c			
	[illegible]	[illegible]	[illegible]	Withdrawn	[illegible]	[illegible]		[illegible]	[illegible]	[illegible]	[illegible]	[illegible]	[illegible]	[illegible]	[illegible]	[illegible]	[illegible]	[illegible]
Leinster.																		
Carlow	[illegible]	[illegible]	[illegible]	[illegible]	[illegible]	[illegible]	[illegible]	[illegible]	[illegible]	[illegible]	[illegible]	[illegible]	[illegible]	[illegible]	[illegible]	[illegible]	[illegible]	[illegible]
Dublin	[illegible]	[illegible]	[illegible]	[illegible]	[illegible]	[illegible]	[illegible]	[illegible]	[illegible]	[illegible]	[illegible]	[illegible]	[illegible]	[illegible]	[illegible]	[illegible]	[illegible]	[illegible]
Kildare	[illegible]	[illegible]	[illegible]	[illegible]	[illegible]	[illegible]	[illegible]	[illegible]	[illegible]	[illegible]	[illegible]	[illegible]	[illegible]	[illegible]	[illegible]	[illegible]	[illegible]	[illegible]
Kilkenny	[illegible]	[illegible]	[illegible]	[illegible]	[illegible]	[illegible]	[illegible]	[illegible]	[illegible]	[illegible]	[illegible]	[illegible]	[illegible]	[illegible]	[illegible]	[illegible]	[illegible]	[illegible]
King's County	[illegible]	[illegible]	[illegible]	[illegible]	[illegible]	[illegible]	[illegible]	[illegible]	[illegible]	[illegible]	[illegible]	[illegible]	[illegible]	[illegible]	[illegible]	[illegible]	[illegible]	[illegible]
Longford	[illegible]	[illegible]	[illegible]	[illegible]	[illegible]	[illegible]	[illegible]	[illegible]	[illegible]	[illegible]	[illegible]	[illegible]	[illegible]	[illegible]	[illegible]	[illegible]	[illegible]	[illegible]
Louth	[illegible]	[illegible]	[illegible]	[illegible]	[illegible]	[illegible]	[illegible]	[illegible]	[illegible]	[illegible]	[illegible]	[illegible]	[illegible]	[illegible]	[illegible]	[illegible]	[illegible]	[illegible]
Meath	[illegible]	[illegible]	[illegible]	[illegible]	[illegible]	[illegible]	[illegible]	[illegible]	[illegible]	[illegible]	[illegible]	[illegible]	[illegible]	[illegible]	[illegible]	[illegible]	[illegible]	[illegible]
Queen's County	[illegible]	[illegible]	[illegible]	[illegible]	[illegible]	[illegible]	[illegible]	[illegible]	[illegible]	[illegible]	[illegible]	[illegible]	[illegible]	[illegible]	[illegible]	[illegible]	[illegible]	[illegible]
Westmeath	[illegible]	[illegible]	[illegible]	[illegible]	[illegible]	[illegible]	[illegible]	[illegible]	[illegible]	[illegible]	[illegible]	[illegible]	[illegible]	[illegible]	[illegible]	[illegible]	[illegible]	[illegible]
Wexford	[illegible]	[illegible]	[illegible]	[illegible]	[illegible]	[illegible]	[illegible]	[illegible]	[illegible]	[illegible]	[illegible]	[illegible]	[illegible]	[illegible]	[illegible]	[illegible]	[illegible]	[illegible]
Wicklow	[illegible]	[illegible]	[illegible]	[illegible]	[illegible]	[illegible]	[illegible]	[illegible]	[illegible]	[illegible]	[illegible]	[illegible]	[illegible]	[illegible]	[illegible]	[illegible]	[illegible]	[illegible]
Total of Leinster	[illegible]	[illegible]	[illegible]	[illegible]	[illegible]	[illegible]	[illegible]	[illegible]	[illegible]	[illegible]	[illegible]	[illegible]	[illegible]	[illegible]	[illegible]	[illegible]	[illegible]	[illegible]
Munster.																		
Clare	[illegible]	[illegible]	[illegible]	[illegible]	[illegible]	[illegible]	[illegible]	[illegible]	[illegible]	[illegible]	[illegible]	[illegible]	[illegible]	[illegible]	[illegible]	[illegible]	[illegible]	[illegible]
Cork	[illegible]	[illegible]	[illegible]	[illegible]	[illegible]	[illegible]	[illegible]	[illegible]	[illegible]	[illegible]	[illegible]	[illegible]	[illegible]	[illegible]	[illegible]	[illegible]	[illegible]	[illegible]
Kerry	[illegible]	[illegible]	[illegible]	[illegible]	[illegible]	[illegible]	[illegible]	[illegible]	[illegible]	[illegible]	[illegible]	[illegible]	[illegible]	[illegible]	[illegible]	[illegible]	[illegible]	[illegible]
Limerick	[illegible]	[illegible]	[illegible]	[illegible]	[illegible]	[illegible]	[illegible]	[illegible]	[illegible]	[illegible]	[illegible]	[illegible]	[illegible]	[illegible]	[illegible]	[illegible]	[illegible]	[illegible]
Tipperary	[illegible]	[illegible]	[illegible]	[illegible]	[illegible]	[illegible]	[illegible]	[illegible]	[illegible]	[illegible]	[illegible]	[illegible]	[illegible]	[illegible]	[illegible]	[illegible]	[illegible]	[illegible]
Waterford	[illegible]	[illegible]	[illegible]	[illegible]	[illegible]	[illegible]	[illegible]	[illegible]	[illegible]	[illegible]	[illegible]	[illegible]	[illegible]	[illegible]	[illegible]	[illegible]	[illegible]	[illegible]
Total of Munster	[illegible]	[illegible]	[illegible]	[illegible]	[illegible]	[illegible]	[illegible]	[illegible]	[illegible]	[illegible]	[illegible]	[illegible]	[illegible]	[illegible]	[illegible]	[illegible]	[illegible]	[illegible]
Ulster.																		
Antrim	[illegible]	[illegible]	[illegible]	[illegible]	[illegible]	[illegible]	[illegible]	[illegible]	[illegible]	[illegible]	[illegible]	[illegible]	[illegible]	[illegible]	[illegible]	[illegible]	[illegible]	[illegible]
Armagh	[illegible]	[illegible]	[illegible]	[illegible]	[illegible]	[illegible]	[illegible]	[illegible]	[illegible]	[illegible]	[illegible]	[illegible]	[illegible]	[illegible]	[illegible]	[illegible]	[illegible]	[illegible]
Cavan	[illegible]	[illegible]	[illegible]	[illegible]	[illegible]	[illegible]	[illegible]	[illegible]	[illegible]	[illegible]	[illegible]	[illegible]	[illegible]	[illegible]	[illegible]	[illegible]	[illegible]	[illegible]
Donegal	[illegible]	[illegible]	[illegible]	[illegible]	[illegible]	[illegible]	[illegible]	[illegible]	[illegible]	[illegible]	[illegible]	[illegible]	[illegible]	[illegible]	[illegible]	[illegible]	[illegible]	[illegible]
Down	[illegible]	[illegible]	[illegible]	[illegible]	[illegible]	[illegible]	[illegible]	[illegible]	[illegible]	[illegible]	[illegible]	[illegible]	[illegible]	[illegible]	[illegible]	[illegible]	[illegible]	[illegible]
Fermanagh	[illegible]	[illegible]	[illegible]	[illegible]	[illegible]	[illegible]	[illegible]	[illegible]	[illegible]	[illegible]	[illegible]	[illegible]	[illegible]	[illegible]	[illegible]	[illegible]	[illegible]	[illegible]
Londonderry	[illegible]	[illegible]	[illegible]	[illegible]	[illegible]	[illegible]	[illegible]	[illegible]	[illegible]	[illegible]	[illegible]	[illegible]	[illegible]	[illegible]	[illegible]	[illegible]	[illegible]	[illegible]
Monaghan	[illegible]	[illegible]	[illegible]	[illegible]	[illegible]	[illegible]	[illegible]	[illegible]	[illegible]	[illegible]	[illegible]	[illegible]	[illegible]	[illegible]	[illegible]	[illegible]	[illegible]	[illegible]
Tyrone	[illegible]	[illegible]	[illegible]	[illegible]	[illegible]	[illegible]	[illegible]	[illegible]	[illegible]	[illegible]	[illegible]	[illegible]	[illegible]	[illegible]	[illegible]	[illegible]	[illegible]	[illegible]
Total of Ulster	[illegible]	[illegible]	[illegible]	[illegible]	[illegible]	[illegible]	[illegible]	[illegible]	[illegible]	[illegible]	[illegible]	[illegible]	[illegible]	[illegible]	[illegible]	[illegible]	[illegible]	[illegible]
Connaught.																		
Galway	[illegible]	[illegible]	[illegible]	[illegible]	[illegible]	[illegible]	[illegible]	[illegible]	[illegible]	[illegible]	[illegible]	[illegible]	[illegible]	[illegible]	[illegible]	[illegible]	[illegible]	[illegible]
Leitrim	[illegible]	[illegible]	[illegible]	[illegible]	[illegible]	[illegible]	[illegible]	[illegible]	[illegible]	[illegible]	[illegible]	[illegible]	[illegible]	[illegible]	[illegible]	[illegible]	[illegible]	[illegible]
Mayo	[illegible]	[illegible]	[illegible]	[illegible]	[illegible]	[illegible]	[illegible]	[illegible]	[illegible]	[illegible]	[illegible]	[illegible]	[illegible]	[illegible]	[illegible]	[illegible]	[illegible]	[illegible]
Roscommon	[illegible]	[illegible]	[illegible]	[illegible]	[illegible]	[illegible]	[illegible]	[illegible]	[illegible]	[illegible]	[illegible]	[illegible]	[illegible]	[illegible]	[illegible]	[illegible]	[illegible]	[illegible]
Sligo	[illegible]	[illegible]	[illegible]	[illegible]	[illegible]	[illegible]	[illegible]	[illegible]	[illegible]	[illegible]	[illegible]	[illegible]	[illegible]	[illegible]	[illegible]	[illegible]	[illegible]	[illegible]
Total of Connaught	[illegible]	[illegible]	[illegible]	[illegible]	[illegible]	[illegible]	[illegible]	[illegible]	[illegible]	[illegible]	[illegible]	[illegible]	[illegible]	[illegible]	[illegible]	[illegible]	[illegible]	[illegible]
Total of Ireland	[illegible]	[illegible]	[illegible]	[illegible]	[illegible]	[illegible]	[illegible]	[illegible]	[illegible]	[illegible]	[illegible]	[illegible]	[illegible]	[illegible]	[illegible]	[illegible]	[illegible]	[illegible]

[illegible] 1881, for the Year ended 31st day of December, 18[illegible].

Result of Appeals Heard					Fair Rent Fixed: In Court: Former Rent	In Court: Judicial Rent	Out of Court: Former Rent	Out of Court: Judicial Rent	Totals: Former Rent	Totals: Judicial Rent	Counties Arranged in Provinces
					£ s. d.	£ s. d.	£ s. d.	£ s. d.	£ s. d.	£ s. d.	Leinster
[illegible]	[illegible]	[illegible]	[illegible]	[illegible]	[illegible]	[illegible]	[illegible]	[illegible]	[illegible]	[illegible]	Carlow
[illegible]	[illegible]	[illegible]	[illegible]	[illegible]	[illegible]	[illegible]	[illegible]	[illegible]	[illegible]	[illegible]	Dublin
[illegible]	[illegible]	[illegible]	[illegible]	[illegible]	[illegible]	[illegible]	[illegible]	[illegible]	[illegible]	[illegible]	Kildare
[illegible]	[illegible]	[illegible]	[illegible]	[illegible]	[illegible]	[illegible]	[illegible]	[illegible]	[illegible]	[illegible]	Kilkenny
[illegible]	[illegible]	[illegible]	[illegible]	[illegible]	[illegible]	[illegible]	[illegible]	[illegible]	[illegible]	[illegible]	King's County
	[illegible]		[illegible]	[illegible]	[illegible]	[illegible]	[illegible]	[illegible]	[illegible]	[illegible]	Longford
[illegible]	[illegible]	[illegible]	[illegible]	[illegible]	[illegible]	[illegible]	[illegible]	[illegible]	[illegible]	[illegible]	Louth
[illegible]	[illegible]	[illegible]	[illegible]	[illegible]	[illegible]	[illegible]	[illegible]	[illegible]	[illegible]	[illegible]	Meath
	[illegible]	[illegible]	[illegible]	[illegible]	[illegible]	[illegible]	[illegible]	[illegible]	[illegible]	[illegible]	Queen's County
[illegible]	[illegible]	[illegible]	[illegible]	[illegible]	[illegible]	[illegible]	[illegible]	[illegible]	[illegible]	[illegible]	Westmeath
	[illegible]	[illegible]	[illegible]	[illegible]	[illegible]	[illegible]	[illegible]	[illegible]	[illegible]	[illegible]	Wexford
[illegible]	[illegible]	[illegible]	[illegible]	[illegible]	[illegible]	[illegible]	[illegible]	[illegible]	[illegible]	[illegible]	Wicklow
[illegible]	[illegible]	[illegible]	[illegible]	[illegible]	[illegible]	[illegible]	[illegible]	[illegible]	[illegible]	[illegible]	Total of Leinster
											Munster
[illegible]	[illegible]	[illegible]	[illegible]	[illegible]	[illegible]	[illegible]	[illegible]	[illegible]	[illegible]	[illegible]	Clare
[illegible]	[illegible]	[illegible]	[illegible]	[illegible]	[illegible]	[illegible]	[illegible]	[illegible]	[illegible]	[illegible]	Cork
[illegible]	[illegible]	[illegible]	[illegible]	[illegible]	[illegible]	[illegible]	[illegible]	[illegible]	[illegible]	[illegible]	Kerry
	[illegible]	[illegible]		[illegible]	[illegible]	[illegible]	[illegible]	[illegible]	[illegible]	[illegible]	Limerick

ARREARS OF RENT

TABLE [illegible].—Return of Proceedings in the County [illegible]

Counties Arranged in Provinces	Section 1. Number of Holdings included in Applications Received	Number of Holdings in respect of which Applications were Granted	Number of Holdings in respect of which Applications were Dismissed or Withdrawn	Section 16. Number of Holdings included in Applications Received	Number of Holdings in respect of which Applications were Granted	Number of Holdings in respect of which Applications were Dismissed or Withdrawn	Number of Holdings included in Applications Received
Leinster.							
Carlow,	577	[illegible]	61	16	14	.	4
Dublin,	88	10	4	.	.	.	.
Kildare,	355	346	75	3	3	.	.
Kilkenny,	1,456	[illegible]	79	17	16	4	10
King's,	1,740	[illegible]	71	44	30	8	10
Longford,	[illegible]	[illegible]	101	5	6	.	10
Louth,	498	[illegible]	15	17	17	.	.
Meath,	[illegible]	[illegible]	61	36	30	5	7
Queen's,	1,795	[illegible]	91	74	53	5	.
Westmeath,	[illegible]	[illegible]	41	51	37	5	13
Wexford,	[illegible]	[illegible]	41	74	30	4	4
Wicklow,	358	348	27	15	15		.
Total of Leinster,	[illegible]	[illegible]	779	356	[illegible]	28	77
Munster.							
Clare,	4,545	4,448	139	11	10	1	1
Cork,	[illegible]	[illegible]	304	116	100	6	5
Kerry,	[illegible]	[illegible]	56	30	21	1	4
Limerick,	[illegible]	[illegible]	166	46	45	1	.
Tipperary,	[illegible]	[illegible]	111	136	125	5	15
Waterford,	779	140	17	73	59	5	.
Total of Munster,	[illegible]	[illegible]	779	[illegible]	353	17	71
Ulster.							
Antrim,	[illegible]	[illegible]	[illegible]	71	6	94	.
Armagh,	[illegible]	[illegible]	144	36	30	.	66
Cavan,	[illegible]	[illegible]	15	14	11	5	[illegible]
Donegal,	[illegible]	[illegible]	[illegible]	16	16	1	64
Down,	[illegible]	[illegible]	[illegible]	6	5	9	
Fermanagh,	[illegible]	[illegible]	[illegible]	17	15	.	1
Londonderry,	[illegible]	3,777	[illegible]	4	3	1	
Monaghan,	[illegible]	[illegible]	[illegible]	19	18	5	115
Tyrone,	[illegible]	[illegible]	[illegible]	77	52	.	.
Total of Ulster,	[illegible]	[illegible]	[illegible]	[illegible]	[illegible]	[illegible]	[illegible]
Connaught.							
Galway,	[illegible]	[illegible]	[illegible]	30	[illegible]	5	[illegible]
Leitrim,	[illegible]	1,974	155	35	1	[illegible]	[illegible]
Mayo,	[illegible]	[illegible]	[illegible]	30	[illegible]	3	[illegible]
Roscommon,	[illegible]	[illegible]	113	70	59		[illegible]
Sligo,	[illegible]	[illegible]	170	34	13	1	[illegible]
Total of Connaught,	[illegible]	[illegible]	[illegible]	[illegible]	[illegible]	[illegible]	[illegible]
Total of Ireland,	[illegible]	[illegible]	[illegible]	[illegible]	[illegible]	[illegible]	[illegible]

Note.—Pursuant to the [illegible] Section of the Act, the Sum of [illegible] has been charged

(IRELAND) ACT, [illegible],

of the Irish Land Commission.

Section 15. Number of Holdings in respect of which Applications were Granted.	Section 15. Number of Holdings in respect of which Applications were Declined or Withdrawn.	Total under Sections 1, 14, and 15. Number of Holdings included in Applications Received.	Total under Sections 1, 14, and 15. Number of Holdings in respect of which Applications were Granted.	Total under Sections 1, 14, and 15. Number of Holdings in respect of which Applications were Declined or Withdrawn.	Amount paid under Section 1.	Amount advanced under Section 14.	Counties arranged in Provinces.
					£ s. d.	£ s. d.	Leinster.
[illegible]	.	[illegible]	[illegible]	[illegible]	[illegible]	[illegible]	Carlow.
.	.	[illegible]	[illegible]	[illegible]	[illegible]	—	Dublin.
.	.	[illegible]	[illegible]	[illegible]	[illegible]	[illegible]	Kildare.
[illegible]	.	[illegible]	[illegible]	[illegible]	[illegible]	[illegible]	Kilkenny.
[illegible]	.	[illegible]	[illegible]	[illegible]	[illegible]	[illegible]	King's.
[illegible]	[illegible]	[illegible]	[illegible]	[illegible]	[illegible]	[illegible]	Longford.
.	.	[illegible]	[illegible]	[illegible]	[illegible]	[illegible]	Louth.
[illegible]	[illegible]	[illegible]	[illegible]	[illegible]	[illegible]	[illegible]	Meath.
.	.	[illegible]	[illegible]	[illegible]	[illegible]	[illegible]	Queen's.
[illegible]	[illegible]	[illegible]	[illegible]	[illegible]	[illegible]	[illegible]	Westmeath.
[illegible]		[illegible]	[illegible]	[illegible]	[illegible]	[illegible]	Wexford.
.	.	[illegible]	[illegible]	[illegible]	[illegible]	[illegible]	Wicklow.
[illegible]	[illegible]	[illegible]	[illegible]	[illegible]	[illegible]	[illegible]	Total of Leinster.
							Munster.
[illegible]	[illegible]	[illegible]	[illegible]	[illegible]	[illegible]	[illegible]	Clare.
[illegible]		[illegible]	[illegible]	[illegible]	[illegible]	[illegible]	Cork.
[illegible]	.	[illegible]	[illegible]	[illegible]	[illegible]	[illegible]	Kerry.
.	.	[illegible]	[illegible]	[illegible]	[illegible]	[illegible]	Limerick.
[illegible]	.	[illegible]	[illegible]	[illegible]	[illegible]	[illegible]	Tipperary.
	.	[illegible]	[illegible]	[illegible]	[illegible]	[illegible]	Waterford.
[illegible]	[illegible]	[illegible]	[illegible]	[illegible]	[illegible]	[illegible]	Total of Munster.
							Ulster.
.	.	[illegible]	[illegible]	[illegible]	[illegible]	[illegible]	Antrim.
[illegible]	[illegible]	[illegible]	[illegible]	[illegible]	[illegible]	[illegible]	Armagh.
[illegible]	[illegible]	[illegible]	[illegible]	[illegible]	[illegible]	[illegible]	Cavan.
[illegible]	.	[illegible]	[illegible]	[illegible]	[illegible]	[illegible]	Donegal.
.	.	[illegible]	[illegible]	[illegible]	[illegible]	[illegible]	Down.
[illegible]	.	[illegible]	[illegible]	[illegible]	[illegible]	[illegible]	Fermanagh.
.	.	[illegible]	[illegible]	[illegible]	[illegible]	[illegible]	Londonderry.
[illegible]	[illegible]	[illegible]	[illegible]	[illegible]	[illegible]	[illegible]	Monaghan.
.	.	[illegible]	[illegible]	[illegible]	[illegible]	[illegible]	Tyrone.
[illegible]	[illegible]	[illegible]	[illegible]	[illegible]	[illegible]	[illegible]	Total of Ulster.
							Connaught.
[illegible]	[illegible]	[illegible]	[illegible]	[illegible]	[illegible]	[illegible]	Galway.
[illegible]	.	[illegible]	[illegible]	[illegible]	[illegible]	[illegible]	Leitrim.
[illegible]	[illegible]	[illegible]	[illegible]	[illegible]	[illegible]	[illegible]	Mayo.
[illegible]	[illegible]	[illegible]	[illegible]	[illegible]	[illegible]	[illegible]	Roscommon.
[illegible]	.	[illegible]	[illegible]	[illegible]	[illegible]	[illegible]	Sligo.
[illegible]	[illegible]	[illegible]	[illegible]	[illegible]	[illegible]	[illegible]	Total of Connaught.
[illegible]	[illegible]	[illegible]	[illegible]	[illegible]	[illegible]	[illegible]	Total of Ireland.

[illegible] the Irish Church Temporalities Funds, in respect of the [illegible]

TABLE [illegible].—SHERIFFS' PROCEEDINGS in the Year [illegible], each Bailiwick by

PROCEEDINGS	Total of Ireland	LEINSTER: Total of Leinster	Carlow	Drogheda Town	Dublin	Dublin City	Kildare	Kilkenny	Kilkenny City	King's County	Longford	Louth	Meath	Queen's County
I.—Proceedings other than those for Ejectment or Taking Possession of Land														
Courts held for Election of Coroners,	[illegible]	[illegible]	[illegible]	[illegible]	[illegible]	[illegible]	[illegible]	[illegible]	[illegible]	[illegible]	[illegible]	[illegible]	[illegible]	[illegible]
Courts held for Election of Members of Parliament,	[illegible]	[illegible]	[illegible]	[illegible]	[illegible]	[illegible]	[illegible]	[illegible]	[illegible]	[illegible]	[illegible]	[illegible]	[illegible]	[illegible]
Courts held under Writs of Trial or Inquiry,	[illegible]	[illegible]	[illegible]	[illegible]	[illegible]	[illegible]	[illegible]	[illegible]	[illegible]	[illegible]	[illegible]	[illegible]	[illegible]	[illegible]
Courts held under Land Clauses Consolidation Act, &c.,	[illegible]	[illegible]	[illegible]	[illegible]	[illegible]	[illegible]	[illegible]	[illegible]	[illegible]	[illegible]	[illegible]	[illegible]	[illegible]	[illegible]
Civil Bill Decrees and Dismisses executed by Sheriff,	[illegible]	[illegible]	[illegible]	[illegible]	[illegible]	[illegible]	[illegible]	[illegible]	[illegible]	[illegible]	[illegible]	[illegible]	[illegible]	[illegible]
" " " by Special Bailiffs,	[illegible]	[illegible]	[illegible]	[illegible]	[illegible]	[illegible]	[illegible]	[illegible]	[illegible]	[illegible]	[illegible]	[illegible]	[illegible]	[illegible]
[illegible] Certificates taken,	[illegible]	[illegible]	[illegible]	[illegible]	[illegible]	[illegible]	[illegible]	[illegible]	[illegible]	[illegible]	[illegible]	[illegible]	[illegible]	[illegible]
Persons [illegible] to Queen's Bench:—														
(1.) [illegible],	[illegible]	[illegible]	[illegible]	[illegible]	[illegible]	[illegible]	[illegible]	[illegible]	[illegible]	[illegible]	[illegible]	[illegible]	[illegible]	[illegible]
(2.) [illegible],	[illegible]	[illegible]	[illegible]	[illegible]	[illegible]	[illegible]	[illegible]	[illegible]	[illegible]	[illegible]	[illegible]	[illegible]	[illegible]	[illegible]
(3.) All other Cases,	[illegible]	[illegible]	[illegible]	[illegible]	[illegible]	[illegible]	[illegible]	[illegible]	[illegible]	[illegible]	[illegible]	[illegible]	[illegible]	[illegible]
Writs of Habeas Corpus, Proceedings on,	[illegible]	[illegible]	[illegible]	[illegible]	[illegible]	[illegible]	[illegible]	[illegible]	[illegible]	[illegible]	[illegible]	[illegible]	[illegible]	[illegible]
Writs of [illegible], Proceedings in,	[illegible]	[illegible]	[illegible]	[illegible]	[illegible]	[illegible]	[illegible]	[illegible]	[illegible]	[illegible]	[illegible]	[illegible]	[illegible]	[illegible]
All other Writs, not being Writs of Execution,	[illegible]	[illegible]	[illegible]	[illegible]	[illegible]	[illegible]	[illegible]	[illegible]	[illegible]	[illegible]	[illegible]	[illegible]	[illegible]	[illegible]
Applications to Court in Proceedings by way of Interpleader,	[illegible]	[illegible]	[illegible]	[illegible]	[illegible]	[illegible]	[illegible]	[illegible]	[illegible]	[illegible]	[illegible]	[illegible]	[illegible]	[illegible]
Issues directed thereon,	[illegible]	[illegible]	[illegible]	[illegible]	[illegible]	[illegible]	[illegible]	[illegible]	[illegible]	[illegible]	[illegible]	[illegible]	[illegible]	[illegible]
Replevin Bonds taken, or Affidavits of Value drawn,	[illegible]	[illegible]	[illegible]	[illegible]	[illegible]	[illegible]	[illegible]	[illegible]	[illegible]	[illegible]	[illegible]	[illegible]	[illegible]	[illegible]
Writs of Execution from High Court of Justice:—														
[illegible],	[illegible]	[illegible]	[illegible]	[illegible]	[illegible]	[illegible]	[illegible]	[illegible]	[illegible]	[illegible]	[illegible]	[illegible]	[illegible]	[illegible]
[illegible],	[illegible]	[illegible]	[illegible]	[illegible]	[illegible]	[illegible]	[illegible]	[illegible]	[illegible]	[illegible]	[illegible]	[illegible]	[illegible]	[illegible]
II.—For Ejectment or Taking Possession of Land.														
Total number of Ejectments for Non-payment of Rent,	[illegible]	[illegible]	[illegible]	[illegible]	[illegible]	[illegible]	[illegible]	[illegible]	[illegible]	[illegible]	[illegible]	[illegible]	[illegible]	[illegible]
Viz.—Writs of Habere of High Court of Justice executed by Sheriff	[illegible]	[illegible]	[illegible]	[illegible]	[illegible]	[illegible]	[illegible]	[illegible]	[illegible]	[illegible]	[illegible]	[illegible]	[illegible]	[illegible]
Writs of Habere of High Court of Justice executed by Special Bailiffs	[illegible]	[illegible]	[illegible]	[illegible]	[illegible]	[illegible]	[illegible]	[illegible]	[illegible]	[illegible]	[illegible]	[illegible]	[illegible]	[illegible]
Civil Bill Ejectments executed,	[illegible]	[illegible]	[illegible]	[illegible]	[illegible]	[illegible]	[illegible]	[illegible]	[illegible]	[illegible]	[illegible]	[illegible]	[illegible]	[illegible]
Total Number of Ejectments between Landlord and Tenant, other than for Non-payment of Rent	[illegible]	[illegible]	[illegible]	[illegible]	[illegible]	[illegible]	[illegible]	[illegible]	[illegible]	[illegible]	[illegible]	[illegible]	[illegible]	[illegible]
Viz.—Writs of Habere of High Court of Justice executed by Sheriff	[illegible]	[illegible]	[illegible]	[illegible]	[illegible]	[illegible]	[illegible]	[illegible]	[illegible]	[illegible]	[illegible]	[illegible]	[illegible]	[illegible]
Writs of Habere of High Court of Justice executed by Special Bailiffs	[illegible]	[illegible]	[illegible]	[illegible]	[illegible]	[illegible]	[illegible]	[illegible]	[illegible]	[illegible]	[illegible]	[illegible]	[illegible]	[illegible]
Civil Bill Ejectments executed,	[illegible]	[illegible]	[illegible]	[illegible]	[illegible]	[illegible]	[illegible]	[illegible]	[illegible]	[illegible]	[illegible]	[illegible]	[illegible]	[illegible]
Total Number of Ejectments other than between Landlord and Tenant	[illegible]	[illegible]	[illegible]	[illegible]	[illegible]	[illegible]	[illegible]	[illegible]	[illegible]	[illegible]	[illegible]	[illegible]	[illegible]	[illegible]
Viz.—Writs of Habere of High Court of Justice executed by Sheriff	[illegible]	[illegible]	[illegible]	[illegible]	[illegible]	[illegible]	[illegible]	[illegible]	[illegible]	[illegible]	[illegible]	[illegible]	[illegible]	[illegible]
Writs of Habere of High Court of Justice executed by Special Bailiffs	[illegible]	[illegible]	[illegible]	[illegible]	[illegible]	[illegible]	[illegible]	[illegible]	[illegible]	[illegible]	[illegible]	[illegible]	[illegible]	[illegible]
Civil Bill Ejectments executed,	[illegible]	[illegible]	[illegible]	[illegible]	[illegible]	[illegible]	[illegible]	[illegible]	[illegible]	[illegible]	[illegible]	[illegible]	[illegible]	[illegible]
Total Number of Ejectments of all classes,	[illegible]	[illegible]	[illegible]	[illegible]	[illegible]	[illegible]	[illegible]	[illegible]	[illegible]	[illegible]	[illegible]	[illegible]	[illegible]	[illegible]
Weekly Tenants and Tenants [illegible]	[illegible]	[illegible]	[illegible]	[illegible]	[illegible]	[illegible]	[illegible]	[illegible]	[illegible]	[illegible]	[illegible]	[illegible]	[illegible]	[illegible]
[illegible]	[illegible]	[illegible]	[illegible]	[illegible]	[illegible]	[illegible]	[illegible]	[illegible]	[illegible]	[illegible]	[illegible]	[illegible]	[illegible]	[illegible]
Number of Writs of [illegible]	[illegible]	[illegible]	[illegible]	[illegible]	[illegible]	[illegible]	[illegible]	[illegible]	[illegible]	[illegible]	[illegible]	[illegible]	[illegible]	[illegible]
Fresh Execution of Writs on Former Certificates, [illegible]	[illegible]	[illegible]	[illegible]	[illegible]	[illegible]	[illegible]	[illegible]	[illegible]	[illegible]	[illegible]	[illegible]	[illegible]	[illegible]	[illegible]
Writs of Assistance from the Chancery Division,	[illegible]	[illegible]	[illegible]	[illegible]	[illegible]	[illegible]	[illegible]	[illegible]	[illegible]	[illegible]	[illegible]	[illegible]	[illegible]	[illegible]
Writs of Assistance from the Probate and Matrimonial Division,	[illegible]	[illegible]	[illegible]	[illegible]	[illegible]	[illegible]	[illegible]	[illegible]	[illegible]	[illegible]	[illegible]	[illegible]	[illegible]	[illegible]
[illegible] from Land Judges,	[illegible]	[illegible]	[illegible]	[illegible]	[illegible]	[illegible]	[illegible]	[illegible]	[illegible]	[illegible]	[illegible]	[illegible]	[illegible]	[illegible]
Process under Land Clauses Acts,	[illegible]	[illegible]	[illegible]	[illegible]	[illegible]	[illegible]	[illegible]	[illegible]	[illegible]	[illegible]	[illegible]	[illegible]	[illegible]	[illegible]
Other Process or Orders,	[illegible]	[illegible]	[illegible]	[illegible]	[illegible]	[illegible]	[illegible]	[illegible]	[illegible]	[illegible]	[illegible]	[illegible]	[illegible]	[illegible]

8	7		.	.	.	Courts held for Election of Coroners.
.	.	1	1	.	.	Courts held for Election of Members of Parliament.
.	.	.	4	.	.	Courts held under Writs of Trial or Inquiry.
.	.	.	.	.	.	Courts held under Land Clauses, Consolidation Act, &c.
.	[illegible]	[illegible]	441	146	.	Civil Bill Decrees and Dismisses executed by Bailiff
.	137	9	[illegible]	16	[illegible]	" " " by Special
.	.	.	.			[illegible]
						[illegible] classified as Queen's Rights —
.	.	.	.	.	.	(1) Forfeitures
.	.	.	.	.	.	(2) Wreck of the Sea
.	.	.		.	.	(3) All other Cases.
.	.	.	.	.	.	Writs of Habeas Corpus, Proceedings on
.	.		.	.	.	Writs of De Lunatico Inquirendo, Proceedings on.
.	.	.	.	.	.	All other Writs, and [illegible] Writs of [illegible]
2	7	.	14	.	.	Applications to Court re Proceedings by way of [illegible]
1	1	.	.	.		[illegible] of [illegible]
.	.	1	.	.	.	Replevin Bonds taken, or Affidavits of Value drawn

…other Writs, and … Writs of Execution,	6	.	-	.	.	1	.	-	-	1
…to Court in Proceedings by way of Interpleader,	1	.	-	.	.	.	1	.	.	.
…recorded Reports,	1	-	-		.	.	1	.	.	.
…Bonds taken, or Affidavits …	.	-	.			-	.	.		
…of Execution from High Court of Justice,—										
Fieri Facias,	[illegible]	[illegible]	[illegible]	[illegible]	[illegible]	[illegible]	[illegible]	[illegible]	[illegible]	[illegible]
Capias ad Satisfaciendum,	1	.	.	-	.	.	-	.	.	.
II.—For Recovery or Taking Possession of Land										
…Number of Ejectments for Non-payment of Rent,	[illegible]	[illegible]	[illegible]	.	[illegible]	[illegible]	[illegible]	[illegible]	[illegible]	[illegible]
…—Writs of Habere of High Court of Justice executed by Sheriff,	[illegible]	[illegible]	[illegible]	.	[illegible]	.	.	[illegible]	[illegible]	
by Special Bailiffs,	[illegible]	-	.	-	.	[illegible]	.	.	.	
Civil Bill Ejectments executed,	[illegible]	[illegible]	[illegible]	-	[illegible]	[illegible]	[illegible]	[illegible]	[illegible]	
…Number of Ejectments between Landlord and Tenant, other than for Non-payment of Rent.	[illegible]	[illegible]	[illegible]	.	[illegible]	[illegible]	.	[illegible]	[illegible]	
—Writs of Habere of High Court of Justice executed by Sheriff,	[illegible]	1	.	.	[illegible]	-	.	[illegible]	[illegible]	
by Special Bailiffs,	[illegible]	-	.	.	.	[illegible]	.	.	.	
Civil Bill Ejectments executed,	[illegible]	.	[illegible]	-	[illegible]	[illegible]	.	[illegible]	[illegible]	
…Number of Ejectments other than between Landlord and Tenant	[illegible]	[illegible]	7	-	[illegible]	[illegible]	[illegible]	-	[illegible]	
…—Writs of Habere of High Court of Justice executed by Sheriff,	[illegible]	[illegible]	[illegible]	-	-	-	[illegible]		[illegible]	
by Special Bailiffs	4	.	.	.	.	[illegible]	.	-	.	
Civil Bill Ejectments executed,	[illegible]	[illegible]	.	.	[illegible]	[illegible]	[illegible]	-	[illegible]	
…Number of Ejectments of all classes,	[illegible]	[illegible]	[illegible]	-	[illegible]	[illegible]	[illegible]	[illegible]	[illegible]	
…of Habere and Decrees executed by consent in writing … under … Vic., c. 154, s. …	[illegible]		.	-	[illegible]	[illegible]	.	.	.	
…of Under-tenants … under … Vic., c. …, s. …	[illegible]	.	-	-	[illegible]	[illegible]	.	.	-	
…of Writs of Habere after Formal Execution, … Vic., c. 154, s. …	[illegible]	.	.	-	.	[illegible]	.	-	.	
…Execution of Writs on Justices' Certificates, … Vic.	.	.	.	.	.	-	.	-		

Fees—Continued, viz.

Writs executed in [illegible]:—

(1.) [illegible]

(2.) Writs of [illegible]

(3.) All other Cases

Writs of Habeas Corpus, Proceedings on.

Writs of De Lunatico Inquirendo, Proceedings in.

All other Writs, not being Writs of Execution.

Applications to Court on Proceedings by way of Interpleader.

Issues directed thereon.

Replevin Bonds taken, or Affidavits of Value drawn.

Writs of Execution from High Court of Justice:—

Fieri Facias

[illegible]

[illegible] Counties of Cities and Towns, and Boroughs having separate Commissions of the Peace, arranged in Provinces	[illegible]	Added by [illegible]	Struck off by [illegible]	[illegible]	[illegible]	Total [illegible]	Qualified as				
							[illegible]	[illegible]	[illegible]	[illegible]	[illegible]
Leinster:											
Carlow,	[illegible]	.	[illegible]	.	.	[illegible]	[illegible]	[illegible]	[illegible]	.	.
Drogheda, Town of,	[illegible]	.	[illegible]	.	.	[illegible]	[illegible]	[illegible]	[illegible]	.	.
Dublin,	[illegible]	.	[illegible]	[illegible]	.	[illegible]	[illegible]	[illegible]	[illegible]	11	.
— City,	[illegible]	[illegible]	[illegible]	.	.	[illegible]	[illegible]	[illegible]	[illegible]	[illegible]	[illegible]
Kildare,	[illegible]	.	[illegible]	.	.	[illegible]	[illegible]	[illegible]	[illegible]	[illegible]	.
Kilkenny,	[illegible]	.	[illegible]	.	.	[illegible]	.	[illegible]	[illegible]	[illegible]	.
— City,	[illegible]	.	[illegible]	.	.	[illegible]	[illegible]	.	[illegible]	.	.
King's County,	[illegible]	.	[illegible]	.	.	[illegible]	[illegible]	[illegible]	[illegible]	.	.
Longford,	[illegible]	.	[illegible]	.	.	[illegible]	[illegible]	[illegible]	[illegible]	[illegible]	.
Louth,	[illegible]	.	[illegible]	1	.	[illegible]	[illegible]	[illegible]	[illegible]	[illegible]	.
Meath,	[illegible]	.	[illegible]	.	.	[illegible]	.	.	[illegible]	[illegible]	.
Queen's County,	[illegible]	.	[illegible]	.	.	[illegible]	[illegible]	[illegible]	[illegible]	[illegible]	.
Westmeath,	[illegible]	.	[illegible]	.	.	[illegible]	[illegible]	[illegible]	[illegible]	[illegible]	.
Wexford,	[illegible]	.	[illegible]	.	.	[illegible]	[illegible]	.	[illegible]	.	[illegible]
Wicklow,	[illegible]	.	[illegible]	[illegible]	.	[illegible]	[illegible]	[illegible]	[illegible]	.	.
Total of Leinster,	[illegible]	[illegible]	[illegible]	[illegible]	.	[illegible]	[illegible]	[illegible]	[illegible]	[illegible]	[illegible]
Munster:											
Clare,	[illegible]	.	[illegible]	.	.	[illegible]	[illegible]	[illegible]	[illegible]	[illegible]	.
Cork, E.R.,	[illegible]	.	[illegible]	.	.	[illegible]	[illegible]	[illegible]	[illegible]	[illegible]	.
— W.R.,	[illegible]	.	[illegible]	.	.	[illegible]	[illegible]	[illegible]	[illegible]	[illegible]	.
— City,	[illegible]	.	[illegible]	.	.	[illegible]	.	[illegible]	[illegible]	[illegible]	[illegible]
Kerry,	[illegible]	.	[illegible]	.	.	[illegible]	[illegible]	[illegible]	[illegible]	.	.
Limerick,	[illegible]	.	[illegible]	.	.	[illegible]	[illegible]	[illegible]	[illegible]	[illegible]	.
— City,	[illegible]	.	[illegible]	.	.	[illegible]	[illegible]	[illegible]	[illegible]	[illegible]	.
Tipperary,	[illegible]	.	[illegible]	.	.	[illegible]	[illegible]	[illegible]	[illegible]	[illegible]	.
Waterford,	[illegible]	.	[illegible]	[illegible]	.	[illegible]	[illegible]	[illegible]	[illegible]	[illegible]	.
— City,	[illegible]	.	[illegible]	.	.	[illegible]	.	.	[illegible]	[illegible]	.
Total of Munster,	[illegible]	.	[illegible]	[illegible]	.	[illegible]	[illegible]	[illegible]	[illegible]	[illegible]	.
Ulster:											
Antrim,	[illegible]	.	[illegible]	.	.	[illegible]	[illegible]	[illegible]	[illegible]	[illegible]	.
Armagh,	[illegible]	.	[illegible]	.	.	[illegible]	[illegible]	[illegible]	[illegible]	.	.
Belfast, Borough,	[illegible]	.	[illegible]	.	.	[illegible]	.	.	[illegible]	.	.
Carrickfergus, Town of,	[illegible]	.	[illegible]	.	.	[illegible]	.	.	[illegible]	.	.
Cavan,	[illegible]	.	[illegible]	.	.	[illegible]	[illegible]	[illegible]	[illegible]	[illegible]	.
Donegal,	[illegible]	.	[illegible]	.	.	[illegible]	[illegible]	[illegible]	[illegible]	[illegible]	.
Down,	[illegible]	.	[illegible]	.	.	[illegible]	[illegible]	[illegible]	[illegible]	[illegible]	.
Fermanagh,	[illegible]	.	[illegible]	.	.	[illegible]	[illegible]	[illegible]	[illegible]	[illegible]	
Londonderry,	[illegible]	.	[illegible]	.	.	[illegible]	[illegible]	[illegible]	[illegible]	[illegible]	
— Borough,	[illegible]	.	[illegible]	.	.	[illegible]	[illegible]	[illegible]	[illegible]	[illegible]	
Monaghan,	[illegible]	.	[illegible]	.	.	[illegible]	[illegible]	.	[illegible]	[illegible]	.
Tyrone,	[illegible]	.	[illegible]	.	.	[illegible]	[illegible]	[illegible]	[illegible]	[illegible]	.
Total of Ulster,	[illegible]	.	[illegible]	.	.	[illegible]	[illegible]	[illegible]	[illegible]	[illegible]	
Connaught:											
Galway,	[illegible]	.	[illegible]	.	.	[illegible]	[illegible]	[illegible]	[illegible]	[illegible]	.
— Town of,	[illegible]	.	[illegible]	.	.	[illegible]	[illegible]	[illegible]	[illegible]	.	.
Leitrim,	[illegible]	.	[illegible]	.	.	[illegible]	[illegible]	[illegible]	[illegible]	[illegible]	.
Mayo,	[illegible]	1	[illegible]	.	.	[illegible]	[illegible]	[illegible]	[illegible]	[illegible]	[illegible]
Roscommon,	[illegible]	.	[illegible]	.	.	[illegible]	[illegible]	[illegible]	[illegible]	[illegible]	.
Sligo,	[illegible]	.	[illegible]	.	.	[illegible]	[illegible]	[illegible]	[illegible]	[illegible]	.
Total of Connaught,	[illegible]	[illegible]	[illegible]	.	.	[illegible]	[illegible]	[illegible]	[illegible]	[illegible]	[illegible]
Total of Ireland,	[illegible]	[illegible]	[illegible]	[illegible]	.	[illegible]	[illegible]	[illegible]	[illegible]	[illegible]	[illegible]

in respect of the Preparation, Revision, and Correction, in 1868, of Jurors' Lists and Jurors' Books, from Returns of the Peace.

General Jurors' Lists [illegible]					Special Jurors' Book [illegible]	[illegible]				COUNTIES, COUNTIES OF CITIES AND TOWNS AND BOROUGHS HAVING SEPARATE CLERKS OF THE PEACE, ARRANGED IN PROVINCES
On List as prepared by Clerk of Peace.	Added by Revision Court.	Struck off by Revision Court.	Exempted by Clerk of Peace.	Struck off Book by Judges.	Total on Book when [illegible]	General Jurors added.	[illegible]	Special Jurors added.	Special Jurors [illegible]	
										LEINSTER:
[illegible]		[illegible]	-	[illegible]	[illegible]	-	-	-		Carlow.
[illegible]	-	[illegible]	-	-	[illegible]	-	-	-	-	Drogheda, Town of.
[illegible]	-	-	[illegible]	-	[illegible]	-	-	-	-	Dublin.
[illegible]	[illegible]	[illegible]	-	-	[illegible]	-	-	-	[illegible]	" City.
[illegible]	[illegible]	[illegible]	-	-	[illegible]	-	-	-	-	Kildare.
[illegible]	-	[illegible]	-	-	[illegible]	-	-		-	Kilkenny.
[illegible]	[illegible]	[illegible]	-	-	[illegible]	-	-	-	-	" City.
[illegible]	-	[illegible]	-	-	[illegible]	-	-		-	King's County.
[illegible]	-	-	-	-	[illegible]	-	-		-	Longford.
[illegible]	-	[illegible]	[illegible]	-	[illegible]	-	[illegible]	-		Louth.
[illegible]	-	[illegible]	-	-	[illegible]	-	-		-	Meath.
[illegible]	-	[illegible]	-	-	[illegible]	-	-	-	-	Queen's County.
[illegible]	-	[illegible]	-	-	[illegible]	-	[illegible]	-	[illegible]	Westmeath.
[illegible]	-	[illegible]	-	-	[illegible]	-	-	-	-	Wexford.
[illegible]	-	[illegible]	[illegible]	-	[illegible]	-	[illegible]	-	-	Wicklow.
[illegible]	[illegible]	[illegible]	[illegible]	-	[illegible]	-	[illegible]	-	[illegible]	Total of Leinster.
										MUNSTER:
[illegible]	-	[illegible]	-	-	[illegible]	-	-	-	-	Clare.
[illegible]	-	[illegible]	-	-	[illegible]	-	-	-	-	Cork, E.R.
[illegible]	-	-	-	-	[illegible]	-	-	-	-	" W.R.
[illegible]	-	[illegible]	-	-	[illegible]	-	-	-	-	" City.
[illegible]	-	[illegible]	-	-	[illegible]	-	-	-	-	Kerry.
[illegible]	[illegible]	[illegible]	-	-	[illegible]	-	-	-	-	Limerick.
[illegible]	[illegible]	[illegible]	-	-	[illegible]	-		-	-	" City.
[illegible]	-	[illegible]	-	-	[illegible]	-		-	-	Tipperary.
[illegible]	-	[illegible]	-	-	[illegible]	-	-	-	-	Waterford.
[illegible]	-	[illegible]	-	-	[illegible]	-	-			" City.
[illegible]	[illegible]	[illegible]	-	-	[illegible]		-	-	-	Total of Munster.
										ULSTER:
[illegible]	[illegible]	[illegible]			[illegible]	-	-		-	Antrim.
[illegible]	-	[illegible]	-	-	[illegible]	-	-	-	-	Armagh.
-	-	-	-	-	-	-	[illegible]	-	-	Belfast, Borough.
[illegible]	-	[illegible]	-	-	[illegible]	-	-	-	-	Carrickfergus, Town of.
[illegible]	-	-	-	-	[illegible]	-	[illegible]	-	[illegible]	Cavan.
[illegible]	[illegible]	[illegible]	-	-	[illegible]	-	[illegible]	-	[illegible]	Donegal.
[illegible]	[illegible]	-	-	-	[illegible]	-		-	-	Down.
[illegible]	[illegible]	-	-	-	[illegible]	-	-	-	-	Fermanagh.
[illegible]	-	[illegible]	-	-	[illegible]	-	-	-	-	Londonderry.
[illegible]	-	[illegible]	-	-	[illegible]	-	-	-	-	" Borough.
[illegible]	-	[illegible]	-	-	[illegible]	-	-		-	Monaghan.
[illegible]	-	[illegible]	-	-	[illegible]	-			-	Tyrone.
[illegible]	[illegible]	[illegible]	-	-	[illegible]	-	[illegible]	-	[illegible]	Total of Ulster.
										CONNAUGHT:
[illegible]	-	[illegible]	-	-	[illegible]	-		-	-	Galway.
[illegible]	-	[illegible]	-	-	[illegible]	-	-	-	-	" Town of.
[illegible]	[illegible]	-	-	-	[illegible]	-				Leitrim.
[illegible]	[illegible]	[illegible]	-	-	[illegible]	-	[illegible]		[illegible]	Mayo.
[illegible]	-	-	-	-	[illegible]	-	-	-		Roscommon.
[illegible]	-	[illegible]	-	-	[illegible]	-	-	-		Sligo.
[illegible]	[illegible]	[illegible]	-	-	[illegible]	-	[illegible]	-	[illegible]	Total of Connaught.
[illegible]	[illegible]	[illegible]	[illegible]	-	[illegible]	-	[illegible]	-	[illegible]	Total of Ireland.

Counties, Counties of Cities and Towns, and Boroughs having separate Sessions of the Peace, arranged in Provinces.	Total Number of [illegible] during the year	General Sessions			Town and Commission Sessions			Special Sessions		
		January to June	July to December	Total	January to June	July to December	Total	January to June	July to December	Total
Leinster: Dublin										
Crown Side of Queen's Bench Division, Winter Assizes, and Commission Court	[illegible]	[illegible]	[illegible]	[illegible]	[illegible]	[illegible]	[illegible]	[illegible]	[illegible]	[illegible]
Civil Side of Queen's Bench Division, Common Pleas Division, Exchequer Division, Probate and Matrimonial Division	[illegible]	[illegible]	[illegible]	[illegible]	[illegible]	[illegible]	[illegible]	[illegible]	[illegible]	[illegible]
Bankruptcy	[illegible]	[illegible]	[illegible]	[illegible]	[illegible]	[illegible]	[illegible]	[illegible]	[illegible]	[illegible]
[illegible]	[illegible]	[illegible]	[illegible]	[illegible]	[illegible]	[illegible]	[illegible]	[illegible]	[illegible]	[illegible]
Other purposes from Quarter Sessions or Civil Bill [illegible]	[illegible]	[illegible]	[illegible]	[illegible]	[illegible]	[illegible]	[illegible]	[illegible]	[illegible]	[illegible]
Total of Dublin County,	[illegible]	[illegible]	[illegible]	[illegible]	[illegible]	[illegible]	[illegible]	[illegible]	[illegible]	[illegible]
Dublin City										
Crown Side of Queen's Bench Division, Winter Assizes, and Commission Court	[illegible]	[illegible]	[illegible]	[illegible]	[illegible]	[illegible]	[illegible]	[illegible]	[illegible]	[illegible]
Civil Side of Queen's Bench Division, Common Pleas Division, Exchequer Division	[illegible]	[illegible]	[illegible]	[illegible]	[illegible]	[illegible]	[illegible]	[illegible]	[illegible]	[illegible]
Probate and Matrimonial Division	[illegible]	[illegible]	[illegible]	[illegible]	[illegible]	[illegible]	[illegible]	[illegible]	[illegible]	[illegible]
Bankruptcy	[illegible]	[illegible]	[illegible]	[illegible]	[illegible]	[illegible]	[illegible]	[illegible]	[illegible]	[illegible]
[illegible]	[illegible]	[illegible]	[illegible]	[illegible]	[illegible]	[illegible]	[illegible]	[illegible]	[illegible]	[illegible]
Other purposes from Quarter Sessions or Civil Bill [illegible]	[illegible]	[illegible]	[illegible]	[illegible]	[illegible]	[illegible]	[illegible]	[illegible]	[illegible]	[illegible]
Total of Dublin City,	[illegible]	[illegible]	[illegible]	[illegible]	[illegible]	[illegible]	[illegible]	[illegible]	[illegible]	[illegible]
Carlow,	[illegible]	[illegible]	[illegible]	[illegible]	[illegible]	[illegible]	[illegible]	[illegible]	[illegible]	[illegible]
Drogheda, Town of,	[illegible]	[illegible]	[illegible]	[illegible]	[illegible]	[illegible]	[illegible]	[illegible]	[illegible]	[illegible]
Kildare,	[illegible]	[illegible]	[illegible]	[illegible]	[illegible]	[illegible]	[illegible]	[illegible]	[illegible]	[illegible]
Kilkenny,	[illegible]	[illegible]	[illegible]	[illegible]	[illegible]	[illegible]	[illegible]	[illegible]	[illegible]	[illegible]
" City,	[illegible]	[illegible]	[illegible]	[illegible]	[illegible]	[illegible]	[illegible]	[illegible]	[illegible]	[illegible]
King's County,	[illegible]	[illegible]	[illegible]	[illegible]	[illegible]	[illegible]	[illegible]	[illegible]	[illegible]	[illegible]
Longford,	[illegible]	[illegible]	[illegible]	[illegible]	[illegible]	[illegible]	[illegible]	[illegible]	[illegible]	[illegible]
Louth,	[illegible]	[illegible]	[illegible]	[illegible]	[illegible]	[illegible]	[illegible]	[illegible]	[illegible]	[illegible]
Meath,	[illegible]	[illegible]	[illegible]	[illegible]	[illegible]	[illegible]	[illegible]	[illegible]	[illegible]	[illegible]
Queen's County,	[illegible]	[illegible]	[illegible]	[illegible]	[illegible]	[illegible]	[illegible]	[illegible]	[illegible]	[illegible]
Westmeath,	[illegible]	[illegible]	[illegible]	[illegible]	[illegible]	[illegible]	[illegible]	[illegible]	[illegible]	[illegible]
Wexford,	[illegible]	[illegible]	[illegible]	[illegible]	[illegible]	[illegible]	[illegible]	[illegible]	[illegible]	[illegible]
Wicklow,	[illegible]	[illegible]	[illegible]	[illegible]	[illegible]	[illegible]	[illegible]	[illegible]	[illegible]	[illegible]
Total of Leinster,	[illegible]	[illegible]	[illegible]	[illegible]	[illegible]	[illegible]	[illegible]	[illegible]	[illegible]	[illegible]
Munster:										
Clare,	[illegible]	[illegible]	[illegible]	[illegible]	[illegible]	[illegible]	[illegible]	[illegible]	[illegible]	[illegible]
Cork,	[illegible]	[illegible]	[illegible]	[illegible]	[illegible]	[illegible]	[illegible]	[illegible]	[illegible]	[illegible]
" City,	[illegible]	[illegible]	[illegible]	[illegible]	[illegible]	[illegible]	[illegible]	[illegible]	[illegible]	[illegible]
Kerry,	[illegible]	[illegible]	[illegible]	[illegible]	[illegible]	[illegible]	[illegible]	[illegible]	[illegible]	[illegible]
Limerick,	[illegible]	[illegible]	[illegible]	[illegible]	[illegible]	[illegible]	[illegible]	[illegible]	[illegible]	[illegible]
" City,	[illegible]	[illegible]	[illegible]	[illegible]	[illegible]	[illegible]	[illegible]	[illegible]	[illegible]	[illegible]
Tipperary,	[illegible]	[illegible]	[illegible]	[illegible]	[illegible]	[illegible]	[illegible]	[illegible]	[illegible]	[illegible]
Waterford,	[illegible]	[illegible]	[illegible]	[illegible]	[illegible]	[illegible]	[illegible]	[illegible]	[illegible]	[illegible]
" City,	[illegible]	[illegible]	[illegible]	[illegible]	[illegible]	[illegible]	[illegible]	[illegible]	[illegible]	[illegible]
Total of Munster,	[illegible]	[illegible]	[illegible]	[illegible]	[illegible]	[illegible]	[illegible]	[illegible]	[illegible]	[illegible]
Ulster:										
Antrim,	[illegible]	[illegible]	[illegible]	[illegible]	[illegible]	[illegible]	[illegible]	[illegible]	[illegible]	[illegible]
Armagh,	[illegible]	[illegible]	[illegible]	[illegible]	[illegible]	[illegible]	[illegible]	[illegible]	[illegible]	[illegible]
Belfast, Borough,	[illegible]	[illegible]	[illegible]	[illegible]	[illegible]	[illegible]	[illegible]	[illegible]	[illegible]	[illegible]
Carrickfergus, Town of,	[illegible]	[illegible]	[illegible]	[illegible]	[illegible]	[illegible]	[illegible]	[illegible]	[illegible]	[illegible]
Cavan,	[illegible]	[illegible]	[illegible]	[illegible]	[illegible]	[illegible]	[illegible]	[illegible]	[illegible]	[illegible]
Donegal,	[illegible]	[illegible]	[illegible]	[illegible]	[illegible]	[illegible]	[illegible]	[illegible]	[illegible]	[illegible]
Down,	[illegible]	[illegible]	[illegible]	[illegible]	[illegible]	[illegible]	[illegible]	[illegible]	[illegible]	[illegible]
Fermanagh,	[illegible]	[illegible]	[illegible]	[illegible]	[illegible]	[illegible]	[illegible]	[illegible]	[illegible]	[illegible]
Londonderry,	[illegible]	[illegible]	[illegible]	[illegible]	[illegible]	[illegible]	[illegible]	[illegible]	[illegible]	[illegible]
" City,	[illegible]	[illegible]	[illegible]	[illegible]	[illegible]	[illegible]	[illegible]	[illegible]	[illegible]	[illegible]
Monaghan,	[illegible]	[illegible]	[illegible]	[illegible]	[illegible]	[illegible]	[illegible]	[illegible]	[illegible]	[illegible]
Tyrone,	[illegible]	[illegible]	[illegible]	[illegible]	[illegible]	[illegible]	[illegible]	[illegible]	[illegible]	[illegible]
Total of Ulster,	[illegible]	[illegible]	[illegible]	[illegible]	[illegible]	[illegible]	[illegible]	[illegible]	[illegible]	[illegible]

Common Pleas Division	[illegible]	[illegible]	[illegible]	[illegible]	[illegible]	[illegible]	[illegible]	[illegible]	[illegible]	[illegible]
Exchequer Division	[illegible]	[illegible]	[illegible]	[illegible]	[illegible]	[illegible]	[illegible]	[illegible]	[illegible]	[illegible]
Probate and Matrimonial Division	[illegible]	[illegible]	[illegible]	[illegible]	[illegible]	[illegible]	[illegible]	[illegible]	[illegible]	[illegible]
Bankruptcy	[illegible]	[illegible]	[illegible]	[illegible]	[illegible]	[illegible]	[illegible]	[illegible]	[illegible]	[illegible]
Records	[illegible]	[illegible]	[illegible]	[illegible]	[illegible]	[illegible]	[illegible]	[illegible]	[illegible]	[illegible]
Other appeals from Quarter Sessions or Civil Bills before County Court Judge	[illegible]	[illegible]	[illegible]	[illegible]	[illegible]	[illegible]	[illegible]	[illegible]	[illegible]	[illegible]
Total of Dublin County	[illegible]	[illegible]	[illegible]	[illegible]	[illegible]	[illegible]	[illegible]	[illegible]	[illegible]	[illegible]
Dublin City										
Queen's Bench of Queen's Bench Division, Assizes, and Commission Court	[illegible]	[illegible]	[illegible]	[illegible]	[illegible]	[illegible]	[illegible]	[illegible]	[illegible]	[illegible]
Civil Bills of Queen's Bench Division	[illegible]	[illegible]	[illegible]	[illegible]	[illegible]	[illegible]	[illegible]	[illegible]	[illegible]	[illegible]
Common Pleas Division	[illegible]	[illegible]	[illegible]	[illegible]	[illegible]	[illegible]	[illegible]	[illegible]	[illegible]	[illegible]
Exchequer Division	[illegible]	[illegible]	[illegible]	[illegible]	[illegible]	[illegible]	[illegible]	[illegible]	[illegible]	[illegible]
Probate and Matrimonial Division	[illegible]	[illegible]	[illegible]	[illegible]	[illegible]	[illegible]	[illegible]	[illegible]	[illegible]	[illegible]
Bankruptcy	[illegible]	[illegible]	[illegible]	[illegible]	[illegible]	[illegible]	[illegible]	[illegible]	[illegible]	[illegible]
Records	[illegible]	[illegible]	[illegible]	[illegible]	[illegible]	[illegible]	[illegible]	[illegible]	[illegible]	[illegible]
Other appeals from Quarter Sessions or Civil Bills before Recorder	[illegible]	[illegible]	[illegible]	[illegible]	[illegible]	[illegible]	[illegible]	[illegible]	[illegible]	[illegible]
Total of Dublin City	[illegible]	[illegible]	[illegible]	[illegible]	[illegible]	[illegible]	[illegible]	[illegible]	[illegible]	[illegible]
Carlow	[illegible]	[illegible]	[illegible]	[illegible]	[illegible]	[illegible]	[illegible]	[illegible]	[illegible]	[illegible]
Drogheda, Town of	[illegible]	[illegible]	[illegible]	[illegible]	[illegible]	[illegible]	[illegible]	[illegible]	[illegible]	[illegible]
Kildare	[illegible]	[illegible]	[illegible]	[illegible]	[illegible]	[illegible]	[illegible]	[illegible]	[illegible]	[illegible]
Kilkenny	[illegible]	[illegible]	[illegible]	[illegible]	[illegible]	[illegible]	[illegible]	[illegible]	[illegible]	[illegible]
" City	[illegible]	[illegible]	[illegible]	[illegible]	[illegible]	[illegible]	[illegible]	[illegible]	[illegible]	[illegible]
King's County	[illegible]	[illegible]	[illegible]	[illegible]	[illegible]	[illegible]	[illegible]	[illegible]	[illegible]	[illegible]
Longford	[illegible]	[illegible]	[illegible]	[illegible]	[illegible]	[illegible]	[illegible]	[illegible]	[illegible]	[illegible]
Louth	[illegible]	[illegible]	[illegible]	[illegible]	[illegible]	[illegible]	[illegible]	[illegible]	[illegible]	[illegible]
Meath	[illegible]	[illegible]	[illegible]	[illegible]	[illegible]	[illegible]	[illegible]	[illegible]	[illegible]	[illegible]
Queen's County	[illegible]	[illegible]	[illegible]	[illegible]	[illegible]	[illegible]	[illegible]	[illegible]	[illegible]	[illegible]
Westmeath	[illegible]	[illegible]	[illegible]	[illegible]	[illegible]	[illegible]	[illegible]	[illegible]	[illegible]	[illegible]
Wexford	[illegible]	[illegible]	[illegible]	[illegible]	[illegible]	[illegible]	[illegible]	[illegible]	[illegible]	[illegible]
Wicklow	[illegible]	[illegible]	[illegible]	[illegible]	[illegible]	[illegible]	[illegible]	[illegible]	[illegible]	[illegible]
Total of Leinster	[illegible]	[illegible]	[illegible]	[illegible]	[illegible]	[illegible]	[illegible]	[illegible]	[illegible]	[illegible]
Munster:										
Clare	[illegible]	[illegible]	[illegible]	[illegible]	[illegible]	[illegible]	[illegible]	[illegible]	[illegible]	[illegible]
Cork	[illegible]	[illegible]	[illegible]	[illegible]	[illegible]	[illegible]	[illegible]	[illegible]	[illegible]	[illegible]
" City	[illegible]	[illegible]	[illegible]	[illegible]	[illegible]	[illegible]	[illegible]	[illegible]	[illegible]	[illegible]
Kerry	[illegible]	[illegible]	[illegible]	[illegible]	[illegible]	[illegible]	[illegible]	[illegible]	[illegible]	[illegible]
Limerick	[illegible]	[illegible]	[illegible]	[illegible]	[illegible]	[illegible]	[illegible]	[illegible]	[illegible]	[illegible]
" City	[illegible]	[illegible]	[illegible]	[illegible]	[illegible]	[illegible]	[illegible]	[illegible]	[illegible]	[illegible]
Tipperary	[illegible]	[illegible]	[illegible]	[illegible]	[illegible]	[illegible]	[illegible]	[illegible]	[illegible]	[illegible]
Waterford	[illegible]	[illegible]	[illegible]	[illegible]	[illegible]	[illegible]	[illegible]	[illegible]	[illegible]	[illegible]
" City	[illegible]	[illegible]	[illegible]	[illegible]	[illegible]	[illegible]	[illegible]	[illegible]	[illegible]	[illegible]
Total of Munster	[illegible]	[illegible]	[illegible]	[illegible]	[illegible]	[illegible]	[illegible]	[illegible]	[illegible]	[illegible]
Ulster:										
Antrim	[illegible]	[illegible]	[illegible]	[illegible]	[illegible]	[illegible]	[illegible]	[illegible]	[illegible]	[illegible]
Armagh	[illegible]	[illegible]	[illegible]	[illegible]	[illegible]	[illegible]	[illegible]	[illegible]	[illegible]	[illegible]
Belfast, Borough	[illegible]	[illegible]	[illegible]	[illegible]	[illegible]	[illegible]	[illegible]	[illegible]	[illegible]	[illegible]
Carrickfergus, Town of	[illegible]	[illegible]	[illegible]	[illegible]	[illegible]	[illegible]	[illegible]	[illegible]	[illegible]	[illegible]
Cavan	[illegible]	[illegible]	[illegible]	[illegible]	[illegible]	[illegible]	[illegible]	[illegible]	[illegible]	[illegible]
Donegal	[illegible]	[illegible]	[illegible]	[illegible]	[illegible]	[illegible]	[illegible]	[illegible]	[illegible]	[illegible]
Down	[illegible]	[illegible]	[illegible]	[illegible]	[illegible]	[illegible]	[illegible]	[illegible]	[illegible]	[illegible]
Fermanagh	[illegible]	[illegible]	[illegible]	[illegible]	[illegible]	[illegible]	[illegible]	[illegible]	[illegible]	[illegible]
Londonderry	[illegible]	[illegible]	[illegible]	[illegible]	[illegible]	[illegible]	[illegible]	[illegible]	[illegible]	[illegible]
" City	[illegible]	[illegible]	[illegible]	[illegible]	[illegible]	[illegible]	[illegible]	[illegible]	[illegible]	[illegible]
Monaghan	[illegible]	[illegible]	[illegible]	[illegible]	[illegible]	[illegible]	[illegible]	[illegible]	[illegible]	[illegible]
Tyrone	[illegible]	[illegible]	[illegible]	[illegible]	[illegible]	[illegible]	[illegible]	[illegible]	[illegible]	[illegible]
Total of Ulster	[illegible]	[illegible]	[illegible]	[illegible]	[illegible]	[illegible]	[illegible]	[illegible]	[illegible]	[illegible]
Connaught:										
Galway	[illegible]	[illegible]	[illegible]	[illegible]	[illegible]	[illegible]	[illegible]	[illegible]	[illegible]	[illegible]
" Town of	[illegible]	[illegible]	[illegible]	[illegible]	[illegible]	[illegible]	[illegible]	[illegible]	[illegible]	[illegible]
Leitrim	[illegible]	[illegible]	[illegible]	[illegible]	[illegible]	[illegible]	[illegible]	[illegible]	[illegible]	[illegible]
Mayo	[illegible]	[illegible]	[illegible]	[illegible]	[illegible]	[illegible]	[illegible]	[illegible]	[illegible]	[illegible]
Roscommon	[illegible]	[illegible]	[illegible]	[illegible]	[illegible]	[illegible]	[illegible]	[illegible]	[illegible]	[illegible]
Sligo	[illegible]	[illegible]	[illegible]	[illegible]	[illegible]	[illegible]	[illegible]	[illegible]	[illegible]	[illegible]
Total of Connaught	[illegible]	[illegible]	[illegible]	[illegible]	[illegible]	[illegible]	[illegible]	[illegible]	[illegible]	[illegible]
Total of Ireland	[illegible]	[illegible]	[illegible]	[illegible]	[illegible]	[illegible]	[illegible]	[illegible]	[illegible]	[illegible]

TABLE —TABLE of PROCEEDINGS in the Year [illegible], as to the ATTENDANCES of MAGISTRATES and the [illegible] under STATUTE [illegible] VIII, c. [illegible], and as to OVERHOLDING TENANTS [illegible]

PETTY SESSIONS DISTRICTS, ARRANGED IN COUNTIES, COUNTIES OF CITIES OR OF TOWNS, AND PROVINCES.	No. of places at which Petty Sessions held	Attendances of Magistrates				[illegible]			
		Number of days on which Petty Sessions held	Number of days on which only one Magistrate attended	Number of days on which only [illegible] Magistrate attended	Number of days on which [illegible] Magistrates	[illegible]	[illegible]	[illegible]	[illegible]
LEINSTER.									
Carlow,	6	[illegible]	[illegible]	[illegible]	[illegible]	[illegible]	[illegible]	[illegible]	[illegible]
Drogheda, Town of,	1	[illegible]	-	-	[illegible]	[illegible]	[illegible]	[illegible]	[illegible]
Dublin, Southside Metropolitan Police District	[illegible]	[illegible]	[illegible]	[illegible]	[illegible]	[illegible]	[illegible]	[illegible]	[illegible]
Dublin, Metropolitan Police District, excluding [illegible]	[illegible]	[illegible]	[illegible]	[illegible]	[illegible]	[illegible]	[illegible]	[illegible]	[illegible]
Kildare,	[illegible]	[illegible]	[illegible]	[illegible]	[illegible]	[illegible]	[illegible]	[illegible]	[illegible]
Kilkenny,	[illegible]	[illegible]	[illegible]	[illegible]	[illegible]	[illegible]	[illegible]	[illegible]	[illegible]
Kilkenny City,	1	[illegible]	-	-	-	[illegible]	[illegible]	[illegible]	
King's County,	[illegible]	[illegible]	[illegible]	[illegible]	[illegible]	[illegible]	[illegible]	[illegible]	[illegible]
Longford,	[illegible]	[illegible]	[illegible]	[illegible]	[illegible]	[illegible]	[illegible]	[illegible]	[illegible]
Louth,	[illegible]	[illegible]	[illegible]	[illegible]	[illegible]	[illegible]	[illegible]	[illegible]	[illegible]
Meath,	[illegible]	[illegible]	[illegible]	[illegible]	[illegible]	[illegible]	[illegible]	[illegible]	[illegible]
Queen's County,	[illegible]	[illegible]	[illegible]	[illegible]	[illegible]	[illegible]	[illegible]	[illegible]	[illegible]
Westmeath,	[illegible]	[illegible]	[illegible]	[illegible]	[illegible]	[illegible]	[illegible]	[illegible]	[illegible]
Wexford,	[illegible]	[illegible]	[illegible]	[illegible]	[illegible]	[illegible]	[illegible]	[illegible]	[illegible]
Wicklow,	[illegible]	[illegible]	[illegible]	[illegible]	[illegible]	[illegible]	[illegible]	[illegible]	[illegible]
Total,	[illegible]	[illegible]	[illegible]	[illegible]	[illegible]	[illegible]	[illegible]	[illegible]	[illegible]
MUNSTER.									
Clare,	[illegible]	[illegible]	[illegible]	[illegible]	[illegible]	[illegible]	[illegible]	[illegible]	[illegible]
Cork,	[illegible]	[illegible]	[illegible]	[illegible]	[illegible]	[illegible]	[illegible]	[illegible]	[illegible]
Cork City,	1	[illegible]	[illegible]	[illegible]		[illegible]	[illegible]	[illegible]	[illegible]
Kerry,	[illegible]	[illegible]	[illegible]	[illegible]	[illegible]	[illegible]	[illegible]	[illegible]	[illegible]
Limerick,	[illegible]	[illegible]	[illegible]	[illegible]	[illegible]	[illegible]	[illegible]	[illegible]	[illegible]
Limerick City,	1	[illegible]	-	-	-	[illegible]	[illegible]	[illegible]	[illegible]
Tipperary,	[illegible]	[illegible]	[illegible]	[illegible]	[illegible]	[illegible]	[illegible]	[illegible]	[illegible]
Waterford,	[illegible]	[illegible]	[illegible]	[illegible]	[illegible]	[illegible]	[illegible]	[illegible]	[illegible]
Waterford City and Police Court	1	[illegible]	[illegible]	[illegible]	-	[illegible]	[illegible]	[illegible]	[illegible]
Total,	[illegible]	[illegible]	[illegible]	[illegible]	[illegible]	[illegible]	[illegible]	[illegible]	[illegible]
ULSTER.									
Antrim,	[illegible]	[illegible]	[illegible]	[illegible]	[illegible]	[illegible]	[illegible]	[illegible]	[illegible]
Armagh,	[illegible]	[illegible]	[illegible]	[illegible]	[illegible]	[illegible]	[illegible]	[illegible]	[illegible]
Carrickfergus, County of the Town of	1	[illegible]	[illegible]	[illegible]	-	[illegible]	[illegible]	[illegible]	[illegible]
Cavan,	[illegible]	[illegible]	[illegible]	[illegible]	[illegible]	[illegible]	[illegible]	[illegible]	[illegible]
Donegal,	[illegible]	[illegible]	[illegible]	[illegible]	[illegible]	[illegible]	[illegible]	[illegible]	[illegible]
Down,	[illegible]	[illegible]	[illegible]	[illegible]	[illegible]	[illegible]	[illegible]	[illegible]	[illegible]
Fermanagh,	[illegible]	[illegible]	[illegible]	[illegible]	[illegible]	[illegible]	[illegible]	[illegible]	[illegible]
Londonderry,	[illegible]	[illegible]	[illegible]	[illegible]	-	[illegible]	[illegible]	[illegible]	[illegible]
Londonderry City,	1	[illegible]	[illegible]	[illegible]	-	[illegible]	[illegible]	[illegible]	[illegible]
Monaghan,	[illegible]	[illegible]	[illegible]	[illegible]	[illegible]	[illegible]	[illegible]	[illegible]	[illegible]
Tyrone,	[illegible]	[illegible]	[illegible]	[illegible]	[illegible]	[illegible]	[illegible]	[illegible]	[illegible]
Total,	[illegible]	[illegible]	[illegible]	[illegible]	[illegible]	[illegible]	[illegible]	[illegible]	[illegible]
CONNAUGHT.									
Galway,	[illegible]	[illegible]	[illegible]	[illegible]	[illegible]	[illegible]	[illegible]	[illegible]	[illegible]
Galway, County of Town,	[illegible]	[illegible]	-	[illegible]	[illegible]	[illegible]	[illegible]	[illegible]	[illegible]
Leitrim,	[illegible]	[illegible]	[illegible]	[illegible]	[illegible]	[illegible]	[illegible]	[illegible]	[illegible]
Mayo,	[illegible]	[illegible]	[illegible]	[illegible]	[illegible]	[illegible]	[illegible]	[illegible]	[illegible]
Roscommon,	[illegible]	[illegible]	[illegible]	[illegible]	[illegible]	[illegible]	[illegible]	[illegible]	[illegible]
Sligo,	[illegible]	[illegible]	[illegible]	[illegible]	[illegible]	[illegible]	[illegible]	[illegible]	[illegible]
Total,	[illegible]	[illegible]	[illegible]	[illegible]	[illegible]	[illegible]	[illegible]	[illegible]	[illegible]
Total of Ireland,	[illegible]	[illegible]	[illegible]	[illegible]	[illegible]	[illegible]	[illegible]	[illegible]	[illegible]

NUMBER of CIVIL CASES other than PROCEEDINGS as to COTTIER TENANTS, and as to COTTIER TENANTS [illegible] TOWNS under 14 & 15 VIC., c. [illegible], from Returns made by Clerks of Petty Sessions.

Summary Recovery of Possession of Tenements, [illegible]								Summary Recovery of Possession [illegible] 14 & 15 Vic., c. [illegible]				PETTY SESSIONS DISTRICTS, ARRANGED IN COUNTIES, COUNTIES OF CITIES AND OF TOWNS, AND PROVINCES.
Section [illegible] Waste		Section [illegible] Rent		Section [illegible] Overholding		[illegible]	[illegible]	[illegible]	[illegible]	[illegible]	[illegible]	
[illegible]	[illegible]	[illegible]	[illegible]	[illegible]	[illegible]							
												LEINSTER.
[illegible]	[illegible]	[illegible]	[illegible]	[illegible]	[illegible]	[illegible]	[illegible]	[illegible]	[illegible]	[illegible]	[illegible]	Carlow.
[illegible]	[illegible]	[illegible]	[illegible]	[illegible]	[illegible]	[illegible]	[illegible]	[illegible]	[illegible]	[illegible]	[illegible]	Drogheda, Town of.
[illegible]	[illegible]	[illegible]	[illegible]	[illegible]	[illegible]	[illegible]	[illegible]	[illegible]	[illegible]	[illegible]	[illegible]	Dublin [illegible] (Dublin)
[illegible]	[illegible]	[illegible]	[illegible]	[illegible]	[illegible]	[illegible]	[illegible]	[illegible]	[illegible]	[illegible]	[illegible]	Dublin [illegible]
[illegible]	[illegible]	[illegible]	[illegible]	[illegible]	[illegible]	[illegible]	[illegible]	[illegible]	[illegible]	[illegible]	[illegible]	Kildare.
[illegible]	[illegible]	[illegible]	[illegible]	[illegible]	[illegible]	[illegible]	[illegible]	[illegible]	[illegible]	[illegible]	[illegible]	Kilkenny.
[illegible]	[illegible]	[illegible]	[illegible]	[illegible]	[illegible]	[illegible]	[illegible]	[illegible]	[illegible]	[illegible]	[illegible]	Kilkenny City.
[illegible]	[illegible]	[illegible]	[illegible]	[illegible]	[illegible]	[illegible]	[illegible]	[illegible]	[illegible]	[illegible]	[illegible]	King's County.
[illegible]	[illegible]	[illegible]	[illegible]	[illegible]	[illegible]	[illegible]	[illegible]	[illegible]	[illegible]	[illegible]	[illegible]	Longford.
[illegible]	[illegible]	[illegible]	[illegible]	[illegible]	[illegible]	[illegible]	[illegible]	[illegible]	[illegible]	[illegible]	[illegible]	Louth.
[illegible]	[illegible]	[illegible]	[illegible]	[illegible]	[illegible]	[illegible]	[illegible]	[illegible]	[illegible]	[illegible]	[illegible]	Meath.
[illegible]	[illegible]	[illegible]	[illegible]	[illegible]	[illegible]	[illegible]	[illegible]	[illegible]	[illegible]	[illegible]	[illegible]	Queen's County.
[illegible]	[illegible]	[illegible]	[illegible]	[illegible]	[illegible]	[illegible]	[illegible]	[illegible]	[illegible]	[illegible]	[illegible]	Westmeath.
[illegible]	[illegible]	[illegible]	[illegible]	[illegible]	[illegible]	[illegible]	[illegible]	[illegible]	[illegible]	[illegible]	[illegible]	Wexford.
[illegible]	[illegible]	[illegible]	[illegible]	[illegible]	[illegible]	[illegible]	[illegible]	[illegible]	[illegible]	[illegible]	[illegible]	Wicklow.
[illegible]	[illegible]	[illegible]	[illegible]	[illegible]	[illegible]	[illegible]	[illegible]	[illegible]	[illegible]	[illegible]	[illegible]	Total.
												MUNSTER.
[illegible]	[illegible]	[illegible]	[illegible]	[illegible]	[illegible]	[illegible]	[illegible]	[illegible]	[illegible]	[illegible]	[illegible]	Clare.
[illegible]	[illegible]	[illegible]	[illegible]	[illegible]	[illegible]	[illegible]	[illegible]	[illegible]	[illegible]	[illegible]	[illegible]	Cork.
[illegible]	[illegible]	[illegible]	[illegible]	[illegible]	[illegible]	[illegible]	[illegible]	[illegible]	[illegible]	[illegible]	[illegible]	Cork City.
[illegible]	[illegible]	[illegible]	[illegible]	[illegible]	[illegible]	[illegible]	[illegible]	[illegible]	[illegible]	[illegible]	[illegible]	Kerry.
[illegible]	[illegible]	[illegible]	[illegible]	[illegible]	[illegible]	[illegible]	[illegible]	[illegible]	[illegible]	[illegible]	[illegible]	Limerick.
[illegible]	[illegible]	[illegible]	[illegible]	[illegible]	[illegible]	[illegible]	[illegible]	[illegible]	[illegible]	[illegible]	[illegible]	Limerick City.
[illegible]	[illegible]	[illegible]	[illegible]	[illegible]	[illegible]	[illegible]	[illegible]	[illegible]	[illegible]	[illegible]	[illegible]	Tipperary.
[illegible]	[illegible]	[illegible]	[illegible]	[illegible]	[illegible]	[illegible]	[illegible]	[illegible]	[illegible]	[illegible]	[illegible]	Waterford.
[illegible]	[illegible]	[illegible]	[illegible]	[illegible]	[illegible]	[illegible]	[illegible]	[illegible]	[illegible]	[illegible]	[illegible]	Waterford City and Police Court.
[illegible]	[illegible]	[illegible]	[illegible]	[illegible]	[illegible]	[illegible]	[illegible]	[illegible]	[illegible]	[illegible]	[illegible]	Total.
												ULSTER.
[illegible]	[illegible]	[illegible]	[illegible]	[illegible]	[illegible]	[illegible]	[illegible]	[illegible]	[illegible]	[illegible]	[illegible]	Antrim.
[illegible]	[illegible]	[illegible]	[illegible]	[illegible]	[illegible]	[illegible]	[illegible]	[illegible]	[illegible]	[illegible]	[illegible]	Armagh.
[illegible]	[illegible]	[illegible]	[illegible]	[illegible]	[illegible]	[illegible]	[illegible]	[illegible]	[illegible]	[illegible]	[illegible]	Carrickfergus, County of the Town of.
[illegible]	[illegible]	[illegible]	[illegible]	[illegible]	[illegible]	[illegible]	[illegible]	[illegible]	[illegible]	[illegible]	[illegible]	Cavan.
[illegible]	[illegible]	[illegible]	[illegible]	[illegible]	[illegible]	[illegible]	[illegible]	[illegible]	[illegible]	[illegible]	[illegible]	Donegal.
[illegible]	[illegible]	[illegible]	[illegible]	[illegible]	[illegible]	[illegible]	[illegible]	[illegible]	[illegible]	[illegible]	[illegible]	Down.
[illegible]	[illegible]	[illegible]	[illegible]	[illegible]	[illegible]	[illegible]	[illegible]	[illegible]	[illegible]	[illegible]	[illegible]	Fermanagh.
[illegible]	[illegible]	[illegible]	[illegible]	[illegible]	[illegible]	[illegible]	[illegible]	[illegible]	[illegible]	[illegible]	[illegible]	Londonderry.
[illegible]	[illegible]	[illegible]	[illegible]	[illegible]	[illegible]	[illegible]	[illegible]	[illegible]	[illegible]	[illegible]	[illegible]	Londonderry City.
[illegible]	[illegible]	[illegible]	[illegible]	[illegible]	[illegible]	[illegible]	[illegible]	[illegible]	[illegible]	[illegible]	[illegible]	Monaghan.
[illegible]	[illegible]	[illegible]	[illegible]	[illegible]	[illegible]	[illegible]	[illegible]	[illegible]	[illegible]	[illegible]	[illegible]	Tyrone.
[illegible]	[illegible]	[illegible]	[illegible]	[illegible]	[illegible]	[illegible]	[illegible]	[illegible]	[illegible]	[illegible]	[illegible]	Total.
												CONNAUGHT.
[illegible]	[illegible]	[illegible]	[illegible]	[illegible]	[illegible]	[illegible]	[illegible]	[illegible]	[illegible]	[illegible]	[illegible]	Galway.
[illegible]	[illegible]	[illegible]	[illegible]	[illegible]	[illegible]	[illegible]	[illegible]	[illegible]	[illegible]	[illegible]	[illegible]	Galway, County of the Town.
[illegible]	[illegible]	[illegible]	[illegible]	[illegible]	[illegible]	[illegible]	[illegible]	[illegible]	[illegible]	[illegible]	[illegible]	Leitrim.
[illegible]	[illegible]	[illegible]	[illegible]	[illegible]	[illegible]	[illegible]	[illegible]	[illegible]	[illegible]	[illegible]	[illegible]	Mayo.
[illegible]	[illegible]	[illegible]	[illegible]	[illegible]	[illegible]	[illegible]	[illegible]	[illegible]	[illegible]	[illegible]	[illegible]	Roscommon.
[illegible]	[illegible]	[illegible]	[illegible]	[illegible]	[illegible]	[illegible]	[illegible]	[illegible]	[illegible]	[illegible]	[illegible]	Sligo.
[illegible]	[illegible]	[illegible]	[illegible]	[illegible]	[illegible]	[illegible]	[illegible]	[illegible]	[illegible]	[illegible]	[illegible]	Total.
[illegible]	[illegible]	[illegible]	[illegible]	[illegible]	[illegible]	[illegible]	[illegible]	[illegible]	[illegible]	[illegible]	[illegible]	Total of Ireland.

TABLE [illegible].—QUARTER SESSIONS COURTS.—TABLE showing NUMBER of APPEALS [illegible] APPLICATIONS for SPIRIT LICENCES in the Year [illegible], from Returns made by [illegible].

COUNTY, COUNTY OF CITY or of TOWN, AND PROVINCE.	Appeals from Magistrates: Total.	Affirmed.	Reversed.	Varied.	Otherwise disposed of	Applications for Spirit Licences: Total.	Granted: On original application	Granted: On application for renewal	Refused: On original application	Refused: On application for renewal	[illegible]	[illegible]	[illegible]
LEINSTER:													
Carlow,	[illegible]	[illegible]	[illegible]	[illegible]	[illegible]	[illegible]	[illegible]	[illegible]	[illegible]	[illegible]	[illegible]	[illegible]	[illegible]
Drogheda, Town of,	[illegible]	[illegible]	[illegible]	[illegible]	[illegible]	[illegible]	[illegible]	[illegible]	[illegible]	[illegible]	[illegible]	[illegible]	[illegible]
Dublin,	[illegible]	[illegible]	[illegible]	[illegible]	[illegible]	[illegible]	[illegible]	[illegible]	[illegible]	[illegible]	[illegible]	[illegible]	[illegible]
Dublin City,	[illegible]	[illegible]	[illegible]	[illegible]	[illegible]	[illegible]	[illegible]	[illegible]	[illegible]	[illegible]	[illegible]	[illegible]	[illegible]
Kildare,	[illegible]	[illegible]	[illegible]	[illegible]	[illegible]	[illegible]	[illegible]	[illegible]	[illegible]	[illegible]	[illegible]	[illegible]	[illegible]
Kilkenny,	[illegible]	[illegible]	[illegible]	[illegible]	[illegible]	[illegible]	[illegible]	[illegible]	[illegible]	[illegible]	[illegible]	[illegible]	[illegible]
Kilkenny City,	[illegible]	[illegible]	[illegible]	[illegible]	[illegible]	[illegible]	[illegible]	[illegible]	[illegible]	[illegible]	[illegible]	[illegible]	[illegible]
King's County,	[illegible]	[illegible]	[illegible]	[illegible]	[illegible]	[illegible]	[illegible]	[illegible]	[illegible]	[illegible]	[illegible]	[illegible]	[illegible]
Longford,	[illegible]	[illegible]	[illegible]	[illegible]	[illegible]	[illegible]	[illegible]	[illegible]	[illegible]	[illegible]	[illegible]	[illegible]	[illegible]
Louth,	[illegible]	[illegible]	[illegible]	[illegible]	[illegible]	[illegible]	[illegible]	[illegible]	[illegible]	[illegible]	[illegible]	[illegible]	[illegible]
Meath,	[illegible]	[illegible]	[illegible]	[illegible]	[illegible]	[illegible]	[illegible]	[illegible]	[illegible]	[illegible]	[illegible]	[illegible]	[illegible]
Queen's County,	[illegible]	[illegible]	[illegible]	[illegible]	[illegible]	[illegible]	[illegible]	[illegible]	[illegible]	[illegible]	[illegible]	[illegible]	[illegible]
Westmeath,	[illegible]	[illegible]	[illegible]	[illegible]	[illegible]	[illegible]	[illegible]	[illegible]	[illegible]	[illegible]	[illegible]	[illegible]	[illegible]
Wexford,	[illegible]	[illegible]	[illegible]	[illegible]	[illegible]	[illegible]	[illegible]	[illegible]	[illegible]	[illegible]	[illegible]	[illegible]	[illegible]
Wicklow,	[illegible]	[illegible]	[illegible]	[illegible]	[illegible]	[illegible]	[illegible]	[illegible]	[illegible]	[illegible]	[illegible]	[illegible]	[illegible]
Total,	[illegible]	[illegible]	[illegible]	[illegible]	[illegible]	[illegible]	[illegible]	[illegible]	[illegible]	[illegible]	[illegible]	[illegible]	[illegible]
MUNSTER:													
Clare,	[illegible]	[illegible]	[illegible]	[illegible]	[illegible]	[illegible]	[illegible]	[illegible]	[illegible]	[illegible]	[illegible]	[illegible]	[illegible]
Cork, East Riding,	[illegible]	[illegible]	[illegible]	[illegible]	[illegible]	[illegible]	[illegible]	[illegible]	[illegible]	[illegible]	[illegible]	[illegible]	[illegible]
Cork, West Riding,	[illegible]	[illegible]	[illegible]	[illegible]	[illegible]	[illegible]	[illegible]	[illegible]	[illegible]	[illegible]	[illegible]	[illegible]	[illegible]
Cork City,	[illegible]	[illegible]	[illegible]	[illegible]	[illegible]	[illegible]	[illegible]	[illegible]	[illegible]	[illegible]	[illegible]	[illegible]	[illegible]
Kerry,	[illegible]	[illegible]	[illegible]	[illegible]	[illegible]	[illegible]	[illegible]	[illegible]	[illegible]	[illegible]	[illegible]	[illegible]	[illegible]
Limerick,	[illegible]	[illegible]	[illegible]	[illegible]	[illegible]	[illegible]	[illegible]	[illegible]	[illegible]	[illegible]	[illegible]	[illegible]	[illegible]
Limerick City,	[illegible]	[illegible]	[illegible]	[illegible]	[illegible]	[illegible]	[illegible]	[illegible]	[illegible]	[illegible]	[illegible]	[illegible]	[illegible]
Tipperary,	[illegible]	[illegible]	[illegible]	[illegible]	[illegible]	[illegible]	[illegible]	[illegible]	[illegible]	[illegible]	[illegible]	[illegible]	[illegible]
Waterford,	[illegible]	[illegible]	[illegible]	[illegible]	[illegible]	[illegible]	[illegible]	[illegible]	[illegible]	[illegible]	[illegible]	[illegible]	[illegible]
Waterford City,	[illegible]	[illegible]	[illegible]	[illegible]	[illegible]	[illegible]	[illegible]	[illegible]	[illegible]	[illegible]	[illegible]	[illegible]	[illegible]
Total,	[illegible]	[illegible]	[illegible]	[illegible]	[illegible]	[illegible]	[illegible]	[illegible]	[illegible]	[illegible]	[illegible]	[illegible]	[illegible]
ULSTER:													
Antrim,	[illegible]	[illegible]	[illegible]	[illegible]	[illegible]	[illegible]	[illegible]	[illegible]	[illegible]	[illegible]	[illegible]	[illegible]	[illegible]
Armagh,	[illegible]	[illegible]	[illegible]	[illegible]	[illegible]	[illegible]	[illegible]	[illegible]	[illegible]	[illegible]	[illegible]	[illegible]	[illegible]
Belfast, Town of,	[illegible]	[illegible]	[illegible]	[illegible]	[illegible]	[illegible]	[illegible]	[illegible]	[illegible]	[illegible]	[illegible]	[illegible]	[illegible]
Carrickfergus, Town of,	[illegible]	[illegible]	[illegible]	[illegible]	[illegible]	[illegible]	[illegible]	[illegible]	[illegible]	[illegible]	[illegible]	[illegible]	[illegible]
Cavan,	[illegible]	[illegible]	[illegible]	[illegible]	[illegible]	[illegible]	[illegible]	[illegible]	[illegible]	[illegible]	[illegible]	[illegible]	[illegible]
Donegal,	[illegible]	[illegible]	[illegible]	[illegible]	[illegible]	[illegible]	[illegible]	[illegible]	[illegible]	[illegible]	[illegible]	[illegible]	[illegible]
Down,	[illegible]	[illegible]	[illegible]	[illegible]	[illegible]	[illegible]	[illegible]	[illegible]	[illegible]	[illegible]	[illegible]	[illegible]	[illegible]
Fermanagh,	[illegible]	[illegible]	[illegible]	[illegible]	[illegible]	[illegible]	[illegible]	[illegible]	[illegible]	[illegible]	[illegible]	[illegible]	[illegible]
Londonderry,	[illegible]	[illegible]	[illegible]	[illegible]	[illegible]	[illegible]	[illegible]	[illegible]	[illegible]	[illegible]	[illegible]	[illegible]	[illegible]
Londonderry City,	[illegible]	[illegible]	[illegible]	[illegible]	[illegible]	[illegible]	[illegible]	[illegible]	[illegible]	[illegible]	[illegible]	[illegible]	[illegible]
Monaghan,	[illegible]	[illegible]	[illegible]	[illegible]	[illegible]	[illegible]	[illegible]	[illegible]	[illegible]	[illegible]	[illegible]	[illegible]	[illegible]
Tyrone,	[illegible]	[illegible]	[illegible]	[illegible]	[illegible]	[illegible]	[illegible]	[illegible]	[illegible]	[illegible]	[illegible]	[illegible]	[illegible]
Total,	[illegible]	[illegible]	[illegible]	[illegible]	[illegible]	[illegible]	[illegible]	[illegible]	[illegible]	[illegible]	[illegible]	[illegible]	[illegible]
CONNAUGHT:													
Galway,	[illegible]	[illegible]	[illegible]	[illegible]	[illegible]	[illegible]	[illegible]	[illegible]	[illegible]	[illegible]	[illegible]	[illegible]	[illegible]
Galway, Town of,	[illegible]	[illegible]	[illegible]	[illegible]	[illegible]	[illegible]	[illegible]	[illegible]	[illegible]	[illegible]	[illegible]	[illegible]	[illegible]
Leitrim,	[illegible]	[illegible]	[illegible]	[illegible]	[illegible]	[illegible]	[illegible]	[illegible]	[illegible]	[illegible]	[illegible]	[illegible]	[illegible]
Mayo,	[illegible]	[illegible]	[illegible]	[illegible]	[illegible]	[illegible]	[illegible]	[illegible]	[illegible]	[illegible]	[illegible]	[illegible]	[illegible]
Roscommon,	[illegible]	[illegible]	[illegible]	[illegible]	[illegible]	[illegible]	[illegible]	[illegible]	[illegible]	[illegible]	[illegible]	[illegible]	[illegible]
Sligo,	[illegible]	[illegible]	[illegible]	[illegible]	[illegible]	[illegible]	[illegible]	[illegible]	[illegible]	[illegible]	[illegible]	[illegible]	[illegible]
Total,	[illegible]	[illegible]	[illegible]	[illegible]	[illegible]	[illegible]	[illegible]	[illegible]	[illegible]	[illegible]	[illegible]	[illegible]	[illegible]
TOTAL OF IRELAND,	[illegible]	[illegible]	[illegible]	[illegible]	[illegible]	[illegible]	[illegible]	[illegible]	[illegible]	[illegible]	[illegible]	[illegible]	[illegible]

(a) [illegible]
(b) [illegible]
(c) [illegible]
(d) [illegible]
(e) [illegible]
(f) [illegible]
(g) [illegible]

www.ingramcontent.com/pod-product-compliance
Lightning Source LLC
Chambersburg PA
CBHW020558270326
41927CB00006B/889
* 9 7 8 3 7 4 2 8 1 0 3 7 3 *